Programming ASP.NET AJAX

Other Microsoft Windows resources from O'Reilly

Related titles

Essential SharePoint 2007

Learning ASP.NET 2.0 with AJAX

Learning C# 2008

Programming WPF

SharePoint 2007: The Definitive Guide

Windows Vista: The Definitive Guide

Windows Vista in a Nutshell

Windows Books Resource Center

windows.oreilly.com is a complete catalog of O'Reilly's Windows and Office books, including sample chapters and code examples.

oreillynet.com is the essential portal for developers interested in open and emerging technologies, including new platforms, programming languages, and operating systems.

Conferences

O'Reilly brings diverse innovators together to nurture the ideas that spark revolutionary industries. We specialize in documenting the latest tools and systems, translating the innovator's knowledge into useful skills for those in the trenches. Visit *conferences.oreilly.com* for our upcoming events.

Safari Bookshelf (*safari.oreilly.com*) is the premier online reference library for programmers and IT professionals. Conduct searches across more than 1,000 books. Subscribers can zero in on answers to time-critical questions in a matter of seconds. Read the books on your Bookshelf from cover to cover or simply flip to the page you need. Try it today for free.

Programming ASP.NET AJAX

Christian Wenz

Beijing · Cambridge · Farnham · Köln · Paris · Sebastopol · Taipei · Tokyo

Programming ASP.NET AJAX
by Christian Wenz

Copyright © 2007 Christian Wenz. All rights reserved.
Printed in the United States of America.

Published by O'Reilly Media, Inc., 1005 Gravenstein Highway North, Sebastopol, CA 95472.

O'Reilly books may be purchased for educational, business, or sales promotional use. Online editions are also available for most titles (*safari.oreilly.com*). For more information, contact our corporate/institutional sales department: (800) 998-9938 or *corporate@oreilly.com*.

Editor: John Osborn
Technical Editor: Mike Pope
Production Editor: Rachel Monaghan
Production Services: Octal Publishing, Inc.

Cover Designer: Karen Montgomery
Interior Designer: David Futato
Illustrators: Robert Romano and Jessamyn Read

Printing History:

September 2007:   First Edition.

 This book uses RepKover,™ a durable and flexible lay-flat binding.

ISBN-10: 0-596-51424-7
ISBN-13: 978-0-596-51424-2
[M]

Table of Contents

Part II.   ASP.NET AJAX Extensions

Part IV. ASP.NET AJAX Futures

Part V.   Microsoft AJAX Library

Part VI.   Appendixes

Preface

The Wikipedia page for Ajax (*http://en.wikipedia.org/wiki/Ajax*) provides more than 40 meanings for the word, including the names of two characters in Homer's *Iliad* (Ajax the Great and Ajax the Lesser), the name of an Amsterdam soccer team, a couple of automobiles, a horse, and—my personal favorite—a household cleaner made by Colgate. However, Ajax is also the term for a collection of technologies many say could revolutionize the Web. If various weblogs and online and print commentaries are to be believed, Ajax is the future of web development, the enabler of Web 2.0, and probably a cure for fatal diseases, as well.

Many web developers want to provide their users with a far richer client experience but don't want to write a Windows client application (or, for practical reasons, cannot write one). Ajax could be just what they need. It allows web applications to behave almost like desktop applications, with features such as keyboard shortcuts and drag-and-drop placement.

ASP.NET "Atlas" was the code name for a new set of technologies from Microsoft that provide Ajax-like functionality for the ASP.NET developer. It offered many of the same benefits for Ajax development that ASP.NET provides for server-side development. In autumn of 2006, the final product name was announced: ASP.NET AJAX. (However, Atlas *is* much easier to pronounce.)

I resisted writing about Ajax for quite some time. For years, I had used and written about the technologies that make up Ajax, but the term itself had to be coined in early 2005 before the technology really took off. In my opinion, Clemens Vasters said it best: "Web 2.0 yadda yadda AJAX yaddayadda Profit!(?)" (see *http://vasters.com/clemensv/PermaLink,guid,d88c1112-d8da-496e-9fd0-8cf03cf55c32.aspx*).

The hype reminds me of the buzz that accompanied XML and web services a few years back: everybody was talking about them, but few had ever read their specs. Once reality settled in, the hype vanished and actual real-world' applications appeared that made effective use of both technologies.

I am convinced that Ajax will follow a similar path but will travel it more quickly. A tour of the Web will prove that there are already loads of useful Ajax applications available today.

But, back to my reluctance to write a book about Ajax.

I kept saying that Ajax itself could be explained in 20 to 30 pages. Adding some background information and examples might produce 75 pages, maybe 100. But how could I fill the rest of the book? Many of the Ajax books currently on the market have to go through contortions to reach a reasonable page count.

My thinking about all of this changed when in September 2005 I attended the Microsoft Professional Developers Conference conference in Los Angeles and saw Atlas for the first time. Microsoft was announcing a framework that provided Ajax functionality but added controls and other tools to make development of modern web applications easier. Now this was something to write about, I thought. I started working on a manuscript based on the early, prerelease version of Atlas. It had to be rewritten several times with every new prerelease drop of Atlas I could get my hands on. The lack of documentation for the preliminary releases required me to reverse-engineer the inner workings of Atlas. As a result, this book may describe a few unofficial ways to accomplish things.

Programming Atlas was published in September of 2006. As one of the first books on the topic, it provided detailed information on the yet still changing framework. At the end of January 2007, ASP.NET AJAX was released in its final 1.0 version. Beyond the name change, the internal changes were so vast it actually required a new edition of the book as each and every existing application had to be adapted.

This book will teach you how to create professional, dynamic web pages using the Microsoft ASP.NET AJAX framework. A certain amount of JavaScript and ASP.NET knowledge is required. For your convenience, some JavaScript basics are covered at the beginning of the book.

I am a big believer in the "show, don't tell" principle. Therefore, this book contains a large number of examples showing you the key aspects of the ASP.NET AJAX framework. I am also a fan of focusing on the relevant facts. So, I have created small examples, each conveying one or two points; I deliberately avoided putting as many facts as possible into one very long listing. In my experience as an author and trainer, shorter examples produce better results and make learning easier.

Also, note that the examples are always very generic. This allows you to add them directly to your own projects and modify and tweak them to meet your needs. Every example is self-contained, making it very easy to use and reuse.

Who This Book Is For

This book was written for two groups of web developers: those who are using ASP.NET and would like to take their applications a step further through the Ajax technology, and those who are using another technology but are interested in the ASP.NET AJAX framework. It is also suitable for JavaScript programmers who would like to avoid some of the headaches caused by the necessity of writing cross-browser code. The languages used in this book are C# and JavaScript. If you need background on these languages, O'Reilly has some solid introductions to both, including *Learning C# 2005*, by Jesse Liberty and Brian MacDonald, and *Learning JavaScript*, by Shelley Powers.

How This Book Is Organized

Chapter 1, *ASP.NET AJAX, Ajax, and ASP.NET*, gives a broad overview of Ajax and the ASP.NET AJAX framework and then covers the installation of ASP.NET AJAX, a review of its structure, and a first simple example.

Chapter 2, *JavaScript*, is a concise introduction to JavaScript. Although ASP.NET AJAX does its best to hide the functional details from ASP.NET programmers, a certain knowledge of JavaScript is required to really master ASP.NET AJAX.

Chapter 3, *Ajax*, explains the technologies beyond the hype. You learn what happens in the background, how Ajax works, and what it really is all about, in fewer than 20 pages.

Chapter 4, *Using ASP.NET AJAX JavaScript Extensions*, describes how ASP.NET AJAX enriches the functionality of client-side JavaScript by adding new OOP-like features and even reimplementing some classes of the .NET Framework so they can be used on the client side.

Chapter 5, *Web Services*, deals with XML web services. Even though ASP.NET AJAX focuses on client-based development, it also adds features for server-side web services. This includes features for error management and session support.

Chapter 6, *UpdatePanel: Refreshing Only Parts of a Page*, introduces the UpdatePanel control that makes individual parts of a web page updateable independent from the rest of the page, without a page refresh. This is one of the most important elements of ASP.NET AJAX.

Chapter 7, *Using the ASP.NET AJAX Profile Service*, details how ASP.NET AJAX provides a JavaScript access to the ASP.NET 2.0 Profile API.

Chapter 8, *Using the ASP.NET AJAX Authentication Service*, explains the JavaScript hook into the ASP.NET 2.0 Forms Authentication API.

Chapter 9, *Localizing and Globalizing Applications*, covers the emerging topic of providing a web application that works with different languages and regional settings.

Chapter 10, *Using the Control Toolkit*, introduces the ASP.NET AJAX Control Toolkit, a collection of impressive server controls enriched with Ajax features.

Chapter 11, *Adding Animation to a Web Page*, introduces the animation framework that is part of the ASP.NET AJAX Control Toolkit.

Chapter 12, *Autocompleting User Input, Fighting Spam, and More*, shows the (debatable) highlights of the ASP.NET AJAX Control Toolkit, showcasing the diversity of the toolkit and also covering some best practices and tips.

Chapter 13, *Writing Custom Controls and Contributing to the Community*, explains how to write your own controls using the Control Toolkit infrastructure, and how to integrate them, or patches, to existing controls in the toolkit project.

Chapter 14, *Client Controls*, describes the client-side controls that come with the ASP.NET AJAX Futures CTP. These make accessing HTML elements from JavaScript easy using a consistent API.

Chapter 15, *Binding and Validating Data*, shows how to implement a client-side data binding between (client) controls, courtesy of the ASP.NET AJAX Futures CTP.

Chapter 16, *Using Behaviors and Components*, shows you the built-in behaviors of ASP.NET AJAX and how to attach their functionality to client-side controls and components.

Chapter 17, *Using Server Data*, explains how you connect to databases. ASP.NET AJAX can be linked to a data source via specifically crafted web services, making data binding without page refreshes quite easy. ASP.NET AJAX also provides special client-side controls to display data.

Chapter 18, *Using Remote Web Services*, helps you overcome the same-domain policy of JavaScript and allows you to call remote web services, using a server-side bridge.

Chapter 19, *Using Animations*, showcases some animation features in the ASP.NET AJAX Futures CTP.

Chapter 20, *Fixing Bookmarks and Back/Forward Buttons*, provides possible solutions to two of the most annoying issues with Ajax applications (breaking the standard browser behavior).

Chapter 21, *Web Parts*, demonstrates that ASP.NET AJAX web parts can do things ASP.NET web parts cannot, including, for example, drag-and-drop on any browser.

Chapter 22, *Using ASP.NET AJAX with Other Server Technologies*, proves that some parts of the Microsoft Ajax Library are not tied to ASP.NET 2.0; a sample application in PHP shows how to bridge these two worlds.

Appendix A, *Debugging ASP.NET AJAX Applications*, covers how to find bugs in ASP.NET AJAX applications and introduces some must-have browser tools.

Appendix B, *XMLHttpRequest Reference*, lists important methods and properties of the `XMLHttpRequest` object.

Appendix C, *DOM Reference*, covers important JavaScript DOM methods.

Appendix D, *ASP.NET AJAX Reference*, lists the most important methods provided by the ASP.NET AJAX framework.

Appendix E, *ScriptManager, UpdatePanel, UpdateProgress, and Timer Declarative Reference*, documents the properties of these four key ASP.NET AJAX server controls.

What You Need to Use This Book

The examples in this book require only ASP.NET 2.0, which is included in the free redistributable version of the .NET Framework. However, to make the most of ASP.NET and ASP.NET AJAX, you should use one of the IDE offerings from Microsoft. Visual Web Developer 2005 Express Edition (VWD) is free; Visual Studio 2005 (in its various editions) is the commercial package with more features. Both are perfectly suited for using the examples in this book.

Conventions Used in This Book

The following typographical conventions are used in this book:

Plain text
> Indicates menu titles, menu options, menu buttons, and keyboard accelerators (such as Alt and Ctrl).

Italic
> Indicates new terms, URLs, email addresses, filenames, file extensions, pathnames, directories, and Unix utilities.

`Constant width`
> Indicates commands, options, switches, variables, attributes, keys, functions, types, classes, namespaces, methods, modules, properties, parameters, values, objects, events, event handlers, XML tags, HTML tags, macros, the contents of files, or the output from commands.

`Constant width bold`
> Used to highlight portions of code.

`Constant width italic`
> Shows text that should be replaced with user-supplied values.

This icon signifies a tip, suggestion, or general note.

 This icon indicates a warning or caution.

Using Code Examples

This book is designed to help you get your job done. In general, you may use the code in this book in your programs and documentation. Unless you're reproducing a significant portion of the code you do not need to contact us for permission. For example, writing a program that uses several chunks of code from this book does not require permission. Selling or distributing a CD-ROM of examples from O'Reilly books *does* require permission. Answering a question by citing this book and quoting example code does not require permission. Incorporating a significant amount of example code from this book into your product's documentation *does* require permission.

We appreciate, but do not require, attribution. An attribution usually includes the title, author, publisher, and ISBN. For example: "*Programming ASP.NET AJAX*, by Christian Wenz. Copyright 2007 Christian Wenz, 978-0-596-51424-2."

If you feel your use of code examples falls outside fair use or the permission given above, feel free to contact us at *permissions@oreilly.com*.

How to Contact Us

Please address comments and questions concerning this book to the publisher:

O'Reilly Media, Inc.
1005 Gravenstein Highway North
Sebastopol, CA 95472
800-998-9938 (in the United States or Canada)
707-829-0515 (international or local)
707-829-0104 (fax)

A web page is available for this book where we list errata, code examples, and any additional information. Corresponding files for code examples are mentioned on the first line of the example. You can access this page at:

http://www.oreilly.com/catalog/9780596514242

To comment or ask technical questions about this book, send email to:

bookquestions@oreilly.com

For more information about our books, conferences, Resource Centers, and the O'Reilly Network, see our web site at:

http://www.oreilly.com

Safari® Books Online

 When you see a Safari® Books Online icon on the cover of your favorite technology book, that means the book is available online through the O'Reilly Network Safari Bookshelf.

Safari offers a solution that's better than e-books. It's a virtual library that lets you easily search thousands of top tech books, cut and paste code samples, download chapters, and find quick answers when you need the most accurate, current information. Try it for free at *http://safari.oreilly.com*.

Acknowledgments (Programming Atlas)

Working on this book turned out to be an enormous task. The lack of documentation changes from one release to the next, and complicated JavaScript debugging led to a lot of trial and error. Although I had worked with ASP.NET and JavaScript for a very long time, I had to learn Atlas from scratch. Luckily, the Atlas team has been very supportive and open, especially in the public forums at *http://forums.asp.net/ default.aspx?GroupID=34*.

I am grateful to the impressive roster of tech editors who helped me shape this book and provided me with feedback. In alphabetical order by first name, the ones who saved my reputation in a couple of instances are: Adonis Bitar, Arsen Yeremin, Bertrand Le Roy, Christoph Wille, Mike Pope, and Tobias Hauser.

Also, I am indebted to my editor, John Osborn, who guided me through this project. He is the only editor I know who ever complained when I was submitting material *before* the negotiated deadline. But it was his excellent project management that allowed me to focus on writing and staying on—and even going ahead—of schedule.

Finally, I have to admit that I am not too keen on personal acknowledgments, thanking family members, husbands/wives/fiancées/partners, and cats/dogs. (The only exception is Richard Hundhausen, who once expressed his gratitude that there were no 24-hour divorce services where he lived.) However, I would like to take this opportunity to thank my parents. They were very supportive when I wrote my first book, and now, some 50-odd books later, I finally show some appreciation. Embarrassingly, they sometimes even find mistakes without knowing the technologies involved: some time ago, my father noticed that there were more opening than closing parentheses in a listing. So, thanks Mom, thanks Dad. And—now that I am into it—thanks to my friends and family, who do not seem to mind when I have long writing phases or am on the road for yet another conference.

Acknowledgments (Programming ASP.NET AJAX)

Sometimes, your timing is just bad. About two weeks after the first edition—then called *Programming Atlas*—was released, Microsoft changed the name to ASP.NET AJAX. Bad timing, but not only for the new name: apart from changing the name, Microsoft also quite drastically changed the inner workings of the framework. As a consequence, no Atlas code listing works with ASP.NET AJAX. Admittedly, many listings were quite trivial to port, but some functionality was dropped or irreversibly changed.

Therefore, this edition looks completely different from the previous ones. The structure has been completely revamped with many new chapters, and some content has been added, some content dropped, and some chapters rewritten. So, while this is technically a second edition, it is more or less a new book. However, if you have existing code based on Atlas, don't worry: you will receive advice regarding the migration of old code to the new release in several chapters of this edition.

I am indebted to John Osborn, my editor, who managed the project, always sending me new ideas for the book. Mike Pope was the primary tech editor (a role he assumed for the first edition). He not only eliminated most of my Microsoft jokes (sigh), but also provided me with countless suggestions, comments, and ideas for this new edition. It was a lot of work, both for him (finding glitches) and for me (fixing them), but I think that the result has been worth the effort. Thanks to both of you for making the second edition even better than the first.

Thanks also to all the readers from the previous editions who provided me with a lot of feedback and suggestions. And thanks to various developers I taught using this book, who gave great feedback as well.

Basics

ASP.NET AJAX, Ajax, and ASP.NET

This book is about ASP.NET AJAX (known in pre-release versions as "Atlas"), a collection of new Microsoft technologies that enables web developers—particularly ASP.NET 2.0 developers—to more easily create web sites with pages that use Ajax. Ajax-style pages provide a richer user interface. Such a page is also more responsive because it can respond immediately to users, and can interact more or less immediately with the server. ASP.NET AJAX also includes tools for creating *mashups*, web applications that combine content from multiple sites, typically using the APIs provided by third-party web services. We'll be exploring all of these capabilities and more throughout the book. This chapter will get you started with ASP.NET AJAX while providing an overview of the underlying technology, and an architectural view of its operation.

ASP.NET AJAX and Ajax

ASP.NET AJAX expands on accepted browser technologies, including Asynchronous JavaScript and XML. Ajax has itself generated quite a lot of buzz lately (see the Preface for some thoughts about that), as it brings the functionality and user interface (UI) of web applications closer to that of desktop applications.

The main concept behind Ajax is to enable web pages to make HTTP requests in the background, or *asynchronously*, without reloading an entire page (or, in ASP.NET terms, without a round trip, or a postback). Ajax also allows more responsive UIs to be constructed by drawing on the power of commonly supported browser functions such as, JavaScript, Document Object Model (DOM), and Cascading Style Sheets (CSS). Google Suggest (*http://www.google.com/webhp?complete=1&hl=en*) demonstrates how an Ajax-enabled page can provide users with suggested words as text is entered (also known as *auto-completion*). Another example is Microsoft's Virtual Earth (*http://www.virtualearth.com/*).

ASP.NET AJAX can help you create these types of Ajax-enabled applications by programming the browser (client). To work with the client side of Ajax and ASP.NET

AJAX, you will need a solid understanding of the core Ajax technologies. Creating Ajax-enabled web pages by programming the browser requires knowledge of Java-Script, DOM, and the XMLHttpRequest object, which handles the requests from the client to the server. Additional knowledge of XML and XSLT is a plus, but is not mandatory. Neither is covered extensively in this book.)

Chapter 2 introduces JavaScript essentials. Other Ajax technologies are discussed in greater detail in Chapter 3. The example provided later in this chapter ("A First ASP.NET AJAX Example: Hello User") will require only a basic understanding of the Ajax technologies. You will develop these skills as we move forward.

Writing Ajax-based applications without a framework like ASP.NET AJAX is not necessarily easy, and you can find yourself writing the same code over and over to perform tasks such as displaying the data returned from a request to the server, binding controls to data, or working with web services. You can also find yourself writing code to work around different browser implementations of the DOM. One of the goals of ASP.NET AJAX is to reduce or even eliminate the need for writing redundant and tedious code and to deliver a client-side developer experience that matches the experience of ASP.NET 2.0 developers. A related goal is to bring to JavaScript some of the productivity advantages of object-oriented programming (OOP) as well as a framework like .NET. ASP.NET AJAX includes client-script libraries that provide these advantages to the JavaScript/DOM/CSS programmer:

Browser compatibility layer
> Allows ASP.NET AJAX scripts to run in most browsers and eliminates the need to handcraft scripts for each browser you want to target. (However, some browser-specific script is unavoidable, as you'll see in Chapter 3.)

Core services
> Provides JavaScript extensions that make OOP-like scripting possible, including support for classes, namespaces, event handling, inheritance, and object serialization with the formats JSON (JavaScript Object Notation) and XML. The most valuable of these extensions are discussed in Chapter 4.

Base class library
> This library provides a number of .NET-like components, such as string builders and timers. You'll learn about them in Chapter 4.

Script controls and components
> Provides ASP.NET AJAX versions of standard HTML controls that are extended with capabilities like data binding, prepackaged behaviors (for example, drag-and-drop functionality), and tight integration with the ASP.NET AJAX client libraries. You can program these controls and components directly, or you can use a new declarative markup called *xml-script*, which we will discuss in several chapters throughout the book. If you are familiar with ASP.NET markup syntax, then you already understand (in general terms) the relationship of HTML controls, abstract programmable versions of these controls, and a declarative syntax.

ASP.NET AJAX and ASP.NET

Although ASP.NET AJAX provides a host of benefits to the client script programmer creating Ajax applications, it is not just about writing JavaScript and making asynchronous calls to the server. As ASP.NET AJAX was created by the ASP.NET team, it's no surprise that one of its prominent features is a server framework that is integrated with (and requires) ASP.NET 2.0.

As with ASP.NET itself, ASP.NET AJAX is designed to deliver functionality—in this case, the benefits of Ajax—without requiring mastery of Ajax technologies. ASP.NET AJAX can manage Ajax functionality for you in much the same way that ASP.NET manages HTTP functionality, such as postbacks, state management, and the client script required to make ASP.NET all "just work."

In addition, on the server side, ASP.NET AJAX works as part of ASP.NET, taking advantage of its inherent features. ASP.NET AJAX controls can interact with other ASP.NET controls and components and participate in the page life cycle. It can be linked to ASP.NET 2.0 features, such as sessions, authentication, and profiles, allowing you to take advantage of these types of capabilities on the client. Finally, with ASP.NET AJAX and ASP.NET, you can reach beyond the page to special web services.

Some of the key elements of the ASP.NET AJAX server framework are described here:

ASP.NET AJAX server controls
> ASP.NET AJAX provides server-based controls resembling those of core ASP.NET 2.0, but which work with the ASP.NET AJAX client framework to deliver their functionality. Two controls in particular are fundamental to ASP.NET AJAX applications: `ScriptManager`, which will be discussed later in this chapter (see "The ScriptManager Control"), and `UpdatePanel`, which is discussed in Chapter 6.

ASP.NET AJAX ASP.NET services
> Provide certain ASP.NET 2.0 application services that are directly available to ASP.NET AJAX client scripts, including profiles, personalization, authentication and membership, and culture-specific services. You can expect the number of ASP.NET services available to ASP.NET AJAX applications to grow with future releases of ASP.NET AJAX.

The Microsoft Ajax Library
> This library provides a JavaScript-only library that does not depend on ASP.NET. Therefore, it can also be used without ASP.NET, as we will discuss in Chapter 22.

Ultimately, ASP.NET AJAX will take its rightful place as a key component of the next release of ASP.NET and will be fully supported with designers, IntelliSense, and debugging tools in a future release of Visual Studio.

ASP.NET AJAX Packages

The ASP.NET AJAX homepage (*http://ajax.asp.net/*) presents several different packages that each have a specific focus:

ASP.NET AJAX Extensions
  Also referred to as "ASP.NET AJAX Core," this is the "main" ASP.NET AJAX package. It is fully supported by Microsoft and contains the ASP.NET AJAX infrastructure (covered in Part II).

ASP.NET AJAX Control Toolkit
  This package contains an extensive collection of server-side components that provide astonishing Ajax functionality with very little effort. The Control Toolkit is an open source effort, although Microsoft still controls the project to ensure quality. However, there is no official Microsoft support for elements within the toolkit. Part III will explore the Control Toolkit.

ASP.NET AJAX Futures Release
  This package provides a sneak peek at features that might become part of ASP.NET and ASP.NET AJAX (or not). The Future Release is also the home of less commonly used functionality that was originally part of pre-release versions of ASP.NET AJAX. The CTP (Community Technology Preview, a pre-release version made available for download) is refreshed more often than the core package. It also is not officially supported, so use it at your own risk. Part IV of this book covers the Futures Release that was current as of the time of printing, namely the ASP.NET Futures (July 2007) release. Also, as of May 2007, the ASP.NET AJAX Futures CTP is part of the ASP.NET Futures CTP, which includes fascinating new (and unsupported) possibilities for classic ASP.NET.

The Microsoft Ajax Library
  The aforementioned JavaScript-only library, which will be covered in Part V.

 In a somewhat surprising move, Microsoft provided the complete source code for ASP.NET AJAX. It can be downloaded from *http://ajax.asp.net/*.

This chapter will introduce and show you how to install the core ASP.NET AJAX Extensions (and will touch briefly on the Futures CTP), before Part II will get into more detail; the remaining packages will be introduced at the beginning of the respective parts.

ASP.NET AJAX Prerequisites and Installation

The best way to understand the power of ASP.NET AJAX is to use it. All you need to develop applications is a JavaScript-enabled browser on the client and an ASP.NET 2.0-enabled web server. A text editor is sufficient to get started. However, when applications get more complex, an IDE with additional features like IntelliSense, code completion, project management, debugging, and WYSIWYG functionality can be real timesavers. In the world of ASP.NET 2.0, the most widely used editor comes from Microsoft in the form of Visual Studio 2005.

Installing the IDE

The good news is that, although the full versions of Visual Studio 2005 are usually your best bet, the free web-centric Express edition of Visual Studio 2005—Microsoft Visual Web Developer 2005 Express Edition—also fully supports ASP.NET AJAX.

In the interest of simplicity, we will sometimes refer to Visual Web Developer as VWD throughout this book. By VWD we mean both the Express edition and the full version of Visual Studio 2005. The web development component of VS 2005 is also called Visual Web Developer (you can see it during installation of Visual Studio), so VWD is the most generic term for creating ASP.NET 2.0 applications with a Microsoft IDE.

If you do not already have an IDE, install either Visual Studio 2005 or Visual Web Developer Express Edition. For the latter, go to *http://msdn.microsoft.com/vstudio/ express/vwd/download*, where you will find a web installer that not only downloads and installs VWD (Figure 1-1), but also takes care of installing the .NET Framework 2.0, if it is not already installed on your system.

If the web installer doesn't work on your machine (e.g., it cannot connect to the Internet from within a corporate environment, or your connection is slow), you can find ISO and IMG images of a CD containing Visual Web Developer and all prerequisites (*http://msdn.microsoft.com/ vstudio/express/support/install*), which you can download to a place with a better connection, then transfer onto a CD.

Installing ASP.NET AJAX

No matter which version of VWD you use, ASP.NET AJAX is integrated directly into the IDE. On the ASP.NET AJAX home page (*http://ajax.asp.net*), you can find a link to ASP.NET AJAX itself in the form of an MSI installer package named *ASPAJAXExtSetup.msi*. Look for the Microsoft ASP.NET 2.0 AJAX Extensions 1.0.

Before you launch the installer, uninstall any previous ASP.NET AJAX versions that may be on your system. The *.msi* installer asks only a few questions. Once you accept the ASP.NET AJAX license agreement, installation will begin, as shown in Figure 1-2.

When installation is complete, a new option for creating a web site—ASP.NET AJAX Web Site—will display within VWD and Visual Studio. This is the best way to get started with the ASP.NET AJAX technology as it copies all required files and

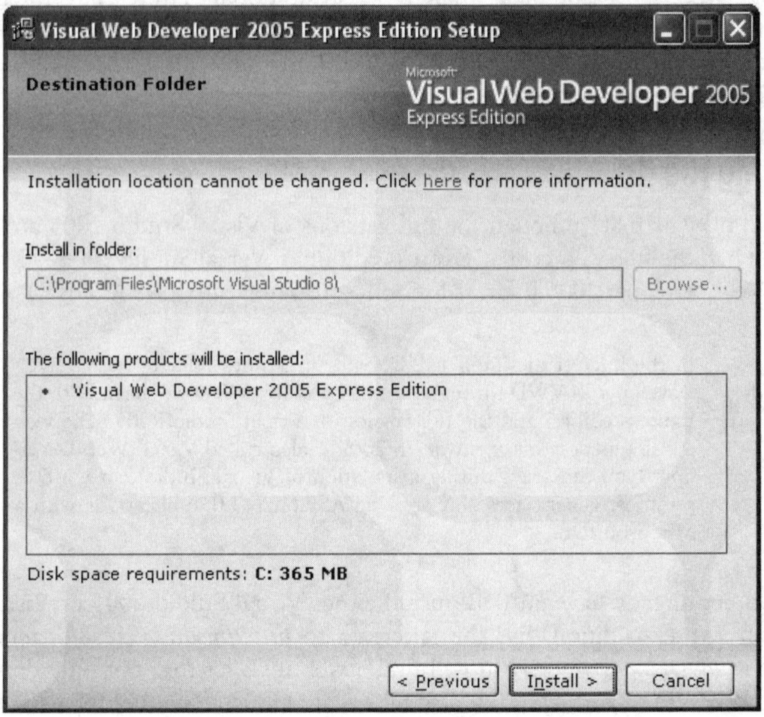

Figure 1-1. Installing Visual Web Developer Express Edition

places them in the proper directories (see Figure 1-3). It also installs the ASP.NET AJAX assembly in the Global Assembly Cache (GAC), so that it is automatically available for all ASP.NET applications.

ASP.NET AJAX also works with the upcoming Visual Studio 2008 and Visual Web Developer 2008 Express Edition. When creating a new web site, just state that you want to use .NET Framework 3.5 (see Figure 1-4), you don't even have to install ASP.NET AJAX, since it comes with the .NET Framework 3.5. For .NET versions prior to 3.5, you still need to install ASP.NET AJAX separately. By the way, if you are working with both Visual Studio 2005 and Visual Studio 2008, or if you want to open ASP.NET AJAX projects in Visual Studio 2008 that were created in Visual Studio 2005, refer to "For Further Reading" at the end of this chapter for some important advice for these scenarios.

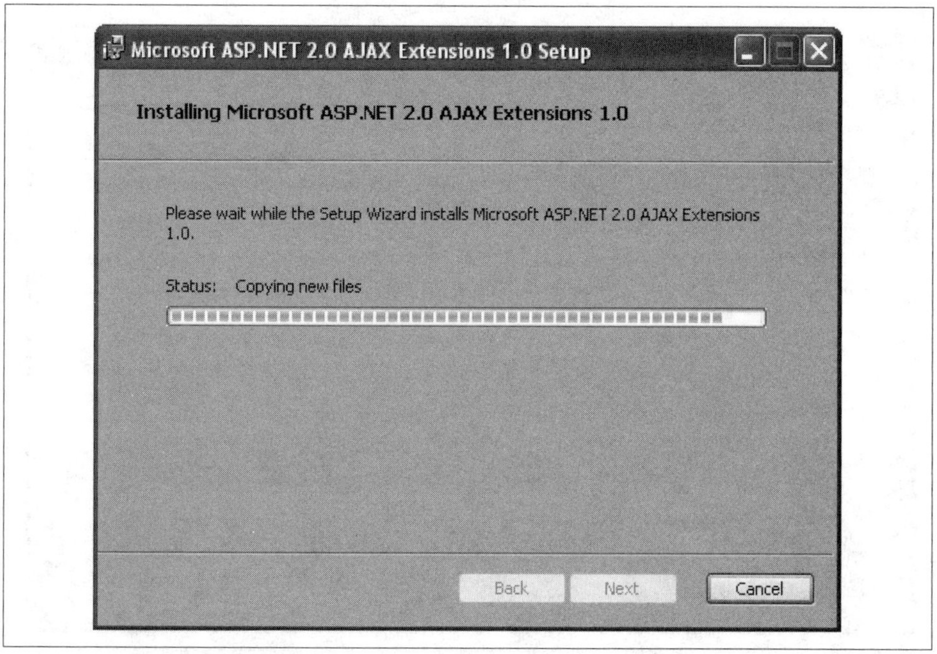

Figure 1-2. Installing the template

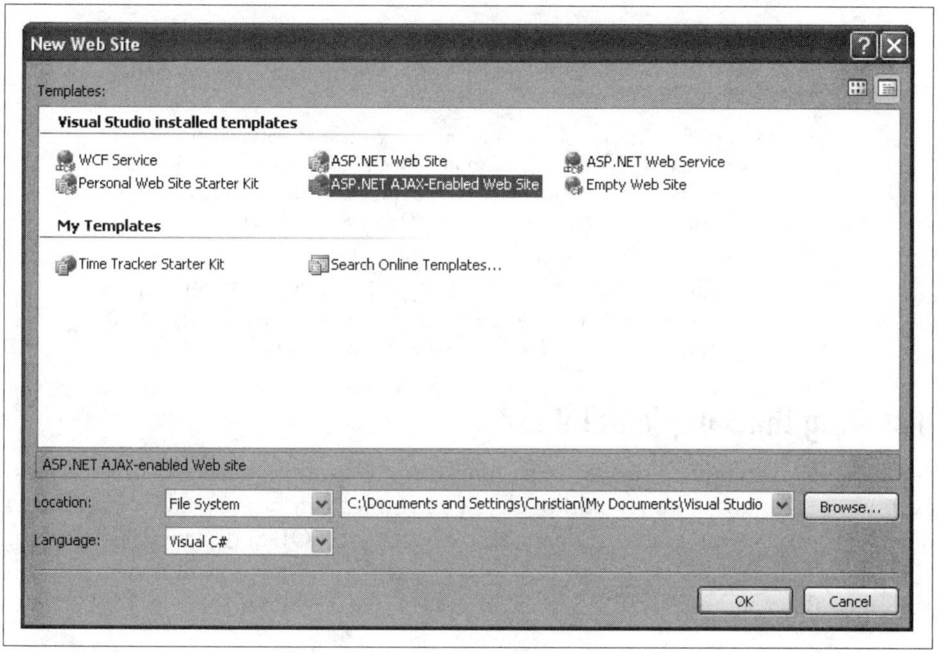

Figure 1-3. After installation, you have a new web site template

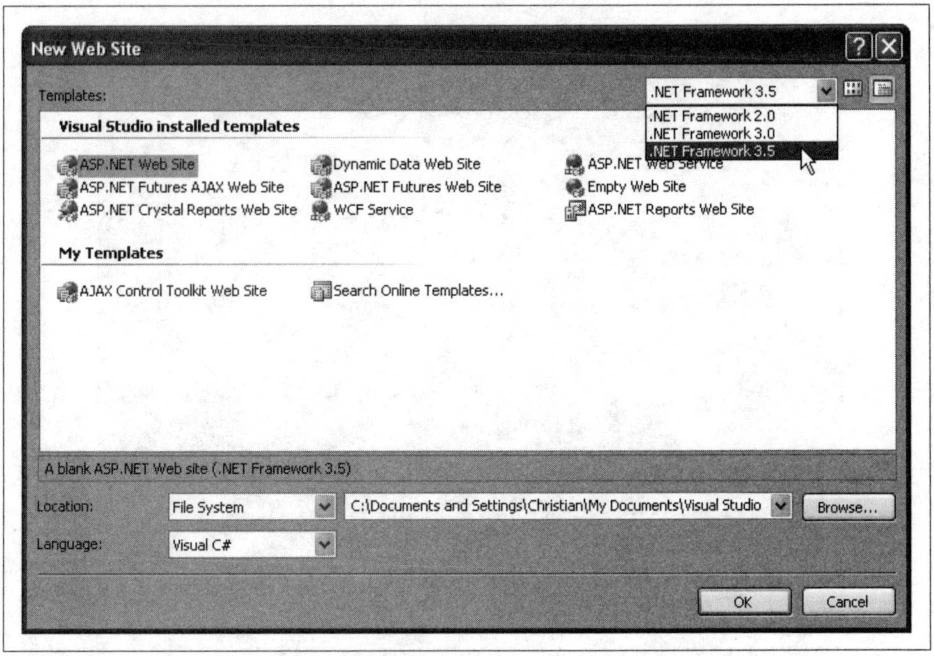

Figure 1-4. A .NET Framework 3.5 web site project automatically uses ASP.NET AJAX

> The ASP.NET AJAX web site offers further information and software related to ASP.NET AJAX. Some of the helpful items you will find on the site are detailed here:
>
> - Documentation that familiarizes you with several aspects of ASP.NET AJAX (*ajax.asp.net/docs*). The documentation also comes in a downloadable form that can be installed on your local computer (*AspNet_AJAX_Documentation.zip*).
> - ASP.NET AJAX samples
> - Links to other ASP.NET AJAX packages: The ASP.NET AJAX Control Toolkit, the Microsoft Ajax Library, the ASP.NET AJAX Futures release, and the ASP.NET AJAX source code.

Installing the Sample Database

Some of the examples in this book assume you are using SQL Server 2005 Express Edition as a database server (although the examples can also be adapted to other data sources). However, if you already have Microsoft SQL Server installed on your computer, you can use that as well. If you do not have Microsoft SQL Server available, download and install SQL Server Express (a free download).

Installing the Futures CTP

The installer for the ASP.NET AJAX Futures CTP (part of the ASP.NET Futures CTP) is quite similar to that of the ASP.NET AJAX Extensions. It also installs a web site template into Visual Studio and Visual Web Developer. It is called *ASP.NET Futures AJAX Web Site* (not to be confused with *ASP.NET Futures Web Site*, which is for Ajax-less sites). Installing the CTP requires that the ASP.NET AJAX Extensions have been installed first.

For samples presented in this book, the ASP.NET AJAX Extensions application uses its standard name, `AJAXEnabledWebSite1`, whereas the CTP web site will be named `AJAXFuturesEnabledWebSite1`. The former will run on port 1234, the latter on port 1236. The port in between, 1235, is reserved for the ASP.NET AJAX Control Toolkit sample application. You can, of course, choose port numbers of your own liking.

To make the setup as easy to deploy as possible, I use the Microsoft sample database *AdventureWorks* for all of the database examples in this book. I also assume that AdventureWorks was installed into a local SQL Server 2005 Express Edition installation, and is accessible using Windows authentication, at *(local)\SQLEXPRESS*.

 You may need to adapt the SQL Express pathname to your local system.

Depending on the version of SQL Server you use, *AdventureWorks* is available for download at either of the following locations:

SQL Server 2005
> *http://www.microsoft.com/downloads/details.aspx?familyid=E719ECF7-9F46-4312-AF89-6AD8702E4E6E&displaylang=en*

SQL Server 2005 Express Edition
> *http://www.microsoft.com/downloads/details.aspx?familyid=9697AAAA-AD4B-416E-87A4-A8B154F92787&displaylang=en*

Select the appropriate link, download and run the installer. When installation is complete, you will have to attach the *AdventureWorks_Data.mdf* file (residing in your SQL Server's *Data* folder) to your SQL Server 2005 installation. The most convenient way to do is by using Microsoft SQL Server Management Studio Express (SSMSE), a free GUI I recommend for administering SQL Server 2005 Express Edition installations. SSMSE is available in both 32-bit and 64-bit versions at *http://www.microsoft.com/downloads/details.aspx?FamilyID=c243a5ae-4bd1-4e3d-94b8-5a0f62bf7796&DisplayLang=en*.

After you've finished installing and configuring *AdventureWorks*, go to the Windows Start menu and launch SQL Server on your system. Enter the information for your SQL Server 2005 Express Edition installation in the dialog box shown in Figure 1-5. The default installation can be accessed using the server name *(local)\ SQLEXPRESS* or *YourMachineName\SQLEXPRESS* and authentication type Windows Authentication.

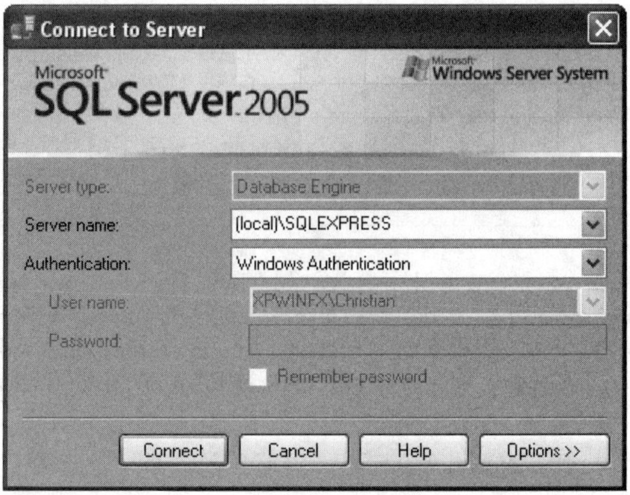

Figure 1-5. The SSMSE login window

Next, right-click on the databases folder within SSMSE and select Attach. In the dialog box that opens (Figure 1-6), click the Add button and select the *AdventureWorks_Data.mdf* file. Click OK twice. The *AdventureWorks* database is now permanently attached to your installation of SQL Server 2005 Express Edition.

ASP.NET AJAX Structure and Architecture

It is now time to actually use ASP.NET AJAX. Start VWD and create a new ASP.NET web site using the ASP.NET AJAX template. If you take a look at Solution Explorer, you will see a regular ASP.NET web site. Don't be surprised; the installer placed the ASP.NET AJAX assembly directly in the GAC. The only thing different about it is the file, *Web.config*, which is preconfigured with the settings required for ASP.NET AJAX to work.

ASP.NET AJAX consists of both server and client components. It is possible to use only the server components, or only the client components. There is one exception: every ASP.NET AJAX application will need the ScriptManager server control, which will be discussed later in this chapter. Usually, you will want to use both the server and client components.

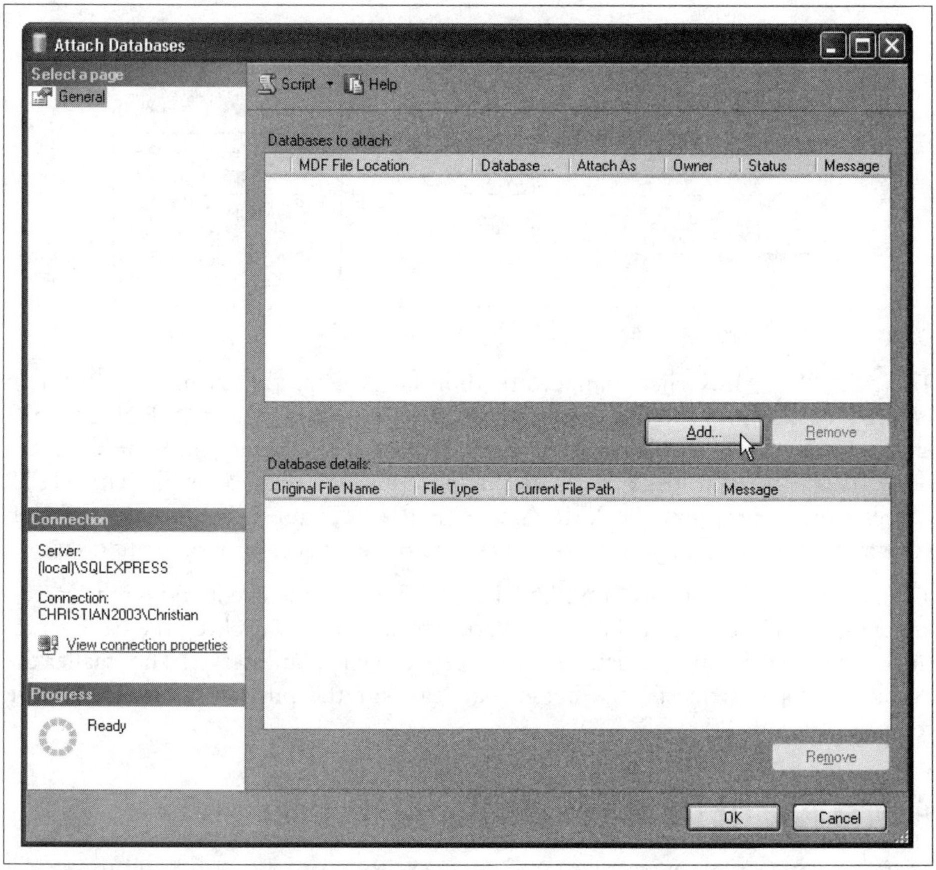

Figure 1-6. Attaching the MDF file to the SQL Server 2005 Express Edition installation

The roles the client and server components play in an ASP.NET AJAX project will become clearer when we take a closer look at how Ajax applications that use XMLHttpRequest really work.

Figure 1-7 shows the basic structure of ASP.NET AJAX. Whereas standard web pages consist of only two parts—one request and one response—Ajax-enabled web pages can continuously exchange data with the server. ASP.NET AJAX helps on both ends of the wire. Client script libraries (which, as you will soon see are dynamically loaded by the ScriptManager control) facilitate communication between browser and web server and make client coding easier. The code implemented in the ASP.NET AJAX server assembly takes care of accepting and handling XMLHttpRequest calls and also implements some convenient server web controls that we will cover later in the book. As a result, client and server components can exchange data with very little effort by the programmer.

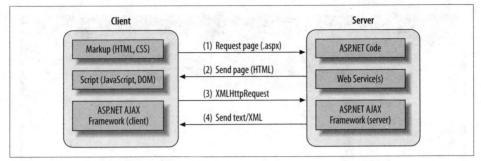

Figure 1-7. The life cycle of an ASP.NET AJAX web page

The ASP.NET AJAX client framework (bottom layer of the client component in Figure 1-7) is sent to the browser from the server the first time an ASP.NET AJAX-enabled page is requested (steps 1 and 2 in Figure 1-7). Subsequent requests to the server from the same page in an Ajax application can then be made with HTTP requests that return text and XML (steps 3 and 4 in Figure 1-7). An ASP.NET web page might use full-page postbacks and asynchronous requests for different tasks.

The individual components of ASP.NET AJAX, both on the client and on the server, are detailed throughout the book. However you should always keep the basic structure in mind, including the data exchange between client and server. The smaller the number of page requests, the better—at least for the purpose of avoiding page refreshes.

A First ASP.NET AJAX Example: Hello User

To test whether your setup of ASP.NET AJAX has been successful and to see the framework in action, let's end this chapter by creating a small sample application. The sample page accepts a username, sends it to the web server (in the background, using XMLHttpRequest), and receives it back with some extra text. The new version of the name is then presented to the user. This sample is a simple demonstrations of how easy it can be to set up an application using the features of ASP.NET AJAX. In later chapters, more detailed descriptions of the inner workings and operation will be provided.

In VWD, create a new web site using the ASP.NET AJAX template. Next, create a new web service (using the web service file template) in the root directory of the web site and call it *WebService.asmx*. In the web service *.asmx* file, implement a simple web method that accepts one string parameter by pasting the code shown in Example 1-1 into the file. Notice that you need the attribute, [ScriptServices], which is actually defined by ASP.NET AJAX (within the namespace System.Web. Script.Services).

Example 1-1. The web service

WebService.asmx

```csharp
<%@ WebService Language="C#" Class="WebService" %>

using System;
using System.Web;
using System.Web.Services;
using System.Web.Services.Protocols;

[WebService(Namespace = "http://hauser-wenz.de/AspNetAJAX/")]
[WebServiceBinding(ConformsTo = WsiProfiles.BasicProfile1_1)]
[System.Web.Script.Services.ScriptService]
public class WebService   : System.Web.Services.WebService {
    [WebMethod]
    public string sayHello(string name) {
    return "Hello " + name + ", says the server!";
    }
}
```

Now call this web service in your web browser, but append */js* to the URL. As shown in Figure 1-8, this URL actually returns JavaScript code. In fact, this code implements a JavaScript proxy class (to be covered in more detail in Chapter 5). Most important, the code produces a variable named WebService that provides a reference to the web service.

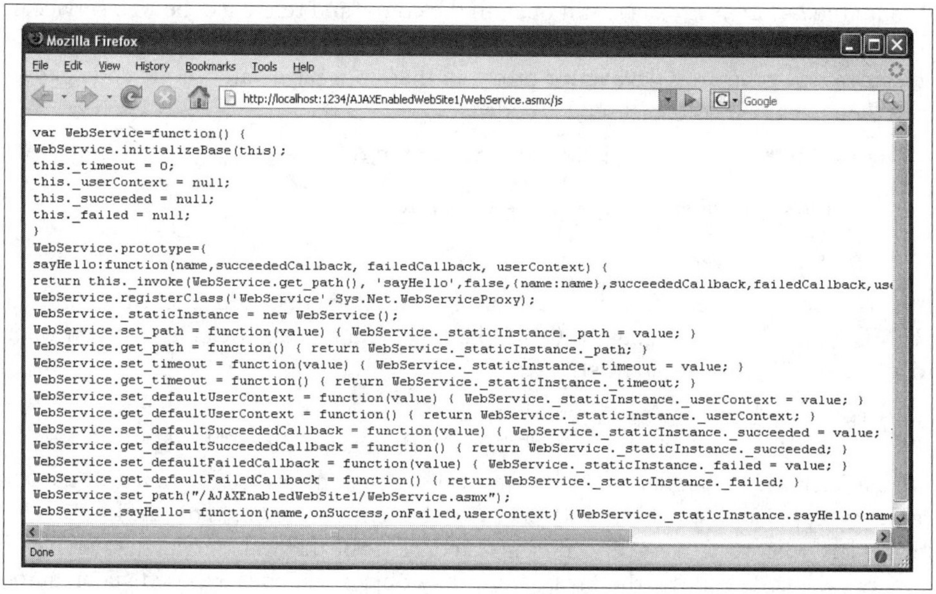

Figure 1-8. ASP.NET AJAX creates this JavaScript code automatically

You will see that the ASP.NET AJAX template already created a file, *Default.aspx*, with some contents that you will expand in the following steps. Following is the code you will see in this file:

```
<%@ Page Language="C#" AutoEventWireup="true" CodeFile="Default.aspx.cs"
Inherits="_Default" %>

<!DOCTYPE html PUBLIC "-//W3C//DTD XHTML 1.1//EN"
"http://www.w3.org/TR/xhtml11/DTD/xhtml11.dtd">
<html xmlns="http://www.w3.org/1999/xhtml">
<head runat="server">
    <title>Untitled Page</title>
</head>
<body>
    <form id="form1" runat="server">
        <asp:ScriptManager ID="ScriptManager1" runat="server" />
        <div>
        </div>
    </form>
</body>
</html>
```

The first thing you will likely notice is a new control: `<asp:ScriptManager>`. This control is the central element of every ASP.NET AJAX web page. We will explore Script-Manager control in greater detail later in this chapter (see "The ScriptManager Control").

Be sure the *Default.aspx* file is still open in the editor and reference the web service in the following fashion within the `ScriptManager` element. When the page runs, this reference will generate a JavaScript proxy so that your page can use the code generated dynamically by the web service code:

```
<asp:ScriptManager ID="ScriptManager1" runat="server">
  <Services>
    <asp:ServiceReference Path="WebService.asmx" />
  </Services>
</asp:ScriptManager>
```

At this point, you need to bring in some HTML elements. Add a text box and an HTML button to the existing `<form>` element (within the `<div>` element, if you want to adhere to XHTML standards):

```
<input type="text" id="name" name="name" />
<input type="button" value="Call Service" onclick="callService(this.form);" />
```

The `onclick` event handler of the button calls a custom JavaScript function named `callService()` and passes a reference to the current form. The `callService()` method is where the web service is invoked. To call the web service's `sayHello()` method, the code can use the JavaScript proxy object, which is exposed via an automatically generated variable named `WebService`. (The name `WebService` matches the name of the web service class you created earlier.)

The sayHello( ) method expects not only a string, but also references to up to three handler functions; one to call when the web service succeeds (callComplete), one to call when an error occurs (callError), and a third to call if the call times out. (For this example, we'll use only the first two.)

Next, place the following code within a client-side <script> element on your page:

```
function callService(f) {
  WebService.sayHello(
    f.elements["name"].value,
    callComplete,
    callError);
}
```

Finally, you need to provide the two handler functions for the callComplete and callError events. To do this, add the following code to the client script block that you just created:

```
function callComplete(result) {
  window.alert(result);
}
function callError(result) {
  window.alert("Error! " + result);
}
```

Example 1-2 shows the complete code for the *Default.aspx* file.

Example 1-2. A simple ASP.NET AJAX page that calls a web service

Default.aspx

```
<%@ Page Language="C#" AutoEventWireup="true" CodeFile="Default.aspx.cs"
Inherits="_Default" %>

<!DOCTYPE html PUBLIC "-//W3C//DTD XHTML 1.1//EN"
"http://www.w3.org/TR/xhtml11/DTD/xhtml11.dtd">
<html xmlns="http://www.w3.org/1999/xhtml">
<head runat="server">
  <title>ASP.NET AJAX</title>

  <script language="Javascript" type="text/javascript">
  function callService(f) {
    WebService.sayHello(
      f.elements["name"].value,
      callComplete,
      callError);
  }

  function callComplete(result) {
    window.alert(result);
  }
```

Example 1-2. A simple ASP.NET AJAX page that calls a web service (continued)

```
  function callError(result) {
    window.alert("Error! " + result);
  }
  </script>

</head>
<body>
  <form id="form1" runat="server">
    <asp:ScriptManager
 ID="ScriptManager1"
runat="server">
      <Services>
        <asp:ServiceReference Path="WebService.asmx" />
      </Services>
    </asp:ScriptManager>
    <div>
      <input type="text" id="name" name="name" />
      <input type="button" value="Call Service" onclick="callService(this.form);" />
    </div>
  </form>

</body>
</html>
```

Figure 1-9 shows the results when the page is loaded and the Call Service button is clicked.

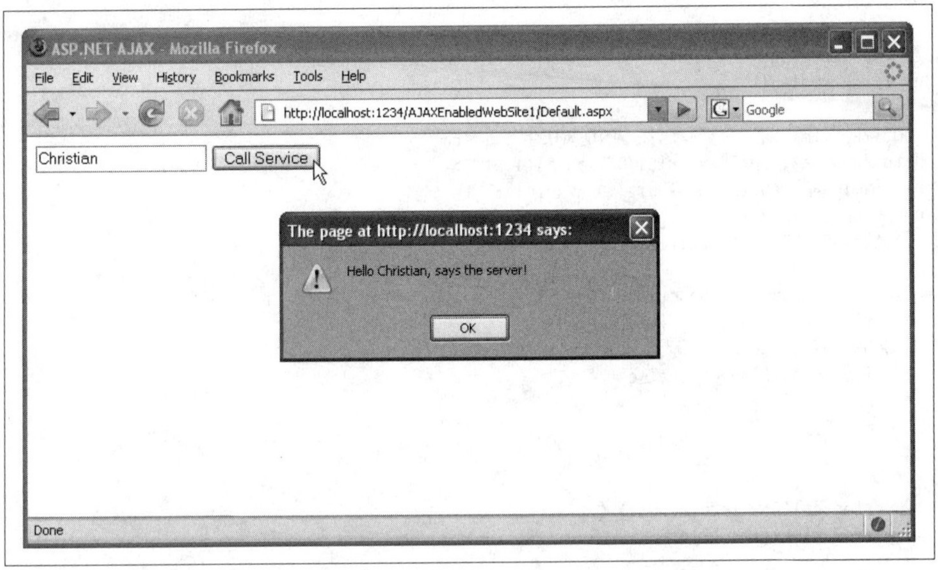

Figure 1-9. The application works as expected

Run the page (F5, or Ctrl+F5 in VWD). As you can see in the browser, the results are predictable—not only with Internet Explorer, but also with other relevant browsers. Click the Call Service button several times, and note carefully that the button does not result in a postback, even though the page is communicating with the web service on the server.

The ScriptManager Control

Now that you've completed the first exercise, here is some more background information about how it worked, and how the other ASP.NET AJAX examples throughout this book work.

The central element of an ASP.NET AJAX-powered ASP.NET page is the ScriptManager control. This control takes care of loading the required JavaScript libraries for ASP.NET AJAX.

If you run an ASP.NET AJAX application and then examine the resulting source code in the browser, you will see that the code has changed quite a bit from what it looked like when you were editing it. The <asp:ScriptManager> element will have been replaced with the following code (although the undecipherable data contained in the URL will be different on your system):

```
<script src="/AJAXEnabledWebSite1/WebResource.axd?d=Jd4j-
uCaCWzJ5gY8Rtbjnw2&amp;t=632962478475625000" type="text/javascript"></script>

<script src="/AJAXEnabledWebSite1/ScriptResource.axd?d=4vKPTV3rK3vcGz1fNEcIXI-
FjnEGgHGMpqfUlmBk4NA5KxnrqcWXFT6hln9QkTuglOUzzonzRPSF5F3_-
OaWhWOb3FCqEciv4AZjgqdK5us1&amp;t=633074690770156250" type="text/javascript">
</script>
<script src="/AJAXEnabledWebSite1/ScriptResource.axd?d=4vKPTV3rK3vcGz1fNEcIXI-
FjnEGgHGMpqfUlmBk4NA5KxnrqcWXFT6hln9QkTuglOUzzonzRPSF5F3_-OaWhdU1qTQPzcChFvbHT6FrI-
81&amp;t=633074690770156250" type="text/javascript"></script>
```

ASP.NET AJAX also generated JavaScript code that initializes some parts of the Ajax framework for you.

 When building the web application in debug mode, the JavaScript code created by ASP.NET is nicely formatted and some errors are caught. This is convenient for developing purposes, but is not required (in fact, is recommended against) when the web site is deployed, since it makes the JavaScript code and therefore the page's size larger.

This ScriptManager element must be present on all pages that use ASP.NET AJAX features.

Loading Additional JavaScript Files

The ScriptManager can also be used to load additional JavaScript libraries, either those that come with ASP.NET AJAX or even your own scripts:

```
<asp:ScriptManager ID="ScriptManager1" runat="server">
  <Scripts>
    <asp:ScriptReference Path="MyScript.js" />
  </Scripts>
</asp:ScriptManager>
```

Note that in the source code from the browser ASP.NET AJAX uses a mechanism to verify whether all external JavaScript files have been properly loaded. If you write custom JavaScript scripts, be sure to add the following code segment to the end of every *.js* file:

```
if (typeof(Sys) != "undefined") {
    Sys.Application.notifyScriptLoaded();
}
```

This segment notifies ASP.NET AJAX that the end of the file has been reached and signals the Ajax framework that all external scripts are fully loaded.

If you are using ASP.NET 2.0 master pages and most of your pages use the ASP.NET AJAX framework, you might consider putting the ScriptManager control on your master page instead of on the individual pages. However, this can cause difficulties when you need to reference additional JavaScript files or web services (like the "Hello User" example earlier) on a content page. Only one ScriptManager control is allowed per page, so you would need to reference the JavaScript file or web service on every page that use ASP.NET AJAX features, even on those that do not need these external resources.

For this scenario, ASP.NET AJAX provides the ScriptManagerProxy control. This control provides ScriptManager functionality when there is already another ScriptManager present.

```
<asp:ScriptManagerProxy ID="ScriptManagerProxy1" runat="server">
  <Scripts>
    <asp:ScriptReference Path="MyScript.js" />
  </Scripts>
</asp:ScriptManagerProxy>
```

The ScriptManagerProxy control can also be useful if you are creating an ASP.NET user control that includes AJAX functionality in cases where there is a ScriptManager control on the host page.

This was just the first step. There's much more to come in the following chapters!

Summary

This chapter introduced ASP.NET AJAX, explained its relationship to Ajax and ASP.NET 2.0, and guided you through its installation and the installation of other software you need for this book, including the *AdventureWorks* database. You also created your first working ASP.NET AJAX example and learned about the ScriptManager control, one of two key server controls that ship with ASP.NET AJAX. In the next chapter, you'll have a look at the JavaScript you will need to work with ASP.NET AJAX.

For Further Reading

http://ajax.asp.net/
> ASP.NET AJAX home page

http://ajax.asp.net/downloads/default.aspx?tabid=47
> ASP.NET AJAX downloads

http://ajax.asp.net/docs/InstallingASPNETAJAX.aspx
> ASP.NET AJAX installation instructions in the Microsoft documentation

http://blogs.msdn.com/webdevtools/archive/2007/07/28/upgrading-asp-net-ajax-1-0-websites-and-web-applications-to-net-framework-3-5.aspx
> Important information for upgrading ASP.NET AJAX web sites created with Visual Studio 2005 to Visual Studio 2008/.NET Framework 3.5

http://weblogs.asp.net/scottgu/archive/2007/08/04/fixes-for-common-vs-2008-and-net-3-5-beta2-issues.aspx
> A list of some known issues in Visual Studio 2008 Beta 2 and their possible workarounds

CHAPTER 2

JavaScript

Interactivity is key to making web pages more useful, dynamic, and interesting to the user. The ability to embed scripts in web pages is key to making them more interactive. Scripts can be used to respond to events, such as when a page loads or a user clicks a button. Scripts are also how you work with and process data sent to and from the server via HTTP requests and responses.

For most web developers, JavaScript is the language of choice as it is the only one supported by all major browsers. A sound knowledge of JavaScript is important to make the most of ASP.NET AJAX. However, an Ajax framework such as ASP.NET AJAX makes it easy to use the technology without requiring extensive familiarity of its details. In fact, ASP.NET AJAX can even help developers who are not at all familiar with JavaScript thanks to the framework approach. Still, as ASP.NET AJAX is simply a framework, without the ability to use JavaScript, you are limited to the functionality offered by the ASP.NET AJAX controls. Some client scenarios may actually require more work in ASP.NET AJAX than creating a custom JavaScript. Therefore, the best strategy for an Ajax-enabled web site is to use the best of both worlds: the ASP.NET AJAX framework that you extend with your JavaScript coding skills.

Of course this book is about ASP.NET AJAX, so a complete tutorial of JavaScript here is beyond our scope. The aim of this chapter is to provide you with a good foundation so you can use and understand the examples in this book. The following details on JavaScript are far from complete and focus only on its most important features. For more information on JavaScript, please refer to the resources listed in the "For Further Reading" section at the end of this chapter.

JavaScript: A History

The JavaScript language was created by Netscape engineer Brendan Eich in the 1990s. Originally called Mocha, it made its first appearance in 1995 as part of the third beta version of Netscape Navigator 2.0. Later that year, Netscape arranged with Sun Microsystems—the originator and owner of the Java language—to use the name JavaScript (prior to this, for some time it was known as LiveScript). This has caused confusion ever since as with the single exception that they're both C-style languages, JavaScript and Java share no other similarities. Sun still owns the trademark to the name JavaScript.

JavaScript allowed HTML pages to be truly dynamic. It offered instant form data validation, graphical effects, user interaction, and much more. At a time when bandwidth was limited (most users were on slow dial-up lines) and server roundtrips were costly, JavaScript gave web developers a tool to make their sites more interactive. When JavaScript took off, Microsoft added scripting capabilities to its own browser, Internet Explorer, as well. For copyright reasons they named their version of the language JScript. It was, for all intents and purposes, a JavaScript work-alike.

In 1997, the browser war between Netscape Navigator (at the time, still the market leader) and Internet Explorer (soon to become the market leader) reached a climax. In June, Netscape 4 was released and included JavaScript Version 1.2 with new capabilities. In the same month, the Ecma (a private standards organization) published the ECMA-262 standard, which formalized the scripting language (see *http://www.ecma-international.org/publications/standards/Ecma-262.htm*). JavaScript, therefore, is an implementation of ECMA-262 or ECMAScript.

In October of that same year, Internet Explorer 4 was released. However, its support was limited to JavaScript 1.1. (It also supported VBScript, a scripting language based on Visual Basic; we do not address VBScript here because it runs only in Internet Explorer and is therefore not relevant for browser-agnostic client scripting.) At that point, the browsers were quite incompatible, particularly when it came to implementing effects like positioning and moving elements. The mix of technologies used to achieve these kinds of effects has been dubbed Dynamic HTML (DHTML). Despite popular belief, DHTML is not a standard at all, but a fabricated term, just like Ajax.

Then, things changed dramatically. Netscape scrapped a near-ready Version 5 of its browser and decided to rewrite it from scratch. This led to an immature Version 6 of Netscape, based on the new open source Mozilla project and the Gecko rendering engine. The delays and the quality issues of the browser (and of course some other factors, as well) cost Netscape their market share, and Internet Explorer took the lead.

—continued—

However, development of Internet Explorer stalled with Version 6, and the Firefox browser (the browser itself was also based on Mozilla, but additional features, such as mail or news reader were not) started claiming some of Internet Explorer's market share. Internet Explorer 7 was the first new release in about six years, so the race is on again.

From a JavaScript point of view, not very much has changed in recent years. After the death of Netscape 4, the major browsers—Internet Explorer and Mozilla, along with Safari, Konqueror, and Opera—are compatible in their support for JavaScript, although some differences and issues remain.

The lack of innovation in browsers has also held back widespread use of JavaScript. Even books on the topic received very few updates in the last couple of years. However, this all changed with the invention of the term Ajax (more on this in Chapter 3). Although the technology behind Ajax has existed since 1998, it only recently moved into mainstream web programming. Chapter 3 covers this in more detail.

The JavaScript Language

JavaScript is loosely based on the C programming language, so programmers coming from a C, C++, C#, or Java background can usually learn the syntax in a short amount of time. There are some aspects of JavaScript that make it quite accessible. For example, it is not strongly typed—the programmer doesn't assign data types. Instead, JavaScript assigns them at runtime. In addition, JavaScript to some extent supports object-oriented programming. However, it does not rely on it, as do other languages such as C# or Java.

JavaScript can be embedded in web pages in three ways: in scripts, in event handlers, and in URLs. The syntax used in each case is different.

Embedding a script in a web page
> Scripts are typically embedded in an HTML page using the HTML <script> element. You can also use the src attribute of <script> to target a URL if you want to load an external script file.

> The major browsers all assume that JavaScript is the default language whenever they encounter a <script> tag on a web page. However, to satisfy W3C (World Wide Web Consortium) standards and the needs of less-used or older browsers (including outdated versions), it's always best to specify the language using the syntax shown here:

```
<script language="JavaScript" type="text/javascript">
    ...
</script>
```

Using a script to handle an event
> JavaScript code can be used for the value of an event handler in an HTML tag attribute (e.g., <input type="button" onclick="doSomething( );" />).

Using JavaScript in a URL
JavaScript can appear in a URL that uses the special `javascript:` pseudoprotocol, making it easy to use JavaScript in hyperlinks (e.g., `<a href="javascript:doSomething( );">click me</a>`).

The first two options are the most commonly used and are demonstrated in the following sections that will also introduce you to key elements of the JavaScript language.

When Browsers Don't Support JavaScript

Years ago, the `<script>` element was used in a different fashion:

```
<script language="JavaScript" type="text/javascript"><!--
    ...//--></script>
```

The HTML comment (`<!--` and `-->`) was used to force browsers without JavaScript capabilities to ignore the JavaScript code. (The two slashes before the end of the HTML comment (`//-->`) denote a JavaScript comment, which caused JavaScript to ignore the closing HTML comment tag.)

However, this is all history. Even browsers that do not support JavaScript now know to ignore `<script>` elements.

Common JavaScript Methods

JavaScript provides two methods that we will use repeatedly in the examples presented in this chapter:

`document.write("Text")`
This method writes the given text to the browser window.

`window.alert("Text")`
This second method opens up a modal window to display an informational message.

Example 2-1 shows markup for a page that uses the second method to display an alert.

Example 2-1. Using JavaScript

`JavaScript.htm`

```
<!DOCTYPE html PUBLIC "-//W3C//DTD XHTML 1.0 Transitional//EN"
"http://www.w3.org/TR/xhtml1/DTD/xhtml1-transitional.dtd">
<html xmlns="http://www.w3.org/1999/xhtml">
<head>
  <title>JavaScript</title>
  <script language="JavaScript" type="text/javascript">
  window.alert("Hello from JavaScript!");
```

Example 2-1. Using JavaScript (continued)

```
   </script>
</head>
<body>
</body>
</html>
```

Figure 2-1 presents the result you can expect when Example 2-1 executes. In Internet Explorer 6 SP 2 onward, you might get a security warning for running active content in the browser from the local filesystem. This message will not appear if the script resides on a remote web server.

Figure 2-1. The modal window created by the JavaScript alert function

Variables

JavaScript variables are defined using the var keyword. They do not require a naming convention such as a prefix to specify their type, as is true in languages such as Perl or PHP. Variables are global unless they are defined in a function. They do not have a fixed data type, which allows them to change their type at runtime. However, JavaScript provides a few built-in data types that you're likely to use repeatedly, including the four listed below:

- Number (1, -2, 3.14159)
- String ("Hello", 'World')
- Boolean (true, false)
- RegEx (/d+/)

There are other data type objects as well. For instance, Date is used for date values. However, this is not an actual data type, but a class that can be used to access the current date and perform calculations with it.

As shown here, values are assigned to a variable using the = operator.

```
var i = 0; //Create variable, set its value to 0
i = "JavaScript"; //Set variable value to a string
i = false; //Set variable value to a Boolean
```

Unlike other languages, such as PHP or Perl, there is no functional difference between single and double quotes in Java-Script. Note that the terminal character (;) is optional, but it's recommended to avoid unintentionally combining statements.

Depending on their current type, JavaScript variables support the class methods associated with that type. For instance, every string you create supports the substring() method, which can locate parts of the string, and the indexOf() method, which can find the occurrence of a substring in the current string.

Arrays

An array is a variable containing a list of values. But because JavaScript is not strongly typed, an array can contain different data types. There are two ways to create an array. One is to use new Array() and provide some values. Array indexes are zero-based, so the following code snippet adds a seventh element to a list:

```
var days = new Array("Sunday", "Monday", "Tuesday", "Wednesday", "Thursday",
"Friday");
days[6] = "Saturday";
```

Alternatively, today's browsers also let you create an array using the shortcut below:

```
var days = ["Sunday", "Monday", "Tuesday", "Wednesday", "Thursday", "Friday",
"Saturday"];
```

Control Structures

JavaScript supports the standard set of control structures, including switch, if... else, and various loops (for, for...in, foreach, while, do...loop, and do...until). Let's begin with the if statement. Example 2-2 generates a random number using Math.random() (something we'll use again later in this book), a built-in function we will use to create a new random number between 0 (inclusive) and 1 (exclusive). Multiplying the value by 6 gives us a random number between 0 (inclusive) and 6 (exclusive). Rounding the number up using the Math.ceil() method generates a value between 1 and 6 (both inclusive), simulating the roll of a single die.

Example 2-2. Using if…else and Math.random

JavaScript-if.htm

```
<!DOCTYPE html PUBLIC "-//W3C//DTD XHTML 1.0 Transitional//EN"
"http://www.w3.org/TR/xhtml1/DTD/xhtml1-transitional.dtd">
<html xmlns="http://www.w3.org/1999/xhtml">
<head>
  <title>JavaScript</title>
  <script language="JavaScript" type="text/javascript">
  var rand = Math.random( );
  rand = Math.ceil(6 * rand);
  if (rand % 2 == 1) {
    document.write("Odd number: ");
  } else {
    document.write("Even number: ");
  }
  document.write(rand);
  </script>
</head>
<body>
</body>
</html>
```

Figure 2-2 shows the results of running the script.

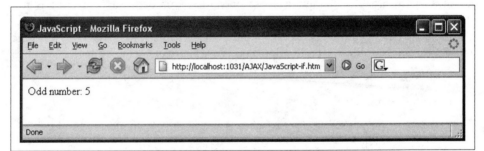

Figure 2-2. Rolling a (virtual) die with JavaScript

Example 2-2 makes use of some additional JavaScript elements that are explained below.

Boolean operators
> ! (exclamation point) the logical negation operator in JavaScript; || is the logical or operator; && is the logical and operator.

Comparison operators
> == checks for equality (whereas = is the assignment operator); other comparison operators include >=, >, <, <=, and !=. A special operator is ===, which not only compares values, but data types as well; its negation is !==.

JavaScript supports a tertiary operator that is a very convenient shortcut for performing an if...else operation. The expression

```
var output = (rand % 2 == 1) ? "odd" : "even";
```

is equivalent to:

```
if (rand % 2 == 1) {
  var output = "odd";
} else {
  var output = "even";
}
```

Rather than using a series of if statements to check the same expression over and over, you can use the switch statement. Have a look at Example 2-3 to see how it works.

Example 2-3. Using switch

JavaScript-switch.htm

```
<!DOCTYPE html PUBLIC "-//W3C//DTD XHTML 1.0 Transitional//EN"
"http://www.w3.org/TR/xhtml1/DTD/xhtml1-transitional.dtd">
<html xmlns="http://www.w3.org/1999/xhtml">
<head>
  <title>JavaScript</title>
  <script language="JavaScript" type="text/javascript">
  var rand = Math.random( );
  rand = Math.ceil(6 * rand);
    switch (rand) {
      case 1:
      case 3:
      case 5:
      document.write("Odd number: ");
      break;
    default:
      document.write("Even number: ");
    }
  document.write(rand);
  </script>
</head>
<body>
</body>
</html>
```

As you can see, only a break statement exits the switch statement. Without it, the JavaScript interpreter would run through the remaining statements even if the switch expression matches one of the case values.

Loops are quite convenient for controlling the number of times code is repeated. For example, the for loop can be used for iterating through arrays. Each array has a property (length) that retrieves the number of elements in the array. The for loop in Example 2-4 displays all data in an array.

Example 2-4. Using a for loop

JavaScript-for.htm

```
<!DOCTYPE html PUBLIC "-//W3C//DTD XHTML 1.0 Transitional//EN"
"http://www.w3.org/TR/xhtml1/DTD/xhtml1-transitional.dtd">
<html xmlns="http://www.w3.org/1999/xhtml">
<head>
  <title>JavaScript</title>
  <script language="JavaScript" type="text/javascript">
  var days = ["Sunday", "Monday", "Tuesday", "Wednesday", "Thursday", "Friday",
"Saturday"];
  for (var i=0; i < days.length; i++) {
    document.write(days[i] + "<br />");
  }
  </script>
</head>
<body>
</body>
</html>
```

Figure 2-3 shows the result of running the script in Example 2-4.

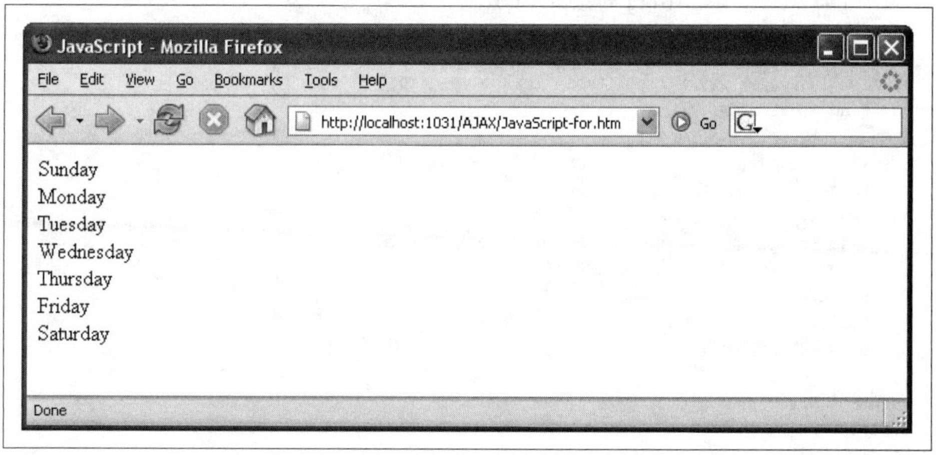

Figure 2-3. The for loop iterates through the array elements

Example 2-4 introduces some additional language features. The expression i++ used to iterate the for loop is a short form for i = i + 1 (i++ is a related expression). Note that the + operator can be used not only to add numbers but to concatenate strings as well.

JavaScript also provides a for...in loop, which works similar to a foreach statement in C# and related languages. Example 2-5 demonstrates its use. At each iteration, the loop variable reads the current element. If you use a foreach statement to retrieve objects, you get access to all properties and methods of the objects.

For arrays, you get the individual array indexes. Therefore, with the days array from the preceding example, the values during an iteration over the array are 0 to 6, not "Sunday" through "Saturday".

Example 2-5. Using a for...in loop

JavaScript-for-in.htm

```
<!DOCTYPE html PUBLIC "-//W3C//DTD XHTML 1.0 Transitional//EN"
"http://www.w3.org/TR/xhtml1/DTD/xhtml1-transitional.dtd">
<html xmlns="http://www.w3.org/1999/xhtml">
<head>
  <title>JavaScript</title>
  <script language="JavaScript" type="text/javascript">
  var days = ["Sunday", "Monday", "Tuesday", "Wednesday", "Thursday", "Friday",
"Saturday"];
  for (var day in days) {
    document.write(days[day] + "<br />");
  }
  </script>
</head>
<body>
</body>
</html>
```

JavaScript provides several other loop statements that each perform similar operations: they run either *while* a particular condition exists or *until* a condition is met. Example 2-6 illustrates the most commonly used of these loops, the while loop.

Example 2-6. Using a while loop

JavaScript-while.htm

```
<!DOCTYPE html PUBLIC "-//W3C//DTD XHTML 1.0 Transitional//EN"
"http://www.w3.org/TR/xhtml1/DTD/xhtml1-transitional.dtd">
<html xmlns="http://www.w3.org/1999/xhtml">
<head>
  <title>JavaScript</title>
  <script language="JavaScript" type="text/javascript">
  var days = ["Sunday", "Monday", "Tuesday", "Wednesday", "Thursday", "Friday",
"Saturday"];
  var i = 0;
  while (i < days.length) {
    document.write(days[i] + "<br />");
    i++;
  }
  </script>
</head>
<body>
</body>
</html>
```

Built-in Methods, Custom Functions, and Event Handling

JavaScript comes with a set of built-in objects, but you can create custom functions (and objects) as well. A function is identified with the `function` keyword. Because you cannot specify a data type for the return value (and as a consequence, there is no void keyword), a function does not necessarily have to return a value. If you do wish to return a value, however, use the `return` statement.

Example 2-7 demonstrates the `replace( )` method available for all strings, which provides regular expression support. As you will see, the script converts several HTML-specific syntax characters to their associated escape-coded entities. The script makes several calls in succession to `replace( )`. First, the & character is replaced by its associated entity (&), then, one by one, the remaining characters (<, >, ", and ') are converted, or "escaped." In the end, any string handled by the script will be transformed into its associated HTML markup, just as the ASP.NET method `Server.HtmlEncode( )` would do.

Example 2-7. Writing a custom function

JavaScript-function.htm

```
<!DOCTYPE html PUBLIC "-//W3C//DTD XHTML 1.0 Transitional//EN"
"http://www.w3.org/TR/xhtml1/DTD/xhtml1-transitional.dtd">
<html xmlns="http://www.w3.org/1999/xhtml">
<head>
  <title>JavaScript</title>
</head>
<body>
  <script language="JavaScript" type="text/javascript">
  function HtmlEscape(s) {
    var result = s.replace(/&/g, "&amp;")
                  .replace(/</g, "&lt;")
                  .replace(/>/g, "&gt;")
                  .replace(/"/g, "&quot;")
                  .replace(/'/g, "&apos;");
    return result;
  }
  document.write(HtmlEscape("<hr />"));
  </script>
</body>
</html>
```

When it executes, Example 2-7 outputs <hr />, which is displayed as <hr /> in the browser, but does not create a horizontal rule.

Although JavaScript does not support function overloading; the number of arguments in a function is not fixed. If more arguments are provided in the function signature than are submitted by the caller, the extra arguments are assigned the value null.

However, as demonstrated in Example 2-8, if more arguments are submitted than expected, the arguments property (short for *<Functionname>*.arguments) provides access to all of them.

Example 2-8. Writing a custom function with a variable number of arguments

JavaScript-function-arguments.htm

```
<!DOCTYPE html PUBLIC "-//W3C//DTD XHTML 1.0 Transitional//EN"
"http://www.w3.org/TR/xhtml1/DTD/xhtml1-transitional.dtd">
<html xmlns="http://www.w3.org/1999/xhtml">
<head>
  <title>JavaScript</title>
</head>
<body>
  <script language="JavaScript" type="text/javascript">
  function OutputList( ) {
    document.write("<ul>");
    for (var i=0; i < arguments.length; i++) {
      document.write("<li>" +
                      arguments[i] +
                      "</li>");
    }
    document.write("</ul>");
  }
  OutputList("one", "two", "three");
  </script>
</body>
</html>
```

Figure 2-4 shows the output that results when Example 2-8 executes.

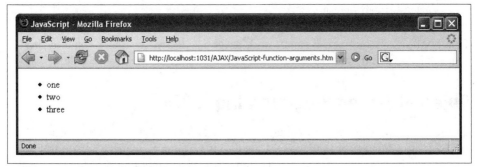

Figure 2-4. The custom function generates the bulleted list

JavaScript also supports *anonymous functions*, functions with no name. Anonymous functions are sometimes used in JavaScript to handle events. For instance, the onload attribute of the <body> tag can be assigned JavaScript code that is executed once the HTML of the page has been completely loaded. (This is, in fact, possible for all events tied to HTML markup.) This is JavaScript's built-in event handling.

You can bind code to an event by concatenating on and the event name and assigning code to be executed when the event occurs. There are other ways to bind code to events, but anonymous methods and HTML attributes are the two most popular choices.

The snippet below displays a window with the word "Loaded" when a page is loaded:

```
<body onload="alert('Loaded.');">
```

Or, more generically stated, the syntax would look as shown below:

```
<body onload="Functionname();">
```

You can also bind an event to a handler in code. The base object of a page is called window, so you can set window.onload to a function, as shown in the following example:

```
function Functionname() {
  // do stuff
}
window.onload = Functionname;
```

If you do not need to use the function for any other reason, you can assign an anonymous function to the event name directly. This will allow you to shorten the preceding example to that presented below:

```
window.onload = function() {
  // do stuff
}
```

Finnally, we present an example of an anonymous function that includes parameters:

```
window.onload = function(a, b) {
  // do stuff with a and b
}
```

This approach is quite convenient and, as you will see, is used frequently by the ASP.NET AJAX framework.

Object-Oriented Programming (OOP)

JavaScript is an *object-based* language, but not an *object-oriented* (OOP) one. There are aspects of JavaScript that are OOP-like, but support for conventional OOP techniques is limited. For instance, visibility of class members (public, private, protected, etc.) can be implemented only in a limited way. Nevertheless, it is possible to create classes in JavaScript and even to provide rudimentary support for class inheritance.

A class in JavaScript is implemented by creating a function. The code within this function is the class constructor. It contains the declarations and definitions of all instance members (i.e., all public and private properties and methods). The keyword this can be used as a reference to the current class instance, thus providing the constructor (and class methods) access to the properties of the current class. This also makes it possible for the class code to set properties and define methods, which are then also available to code outside the class.

Example 2-9 shows a simple class that implements a book. Note that we are using data in private properties which cannot be accessed from outside the class. Next, we define public getter and setter methods to provide access these properties. This is commonly called *encapsulation* and allows a standardized access to properties and offers the possibility to validate values before assigning them to properties.

Example 2-9. Using JavaScript's OOP features

JavaScript-class.htm

```
<!DOCTYPE html PUBLIC "-//W3C//DTD XHTML 1.0 Transitional//EN"
"http://www.w3.org/TR/xhtml1/DTD/xhtml1-transitional.dtd">
<html xmlns="http://www.w3.org/1999/xhtml">
<head>
  <title>JavaScript</title>
</head>
<body>
  <script language="JavaScript" type="text/javascript">
  function Book(isbn, author, title) {
    var _isbn = isbn;
    var _author = author;
    var _title = title;

    this.get_isbn = function( ) {
      return _isbn;
    }
    this.set_isbn = function(value) {
      _isbn = value;
    }
    this.get_author = function( ) {
      return _author;
    }
    this.set_author = function(value) {
      _author = value;
    }
    this.get_title = function( ) {
      return _title;
    }
    this.set_title = function(value) {
      _title = value;
    }

    this.toString = function( ) {
      return this.get_author() + ": " + this.get_title() + " (" + this.get_isbn() + ")";
    }
  }
```

Example 2-9. Using JavaScript's OOP features (continued)

```
   var atlas = new Book("0792275438", "National Geographic");
   atlas.set_title("Atlas of the World");
   document.write(atlas.toString( ));
   </script>
</body>
</html>
```

This code in this example will output the following text:

```
   National Geographic: Atlas of the World (0792275438)
```

Since JavaScript does not support access modifiers (just think of private, protected, and public in C#), we use local variables to implement the private properties. As mentioned, all properties assigned to instances of this are accessible from outside the class; variables that are declared inside the class remain private. The latter variables can be used only from within the class and are not exposed for use by others. This is the only way to implement data hiding and create something similar to private methods and properties.

Inheritance is possible in JavaScript to a limited extent. The prototype property can be used to define a method or property that is available to all instances of inherited objects. The following code would add a new method to all arrays:

```
   Array.prototype.empty = function( ) {
      this.length = 0;
   }
```

Use the following expression to define one class that inherits from another class:

```
   DerivedClass.prototype = new BaseClass( );
```

Example 2-10 extends the Book class with a DigitalBook class, adding one more private field (implemented as a local variable, _size, and accessible via getter and setter methods) and overriding the toString( ) method. Note that in JavaScript there are no protected properties (properties that can be accessed from subclasses), so all field variables from the base class must be defined again. ("Subclass" is presented here in the context of JavaScript—since JavaScript does not support "real" OOP inheritance, there is no such thing as subclasses, but you can create a similar behavior, as in this example.) However, the existing get and set methods are still available. In order to access them, use the call( ) method of the base object (similar to accessing base within a C# class).

Example 2-10. Using inheritance with JavaScript

JavaScript-class-prototype.htm

```
<!DOCTYPE html PUBLIC "-//W3C//DTD XHTML 1.0 Transitional//EN"
"http://www.w3.org/TR/xhtml1/DTD/xhtml1-transitional.dtd">
<html xmlns="http://www.w3.org/1999/xhtml">
<head>
  <title>JavaScript</title>
```

Example 2-10. Using inheritance with JavaScript (continued)

```
</head>
<body>
  <script language="JavaScript" type="text/javascript">
  function Book(isbn, author, title) {
    var _isbn = isbn;
    var _author = author;
    var _title = title;

    this.get_isbn = function() {
      return _isbn;
    }
    this.set_isbn = function(value) {
      _isbn = value;
    }
    this.get_author = function() {
      return _author;
    }
    this.set_author = function(value) {
      _author = value;
    }
    this.get_title = function() {
      return _title;
    }
    this.set_title = function(value) {
      _title = value;
    }

    this.toString = function() {
      return this.get_author() + ": " + this.get_title() + " (" + this.get_isbn() + ")";
    }
  }

  //class to derive from Book
  function DigitalBook(isbn, author, title, size) {
    Book.call(this, isbn, author, title);
    var _size = (size != null) ? size : 0;
    this.get_size = function() {
      return _size;
    }
    this.set_size = function(value) {
      _size = value;
    }

    this.toString = function() {
      return this.get_author() + ": " + this.get_title() + " (" + this.get_isbn() + ")" +
      " - " + this.get_size() + " KB";
    }
  }
  DigitalBook.prototype = new Book(); //Derive from book

  var atlas = new DigitalBook("0123456789", "International Graphics",
"Atlas of the City");
```

Example 2-10. Using inheritance with JavaScript (continued)

```
  atlas.set_size(1024);
  document.write(atlas.toString( ));
  </script>
</body>
</html>
```

Figure 2-5 shows the results displayed when you execute Example 2-10.

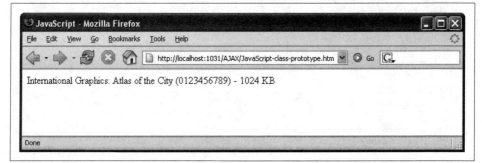

Figure 2-5. The toString( ) method of the derived object

Accessing Page Elements

Although recent browsers support the W3C DOM as a means of accessing elements within the current HTML page, there are, as you will see later, easier ways to work with elements on a page (see "DOM Methods," later in this chapter, for more information). Two of them are covered within this section.

Accessing Form Elements

JavaScript's document object grants access to all elements on the current page. document is a representation of the DOM that is accessible to JavaScript. To make access as convenient as possible, there are several subproperties that allow direct access to special page elements:

document.embeds
    An array containing all embedded media (via <embed>) on the current page

document.forms
    An array containing all <form> elements on the page

document.frames
    An array containing all frames on the current page

document.images
    An array containing all images on the current page

document.links
    An array containing all hyperlinks on the current page

The most commonly used property is document.forms, which allows access to all <form> elements on the current page, such as text boxes and buttons. Usually, there is only a single form on a page. However, the document.forms[0] property grants access to all elements within the first form. Then, the form object supports an elements[] array to access individual form elements. By accessing form elements, it's possible to add special features to a web page, such as a script to perform client-side form data validation as demonstrated below:

```
<form>
  <input type="text" name="TextBox1" />
</form>
```

The expression document.forms[0].elements["TextBox1"] accesses the form element called TextBox1 within the first form on the page. (A shortcut is document.forms[0]. TextBox1; however, this does not work if special characters—spaces or hyphens—are used in the form element's name attribute.) Depending on the type of the form element (e.g., text fields, radio buttons, checkboxes), accessing its value, whether it is text in the text field, or a selected radio button, can differ, but usually the value attribute will contain this information, just as the value HTML attribute does for most form fields.

Example 2-11 displays the output of the data entered into a text field after the user clicks on a button. Here is the markup for the button:

```
<input type="button" onclick="ShowText(this.form);" />
```

When you click the button, the ShowText() function is called. The parameter is this. form, which is a reference to the element's parent form. This makes accessing the data a bit easier as you can avoid using document.forms[0] in the called function. Example 2-11 shows the complete example.

Example 2-11. Accessing form elements

JavaScript-form-textbox.htm

```
<!DOCTYPE html PUBLIC "-//W3C//DTD XHTML 1.0 Transitional//EN"
"http://www.w3.org/TR/xhtml1/DTD/xhtml1-transitional.dtd">
<html xmlns="http://www.w3.org/1999/xhtml">
<head>
  <title>JavaScript</title>
  <script language="JavaScript" type="text/javascript">
  function ShowText(f) {
    alert("Entered text: " + f.elements["TextBox1"].value);
  }
  </script>
</head>
<body>
  <form action="">
    <input type="text" name="TextBox1" />
    <input type="button" value="Show text" onclick="ShowText(this.form);" />
  </form>
</body>
</html>
```

Figure 2-6 shows the result displayed when the script runs.

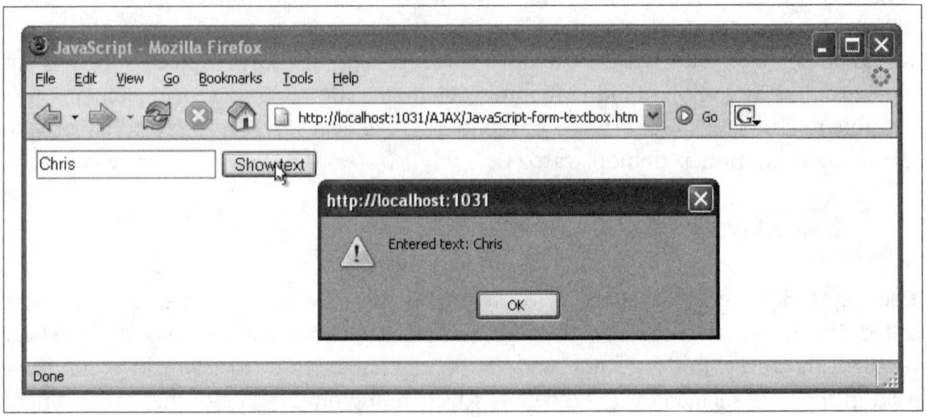

Figure 2-6. The form data is shown in a window

Table 2-1 shows the properties used to access the most commonly used values within the most common form field types. For example, the value of a text box defined with the markup `<input type="text" name="Name" />` can be accessed using the expression `document.forms[0].elements["Name"].value` (assuming that the text box resides in the first or only form in the document).

Table 2-1. HTML form fields and associated properties

Form field	HTML markup	Property

Text fields and password fields	`<input type="text">`
	`<input type="password">`
	`<textarea>`
		`value`: Gets and sets the data in the field

Radio buttons	`<input type="radio">`	`checked`: Gets and sets whether the radio button is checked or not
Checkboxes	`<input type="checkbox">`	`checked`: Gets and sets whether the checkbox is checked or not
Selection lists	`<select>`	`selectedIndex`: Gets and sets the index of the first selected element (or -1 if nothing is selected) `options`: Array containing all list options
Selection list options	`<option>`	`selected`: Gets and sets whether an option is selected or not `value`: Value of an option

Accessing Arbitrary Elements

For reading form data, document.forms is very convenient. One of the main tasks for JavaScript—especially when used as part of an Ajax implementation—is to display data in an element such as a paragraph (<p>) or text span (<span> or <label>). You can do this by following the steps below:

1. Using the name attribute, provide a unique identifier for the paragraph or span element. This is not required or used for the HTTP request when the form is submitted, but often used for accessing element values in JavaScript.

2. In JavaScript, get a reference to the element using the expression document.getElementById( ).

3. Set the element's innerHTML property to display data within the element.

Example 2-12 shows data once again being taken from a text field, but this time writing it into a <span> element.

Example 2-12. Putting HTML and text into an element

JavaScript-form-label.htm

```
<!DOCTYPE html PUBLIC "-//W3C//DTD XHTML 1.0 Transitional//EN"
"http://www.w3.org/TR/xhtml1/DTD/xhtml1-transitional.dtd">
<html xmlns="http://www.w3.org/1999/xhtml">
<head>
  <title>JavaScript</title>
  <script language="JavaScript" type="text/javascript">
  function HtmlEscape(s) {
    var result = s.replace(/&/g, "&amp;")
                  .replace(/</g, "&lt;")
                  .replace(/>/g, "&gt;")
                  .replace(/"/g, "&quot;")
                  .replace(/'/g, "&apos;");
    return result;
  }

  function ShowText(f) {
    var label = document.getElementById("Label1");
    label.innerHTML = HtmlEscape(f.elements["TextBox1"].value);
  }
  </script>
</head>
<body>
  <form action="">
    <input type="text" name="TextBox1" />
    <input type="button" value="Show text" onclick="ShowText(this.form);" />
    <p>Entered text: <span id="Label1">---</span></p>
  </form>
</body>
</html>
```

By default, the <span> element just contains three hyphens (-). When the user clicks on the button, the dashes are replaced with the HTML-encoded data from the text field. Figure 2-7 shows the result.

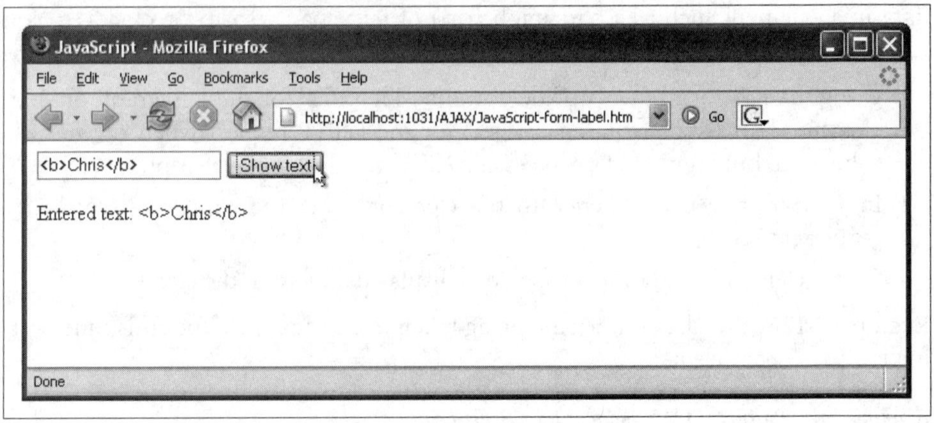

![Screenshot of Mozilla Firefox browser showing a text field containing "<b>Chris</b>" next to a "Show text" button, with the text "Entered text: <b>Chris</b>" displayed below.]

Figure 2-7. The text is HTML-encoded and put into the <span> element

DOM Methods

In most scenarios involving interaction with elements on an HTML page, using the special JavaScript document.forms object and its friends or using document. getElementById() (which returns an element with the given ID) with the innerHTML property suffices. Yet there are some cases where access to the DOM itself is required. The list below describes some of the most important ones:

getElementsByTagName(*name*)
:   Returns an array with all elements of the given element name in the page

createElement(*name*)
:   Creates a new DOM node with the given element name

createAttribute(*name*)
:   Creates a new attribute for the node with the given attribute name

createTextNode(*text*)
:   Creates a new text DOM node (text within an element) with the given text

appendChild(*node*)
:   Appends the node as a child of the current element

Appendix B contains a complete list of supported methods for accessing the DOM.

Example 2-13 shows how to use some of these methods to recreate the preceding example, but this time dynamically creating a new <span> element and a text node. In this example, the appendChild( ) method comes into play. First, the text child is added to the <span> element. Next, the <span> element is added to the paragraph.

Example 2-13. Using DOM with JavaScript

JavaScript-DOM.htm

```
<!DOCTYPE html PUBLIC "-//W3C//DTD XHTML 1.0 Transitional//EN"
"http://www.w3.org/TR/xhtml1/DTD/xhtml1-transitional.dtd">
<html xmlns="http://www.w3.org/1999/xhtml">
<head>
  <title>JavaScript</title>
  <script language="JavaScript" type="text/javascript">
  function ShowText(f) {
    var paragraph = document.getElementsByTagName("p")[0];
    var label = document.createElement("span");
    var text = document.createTextNode(f.elements["TextBox1"].value);
    label.appendChild(text);
    paragraph.appendChild(label);
  }
  </script>
</head>
<body>
  <form action="">
    <input type="text" name="TextBox1" />
    <input type="button" value="Show text" onclick="ShowText(this.form);" />
    <p>Entered text: </p>
  </form>
</body>
</html>
```

Summary

In this chapter, you learned the essentials of JavaScript client-side programming. In the following chapters, you will be introduced to additional JavaScript features. However, this chapter has introduced you to all the fundamental concepts that are required to understand the rest of the book.

For Further Reading

Flanagan, David. JavaScript: The Definitive Guide, Fifth Edition (O'Reilly)
    A complete programmer's guide and reference for the JavaScript language

Flanagan, David. JavaScript Pocket Reference, Second Edition (O'Reilly)
    A concise but thorough overview of the language

CHAPTER 3

Ajax

Ajax is the set of technologies upon which ASP.NET AJAX is built. And although ASP.NET AJAX does its best to hide the technical details of Ajax, to understand what is possible with ASP.NET AJAX and to create advanced applications that extend the framework for your own needs, you must have a detailed knowledge of Ajax.

The term "Ajax" was coined by Jesse James Garrett in early 2005 in his essay "A New Approach to Web Applications" (*http://www.adaptivepath.com/publications/essays/archives/000385.php*). However, only the term is new, not the technology itself. Although XML can be part of an Ajax application (but doesn't need to be!), and some CSS may also be in the mix, the foundation of any Ajax-powered application is JavaScript.

In this chapter, you'll create web pages that involve both client script in the browser and web server processing. Therefore, the examples in this chapter and the rest of the book will involve working with ASP.NET and with *.aspx* pages. We'll also cover the three most important JavaScript technologies used to deliver Ajax behaviors to web apps. These technologies are outlined below:

XMLHttpRequest
: The JavaScript object that takes care of making (asynchronous) HTTP calls

XMLDocument
: The JavaScript object used to parse and access XML data

JavaScript Object Notation (JSON)
: A data format that can be used instead of XML to exchange data between client and server without the burden of XML parsing

The XMLHttpRequest Object

The foundation of Ajax is the XMLHttpRequest object, which enables you to make HTTP requests and receive responses without performing a full page postback and refresh.

History of the XMLHttpRequest Object

The first implementation of XMLHttpRequest can be found in the 1999 release of Internet Explorer 5. That release included an ActiveX object called XMLHttpRequest that did just what the name suggests; make an HTTP request and get a message back. (The format of the returned message could be an XML message, but that was not a requirement.) Originally, Internet Explorer engineers needed this functionality for the web frontend to Outlook (Outlook Web Access [OWA]), so they could make OWA behave more like a desktop application. As useful as it was, for some time the addition of the XMLHttpRequest object to Internet Explorer went unnoticed by web programmers. However, competing browser developers later incorporated a compatible version in their own applications. Because only Internet Explorer supports ActiveX controls, other browsers implemented the XMLHttpRequest object natively in their browser.

After Internet Explorer, the first browser to support XMLHttpRequest was the Mozilla 1.0 browser (not to be confused with the code name for early Netscape browsers). Subsequent versions of Mozilla as well as derivatives, such as the Camino browser for Mac OS X and Firefox, implement XMLHttpRequest. Apple then added appropriate support in the 1.2 version of their Safari browser. Safari is based on the KHTML renderer that is part of Konqueror, the web browser of the KDE desktop environment for Linux. Apple engineers later back-ported support for the XMLHttpRequest object to Konqueror as well.

Opera 8.0 and later also included XMLHttpRequest support in their browser, as did the rather exotic system, Open Laszlo, from IBM.

A significant portion of the web browser market supports XMLHttpRequest and therefore is Ajax-compatible. According to a study conducted in November 2005 by Net Applications (*http://www.netapplications.com*), approximately 99 percent of the browsers in use are Internet Explorer 5 or later, Mozilla 1.0 or later, Firefox 1.0 or later, Opera 8 or later, Safari 1.2 or later, or KDE 3 or later. So does this mean that almost everybody can experience Ajax applications?

The answer, unfortunately, is no. Depending on which study you trust, between 5 to 15 percent of web users have disabled JavaScript in their browser, perhaps because of recurring reports of security vulnerabilities in browsers or because of corporate policies.

XMLHttpRequest and Standards

Despite being supported on most browsers, the XMLHttpRequest object is still nonstandard since it is not part of the ECMAScript specification. There is, however, a W3C specification that defines similar functionality, namely dynamically loading and sending XML back to the server. The specification is called "DOM Level 3 Load and Save," and has been a W3C recommendation since April 2004 (*http://www.w3.org/TR/DOM-Level-3-LS*). This standard has not yet been implemented in any popular browser, and it will probably take time before browser developers start working on it.

On the other hand, W3C recently started an initiative to standardize XMLHttpRequest. Refer to *http://www.w3.org/TR/XMLHttpRequest* for more information.

As a result, it's possible that a significant portion of your users *cannot* use applications that rely on JavaScript, which includes Ajax applications, in spite of the widespread adoption of up-to-date browsers. Therefore, you always need a fallback plan for those times when your application encounters an Ajax-resistant browser.

Programming the XMLHttpRequest Object

How you instantiate the XMLHttpRequest object depends on the browser in which your code executes. For Internet Explorer 5 and later versions, the code shown in the following snippet does the work. It tries two methods to instantiate XMLHttpRequest, because different versions of Internet Explorer have different versions of the Microsoft XML library installed on the system. To avoid error messages when one of the methods fails, two try-catch blocks are used:

```
var XMLHTTP = null;
try {
  XMLHTTP = new ActiveXObject("Msxml2.XMLHTTP");
} catch (e) {
  try {
    XMLHTTP = new ActiveXObject("Microsoft.XMLHTTP");
  } catch (e) {
  }
}
```

For browsers other than Internet Explorer, a simpler syntax is available:

```
XMLHTTP = new XMLHttpRequest();
```

So, all that is required is to determine which browser type is in use and then instantiate the XMLHttpRequest object accordingly. For instance, the following code checks whether an ActiveX object can be instantiated by testing the ActiveXObject property of the window object; if this code works, the browser must be Internet Explorer.

```
if (window.ActiveXObject) {
  // it's probably IE
}
```

Similarly, you can use the following snippet to check for the presence of an XMLHttpRequest object, which, if found, indicates you are using Mozilla and its derivatives, or that you are using Opera, Konqueror, or Safari:

```
if (XMLHttpRequest) {
   // it's probably not IE
}
```

However, as shown in Figure 3-1, checking for the XMLHttpRequest object directly causes Internet Explorer to display the error message "XMLHttpRequest is undefined." This has changed with release of Internet Explorer 7, which provides a native XMLHttpRequest object.

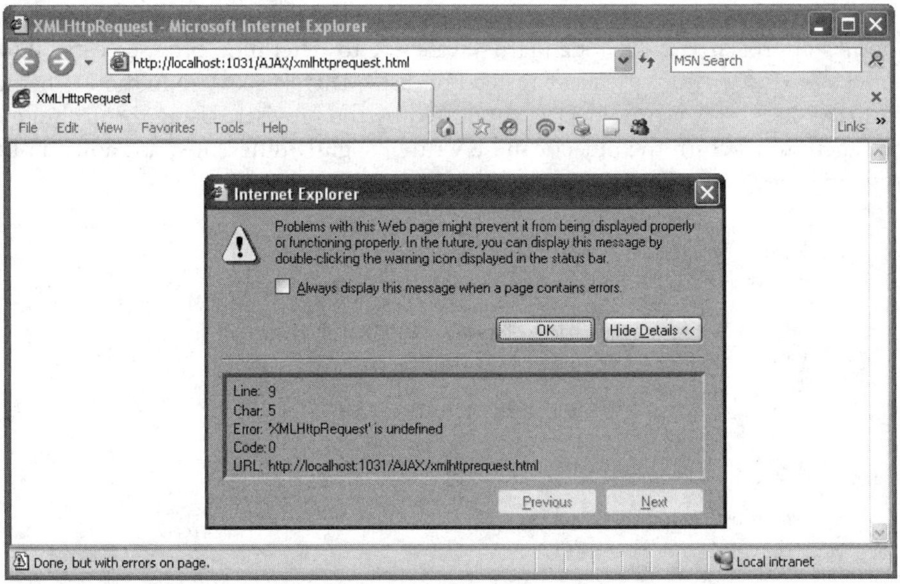

Figure 3-1. Internet Explorer does not like our code

What's needed instead is an approach that uses all of the tests shown here. The JavaScript typeof operator is used to determine the type of an expression and returns "undefined" as a string if the expression evaluates to "undefined." The snippet that follows enables you to detect browsers that are not Internet Explorer:

```
if (typeof XMLHttpRequest != "undefined") {
   //it's not IE <= 6
}
```

Here's code for a function, getXMLHTTP( ), that aggregates the previous snippets to return an XMLHttpRequest object regardless of which Ajax-enabled, JavaScript-activated browser is used.

```
function getXMLHTTP( ) {
  var XMLHTTP = null;
  try {
    XMLHTTP = new ActiveXObject("Msxml2.XMLHTTP");
  } catch (e) {
    try {
      XMLHTTP = new ActiveXObject("Microsoft.XMLHTTP");
    } catch (e) {
      if (typeof XMLHttpRequest != "undefined") {
        XMLHTTP = new XMLHttpRequest( );
      }
    }
  }
  return XMLHTTP;
}
```

Another approach is to use standard JavaScript to determine browser capabilities and check window.XMLHttpRequest instead of just XMLHttpRequest to find out whether the native XMLHttpRequest object is supported by the browser. Using this technique, the function to return the object can be written slightly differently, as shown in the following code:

```
function getXMLHTTP( ) {
  var XMLHTTP = null;
  if (window.ActiveXObject) {
    try {
      XMLHTTP = new ActiveXObject("Msxml2.XMLHTTP");
    } catch (e) {
      try {
        XMLHTTP = new ActiveXObject("Microsoft.XMLHTTP");
      } catch (e) {
      }
    }
  } else if (window.XMLHttpRequest) {
    try {
      XMLHTTP = new XMLHttpRequest( );
    } catch (e) {
    }
  }
  return XMLHTTP;
}
```

The XMLHttpRequest object, no matter which browser created it, has a set of properties and methods that are used for sending HTTP requests and receiving the server's response. In most scenarios, you must follow these four steps to create an HTTP request and evaluate the return values:

1. Create an XMLHttpRequest object as shown in the preceding examples.

2. Call the object's open( ) method to prepare the request.

   The open( ) method expects up to five parameters, but usually you only need the first two: the method type of the request (usually "GET" or "POST"), and the target URL (relative or absolute).

The third parameter of open( ) defaults to true, meaning that the request is an asynchronous one. If you set it to false, the request is synchronous, meaning that the script halts until the response has completed. Generally, you want the asynchronous behavior, so you either omit the parameter or set it to true. If the HTTP request requires authentication, you can use the fourth and fifth parameter to provide a username and a password.

3. Provide a reference to a callback function in the onreadystatechange property.

    This function will be called when the server returns an HTTP response to the HTTP request.

4. Send the HTTP request using the send( ) method.

    This starts the HTTP request. If you are using asynchronous communication, the script continues executing and the user can continue to interact with the page.

 Since all JavaScript code is evaluated on the client-side, there is no reliable way to prevent users from having a look at the source code. Several measures can be taken that can help the situation a bit, including JavaScript code to disable right-clicking, or client-side JavaScript code obfuscation. However, all of these can be defeated. In general, your JavaScript code is not safe, so it is not a good idea to put sensitive information like a username and a password verbatim into the JavaScript code. Therefore, the fourth and fifth parameter of open( ) are very rarely used. Even if you collect the credentials from the user, you still need to use SSL in order to avoid sensitive data being sent in plain text over an unsecured network.

Setting the onreadystatechange property of the XMLHttpRequest object provides the callback mechanism for the HTTP response. The property name suggests its function, which is to specify the action to be taken when a change occurs in the value of another XMLHttpRequest property, readyState, as listed in Table 3-1. The readyState property indicates the state of the XMLHttpRequest object, which can be set to five possible values.

Table 3-1. Possible values for readyState

Value of readyState	Description
0	Object is uninitialized
1	Request is loading
2	Request is fully loaded
3	Request is waiting for user interaction
4	Request is complete

Whenever the value of readyState changes, the function provided in the onreadystatechange property is called. In this function, you first check the value of readyState. Typically, you are testing to determine whether the value is 4, which indicates that the request has returned.

When a function is called in response to a change in readyState, some other properties of the XMLHttpRequest object come into play. The status property contains the HTTP status returned by the request; if everything worked, the status is 200. The statusText property holds the associated textual description of the HTTP status. As an example, for HTTP status 200, the value of statusText is "OK". Checking the status property, however, is a more reliable method, because different web servers might return different text for the status codes.

Two properties provide access to the return value from the server:

responseText
    Returns the response data as a string

responseXML
    Returns the response data as an XML document (detailed later in this chapter in "The XMLDocument Object")

The following script is a small example that illustrates how to use the XMLHttpRequest object. In the example, the request is made to an ASP.NET page named *ajax.aspx*. In the first step, the getXMLHTTP( ) function detailed earlier is used to create the XMLHttpRequest object. If it succeeds (that is, the return value of the function is not null), a GET request is sent to the server with the parameter sendData=ok (an arbitrary value, just for this example). Next, the onreadystatechange property is set to a function, and finally the request is sent to the server.

```
var XMLHTTP = getXMLHTTP( );
if (XMLHTTP != null) {
  XMLHTTP.open("GET", "ajax.aspx?sendData=ok");
  XMLHTTP.onreadystatechange = stateChanged;
  XMLHTTP.send(null);
}
```

The stateChanged( ) function might look something like the following (with error reporting omitted). This script displays whatever text the server has sent as the response.

```
function stateChanged( ) {
  if (XMLHTTP.readyState == 4 &&
      XMLHTTP.status == 200) {
    window.alert(XMLHTTP.responseText);
  }
}
```

Note that the function called when readyState changes does not accept any parameters. Therefore, the XMLHttpRequest object must be global. Otherwise, you cannot access it from within the function invoked by the asynchronous call.

Of course, you must also have server code to handle the request made by the XMLHttpRequest object. The following C# code shows a Page_Load event handler in an ASP.NET page that can respond to the asynchronous request made by the XMLHttpRequest object:

```
void Page_Load( ) {
  if (Request.QueryString["sendData"] != null &&
    Request.QueryString["sendData"] == "ok")
  {
    Response.Write("Hello from the server!");
    Response.End( );
  }
}
```

Anonymous JavaScript Functions

To provide the client-side functionality when readyState changes, instead of referencing
a standalone function you can use JavaScript anonymous functions. These are functions
without names that are declared as part of an expression. The following example shows
how this can look.

```
var XMLHTTP = getXMLHTTP( );
if (XMLHTTP != null) {
  XMLHTTP.open("GET", "ajax.aspx?sendData=ok");
  XMLHTTP.onreadystatechange = function( ) {
    if (XMLHTTP.readyState == 4 &&
        XMLHTTP.status == 200) {
      window.alert(XMLHTTP.responseText);
    }
  };
  XMLHTTP.send(null);
}
```

Example 3-1 shows how you can put all of these pieces together (both client script
and server code) into a single page named *ajax.aspx*.

 To see this example in action, you must run it as a page named *ajax.aspx*
using a web server (IIS or the ASP.NET Development Server that comes
with Visual Studio and VWD) on a computer where the .NET Framework is installed.

Example 3-1. A simple example combining Ajax and ASP.NET

ajax.aspx

```
<%@ Page Language="C#" %>

<!DOCTYPE html PUBLIC "-//W3C//DTD XHTML 1.0 Transitional//EN"
"http://www.w3.org/TR/xhtml1/DTD/xhtml1-transitional.dtd">

<script runat="server">
  void Page_Load( )
  {
    if (Request.QueryString["sendData"] != null &&
        Request.QueryString["sendData"] == "ok")
```

Example 3-1. A simple example combining Ajax and ASP.NET (continued)

```
      {
        Response.Write("Hello from the server!");
        Response.End( );
      }
   }
</script>

<html xmlns="http://www.w3.org/1999/xhtml">
<head runat="server">
  <title>Ajax with ASP.NET</title>

  <script language="Javascript" type="text/javascript">
function getXMLHTTP( ) {
  var XMLHTTP = null;
  if (window.ActiveXObject) {
    try {
      XMLHTTP = new ActiveXObject("Msxml2.XMLHTTP");
    } catch (e) {
      try {
        XMLHTTP = new ActiveXObject("Microsoft.XMLHTTP");
      } catch (e) {
      }
    }
  } else if (window.XMLHttpRequest) {
    try {
      XMLHTTP = new XMLHttpRequest( );
    } catch (e) {
    }
  }
  return XMLHTTP;
}

var XMLHTTP = getXMLHTTP( );
if (XMLHTTP != null) {
  XMLHTTP.open("GET", "ajax.aspx?sendData=ok");
  XMLHTTP.onreadystatechange = stateChanged;
  XMLHTTP.send(null);
}

function stateChanged( ) {
  if (XMLHTTP.readyState == 4 &&
      XMLHTTP.status == 200) {
    window.alert(XMLHTTP.responseText);
  }
}
  </script>

</head>
<body>
  <p>Wait and see ...</p>
</body>
</html>
```

If you see the text "Wait and see…" but the browser never displays a dialog box with "Hello from the server!," double-check that you are working with the filename *ajax.aspx*.

As you can see in Figures 3-2, 3-3, and 3-4, this code works beautifully in Internet Explorer, Firefox, and Konqueror (using Mono for ASP.NET), the most commonly used browsers. It should work equally well in any other browser you choose to test, as long as JavaScript is turned on.

Figure 3-2. The example works in Internet Explorer

Figure 3-3. The example works in Firefox

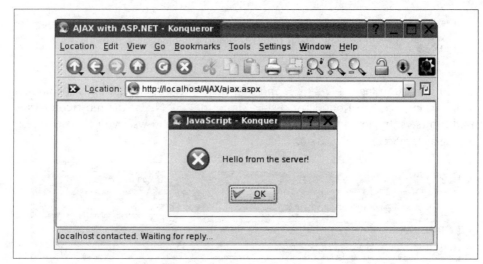

Figure 3-4. *The example works in Konqueror and other browsers*

This is one of the few places in this book where I've taken screenshots for more than one browser. Generally, the listings in this book work with ASP.NET 2.0 on the server and any JavaScript-enabled browser on the client of reasonably recent release. Most screenshots in this book are taken with Firefox 2.0. If we noticed discrepancies in using the examples with different browsers, this is noted.

If you want to use a POST command for the HTTP request, set the first parameter of the open( ) method as needed. Using POST is especially important when you are sending 500 bytes or more of data (you might exceed the maximum URL length for the server) or when you want to avoid caching by proxy servers. The data you want to send is provided in the send( ) function, in name-value pairs and URL-encoded (if needed) as shown in the following snippet:

```
XMLHTTP.open("POST", "ajax.aspx");
XMLHTTP.onreadystatechange = stateChanged;
XMLHTTP.send("sendData=ok&returnValue=123");
```

Data sent with a POST command can be read on the server, in the case of ASP.NET using Request.Form for POST instead of the Request.QueryString property used to read GET requests.

For web service calls that use the SOAP protocol, you may have to send XML directly, without URL-encoding. However, for this to work with the Safari and Konqueror browsers (and therefore to maximize your potential audience), you have to explicitly set the request content type to text/xml. (Other browsers do not require this content specification.) The following snippet shows how to do this:

```
XMLHTTP.open("POST", "ajax.aspx");
XMLHTTP.onreadystatechange = stateChanged;
XMLHTTP.setRequestHeader("Content-Type", "text/xml");
XMLHTTP.send("<soap:Envelope>...</soap:Envelope>");
```

 A complete reference of properties and methods of the XMLHttpRequest object is available in Appendix A.

A word regarding security: by default, XMLHttpRequest can access resources only in the same domain as the page that contains the client script. Unfortunately, this limits the capabilities of the technology since there is no easy way to call a web service using Ajax, unless it resides on your own domain. Mozilla browsers support accessing remote servers in another domain by explicitly prompting the user for additional privileges. Figure 3-5 shows the message that prompts the user for privileges. However, this approach generates several additional issues of its own and is not browser-agnostic, which is why this is very rarely in use today and not used in this book. So, all HTTP requests illustrated in this book are to the server from which the page itself originates.

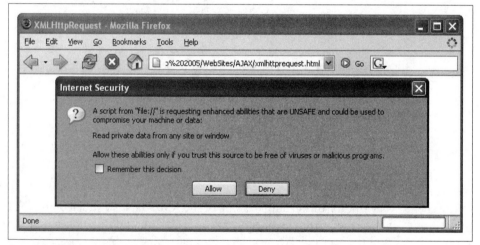

Figure 3-5. Requesting additional privileges in Mozilla browsers

The XMLDocument Object

The responseXML property of the XMLHttpRequest object expects the return value of the remote call to be in the form of an XMLDocument object. This requires the server code to return well-formed XML data so that the client script can parse it. However, it is easy to access this XML data because you have full DOM support.

JavaScript supports a set of DOM features to access specific nodes in the XML file or to navigate the tree structure of the XML document. Appendix B contains a complete list of methods and properties of the XMLDocument object. The following example shows how to use several of them. For the purposes of this example, the return data of the server request is the XML data shown here:

```
<book title="Programming ASP.NET AJAX" author="Christian Wenz">
  <chapters>
    <chapter number="1" title="Introduction" />
    <chapter number="2" title="JavaScript" />
    <chapter number="3" title="Ajax" />
  </chapters>
</book>
```

 It is important that when XML is returned, the Content-type HTTP header of the response is explicitly set to "text/xml". If this header is omitted, some browsers (most notably, Mozilla and its derivatives) refuse to parse the return data, and the responseXML object is set to null. The following C# code in an ASP.NET page shows how to set the content type appropriately:

```
void Page_Load( )
{
    if (Request.QueryString["sendData"] != null &&
        Request.QueryString["sendData"] == "ok")
    {
        string xml = "<book title=\"Programming ASP.NET AJAX\"
        author=\"Christian Wenz\"><chapters><chapter number=\"1\"
title=\"Introduction\"
/><chapter number=\"2\" title=\"JavaScript\" /><chapter
number=\"3\" title=\"Ajax\"
/></chapters></book>";
        Response.ContentType = "text/xml";
        Response.Write(xml);
        Response.End( );
    }
}
```

In the client JavaScript for this example, some of the XML data is extracted and then printed out, such as the attributes of the root node and the information about the various chapters of the book object.

Printing out is intentionally *not* done using document.write( ) because that would clear the current page, which works more or less in Mozilla browsers, but Internet Explorer does not seem to support that. Instead, the script creates new HTML elements. There are two general approaches: set the contents of existing elements or create new elements.

To set the contents of an element, set the innerHTML property of an HTML element. Consider an HTML document that contains the following <p> element:

```
<p id="output">Wait and see ...</p>
```

With the following JavaScript code, you can replace the content of the element:

```
document.getElementById("output").innerHTML = "Now you see!";
```

Alternatively, you can create new elements and add them to the page. The snippet below creates an empty bulleted list:

```
<ul id="list"></ul>
```

The following JavaScript code adds two elements to the list:

```
var list = document.getElementById("list");
var listItem1 = document.createElement("li");
var listItemText1 = document.createTextNode("Item 1");
listItem1.appendChild(listItemText1);
list.appendChild(listItem1);
var listItem2 = document.createElement("li");
var listItemText2 = document.createTextNode("Item 2");
listItem2.appendChild(listItemText2);
list.appendChild(listItem2);
```

Back to the task at hand, reading out data from the XML document. There are actually two approaches you can use. As shown below, the first is to directly access tags by their names and then read their attributes.

```
var xml = XMLHTTP.responseXML;
var root = xml.documentElement;
document.getElementById("output").innerHTML =
  root.getAttribute("title") +
  " by " +
  root.getAttribute("author");

var list = document.getElementById("list");
var chapters = xml.getElementsByTagName("chapter");
for (var i=0; i<chapters.length; i++) {
  var listItem = document.createElement("li");
  var listItemText = document.createTextNode(
    chapters[i].getAttribute("number") +
    ": " +
    chapters[i].getAttribute("title"));
  listItem.appendChild(listItemText);
  list.appendChild(listItem);
}
```

Alternatively, you can walk the XML tree using the structure of the XML document. In the following code snippet, the <chapters> element is selected using getElementsByTagName( ), but then the script navigates along the tree, looking at all subelements of the first <chapters> element. When a <chapter> node is found, its attributes are printed out.

```
var xml = XMLHTTP.responseXML;
var root = xml.documentElement;
document.getElementById("output").innerHTML =
  root.getAttribute("title") +
  " by " +
```

```
    root.getAttribute("author");

  var list = document.getElementById("list");
  var chapters = xml.getElementsByTagName("chapters")[0];
  for (var i=0; i<chapters.childNodes.length; i++) {
    if (chapters.childNodes[i].nodeName == "chapter") {
      var listItem = document.createElement("li");
      var listItemText = document.createTextNode(
        chapters.childNodes[i].getAttribute("number") +
        ": " +
        chapters.childNodes[i].getAttribute("title"));
      listItem.appendChild(listItemText);
      list.appendChild(listItem);
    }
  }
}
```

But this is not the end of our work. Internet Explorer once again behaves differently on some systems (depending on loading or execution speed), especially with the second approach. The reason: the XMLHttpRequest call is executed "too fast" (from the point of view of our example), so that the whole HTML document might not have been parsed by the time the example code runs. Therefore, it is mandatory that the Ajax magic start only when the document has been fully loaded and parsed. You can do this using an anonymous function, as shown below:

```
var XMLHTTP;
window.onload = function( ) {
  XMLHTTP = getXMLHTTP( );
  if (XMLHTTP != null) {
    XMLHTTP.open("GET", "xmldocument2.aspx?sendData=ok");
    XMLHTTP.onreadystatechange = stateChanged;
    XMLHTTP.send(null);
  }
}
```

The preceding code snippet does the XMLHttpRequest call only when the whole HTML page has been loaded.

To sum it up, Example 3-2 shows the complete code for the first approach, which is provided in the file *xmldocument.aspx* in the code download repository for this book (*http://www.oreilly.com/catalog/9780596514242*). The second approach (not illustrated here) can be found in the file *xmldocument2.aspx*.

Example 3-2. Reading and writing data using JavaScript, Ajax, and DOM

xmldocument.aspx

```
<%@ Page Language="C#" %>

<!DOCTYPE html PUBLIC "-//W3C//DTD XHTML 1.0 Transitional//EN"
"http://www.w3.org/TR/xhtml1/DTD/xhtml1-transitional.dtd">

<script runat="server">
  void Page_Load( )
```

Example 3-2. Reading and writing data using JavaScript, Ajax, and DOM (continued)

```
  {
    if (Request.QueryString["sendData"] != null &&
        Request.QueryString["sendData"] == "ok")
    {
      string xml = "<book title=\"Programming ASP.NET AJAX\" author=\"Christian Wenz\">
<chapters><chapter number=\"1\" title=\"Introduction\" /><chapter number=\"2\" title=\
"JavaScript\" /><chapter number=\"3\" title=\"Ajax\" /></chapters></book>";
      Response.ContentType = "text/xml";
      Response.Write(xml);
      Response.End( );
    }
  }
</script>

<html xmlns="http://www.w3.org/1999/xhtml">
<head id="Head1" runat="server">
  <title>Ajax with ASP.NET</title>

  <script language="Javascript" type="text/javascript">
function getXMLHTTP( ) {
  var XMLHTTP = null;
  if (window.ActiveXObject) {
    try {
      XMLHTTP = new ActiveXObject("Msxml2.XMLHTTP");
    } catch (e) {
      try {
        XMLHTTP = new ActiveXObject("Microsoft.XMLHTTP");
      } catch (e) {
      }
    }
  } else if (window.XMLHttpRequest) {
    try {
      XMLHTTP = new XMLHttpRequest( );
    } catch (e) {
    }
  }
  return XMLHTTP;
}

var XMLHTTP;
window.onload = function( ) {
  XMLHTTP = getXMLHTTP( );
  if (XMLHTTP != null) {
    XMLHTTP.open("GET", "xmldocument.aspx?sendData=ok");
    XMLHTTP.onreadystatechange = stateChanged;
    XMLHTTP.send(null);
  }
}

function stateChanged( ) {
  if (XMLHTTP.readyState == 4 &&
      XMLHTTP.status == 200) {
```

Example 3-2. Reading and writing data using JavaScript, Ajax, and DOM (continued)

```
    var xml = XMLHTTP.responseXML;
    var root = xml.documentElement;

    document.getElementById("output").innerHTML =
      root.getAttribute("title") +
      " by " +
      root.getAttribute("author");

    var list = document.getElementById("list");
    var chapters = xml.getElementsByTagName("chapter");
    for (var i=0; i<chapters.length; i++) {
      var listItem = document.createElement("li");
      var listItemText = document.createTextNode(
        chapters[i].getAttribute("number") +
        ": " +
        chapters[i].getAttribute("title"));
      listItem.appendChild(listItemText);
      list.appendChild(listItem);
    }
  }
}
  </script>

</head>
<body>
  <p id="output">Wait and see ...</p>
  <ul id="list"></ul>
</body>
</html>
```

The results of running this script are shown in Figure 3-6.

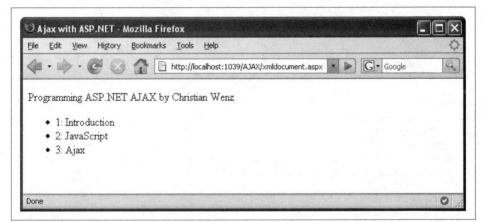

Figure 3-6. The XML data in a readable form

JSON

In addition to the XMLHttpRequest object and XML, a third major technology often used for Ajax applications is JavaScript Object Notation (JSON, *http://www.json.org/*). With JSON, JavaScript objects or data can be persisted (serialized) in a short and easily understandable way, without requiring a lot of JavaScript code to either write or read the data (also true for XML). JSON makes use of a previously often-overlooked feature of JavaScript, or more accurately, of the ECMAScript language specification, also known as ECMA-262.

JSON is used internally by current versions of ASP.NET AJAX and generally can be used to exchange complex data with a server. This allows JavaScript to understand it, and it helps avoid the sometimes cumbersome parsing process of XML. The following code uses JSON to define a book object:

```
{"book": {
  "title": "Programming ASP.NET AJAX",
  "author": "Christian Wenz",
  "chapters": {
    "chapter": [
      {"number": "1", "title": "Introduction"},
      {"number": "2", "title": "JavaScript"},
      {"number": "3", "title": "Ajax"}
    ]
  }
}}
```

This is the same data that you saw defined using XML earlier in this chapter. The object with the book property contains title, author, and chapters properties. The chapters property contains several chapter subelements, each with a number and a title property. This can be best visualized when looking at it as XML data.

```
<book title="Programming ASP.NET AJAX" author="Christian Wenz">
  <chapters>
    <chapter number="1" title="Introduction" />
    <chapter number="2" title="JavaScript" />
    <chapter number="3" title="Ajax" />
  </chapters>
</book>
```

Example 3-3 shows how you can parse JSON data.

Example 3-3. Using JSON to easily create objects

json.html

```
<!DOCTYPE html PUBLIC "-//W3C//DTD XHTML 1.0 Transitional//EN"
"http://www.w3.org/TR/xhtml1/DTD/xhtml1-transitional.dtd">
<html xmlns="http://www.w3.org/1999/xhtml">
```

Example 3-3. Using JSON to easily create objects (continued)

```
<head>
  <title>JSON</title>
</head>
<body>

  <script language="JavaScript" type="text/javascript">
    var json = '{"book": { "title": "Programming ASP.NET AJAX", "author": "Christian
Wenz","chapters": {"chapter": [ {"number": "1", "title": "Introduction"}, {"number": "2",
"title": "JavaScript"}, {"number": "3", "title": "Ajax"} ]} }}';
    var obj = eval("(" + json + ")");
    for (var i=0; i < obj.book.chapters.chapter.length; i++) {
      document.write(
        "<p>" +
        obj.book.chapters.chapter[i].number +
        ": " +
        obj.book.chapters.chapter[i].title +
        "</p>"
      );
    }
  </script>

</body>
</html>
```

Figure 3-7 shows the result of running this script.

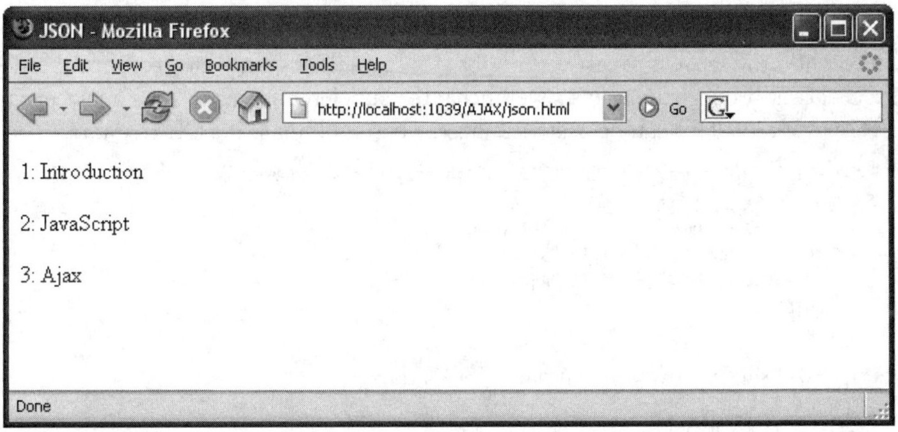

Figure 3-7. The result of evaluating the JSON notation

As you can see in Figure 3-7, the data from the JSON notation—the names of the three chapters—is printed out in the browser. The curly braces that appear in Example 3-3 are used to specify object properties, and square brackets are used to define array lists.

However, you will also note something that looks very dangerous from a security point of view. The following line of code evaluates the JSON code at runtime:

```
eval("var obj = " + json + ";");
```

This line of code uses the built-in eval( ) JavaScript function, which dynamically evaluates code at runtime. Some programmers consider runtime evaluation bad style, but there is an even worse problem here, namely that eval( ) implicitly trusts the code it is running. In the example, the JSON notation is part of the script, so you can trust it. In Ajax applications, usually the JSON data comes from the same server as the client page. The trust implicit in the eval( ) function may be misplaced, especially when you do not control the page the JSON object comes from or when the machine on which the script runs has been misconfigured (i.e., by spyware that redirects requests from one server to another). Therefore, be careful when using eval( ); only use it on code you can really trust.

Using (and Avoiding) Client-Side Caching

Browsers love to cache as it makes pages load faster. Webmasters love to cache as it can take a load off a server. Developers, however, sometimes hate caching. If an outdated version of the page is delivered, it can make debugging very frustrating. In the Ajax world, this is a very common problem. There are two easy solutions to the caching problem. One solution is to append a fake GET parameter to the URL used for the XMLHttpRequest object, which does not affect the results, yet avoids any caching because it changes the URL with each request. The following snippet shows one way to do this.

```
XMLHTTP.open("GET", "xmldocument.aspx?sendData=ok&token="
    + Math.random( ));
```

The snippet appends something like &token=0.19964476288175226 to the URL, making it unique. Alternatively, you can set an additional request header for the HTTP request, If-Modified-Since, to a date in the past, and the browser will fetch the new version each time, as illustrated below:

```
XML.setRequestHeader(
    "If-Modified-Since",
    "Tuesday, 1 Jan 1980 12:00:00 GMT");
```

During development, use one of these techniques to facilitate debugging. On production systems, however, the built-in browser caching mechanism may increase the performance of your application (if it does not generate side effects with your application), and server-side caching can be even more effective. It always depends on the specific scenario in which you want to implement caching.

Summary

This chapter covered three of the technologies that make Ajax work. Of special importance is the XMLHttpRequest object. You also learned how to process complex data returned by the server using JavaScript and either XML or JSON.

For Further Reading

http://www.adaptivepath.com/publications/essays/archives/000385.php
   The article that started it all

http://www.json.org/
   Unofficial home page for JSON

Perry, Bruce W. Ajax Hacks (O'Reilly)
   Tips and tricks for Ajax apps

McLaughlin, Brett. Head Rush Ajax (O'Reilly)
   A fast-paced introduction to Ajax

ASP.NET AJAX Extensions

CHAPTER 4

Using ASP.NET AJAX
JavaScript Extensions

In addition to delivering a considerable amount of Ajax functionality in an easy-to-use framework, ASP.NET AJAX provides a number of additions to JavaScript that can make client coding easier. Among these are OOP-style constructs, such as namespaces, inheritance, and interfaces, as well as client-side reimplementations that resemble .NET constructs such as `StringBuilder`. Also, selected JavaScript objects are enriched with new features.

ASP.NET AJAX Shortcuts and Helper Functions

By including the ASP.NET AJAX `ScriptManager` control into a web page, you automatically get a number of useful helper functions and shortcuts to important JavaScript features. Some of these new functions just save you some typing. Some of them, however, offer a much greater advantage: they are browser-agnostic. For instance, Internet Explorer on one side and all other modern browsers on the other side each provide their unique way to attach event listeners (see Chapter 2). The code in ASP.NET AJAX detects the browser type and automatically uses the appropriate function on every system.

Shortcuts

The method most often used by developers to create a modern JavaScript-powered web site is `document.getElementById()`. Several Ajax toolkits provide a shortcut for this rather lengthy method name called `$()`. ASP.NET AJAX tries to coexist with other frameworks and therefore is using a new name: `$get()`.

Whereas this saves only a few characters, the new event handling helper functions are of greater value. When programmatically assigning a handler function to an event, you can use the `$addHandler()` function.

```
function $addHandler (element, eventName, handler) { }
```

You need to provide the element attribute to attach the handler to the eventName (without the "on" prefix!), and the actual handler (as a function reference or an anonymous function). Below is an example that pops up a warning window when a user clicks on a button:

```
$addHandler("Button1", "click", function() { alert("Ouch!"); } );
```

 When you want to assign handlers for several events for an element, you can either use several $addHandler() calls, or you use $addHandlers(), providing the element and an array of events and handler functions as arguments.

To remove a specific handler, use the $removeHandler() function demonstrated here:

```
function $removeHandler(element, eventName, handler) {}
```

Note that you have to pass the event-handler function again when removing the handler. Therefore, it is more convenient in most cases to call the $clearHandlers() function, which removes all handlers for a given element:

```
function $clearHandlers(element) {}
```

Adding Event Handlers, the Alternative Way

Apart from the $addHandler(), $removeHandler() and $clearHandlers() functions, ASP.NET AJAX also supports a special pattern for attaching handlers to element events: the add_xxx() methods. For instance, Sys.Application is the ASP.NET AJAX JavaScript object that represents the current page. In order to execute code after the page has been fully loaded, you can code as shown here:

```
Sys.Application.add_load(function() {
  /* ... */
}).
```

This is quite useful when using special client classes for DOM elements that are currently part of the ASP.NET AJAX Futures CTP. We will cover this in greater detail in Chapter 15.

The ASP.NET AJAX team tried very hard to recreate to a certain extent the ASP.NET page lifecycle in JavaScript. JavaScript itself only supports a load event, which is not enough for some applications. It also has a serious flaw: the event is fired when the HTML markup of the current page has been fully loaded. However, ASP.NET AJAX sites load several external JavaScript libraries. They are usually not available yet when the HTML has been fully rendered by the browser. Therefore, using the JavaScript load event to start any ASP.NET AJAX coding is too early in the client page lifecycle.

The load event defined by ASP.NET AJAX only runs when all external JavaScript files have been fully loaded. In order to execute code after the event has been fired, you have two options. You can either use the Sys.Application.add_load() method (as described in the sidebar, "Adding Event Handlers, the Alternative Way"), or you can write a JavaScript function named pageLoad(). When ASP.NET AJAX determines that all external files have been fully loaded, it executes the pageLoad() function, if it exists on the current page—quite similar to the way ASP.NET executes the server-side Page_Load() method if it exists. This method provides a safe way to start using ASP.NET AJAX as early as possible.

```
function pageLoad() {
  /* ...*/
}
```

At the end of a page, when the user closes the browser or navigates to another URL, the unload event occurs. You can execute code when this happens by writing a function called pageUnload().

```
function pageUnload() {
  /* ...*/
}
```

ASP.NET AJAX automatically executes such a function at the appropriate time, if it has been implemented.

DOM Element Methods

For DOM elements, ASP.NET AJAX provides special methods for common scenarios like applying CSS classes. These methods are defined in the Sys.UI.DomElement class. For common features like setting CSS classes or removing them, CSS class methods take some keyboarding weight off developers' shoulders.

Sys.UI.DomElement.addCssClass(element, className)
> Adds a CSS class (className) to an HTML element.

Sys.UI.DomElement.containsCssClass(element, className)
> Checks whether the CSS class definition of an element contains a certain CSS class.

Sys.UI.DomElement.removeCssClass
> Removes a CSS class (className) from an HTML element.

Sys.UI.DomElement.toggleCssClass(element, className)
> Checks whether the CSS class definition of an element contains a certain CSS class (className). If it does, it removes this CSS class, otherwise it appends the CSS class. Apart from CSS classes, ASP.NET AJAX provides helper methods for some of the most often accessed properties of general HTML elements: width, height, and position.

Sys.UI.DomElement.getBounds(element)
> Returns an object with the properties x, y, height, width, containing the x coordinate, y coordinate, height, and width of the given element.

`Sys.UI.DomElement.getLocation(element)`
Returns an object with the properties x and y, containing the x and y coordinates of the given element.

`Sys.UI.DomElement.setLocation(element, x, y)`
Sets the x and y coordinates of the given element.

Another method defined within `Sys.UI.DomElement` is `getElementById( )`—but you already know the shortcut for that, `$get( )`.

Extensions to Existing JavaScript Objects

Chapter 2 described how to add methods to JavaScript base objects like `Date`. This feature has also been used heavily by the ASP.NET AJAX developers. As a result, JavaScript base types in the following list have been enriched with additional features:

- `Array`
- `Boolean`
- `Date`
- `Error`
- `Number`
- `Object`
- `String`

None of these extensions alone is worth writing home about, but taken together, they can provide some real value if you write a lot of JavaScript code. Remember that a key idea of any Ajax framework is to dramatically reduce the amount of custom JavaScript code that needs to be written on top of the framework.

Instead of a complete list, we'll present just one easily written example. The new `Array.forEach( )` method applies a function to each element of a given array.

```
function Array$forEach(a, fnct) {
  for (var i = 0; i = a.length; i++) {
    if (typeof(a[i]) != "undefined") {
      fnct.call(null, a[i], i, a);
    }
  }
}
```

However, the built-in ASP.NET AJAX `forEach( )` method saves some typing, a bit of debugging, and a lot of extra maintenance work.

An excellent overview of the new JavaScript object properties are available at no cost as PDF and XPS files. See the "For Further Reading" section at the end of this chapter for details on how to get those files.

ASP.NET AJAX OOP Features for JavaScript

In Chapter 2, we learned JavaScript does have some OOP capabilities, but they are no match for those in programming languages like Visual Basic or C#. However, it's relatively easy to add new features to JavaScript using JavaScript itself, something the ASP.NET AJAX team has exploited.

To facilitate OOP development, ASP.NET AJAX adds to JavaScript some OOP-type features, which are covered in this chapter. These include namespaces, abstract classes, and interfaces. The additional features are designed to help you design and write more structured client-side code. They can apply not only to Ajax applications, but also to any JavaScript code you write.

Namespaces

A key ASP.NET AJAX JavaScript OOP extension is the addition of namespace functionality. Namespaces enable you to encapsulate functionality into logical groups under a single name. They help avoid name collisions with functions that have the same name but fulfill different purposes. The JavaScript language specification does not specify namespaces, so the language itself cannot offer this functionality. However, ASP.NET AJAX uses a simple technique to emulate namespaces. You can create a new class (which serves as the "namespace"), then make another (new) class accessible as a property of the namespace class. This allows you to access your class using *NamespaceClassName.YourClassName*.

One of the base classes in ASP.NET AJAX runtime is the Type class. Two methods of this class come in handy when creating the ASP.NET AJAX namespaces:

`Type.registerNamespace(name)`
> Registers a namespace

`Class.registerClass(name, base type, interface type)`
> Registers a class as a member of the namespace

To demonstrate this technique, let's create an OReilly namespace for a group of classes used in this book. Suppose that one of them is named Software with two properties: name and vendor. First, you must register the OReilly namespace:

```
Type.registerNamespace("OReilly");
```

Next, you create the Software class as a member of OReilly using the following code snippet:

```
OReilly.Software = function(name, vendor) {
  var _name = (name != null) ? name : "unknown";
  var _vendor = (vendor != null) ? vendor : "unknown";

  this.getName = function() {
    return _name;
  }
```

```
  this.setName = function(name) {
    _name = name;
  }

  this.getVendor = function( ) {
    return _vendor;
  }
  this.setVendor = function(vendor) {
    _vendor = vendor;
  }
}
```

The class constructor expects values for the two properties. To perform data hiding, the class member values are saved as separate variables, and the class implements setter and getter methods for the properties. Note that JavaScript does not support private or protected properties. Therefore, all class members are public. The data hiding implemented here does not provide protection from unauthorized access; it is just a helper tool to structure code and make the data access coherent. Of course most technologies that do support private or protected still allow access to those properties using reflection.

Finally, OReilly.Software must be registered as a class so that you can use it in your applications. You do this with the registerClass( ) method. This method can take up to three parameters:

name
> The name of the class

base type
> The base type of the class, if any, as a reference to the type

interface type
> The interface type of the class, if any, as a reference to the type

The OReilly.Software class does not have a base type and does not implement an interface type. The call to registerClass( ) registers the class, omitting the second and third parameters:

```
Type.registerClass("OReilly.Software");
```

ASP.NET AJAX implements several types, but the one you will use most often is Sys.IDisposable (because you can write a dispose( ) method that is called automatically when the script ends), even though JavaScript has only a simple garbage collector. However, you do not necessarily need to implement an interface. If you do not use an interface, the call to Type.registerClass( ) is subsequently not necessary to access the new class. For more advanced features, this method call is mandatory (see the following sections).

Now, you can instantiate the Software class using the new keyword to get and set its properties. Example 4-1 creates two instances; one for Microsoft Internet Explorer and one for Mozilla Foundation Firefox. Example 4-1 also uses a very handy feature of ASP.NET AJAX. After both the page and all libraries used by ASP.NET AJAX have been fully loaded, the pageLoad( ) function is executed (if it exists on the page). Remember that window.onload does not take loading of external files like JavaScript libraries into account. Therefore you should always use pageLoad( ) when using ASP.NET AJAX for that task.

Example 4-1. Using ASP.NET AJAX namespaces

ClientNamespaces.aspx

```
<%@ Page Language="C#" %>

<!DOCTYPE html PUBLIC "-//W3C//DTD XHTML 1.0 Transitional//EN"
"http://www.w3.org/TR/xhtml1/DTD/xhtml1-transitional.dtd">
<html xmlns="http://www.w3.org/1999/xhtml">
<head id="Head1" runat="server">
  <title>ASP.NET AJAX</title>

  <script language="Javascript" type="text/javascript">
  function pageLoad( ) {
    var s = "";

    Type.registerNamespace("OReilly");
    OReilly.Software = function(name, vendor) {
      var _name = (name != null) ? name : "unknown";
      var _vendor = (vendor != null) ? vendor : "unknown";

      this.getName = function( ) {
        return _name;
      }
      this.setName = function(name) {
        _name = name;
      }

      this.getVendor = function( ) {
        return _vendor;
      }
      this.setVendor = function(vendor) {
        _vendor = vendor;
      }
    }

    Type.registerClass("OReilly.Software");

    var ie = new OReilly.Software("Internet Explorer", "Microsoft");
    s = ie.getName() + " from " + ie.getVendor() + "<br />";

    var ff = new OReilly.Software( );
    ff.setName("Firefox");
```

Example 4-1. Using ASP.NET AJAX namespaces (continued)

```
      ff.setVendor("Mozilla Foundation");
      s += ff.getName() + " from " + ff.getVendor();

      document.getElementById("output").innerHTML = s;
   }
  </script>
</head>
<body>
  <form id="form1" runat="server">
    <asp:ScriptManager ID="ScriptManager1" runat="server">
    </asp:ScriptManager>
    <div id="output">
    </div>
  </form>
</body>
</html>
```

Figure 4-1 shows the result displayed when the page is loaded.

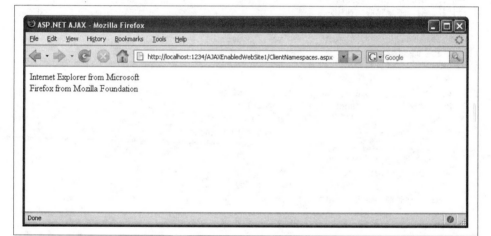

Figure 4-1. Instantiating two objects within the same namespace

Although ASP.NET AJAX namespace classes are not real namespaces, they can make it easier for you to structure complex JavaScript code, with very little overhead.

Class Inheritance

As detailed in Chapter 2, the prototype property provides limited support for class inheritance in JavaScript. ASP.NET AJAX provides more abstraction. The prototype mechanism is supported for namespace classes that were registered using `Class name.registerClass()`. As a second parameter for `registerClass()`, you can specify a base class. Here is where you specify from which class the current class derives.

Derived classes

Let's create a class that inherits from Software. One very specific type of software is a web browser, so let's create a Browser class. In addition to the features of the generic Software class, a browser would benefit from some extra properties. An isJavaScriptSupported property can provide information about whether a particular browser is capable of running JavaScript.

```
OReilly.Browser = function(name, vendor, isJavaScriptSupported) {
  //...
}
```

Here's how to register the class. Note how the new class (the string parameter) derives from the old OReilly.Software class (no string!).

```
OReilly.Browser.registerClass("OReilly.Browser", OReilly.Software);
```

Of course, it would be possible to create getter and setter methods for name and vendor once again, and to write the constructor code as well. However, one of the benefits of class inheritance (actually, the major benefit) is that you can reuse functionality. Because OReilly.Browser inherits from OReilly.Software, you can use the getter and setter methods (i.e., the properties) that are already there, as well as the _name and _vendor "private" members. You do, however, need to add getter and setter methods and private members for the new isJavaScriptSupported property, as shown here:

```
var _isJavaScriptSupported = (isJavaScriptSupported != null) ?
  isJavaScriptSupported : false;

this.getIsJavaScriptSupported = function() {
  return _isJavaScriptSupported;
}
this.setIsJavaScriptSupported = function(isJavaScriptSupported) {
  _isJavaScriptSupported = isJavaScriptSupported;
}
```

All that remains is for us to write the constructor. But instead of writing it again from scratch, you can reuse the base class constructor. To do so, ASP.NET AJAX provides the initializeBase( ) method. The first parameter is the instance of which the base class will be initialized; usually, you provide this as the value. The second parameter is an array of arguments to be passed to the base constructor (the base constructor defines which arguments it expects). In our case, this array consists of the browser name and vendor.

```
OReilly.Browser.initializeBase(this, new Array(name, vendor));
```

 You can save a few characters and use JSON to create the array:

```
OReilly.Browser.initializeBase(this, [name,vendor]);
```

Example 4-2 shows the code needed to create and use the new derived Browser class.

Example 4-2. Using ASP.NET AJAX class inheritance

ClientInheritance.aspx

```
<%@ Page Language="C#" %>

<!DOCTYPE html PUBLIC "-//W3C//DTD XHTML 1.0 Transitional//EN"
"http://www.w3.org/TR/xhtml1/DTD/xhtml1-transitional.dtd">
<html xmlns="http://www.w3.org/1999/xhtml">
<head id="Head1" runat="server">
  <title>ASP.NET AJAX</title>

  <script language="Javascript" type="text/javascript">
  function pageLoad( ) {
    var s = "";

    Type.registerNamespace("OReilly");
    OReilly.Software = function(name, vendor) {
      var _name = (name != null) ? name : "unknown";
      var _vendor = (vendor != null) ? vendor : "unknown";

      this.getName = function( ) {
        return _name;
      }
      this.setName = function(name) {
        _name = name;
      }

      this.getVendor = function( ) {
        return _vendor;
      }
      this.setVendor = function(vendor) {
        _vendor = vendor;
      }
    }
    Type.registerClass("OReilly.Software");


    OReilly.Browser = function(name, vendor, isJavaScriptSupported) {
    OReilly.Browser.initializeBase(this, new Array(name, vendor));
      var _isJavaScriptSupported = (isJavaScriptSupported != null) ?
        isJavaScriptSupported : false;

      this.getIsJavaScriptSupported = function( ) {
        return _isJavaScriptSupported;
      }
      this.setIsJavaScriptSupported = function(isJavaScriptSupported) {
        _isJavaScriptSupported = isJavaScriptSupported;
      }

    }
    OReilly.Browser.registerClass("OReilly.Browser", OReilly.Software);
```

Example 4-2. Using ASP.NET AJAX class inheritance (continued)

```
    var ie = new OReilly.Browser("Internet Explorer", "Microsoft", true);
    s = ie.getName() + " from " + ie.getVendor() +
      (ie.getIsJavaScriptSupported() ? " (w/ JS)" : " (w/o JS)") +
      "<br />";

    var lynx = new OReilly.Browser("Lynx");
    lynx.setIsJavaScriptSupported(false);
    s += lynx.getName() + " from " + lynx.getVendor() +
      (lynx.getIsJavaScriptSupported() ? " (w/ JS)" : " (w/o JS)");

    document.getElementById("output").innerHTML = s;
  }
  </script>

</head>
<body>
  <form id="form1" runat="server">
    <asp:ScriptManager ID="ScriptManager1" runat="server">
    </asp:ScriptManager>
    <div id="output">
    </div>
  </form>
</body>
</html>
```

Figure 4-2 shows the results displayed when the page is loaded and its JavaScript runs.

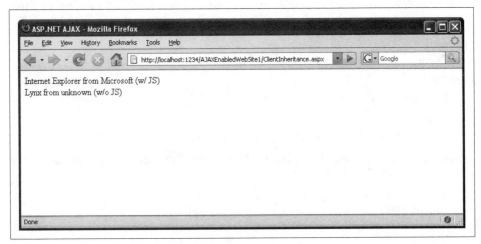

Figure 4-2. Instantiating objects derived from the same base class

 Just in case you are wondering, the Lynx text browser does have a "vendor." The copyright holder is the University of Kansas.

Accessing base methods

When we talk about class inheritance, a logical question is whether methods can be overridden in derived classes. The answer is yes. The next question: is there any way to access the equivalent method of the base class, (i.e., the overridden method)? Even better, the answer is again yes, ASP.NET AJAX allows you to do so. To demonstrate this, let's add a `toString()` method to `OReilly.Software` that outputs the product and vendor names stored by the class. The `prototype` property ensures automated inheritance and also helps demonstrate access to the base method later on.

```
OReilly.Software.prototype.toString = function() {
  return this.getName() + " from " + this.getVendor();
}
```

 You could also directly access the properties _name and _vendor as variables. Using the getter methods is just a personal preference. There is no functional difference in doing so.

In the `OReilly.Browser` class, you could write a similar `toString()` method:

```
OReilly.Browser.prototype.toString = function() {
  return this.getName() + " from " + this.getVendor() +
      (this.getIsJavaScriptSupported() ? " (w/ JS)" : " (w/o JS)");
}
```

However, it is once again advisable to reuse existing code, in this case, the base class's `toString()` method. ASP.NET AJAX provides you with `callBaseMethod()`, a helper method to call a method from the parent class that can take up to three parameters:

instance
 The instance whose parent's method to call (usually `this`)

methodName
 The name of the method (as a string)

baseArguments
 Parameters for the method, if any (as an array)

In this case, the `toString()` method of `OReilly.Browser` can be implemented as the following code demonstrates:

```
OReilly.Browser.prototype.toString = function() {
  return OReilly.Browser.callBaseMethod(this, "toString") +
      (this.getIsJavaScriptSupported() ? " (w/ JS)" : " (w/o JS)");
}
```

Now, the code to output the browser information can be reduced a bit to these commands below:

```
var s = "";
var ie = new OReilly.Browser("Internet Explorer", "Microsoft", true);
s = ie.toString() + "<br />";
```

```
    var lynx = new OReilly.Browser("Lynx", null, false);
    s += lynx.toString();
    document.getElementById("output").innerHTML = s;
```

Example 4-3 shows the complete listing.

Example 4-3. Accessing a base class method

```
ClientBaseMethods.aspx

<%@ Page Language="C#" %>

<!DOCTYPE html PUBLIC "-//W3C//DTD XHTML 1.0 Transitional//EN"
"http://www.w3.org/TR/xhtml1/DTD/xhtml1-transitional.dtd">
<html xmlns="http://www.w3.org/1999/xhtml">
<head id="Head1" runat="server">
  <title>ASP.NET AJAX</title>

  <script language="Javascript" type="text/javascript">
  function pageLoad() {
    var s = "";

    Type.registerNamespace("OReilly");
    OReilly.Software = function(name, vendor) {
      var _name = (name != null) ? name : "unknown";
      var _vendor = (vendor != null) ? vendor : "unknown";

      this.getName = function() {
        return _name;
      }
      this.setName = function(name) {
        _name = name;
      }

      this.getVendor = function() {
        return _vendor;
      }
      this.setVendor = function(vendor) {
        _vendor = vendor;
      }
    }
    Type.registerClass("OReilly.Software");

    OReilly.Browser = function(name, vendor, isJavaScriptSupported) {
      OReilly.Browser.initializeBase(this, new Array(name, vendor));
      var _isJavaScriptSupported = (isJavaScriptSupported != null) ?
isJavaScriptSupported : false;
      this.getIsJavaScriptSupported = function() {
        return _isJavaScriptSupported;
      }
      this.setIsJavaScriptSupported = function(isJavaScriptSupported) {
        _isJavaScriptSupported = isJavaScriptSupported;
      }
```

Example 4-3. Accessing a base class method (continued)

```
    }
    OReilly.Browser.registerClass("OReilly.Browser", OReilly.Software);

    OReilly.Software.prototype.toString = function() {
      return this.getName() + " from " + this.getVendor();
    }
    OReilly.Browser.prototype.toString = function() {
      return OReilly.Browser.callBaseMethod(this, "toString") +
        (this.getIsJavaScriptSupported() ? " (w/ JS)" : " (w/o JS)");
    };

    var ie = new OReilly.Browser("Internet Explorer", "Microsoft", true);
    s = ie.toString() + "<br />";

    var lynx = new OReilly.Browser("Lynx", null, false);
    s += lynx.toString();

    document.getElementById("output").innerHTML = s;
  }
  </script>

</head>
<body>
  <form id="form1" runat="server">
    <asp:ScriptManager ID="ScriptManager1" runat="server">
    </asp:ScriptManager>
    <div id="output">
    </div>
  </form>
</body>
</html>
```

Note that when you run this page, the output of this code is identical to that shown in Figure 4-2.

Interfaces

The final OOP-like feature made available to JavaScript by ASP.NET AJAX is interfaces. An interface does not contain any implementation at all but instead specifies the members that subclasses must implement. Even if you inherit from an interface, there is no implementation you can use. Instead, you must create the methods that are defined in the interface. This is a good way for developers to keep class structure and implementation details separated in their code.

As you have probably already guessed, the method for creating an interface is `Type.registerInterface()`. The interface name you just created is provided as the third (optional) parameter of `registerClass()`. So, starting with the interface itself, we will use the following code:

```
OReilly.IProduct = function( ) {
  this.toString = Function.abstractMethod;
}
Type.registerInterface("OReilly.IProduct");
```

Here, OReilly.Product is an abstract class. Unfortunately, the final version of ASP.NET AJAX does not support abstract classes (pre-release versions did). Therefore, there is no technical difference between abstract classes and regular classes.

In the following example, the OReilly.Product class introduces and implements the properties name and vendor.

```
OReilly.Product = function(name, vendor) {
  var _name = (name != null) ? name : "unknown";
  var _vendor = (vendor != null) ? vendor : "unknown";

  this.getName = function( ) {
    return _name;
  }
  this.setName = function(name) {
    _name = name;
  }
  this.getVendor = function( ) {
    return _vendor;
  }
  this.setVendor = function(vendor) {
    _vendor = vendor;
  }
}
Type.registerClass("OReilly.Product");
```

The next class to be implemented is OReilly.Software. Since we do not want to instantiate this class directly (we have subclasses like OReilly.Browser for that), this can now also be turned into an abstract class. It derives from OReilly.Product (to get name and vendor), but it also implements OReilly.IProduct (for the toString( ) method). After declaring the class, we register it with the following call to Type.registerClass( ):

```
OReilly.Software.registerClass("OReilly.Software", OReilly.Product,
OReilly.IProduct);
```

The rest of the code remains unchanged. It is quite long, so you might consider putting it into an external *.js* file for legibility of the *.aspx* file. Example 4-4 shows the complete listing.

Example 4-4. Using interfaces to structure code

ClientInterface.aspx

```
<%@ Page Language="C#" %>

<!DOCTYPE html PUBLIC "-//W3C//DTD XHTML 1.0 Transitional//EN"
"http://www.w3.org/TR/xhtml1/DTD/xhtml1-transitional.dtd">
```

Example 4-4. Using interfaces to structure code (continued)

```
<html xmlns="http://www.w3.org/1999/xhtml">
<head id="Head1" runat="server">
  <title>ASP.NET AJAX</title>

  <script language="Javascript" type="text/javascript">
  function pageLoad( ) {
    var s = "";

    Type.registerNamespace("OReilly");

    OReilly.IProduct = function( ) {
      this.toString = Function.abstractMethod;
    }
    Type.registerInterface("OReilly.IProduct");

    OReilly.Product = function(name, vendor) {
      var _name = (name != null) ? name : "unknown";
      var _vendor = (vendor != null) ? vendor : "unknown";

      this.getName = function( ) {
        return _name;
      }
      this.setName = function(name) {
        _name = name;
      }
      this.getVendor = function( ) {
        return _vendor;
      }
      this.setVendor = function(vendor) {
        _vendor = vendor;
      }
    }
    Type.registerClass("OReilly.Product");

    OReilly.Software = function(name, vendor) {
      var _name = (name != null) ? name : "unknown";
      var _vendor = (vendor != null) ? vendor : "unknown";
      this.getName = function( ) {
        return _name;
      }
      this.setName = function(name) {
        _name = name;
      }
      this.getVendor = function( ) {
        return _vendor;
      }
      this.setVendor = function(vendor) {
        _vendor = vendor;
      }
    }
    OReilly.Software.registerClass("OReilly.Software", OReilly.Product, OReilly.IProduct);
    OReilly.Software.prototype.toString = function( ) {
    return this.getName() + " from " + this.getVendor();
```

Example 4-4. Using interfaces to structure code (continued)

```
    }

    OReilly.Browser = function(name, vendor, isJavaScriptSupported) {
      OReilly.Browser.initializeBase(this, new Array(name, vendor));
      var _isJavaScriptSupported = (isJavaScriptSupported != null) ? vendor : false;
      this.getIsJavaScriptSupported = function() {
        return _isJavaScriptSupported;
      }
      this.setIsJavaScriptSupported = function(isJavaScriptSupported) {
        _isJavaScriptSupported = isJavaScriptSupported;
      }
    }
    OReilly.Browser.registerClass("OReilly.Browser", OReilly.Software);
    OReilly.Browser.prototype.toString = function() {
      return OReilly.Browser.callBaseMethod(this, "toString") +
            (this.getIsJavaScriptSupported() ? " (w/ JS)" : " (w/o JS)");
    }

    var ie = new OReilly.Browser("Internet Explorer", "Microsoft", true);
    s = ie.toString() + "<br />";
    var lynx = new OReilly.Browser("Lynx", null, false);
    s += lynx.toString();
    document.getElementById("output").innerHTML = s;
  }
  </script>

</head>
<body>
  <form id="form1" runat="server">
    <asp:ScriptManager ID="ScriptManager1" runat="server">
    </asp:ScriptManager>
    <div id="output">
    </div>
  </form>
</body>
</html>
```

Client Versions of .NET Classes

In addition to adding OOP-like features for JavaScript coding, ASP.NET AJAX achieves two goals through client class implementations that are analogs of some .NET classes:

- Functionality missing in JavaScript is provided as part of ASP.NET AJAX.
- .NET developers with little JavaScript experience can use some familiar elements in their code.

In my opinion, this is one of the areas where upcoming ASP.NET AJAX versions will most certainly add more features, so the following list of classes is neither exhaustive nor final. Two useful features that are already available are Sys.StringBuilder and enumerations.

Sys.StringBuilder

One of the new features introduced in .NET 1.0 that really improved performance was the introduction of the StringBuilder class. The downside, however, is that applications are usually full of code such as that illustrated below:

```
string s = "", t;
while () {
  t = <value>;
  s += t;
}
```

The problem lies in the statement s += t, which is equivalent to s = s + t. Whenever this code is executed, a copy of s and a copy of t are created in memory, concatenated, then saved back into s. However, it's inefficient to create a copy of s to achieve these results. Therefore, StringBuilder uses an optimized algorithm for string concatenation.

In JavaScript, this approach does not have any measurable effect on memory (in fact, the implementation seems to be a tick slower than the standard approach). Then again, performance is not as critical an issue for client script as it is for server code. Nevertheless, for consistency with your server coding techniques, you can rely on your knowledge of .NET coding techniques and use StringBuilder on the client. Example 4-5 puts the StringBuilder class to work. It concatenates some strings to build an HTML chessboard.

Example 4-5. Using an ASP.NET AJAX StringBuilder

ClientStringBuilder.aspx

```
<%@ Page Language="C#" %>

<!DOCTYPE html PUBLIC "-//W3C//DTD XHTML 1.0 Transitional//EN"
"http://www.w3.org/TR/xhtml1/DTD/xhtml1-transitional.dtd">
<html xmlns="http://www.w3.org/1999/xhtml">
<head id="Head1" runat="server">
  <title>ASP.NET AJAX</title>

  <script language="Javascript" type="text/javascript">
  window.onload = function() {
    var sb = new Sys.StringBuilder();
    for (var i = 8; i >= 1; i--) {
      for (var j = 97; j <= 104; j++) {
        sb.append(String.fromCharCode(j));
        sb.append(i);
        sb.append(" ");
      }
      sb.appendLine();
      sb.appendLine();
    }
    document.getElementById("output").innerHTML = "<pre>" + sb.toString() + "</pre>";
```

Example 4-5. Using an ASP.NET AJAX StringBuilder (continued)

```
    }
    </script>

</head>
<body>
    <form id="form1" runat="server">
        <asp:ScriptManager ID="ScriptManager1" runat="server">
        </asp:ScriptManager>
        <div id="output"></div>
    </form>
</body>
</html>
```

The built-in JavaScript function String.fromCharCode( ) converts an ASCII code to its associated character, so the inner for loop runs from "a" through "h". As Figure 4-3 reveals, the code in Example 4-7 creates a simple chessboard.

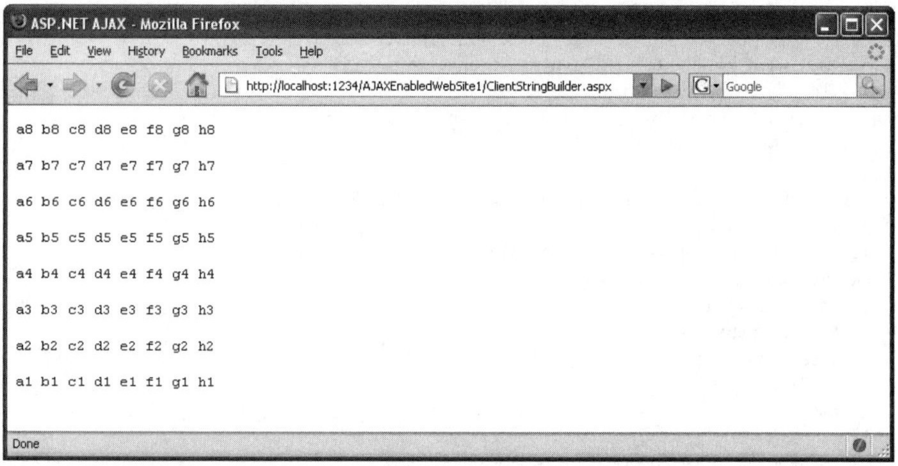

Figure 4-3. A chessboard (with some potential)

Enumerations

Another .NET type that is emulated by ASP.NET AJAX for JavaScript is Enum. You can create a custom enumeration using the createEnum( ) method. The API for this changed quite a bit during the Atlas and ASP.NET AJAX development cycle. In its current form, you can create an enumeration as shown in the following listing, but you cannot iterate over it. You can create a namespace, if you wish to use one:

```
    Type.registerNamespace("ORA.MyEnums");
```

Then, create the enum object, assigning it an (empty) function:

```
    ORA.MyEnums.Ajax = function( ) {};
```

Next, define all values in the enumeration, using the syntax below:

```
ORA.MyEnums.Ajax.prototype = {
  "Asynchronous": 0,
  "JavaScript": 1,
  "and": 2,
  "XML": 3
};
```

Finally, the enumeration needs to be registered:

```
ORA.MyEnums.Ajax.registerEnum("ORA.MyEnums.Ajax");
```

Example 4-6 shows a complete example that creates the enumeration and then accesses it.

Example 4-6. Using an ASP.NET AJAX Enum

ClientEnum.aspx

```
<%@ Page Language="C#" %>

<!DOCTYPE html PUBLIC "-//W3C//DTD XHTML 1.0 Transitional//EN"
"http://www.w3.org/TR/xhtml1/DTD/xhtml1-transitional.dtd">
<html xmlns="http://www.w3.org/1999/xhtml">
<head id="Head1" runat="server">
  <title>ASP.NET AJAX</title>

  <script language="Javascript" type="text/javascript">
  function pageLoad( ) {
    Type.registerNamespace("ORA.MyEnums");
    ORA.MyEnums.Ajax = function( ) {};
    ORA.MyEnums.Ajax.prototype = {
      "Asynchronous": 0,
      "JavaScript": 1,
      "and": 2,
      "XML": 3
    };
    ORA.MyEnums.Ajax.registerEnum("ORA.MyEnums.Ajax");

    document.getElementById("output").innerHTML +=
      ORA.MyEnums.Ajax.Asynchronous + " " +
      ORA.MyEnums.Ajax.JavaScript + " " +
      ORA.MyEnums.Ajax.and + " " +
      ORA.MyEnums.Ajax.XML;
  }
  </script>

</head>
<body>
  <form id="form1" runat="server">
    <asp:ScriptManager ID="ScriptManager1" runat="server">
    </asp:ScriptManager>
    <div id="output"></div>
  </form>
```

Example 4-6. Using an ASP.NET AJAX Enum (continued)

```
</body>
</html>
```

This code outputs the string "0 1 2 3 " (the keys for the enumeration entries) in the
<div> element.

Enumerations are also used internally by ASP.NET AJAX to define mouse button
values (the following code snippet has been edited and reformatted for clarity).

```
Sys.UI.MouseButton = function( ) { };
Sys.UI.MouseButton.prototype = {
  leftButton:0,
  middleButton:1,
  rightButton:2
};
Sys.UI.MouseButton.registerEnum("Sys.UI.MouseButton");
```

Summary

The ASP.NET AJAX client script library implements several convenient features not
present in standard JavaScript, including OOP-like functionality and client-side
equivalents of .NET Framework features. These features can be used by any Java-
Script programmer, without repercussions to ASP.NET or the server-side features of
ASP.NET AJAX.

For Further Reading

http://www.kevlindev.com/tutorials/javascript/inheritance
> Online tutorial for JavaScript's OOP capabilities

http://aspnetresources.com/blog/ms_ajax_cheat_sheets_batch2.aspx
> "Cheat sheets" for ASP.NET AJAX's JavaScript extensions

http://ajax.asp.net/docs/ClientReference/Global/default.aspx
> Documentation for helper functions and JavaScript base type extensions

http://quickstarts.asp.net/Futures/ajax/doc/cssselectors.aspx
> The ASP.NET AJAX Futures provides JavaScript helper functions to select ele-
> ments based on CSS rules

CHAPTER 5

Web Services

In the very first "Hello World" application in Chapter 1, we used a web service to exchange data between a client and server. However, to use web services with JavaScript to their fullest, you need to master some additional skills. These include error handling, inline web services (web service methods in the current *.aspx* page, also called page methods), and using web services and JavaScript without the help of the .NET Framework.

In this chapter, you will learn some special features of ASP.NET AJAX's web services support, including error handling and maintaining session state. You will also see how to use non-ASP.NET web services with JavaScript.

Error Handling

Up to now, when working with web services, we expected our remote calls to work each time. However, the fact that an exception could be thrown has not yet been considered.

When using web services from remote servers (which, for the purposes of this dicussion means servers on another domain), developers often do not include exception-handling code. One reason is that a web service can be implemented with any technology, and every technology has its own way of running exceptions. Some do not raise exceptions at all.

However in the case of ASP.NET AJAX and Ajax, using web services is a bit different. We cannot directly use a remote service, since the security model prohibits us from doing so. By default, JavaScript and the XMLHttpRequest object only allow access to URIs within the same domain as the current page. Thus, when you work with ASP.NET AJAX, you are calling a web service that is in the same domain, meaning it's a web service based on .NET technology (or WCF, the new Windows Communication Foundation). As a consequence, you know which exception model is used.

ASP.NET AJAX allows you to access exceptions in JavaScript code thrown by a web service. To demonstrate this, let's write a simple math service that divides two numbers. You have probably already guessed where this is leading: if the user tries to trigger a divide-by-zero exception, the service throws DivideByZeroException. Example 5-1 shows the code for a web service (*MathService.asmx*) that throws this exception. One point to remember; web services that can be used from ASP.NET AJAX require the [ScriptService] and [WebMethod] attributes.

Example 5-1. A web service that throws an exception

MathService.asmx

```
<%@ WebService Language="C#" Class="MathService" %>

using System;
using System.Web;
using System.Web.Services;
using System.Web.Services.Protocols;

[WebService(Namespace = "http://hauser-wenz.de/AspNetAJAX/")]
[WebServiceBinding(ConformsTo = WsiProfiles.BasicProfile1_1)]
[System.Web.Script.Services.ScriptService]
public class MathService  : System.Web.Services.WebService {

    [WebMethod]
    public float DivideNumbers(int a, int b) {
      if (b == 0) {
        throw new DivideByZeroException( );
      } else {
        return (float)a / b;
      }
    }
}
```

Now, let's assemble a page that calls this web service. We need two input fields in which to enter the values we would like to divide. We also need two output containers: one for the result of the division and one for eventual error messages. A button then calls the client-side function, which in turn, calls the web service.

```
<nobr>
  <input type="text" id="a" name="a" size="2" />
  /
  <input type="text" id="b" name="b" size="2" />
  =
  <span id="c" style="width: 50px;" />
</nobr>
<br />
<input type="button" value="Divide Numbers" onclick="callService(this.form);" />
<br />
<div id="output" style="width: 600px; height: 300px;">
</div>
```

As for server controls on the page, we need two: the `ScriptManager` element and, embedded into it, the reference to the web service we want to use.

```
<asp:ScriptManager ID="ScriptManager1" runat="server">
  <Services>
    <asp:ServiceReference Path="MathService.asmx" />
  </Services>
</asp:ScriptManager>
```

Now when you call the web service, you can use the proxy object `MathService` that was generated automatically. Remember the parameters when calling a web method: first the parameter(s) of the web method, then the callback function for call completion.

However, this time we submit one more parameter to the `DivideNumbers()` method. After a callback to handle call completion, we provide another callback. The new one is executed when an error occurs, which includes timeouts as well.

```
function callService(f) {
  document.getElementById("c").innerHTML = "";
  MathService.DivideNumbers(
    parseInt(f.elements["a"].value),
    parseInt(f.elements["b"].value),
    callComplete,
    callError
  );
}
```

This error handling function retrieves an error object that contains five methods:

get_exceptionType( )
> Retrieves the type of the exception

get_message( )
> Retrieves the error message of the exception

get_stackTrace( )
> Retrieves the stack trace of the error

get_statusCode( )
> Retrieves the status code sent from the server

get_timeOut( )
> Determines whether a timeout has occurred

This information is output in the `<div>` element that we created specifically for receiving it:

```
function callError(result) {
  document.getElementById("output").innerHTML =
    "<b>" +
    result.get_exceptionType() +
    "</b>: " +
    result.get_message() +
    "<br />" +
    result.get_stackTrace();
}
```

The rest of the example is straightforward. When the call to the web service completes successfully, output the result of the division in the <span> element. Example 5-2 shows the complete code for the page.

Example 5-2. A page that displays exceptions thrown by MathService.asmx

Error.aspx

```
<%@ Page Language="C#" %>

<!DOCTYPE html PUBLIC "-//W3C//DTD XHTML 1.0 Transitional//EN"
"http://www.w3.org/TR/xhtml1/DTD/xhtml1-transitional.dtd">

<html xmlns="http://www.w3.org/1999/xhtml">
<head runat="server">
  <title>ASP.NET AJAX</title>

  <script language="Javascript" type="text/javascript">
  function callService(f) {
    document.getElementById("c").innerHTML = "";
    document.getElementById("output").innerHTML = "";
    MathService.DivideNumbers(
      parseInt(f.elements["a"].value),
      parseInt(f.elements["b"].value),
      callComplete,
      callError);
  }

  function callComplete(result) {
    document.getElementById("c").innerHTML = result;
  }

  function callError(result) {
    document.getElementById("output").innerHTML =
      "<b>" +
      result.get_exceptionType() +
      "</b>: " +
      result.get_message() +
      "<br />" +
      result.get_stackTrace();
  }
  </script>

</head>
<body>
  <form id="form1" runat="server">
    <asp:ScriptManager ID="ScriptManager1" runat="server">
      <Services>
        <asp:ServiceReference Path="MathService.asmx" />
      </Services>
    </asp:ScriptManager>
    <div>
      <nobr>
        <input type="text" id="a" name="a" size="2" />
```

```
      /
      <input type="text" id="b" name="b" size="2" />
      =
      <span id="c" style="width: 50px;"></span>
    </nobr>
    <br />
    <input type="button" value="Divide Numbers" onclick="callService(this.form);" />
    <br />
    <div id="output" style="width: 600px; height: 300px;">
    </div>
  </div>
 </form>
</body>
</html>
```

Now when you divide 6 by 7, you get, as expected, 0.8571429. However, if you try to divide 6 by 0, the web service throws the predicted exception. Figure 5-1 shows the output, including a short stack trace.

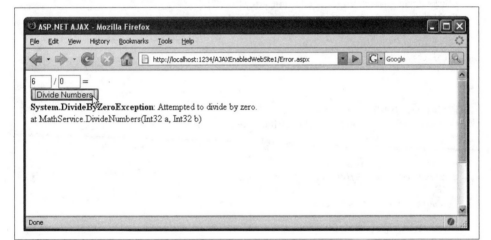

Figure 5-1. Information about the exception is shown

About (Not) Displaying Error Messages

Showing error messages in the client is a nice tool for debugging an application, but it can be really dangerous in a production environment. Error messages may contain sensitive information, like connection strings. Even if you do not display this information, ASP.NET AJAX may send this information to the client anyway. There are two steps you can take to prevent this. First, do not show detailed error messages like stack traces on the client. Second, when throwing exceptions on the server, try to embed as little information as possible in these exceptions.

Page Methods

You have probably found that putting all the web methods for an application in a separate file is a bit cumbersome. From an architectural point of view, this type of file management seems like a good idea. But with simple scripts or applications (like most of the examples in this book), the extra *.asmx* file clutters up the project.

With very little extra code (ultimately, even less code), you can put all of your code in one place, namely in your main *.aspx* file (or its code-behind class file). This technique takes two steps. First, you import the web services namespace into the page file, using an @ Import directive as shown here:

```
<%@ Import Namespace="System.Web.Services" %>
```

Second, you put the code for the web method on your page. To identify it as a web service method (well, more accurately, as a method that works like a web method), use the [WebMethod] attribute as you would do in an *.asmx* file. However, the inline web service methods support of ASP.NET AJAX has the following requirements as well:

- The method must be marked with the ScriptMethod attribute, defined in System.Web.Script.Services.
- The method must be declared as public.
- The method must be declared as static.

Following is the code for a simple method that supports all of these requirements:

```
<script runat="server">
  [WebMethod]
  [System.Web.Script.Services.ScriptMethod]
  public static float DivideNumbers(int a, int b)
  {
    if (b == 0)
    {
      throw new DivideByZeroException();
    }
    else
    {
      return (float)a / b;
    }
  }
</script>
```

ASP.NET AJAX automatically searches for all such methods and encapsulates them in the client PageMethods class. So, to call the method, use PageMethods.DivideNumbers() as illustrated here:

```
function callService(f) {
  document.getElementById("c").innerHTML = "";
  PageMethods.DivideNumbers(
    parseInt(f.elements["a"].value),
    parseInt(f.elements["b"].value),
```

```
        callComplete,
        callError);
  }
```

The final step is to enable calling inline web service methods. ASP.NET AJAX calls them "page methods," and the ScriptManager control supports the EnablePageMethods property to enable page methods support:

```
<asp:ScriptManager ID="a1" runat="server" EnablePageMethods="true" />
```

Example 5-3 shows the complete code for an ASP.NET page in which both the page code and the web service method code is in one file.

Example 5-3. Web service code and ASP.NET AJAX code together in one file

Inline.aspx

```
<%@ Page Language="C#" %>
<%@ Import Namespace="System.Web.Services" %>

<!DOCTYPE html PUBLIC "-//W3C//DTD XHTML 1.0 Transitional//EN"
"http://www.w3.org/TR/xhtml1/DTD/xhtml1-transitional.dtd">

<script runat="server">
  [WebMethod]
  [System.Web.Script.Services.ScriptMethod]
  public static float DivideNumbers(int a, int b)
  {
    if (b == 0)
    {
      throw new DivideByZeroException();
    }
    else
    {
      return (float)a / b;
    }
  }
</script>

<html xmlns="http://www.w3.org/1999/xhtml">
<head runat="server">
  <title>ASP.NET AJAX</title>

  <script language="Javascript" type="text/javascript">
  function callService(f) {
    document.getElementById("c").innerHTML = "";
    PageMethods.DivideNumbers(
      parseInt(f.elements["a"].value),
      parseInt(f.elements["b"].value),
      callComplete,
      callError);
  }

  function callComplete(result) {
    document.getElementById("c").innerHTML = result;
```

```
  }

  function callError(result) {
    document.getElementById("output").innerHTML =
      "<b>" +
      result.get_exceptionType() +
      "</b>: " +
      result.get_message() +
      "<br />" +
      result.get_stackTrace();
  }
  </script>

</head>
<body>
  <form id="form1" runat="server">
    <asp:ScriptManager ID="ScriptManager1" runat="server"
EnablePageMethods="true">
    </asp:ScriptManager>
    <div>
      <nobr>
        <input type="text" id="a" name="a" size="2" />
        /
        <input type="text" id="b" name="b" size="2" />
        = <span id="c" style="width: 50px;"></span>
      </nobr>
      <br />
      <input type="button" value="Divide Numbers" onclick="callService(this.form);" />
      <br />
      <div id="output" style="width: 600px; height: 300px;">
      </div>
    </div>
  </form>
</body>
</html>
```

Figure 5-2 shows the results that are displayed when you load the page, enter two numbers, and click the Divide Numbers button.

Maintaining Session State

Web services are sometimes criticized as being great technology that has nothing to do with the Web itself. But since .NET web services are seamlessly integrated with ASP.NET, if you're using ASP.NET, you're can enable scenarios that web services technology by itself cannot offer.

With .NET web services, for example, you can maintain session state. And even if you are using Ajax, this session state is still available to you from your ASP.NET AJAX application. For instance, ASP.NET AJAX would enable different Ajax applications on the same server share information from the same user.

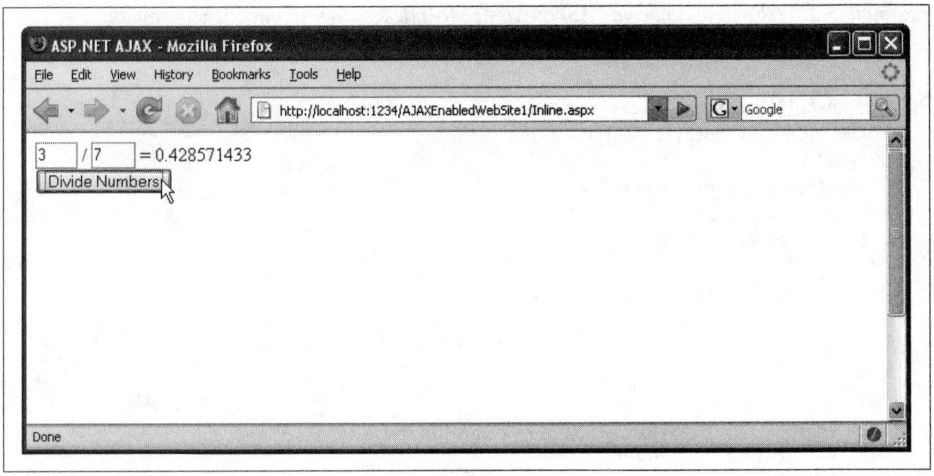

Figure 5-2. One file, one web service, one division operation

Implementing this is easier than describing it. The EnableSession property of the [WebMethod] attribute does the trick—exactly as if you were coding a .NET web method:

```
[WebMethod(EnableSession=true)]
```

You can then directly access the ASP.NET Session object and write data to and read from it. Since the web methods need to be static, you have to use HttpContext.Current. Session, not just Session, which is available only to actual instances of the Page class.

The next code snippet illustrates two functions: one stores the current time in a session, the other determines the difference between the current time and the timestamp in the session. If there is no timestamp in the session, -1 is returned.

```
[WebMethod(EnableSession = true)]
[System.Web.Script.Services.ScriptMethod]
public static bool SaveTime()
{
  HttpContext.Current.Session["PageLoaded"] = DateTime.Now;
  return true;
}

[WebMethod(EnableSession = true)]
[System.Web.Script.Services.ScriptMethod]
public static double CalculateDifference()
{
  if (HttpContext.Current.Session["PageLoaded"] == null) {
    return -1;
  } else {
    DateTime then = (DateTime)HttpContext.Current.Session["PageLoaded"];
    TimeSpan diff = DateTime.Now.Subtract(then);
    return diff.TotalSeconds;
  }
}
```

Now let's return to our application for handling the division of two numbers. When the page containing the code from the preceding snippet loads and the SaveTime( ) method is called, the current time is stored in session state. When division of the two numbers you enter is executed, the time difference is calculated. So, it is possible to determine how long a user had the form open before the division is requested (which, of course, could be done in plain JavaScript as well, but for the sake of demonstration we are using the server detour).

The following JavaScript code calls the web service method to store the time when the page is first loaded by calling the SaveTime( ) method. Because we don't need any return value, we can route the callback to a function that doesn't do anything.

```
function pageLoad( ){
   PageMethods.SaveTime(doNothing, doNothing);
}

function doNothing(result) {
   //nothing :-)
}
```

As you've seen earlier, you'll need a callService( ) method to call the CalculateDifference( ) web service method. The following code makes *two* calls to web service methods. The first calculates the time difference between the initial page load and the current time; the second performs the same math calculation we have been using.

```
function callService(f) {
   document.getElementById("c").innerHTML = "";
   PageMethods.CalculateDifference(
     showDifference,
     callError);
   PageMethods.DivideNumbers(
     parseInt(f.elements["a"].value),
     parseInt(f.elements["b"].value),
     callComplete,
     callError);
}
```

Finally, you need some markup to display the time difference. We will use the output <div> container. Note that the return value -1 from the web method means that there was no timestamp in the session, so there is no time difference to display.

```
function showDifference(result) {
   if (result != -1) {
     document.getElementById("output").innerHTML =
       "The form has been open for " + result + " seconds";
   }
}
```

Example 5-4 shows the complete markup and script you need to implement this example, with changes shown in bold. Note that you must again set the EnablePageMethods="true" attribute of the ScriptManager control. If the attribute is not set, the page methods will not work.

Example 5-4. Maintaining session state with ASP.NET AJAX and ASP.NET

WebServiceSession.aspx

```
<%@ Page Language="C#" %>
<%@ Import Namespace="System.Web.Services" %>

<!DOCTYPE html PUBLIC "-//W3C//DTD XHTML 1.0 Transitional//EN"
"http://www.w3.org/TR/xhtml1/DTD/xhtml1-transitional.dtd">

<script runat="server">
  [WebMethod(EnableSession = true)]
  [System.Web.Script.Services.ScriptMethod]
  public static bool SaveTime()
  {
    HttpContext.Current.Session["PageLoaded"] = DateTime.Now;
    return true;
  }

  [WebMethod(EnableSession = true)]
  [System.Web.Script.Services.ScriptMethod]
  public static double CalculateDifference()
  {
    if (HttpContext.Current.Session["PageLoaded"] == null) {
      return -1;
    } else {
      DateTime then = (DateTime)HttpContext.Current.Session["PageLoaded"];
      TimeSpan diff = DateTime.Now.Subtract(then);
      return diff.TotalSeconds;
    }
  }

  [WebMethod]
  [System.Web.Script.Services.ScriptMethod]  public static float DivideNumbers(int a, int b)
  {
    if (b == 0)
    {
      throw new DivideByZeroException();
    }
    else
    {
      return (float)a / b;
    }
  }
</script>

<html xmlns="http://www.w3.org/1999/xhtml">
<head runat="server">
  <title>ASP.NET AJAX</title>

  <script language="Javascript" type="text/javascript">
  function pageLoad() {
    PageMethods.SaveTime(doNothing, doNothing);
  }
```

```
  function doNothing(result) {
    //nothing :-)
  }

  function callService(f) {
    document.getElementById("c").innerHTML = "";
    PageMethods.CalculateDifference(
      showDifference,
      callError);
    PageMethods.DivideNumbers(
      parseInt(f.elements["a"].value),
      parseInt(f.elements["b"].value),
      callComplete,
      callError);
  }
function showDifference(result) {
    if (result != -1) {
      document.getElementById("output").innerHTML =
        "The form has been open for " + result + " seconds";
    }
  }

  function callComplete(result) {
    document.getElementById("c").innerHTML = result;
  }

  function callError(result) {
    if (result == null) {
      window.alert("Error!");
    } else {
      document.getElementById("output").innerHTML =
        "<b>" +
        result.get_exceptionType() +
        "</b>: " +
        result.get_message() +
        "<br />" +
        result.get_stackTrace();
    }
  }
  </script>

</head>
<body>
  <form id="form1" runat="server">
    <asp:ScriptManager ID="ScriptManager1" runat="server"
      EnablePageMethods="true">
    </asp:ScriptManager>
    <div>
      <nobr>
        <input type="text" id="a" name="a" size="2" />
        /
        <input type="text" id="b" name="b" size="2" />
```

```
      = <span id="c" style="width: 50px;"></span>
    </nobr>
    <br />
    <input type="button" value="Divide Numbers" onclick="callService(this.form);" />
    <br />
    <div id="output" style="width: 600px; height: 300px;">
    </div>
  </div>
  </form>
</body>
</html>
```

When the `DivideNumbers()` method is called in the browser, you'll notice two things differ from earlier examples. First, the web site sends out a session cookie (unless you specified cookieless session management in the *Web.config* file). If your browser prompts you before accepting cookies, you'll see a dialog box like the one displayed in Figure 5-3. Second, the session data is preserved during calls to the web service (Figure 5-4).

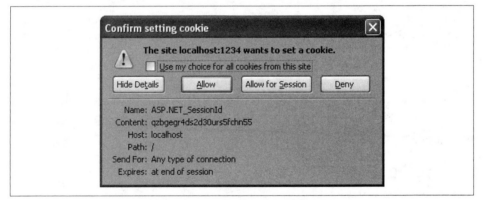

Figure 5-3. ASP.NET now sends out a session cookie on behalf of the page

Exchanging Complex Data with the Server

So far, we have used only strings or primitive types (strings, Booleans, numbers) to exchange between client and server. However, you can use more complex data as well. JavaScript cannot compete with the rich type system offered by the .NET Framework, but the JSON format (introduced in Chapter 3) offers at least rudimentary support for arrays and objects.

ASP.NET AJAX comes with JSON serialization and deserialization features. So let us add a new feature to the division web service from Examples 5-1 and 5-2. We'll create a new web method that returns two pieces of information in one; the result of the division and a current timestamp from the server. For this to work, we first create a new class in *MathService.asmx* that provides us with the object we will later return:

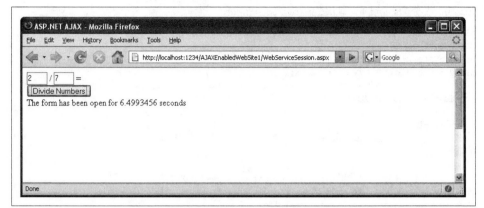

Figure 5-4. Using session state to store a time for calculating elapsed time between page load and user request

```
public class DivisionData
{
  public float result;
  public string calculationTime;
}
```

The method illustrated below then creates and returns the object:

```
[WebMethod]
public DivisionData ExtendedDivideNumbers(int a, int b) {
  if (b == 0) {
    throw new DivideByZeroException( );
  } else {
    float res = (float)a / b;
    string stamp = DateTime.Now.ToLongTimeString( );
    DivisionData d = new DivisionData( );
    d.result = res;
    d.calculationTime = stamp;
    return d;
  }
}
```

In order to make the returned object accessible for JavaScript, ASP.NET AJAX must serialize the data into proper JSON. The GenerateScriptType attribute (defined in System.Web.Script.Services [where the ScriptService and ScriptMethod attributes are also located]) instructs ASP.NET AJAX to pick the correct object definition:

```
[System.Web.Script.Services.GenerateScriptType(typeof(DivisionData))]
```

That's all the extra work that is required on the server. Example 5-5 contains the updated code for *MathService.asmx*.

Example 5-5. The updated MathService file

```
MathService.asmx

<%@ WebService Language="C#" Class="MathService" %>
```

Example 5-5. The updated MathService file (continued)

```csharp
using System;
using System.Web;
using System.Web.Services;
using System.Web.Services.Protocols;

public class DivisionData
{
  public float result;
  public string calculationTime;
}

[WebService(Namespace = "http://hauser-wenz.de/AspNetAJAX/")]
[WebServiceBinding(ConformsTo = WsiProfiles.BasicProfile1_1)]
[System.Web.Script.Services.ScriptService]
[System.Web.Script.Services.GenerateScriptType(typeof(DivisionData))]
public class MathService : System.Web.Services.WebService
{

  [WebMethod]
  public float DivideNumbers(int a, int b)
  {
    if (b == 0)
    {
      throw new DivideByZeroException( );
    }
    else
    {
      return (float)a / b;
    }
  }


  [WebMethod]
  public DivisionData ExtendedDivideNumbers(int a, int b)
  {
    if (b == 0)
    {
      throw new DivideByZeroException( );
    }
    else
    {
      float res = (float)a / b;
      string stamp = DateTime.Now.ToLongTimeString( );
      DivisionData d = new DivisionData( );
      d.result = res;
      d.calculationTime = stamp;
      return d;
    }
  }

}
```

On the client, the deserialization of the DivisionData object is entirely done automatically. The result from the web services call has the same properties, result and calculationTime, as the DivisionData object. Example 5-6 shows the required JavaScript code to call the extended web service.

Example 5-6. A page that receives complex objects from a web method

```
Complex.aspx

<%@ Page Language="C#" %>

<!DOCTYPE html PUBLIC "-//W3C//DTD XHTML 1.0 Transitional//EN"
"http://www.w3.org/TR/xhtml1/DTD/xhtml1-transitional.dtd">

<html xmlns="http://www.w3.org/1999/xhtml">
<head runat="server">
  <title>ASP.NET AJAX</title>

  <script language="Javascript" type="text/javascript">
  function callService(f) {
    document.getElementById("c").innerHTML = "";
    document.getElementById("output").innerHTML = "";
    MathService.ExtendedDivideNumbers(
      parseInt(f.elements["a"].value),
      parseInt(f.elements["b"].value),
      callComplete,
      callError);
  }

  function callComplete(result) {
    document.getElementById("c").innerHTML =
      result.result +
      " (calculated at " +
      result.calculationTime +
      ")";
  }

  function callError(result) {
    document.getElementById("output").innerHTML =
      "<b>" +
      result.get_exceptionType( ) +
      "</b>: " +
      result.get_message( ) +
      "<br />" +
      result.get_stackTrace( );
  }
  </script>

</head>
```

Example 5-6. A page that receives complex objects from a web method (continued)

```
<body>
  <form id="form1" runat="server">
    <asp:ScriptManager ID="ScriptManager1" runat="server">
      <Services>
        <asp:ServiceReference Path="MathService.asmx" />
      </Services>
    </asp:ScriptManager>
    <div>
      <nobr>
        <input type="text" id="a" name="a" size="2" />
        /
        <input type="text" id="b" name="b" size="2" />
        =
        <span id="c" style="width: 50px;"></span>
      </nobr>
      <br />
      <input type="button" value="Divide Numbers" onclick="callService(this.form);" />
      <br />
      <div id="output" style="width: 600px; height: 300px;">
      </div>
    </div>
  </form>
</body>
</html>
```

Figure 5-5 displays both the division result and the time output of this script.

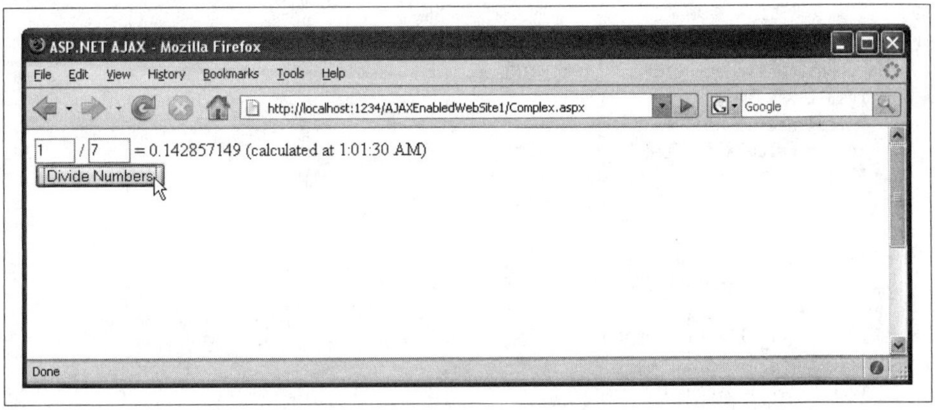

Figure 5-5. The complex information from the server is shown

If you sniff the HTTP traffic that this script generates, you can clearly see how the complex data is transformed into JSON (see Figure 5-6).

So far, you've learned about special web services features offered by ASP.NET AJAX that would be extremely hard to do with JavaScript alone. The ASP.NET AJAX framework integrates very well with .NET web services, making it very convenient to bridge the JavaScript (client) and ASP.NET (server) technologies.

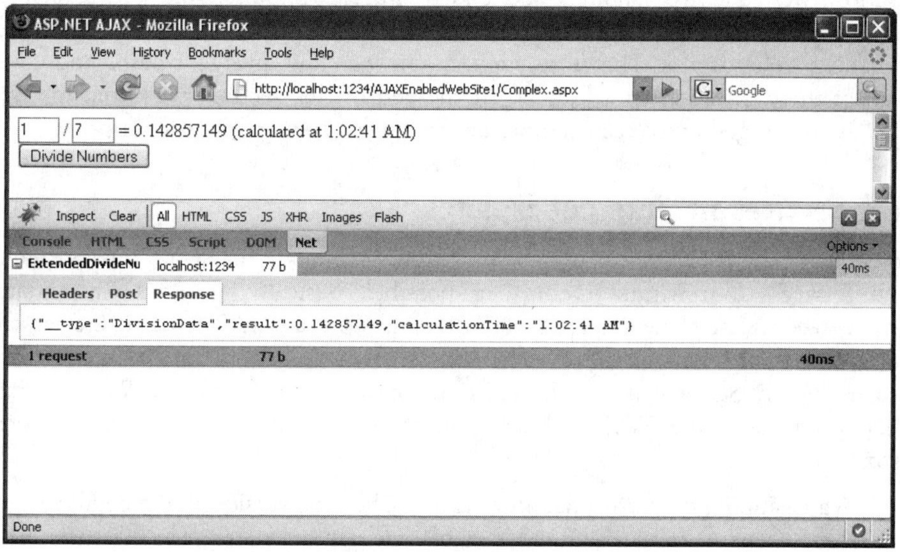

Figure 5-6. The complex information is serialized in JSON

Consuming Web Services with JavaScript

The automatic mechanisms that ASP.NET AJAX provides for accessing web services are quite easy to use as they take care of most of the work. However, there are situations when these mechanisms do not work. For example, imagine you have to call a (same domain) web service that is not written in .NET, but in another server-side technology such as PHP or Java. Or, imagine that you cannot use ASP.NET AJAX for some reason (for instance, due to company policies regarding third-party modules or disagreement with the license). As this book goes beyond using ASP.NET AJAX to write Ajax-empowered ASP.NET applications (and the underlying technologies), this section covers alternative ways to call remote web services from JavaScript.

Before we go into detail, you have to remember once again that the security model of JavaScript forbids cross-domain scripting. This means that you cannot access remote sites using JavaScript (implicitly using XMLHttpRequest).

There are two possible ways to call a web service programmatically using JavaScript. You can either bet on XMLHttpRequest, or write a suitable SOAP HTTP request and then evaluate the data returned from the server. This is quite complicated and very error-prone. A much better approach is to use built-in technology or official add-ons to the browsers that solve this problem for you.

Unfortunately, the two major browser types—Internet Explorer and Mozilla (including Firefox, Epiphany, Camino, and others)—have completely different approaches to calling web services. Therefore, we must now follow divergent paths and cover each of these browsers individually. At the end of this section, we'll join the two models back together to create a more-or-less single browser-agnostic script.

Web Services and Internet Explorer

Some years ago, Microsoft started working on script code that would make calling web services from within its browser possible. Basically, the code instantiates XMLHttpRequest, sets the required HTTP headers for a SOAP request, creates the body of the request, waits for the SOAP response, and transforms that back into something JavaScript can use. In addition, the code can parse the Web Services Description Language (WSDL) description of the web service and generate a local proxy object.

The idea is simple; the implementation is not. The final version of the code (version 1.0.1.1120) consists of nearly 2,300 lines of code. Unfortunately, in 2002, Microsoft abandoned the component it had written. This is a pity, as it still works well today. Luckily, the code is still available in the archives of MSDN, at *http://msdn.microsoft.com/ archive/en-us/samples/internet/behaviors/library/webservice/default.asp*.

Download the file *webservice.htc* and save it to the directory where your example scripts reside. The file extension *.htc* stands for "HTML control," otherwise known as an Internet Explorer behavior. Using a CSS style supported only in Internet Explorer, you can load the file into your application.

```
<div id="WebService" style="behavior:url(webservice.htc);"></div>
```

The name you provide in the id attribute can then be used in JavaScript to access both the HTML control and the web service to which it is linked.

This "linking" can be achieved by providing a link to the WSDL description of the web services you want to use. The method of the *.htc* file you need for this task is useService( ). You also need to provide a unique identifier to access the specific web service later on.

```
WebService.useService("MathService.asmx?WSDL", "MathService");
```

Next, you call the web service. However, the order of the parameters of the associated method, callService( ), is a bit different from the proxy object created by ASP.NET AJAX. The required parameters are :

- A reference to the callback method
- The name of the web method to be called
- The parameter(s) to be submitted to the web service

Note that error handling is not supported (unlike with ASP.NET AJAX where exception information is provided to the client script).

In the case of the MathService web service, the call illustrated here executes the division:

```
WebService.MathService.callService(
  callComplete,
  "DivideNumbers",
  6, 7);
```

The callback function then receives the result as an object whose value attribute contains the return value of the web service:

```
function callComplete(result) {
  document.getElementsById("c").innerHTML = result.value;
}
```

Example 5-7 shows the complete code for this example.

Example 5-7. Calling a web service from Internet Explorer

MathServiceInternetExplorer.htm

```
<!DOCTYPE html PUBLIC "-//W3C//DTD XHTML 1.0 Transitional//EN"
"http://www.w3.org/TR/xhtml1/DTD/xhtml1-transitional.dtd">
<html xmlns="http://www.w3.org/1999/xhtml">
<head>
  <title>ASP.NET AJAX</title>

  <script language="Javascript" type="text/javascript">
  function callService(f) {
    document.getElementById("c").innerHTML = "";
    WebService.useService("MathService.asmx?WSDL", "MathService");
    WebService.MathService.callService(
      callComplete,
      "DivideNumbers",
      f.elements["a"].value, f.elements["b"].value);
  }

  function callComplete(result) {
    document.getElementById("c").innerHTML = result.value;
  }
  </script>

</head>
<body>
  <div id="WebService" style="behavior:url(webservice.htc);">
  </div>
  <form method="post" onsubmit="return false;">
    <div>
      <nobr>
        <input type="text" id="a" name="a" size="2" />
        :
        <input type="text" id="b" name="b" size="2" />
        =
        <span id="c" style="width: 50px;"></span>
      </nobr>
```

Example 5-7. Calling a web service from Internet Explorer (continued)

```
      <br />
      <input type="button" value="Divide Numbers" onclick="callService(this.form);" />
    </div>
  </form>
</body>
</html>
```

You will get some very strange errors if you do not place the web service behavior at the beginning of the <body> element, including error messages claiming that WebService is not defined (although a window.alert(WebService) call works).

Web Services and Mozilla Browsers

Relatively recent versions of Mozilla browsers also contain support for web services as a built-in extension to the browser. Unfortunately, the component for handling web services does not seem to have received much attention recently from the community, but at least it does its job well. However, it is virtually undocumented, and you'll find a lot of strange advice on how to make it work. The approach we'll use in this section does the job, but involves quite a bit of extra code.

Mozilla's SOAPCall class handles all communication with a remote service. As it uses SOAP 1.1, you need to set the SOAPAction header (which, conveniently, is a property of the SOAPCall class) and the URL of the web service file. Following is the code to do this as it relates to our example:

```
var soapcall = new SOAPCall();
soapcall.actionURI = "http://hauser-wenz.de/AspNetAJAX/DivideNumbers";
soapcall.transportURI = "http://localhost:1234/AJAXEnabledWebSite1/MathServiceDocEnc.
asmx";
```

The value of the transportURI property must be an absolute URL. Make sure you change the URI (especially the port number, if using the development server of Visual Studio/Visual Web Developer) to your local system.

All parameters that you provide to the web service are of type SOAPParameter. In the class constructor, you provide first the value of the parameter, then its name.

```
var p1 = new SOAPParameter(6, "a");
var p2 = new SOAPParameter(7, "b");
```

Now comes the tricky part. If you omit the next step, the SOAP call is sent (and the returned values are received), but on the server, the service receives only empty parameters. In the case of our division calculation, this leads to a "divide by zero" exception, but this time an unwanted one.

The trick is to manually set the correct encoding for the integer values. To do so, you need to load the appropriate namespaces for the SOAP integer data type. Then, set the schemaType property of the parameters you want to send to the web service to the generated data type. Here's the code to complete those steps:

```
var senc = new SOAPEncoding();
assenc = senc.getAssociatedEncoding(
  "http://schemas.xmlsoap.org/soap/encoding/",
  false);
var scoll = assenc.schemaCollection;
var stype = scoll.getType(
  "integer",
  "http://www.w3.org/2001/XMLSchema");
p1.schemaType = stype;
p2.schemaType = stype;
```

Next, you need to assemble the web service call. The encode( ) method takes care of that, but only after you have provided several parameters, as shown in the following snippet:

```
soapcall.encode(
  0,                                      //default value for SOAP version 1.1
  "DivideNumbers",                        //name of web method
  "http://hauser-wenz.de/AspNetAJAX/",    //Namespace
  0,                                      //number of additional headers
  new Array(),                            //additional headers
  2,                                      //number of parameters
  new Array(p1, p2)                       //parameters
);
```

Finally, you need to asynchronously invoke the web service using the asyncInvoke( ) method. As a parameter you must provide a reference to the callback function.

```
soapcall.asyncInvoke(callComplete);
```

Three parameters are received by the callback function:

- The XML resulting from the web service call
- The SOAPCall object (in case you are interested in its SOAP headers)
- The HTTP status code of the call

The only remaining task is to extract the information you need from the returned XML. So, let's have a look at a sample of the XML that is returned from a call to MathService—data you can retrieve using software like the Windows tool Fiddler (*http://www.fiddlertool.com/fiddler*) or the Mozilla extension Live HTTP headers (*http://livehttpheaders.mozdev.org/*):

```
<?xml version="1.0" encoding="utf-8"?>
<soap:Envelope xmlns:xsi="http://www.w3.org/2001/XMLSchema-instance"
xmlns:xsd="http://www.w3.org/2001/XMLSchema" xmlns:soap="http://schemas.xmlsoap
.org/soap/envelope/">
  <soap:Body>
```

```
        <DivideNumbersResponse xmlns="http://hauser-wenz.de/AspNetAJAX/">
          <DivideNumbersResult>0.857142866</DivideNumbersResult>
        </DivideNumbersResponse>
      </soap:Body>
    </soap:Envelope>
```

 Refer to Appendix A for more information on getting access to the HTTP requests sent by Ajax applications and on debugging Ajax applications in general.

Working from the representation of the XML data, we can see that the following steps are required to access the actual return value, 0.857142866:

- Use the property body to get access to the <soap:Body> element
- Use the property firstChild to access the <DivideNumberResponse> element
- Use firstChild again to access the <DivideNumbersResult> element
- Use a third firstChild reference to access the text node under the <DivideNumbersResult> element
- Use the data property to access the text within the text node

The JavaScript code you need to retrieve the result of the web service call is illustrated here:

```
function callComplete(result, soapcall, status) {
  document.getElementById("c").innerHTML =
    result.body.firstChild.firstChild.firstChild.data;
}
```

Putting all of these elements together, you get the code shown in Example 5-8. Note that you need to have an Internet connection for this to work, since Mozilla accesses the SOAP schema information.

Example 5-8. Calling a web service in Mozilla browsers

MathServiceMozilla.htm

```
<!DOCTYPE html PUBLIC "-//W3C//DTD XHTML 1.0 Transitional//EN"
"http://www.w3.org/TR/xhtml1/DTD/xhtml1-transitional.dtd">
<html xmlns="http://www.w3.org/1999/xhtml">
<head>
  <title>ASP.NET AJAX</title>

  <script language="Javascript" type="text/javascript">
  function callService(f) {
    document.getElementById("c").innerHTML = "";
    var soapcall = new SOAPCall();
    soapcall.actionURI = "http://hauser-wenz.de/AspNetAJAX/DivideNumbers";
    soapcall.transportURI = "http://localhost:1234/AJAXEnabledWebSite1/MathService.asmx";
```

Example 5-8. Calling a web service in Mozilla browsers (continued)

```
    var p1 = new SOAPParameter(parseInt(f.elements["a"].value), "a");
    var p2 = new SOAPParameter(parseInt(f.elements["b"].value), "b");

    var senc = new SOAPEncoding( );
    assenc = senc.getAssociatedEncoding(
      "http://schemas.xmlsoap.org/soap/encoding/",
      false);
    var scoll = assenc.schemaCollection;
    var stype = scoll.getType(
      "integer",
      "http://www.w3.org/2001/XMLSchema");
    p1.schemaType = stype;
    p2.schemaType = stype;

    soapcall.encode(
      0,                                        //default value for SOAP version 1.1
      "DivideNumbers",                          //name of web method
      "http://hauser-wenz.de/AspNetAJAX/",      //Namespace
      0,                                        //number of additional headers
      new Array( ),                             //additional headers
      2,                                        //number of parameters
      new Array(p1, p2)                         //parameters
    );
    soapcall.asyncInvoke(callComplete);
  }
  function callComplete(result, soapcall, status) {
    document.getElementById("c").innerHTML =
      result.body.firstChild.firstChild.firstChild.data;
  }
  </script>

</head>
<body>
  <form method="post" onsubmit="return false;">
    <div>
      <nobr>
        <input type="text" id="a" name="a" size="2" />
        :
        <input type="text" id="b" name="b" size="2" />
        =
        <span id="c" style="width: 50px;"></span>
      </nobr>
      <br />
      <input type="button" value="Divide Numbers" onclick="callService(this.form);" />
    </div>
  </form>
</body>
</html>
```

Remote Web Services with Mozilla

The Mozilla security model does allow you to call remote services. However, the script prompts the user for additional privileges (see Figure 5-7). The specific privilege required in this case is UniversalBrowserRead, meaning that the browser may read from anywhere (including remote servers and the local filesystem).

```
netscape.security.PrivilegeManager.enablePrivilege(
    "UniversalBrowserRead");
```

The default configuration of Mozilla, Firefox, and other browsers only grants this privilege for local files (using the *file://* protocol), so this approach is basically applicable only to intranet applications. Figure 5-7 shows the message Mozilla browsers display when these elevated privileges are requested.

Web Services with Both Browsers

To wrap up our look at techniques for accessing web services using JavaScript in either Internet Explorer or in the Mozilla family of browsers, let's combine both approaches in a single page. To do this, you first have to decide how to implement browser detection. As discussed in Chapter 2, the best way of doing so is to check for browser capabilities, not for browser types. In Example 5-9, we use the approach that worked for us in Chapter 2 where you learned how to create the XMLHttpRequest object. The goal is to try to create one of the browser-specific objects. If that succeeds, we continue as planned. If it fails, we use a method that works in the other browser. We'll use two nested try...catch constructs to make the calls.

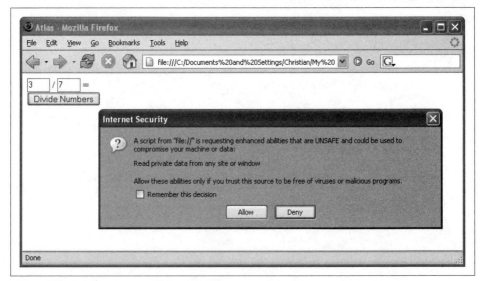

Figure 5-7. Firefox requests additional privileges to call the remote service

Example 5-9 shows the complete markup and script needed to carry out the task. Be sure to test this code in different browsers, and remember to set the soapcall. transportURI property to the URL of the site (and, if required, port) that you're using.

Example 5-9. Calling a web service in either Internet Explorer or Mozilla

MathService.htm

```
<!DOCTYPE html PUBLIC "-//W3C//DTD XHTML 1.0 Transitional//EN"
"http://www.w3.org/TR/xhtml1/DTD/xhtml1-transitional.dtd">
<html xmlns="http://www.w3.org/1999/xhtml">
<head>
  <title>ASP.NET AJAX</title>

  <script language="Javascript" type="text/javascript">
  function callService(f) {
    document.getElementById("c").innerHTML = "";
    try {
      WebService.useService("MathService.asmx?WSDL", "MathService");
      WebService.MathService.callService(
        callComplete,
        "DivideNumbers",
        parseInt(f.elements["a"].value), parseInt(f.elements["b"].value));
    } catch (e) {
      try {
        var soapcall = new SOAPCall();
        soapcall.actionURI = "http://hauser-wenz.de/AspNetAJAX/DivideNumbers";
        soapcall.transportURI = "http://localhost:1234/AJAXEnabledWebSite1/MathService.
asmx";

        var p1 = new SOAPParameter(parseInt(f.elements["a"].value), "a");
        var p2 = new SOAPParameter(parseInt(f.elements["b"].value), "b");

        var senc = new SOAPEncoding();
        assenc = senc.getAssociatedEncoding(
          "http://schemas.xmlsoap.org/soap/encoding/",
          false);
        var scoll = assenc.schemaCollection;
        var stype = scoll.getType(
          "integer",
          "http://www.w3.org/2001/XMLSchema");
        p1.schemaType = stype;
        p2.schemaType = stype;

        soapcall.encode(
          0,                                 //default value for SOAP version 1.1
          "DivideNumbers",                   //name of web method
          "http://hauser-wenz.de/AspNetAJAX/", //Namespace
          0,                                 //number of additional headers
          new Array(),                       //additional headers
          2,                                 //number of parameters
          new Array(p1, p2)                  //parameters
        );
```

Example 5-9. Calling a web service in either Internet Explorer or Mozilla (continued)

```
        soapcall.asyncInvoke(callComplete);
      } catch (e) {
        window.alert("Your browser is not supported.");
      }
    }
  }

  function callComplete(result, soapcall, status) {
    if (result.value != null) {
      document.getElementById("c").innerHTML = result.value;
    } else {
      document.getElementById("c").innerHTML =
        result.body.firstChild.firstChild.firstChild.data;
    }
  }
  </script>

</head>
<body>
  <div id="WebService" style="behavior: url(webservice.htc);">
  </div>
  <form method="post" onsubmit="return false;">
    <div>
      <nobr>
        <input type="text" id="a" name="a" size="2" />
        :
        <input type="text" id="b" name="b" size="2" />
        = <span id="c" style="width: 50px;" ></span>
      </nobr>
      <br />
      <input type="button" value="Divide Numbers" onclick="callService(this.form);" />
    </div>
  </form>
</body>
</html>
```

As you can see in Figures 5-8 and 5-9, Example 5-9 works in both major browser types.

All that remains is to reflect on whether it is all worth it—do you really want to use a browser-specific approach to call a web service? Web sites whose server platform is ASP.NET can stick with ASP.NET AJAX. Since ASP.NET AJAX is easy to deploy, the approach taken in the final section should be seen as a last resort only, especially since development of the Mozilla web service functionality is obviously stalled.

Summary

This chapter featured several scenarios for web services: first, we covered error handling and maintaining session state, then we exchanged complex data between client applications and web service. Finally, you saw how to access non-ASP.NET web services with JavaScript.

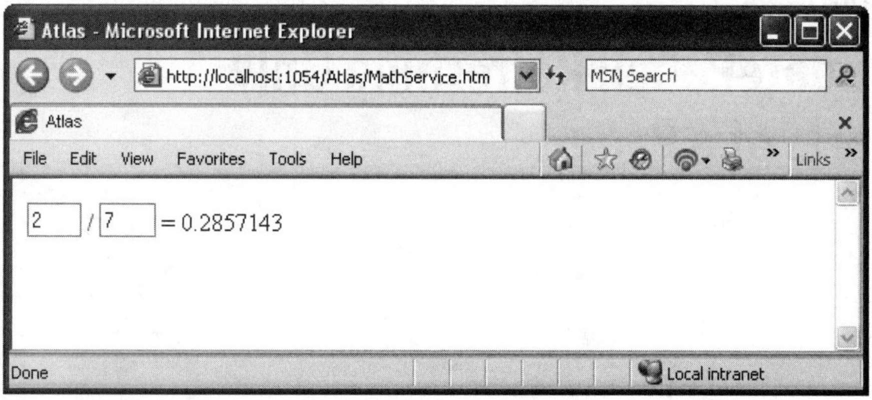

Figure 5-8. The script now works in Internet Explorer

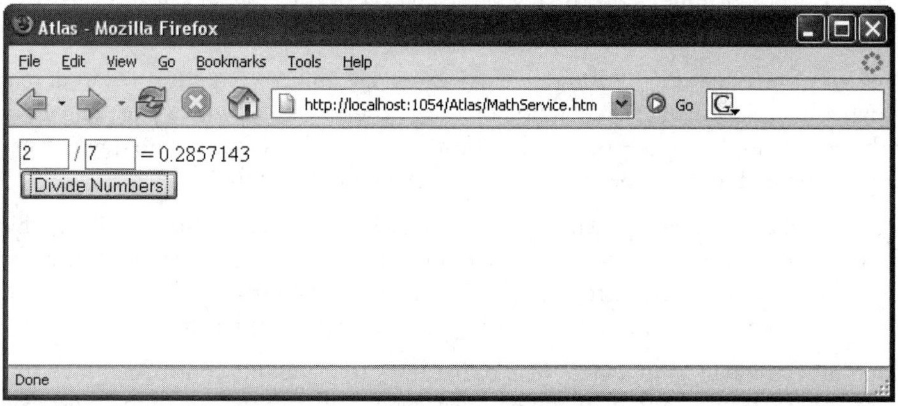

Figure 5-9. The script also works in Mozilla browsers like Firefox

For Further Reading

http://msdn.microsoft.com/archive/en-us/samples/internet/behaviors/library/webservice/default.asp

Archived version of *webservice.htc*

http://ajax.asp.net/docs/tutorials/ASPNETAJAXWebServicesTutorials.aspx

Web Services tutorial in the Microsoft ASP.NET AJAX documentation

CHAPTER 6

UpdatePanel: Refreshing Only Parts of a Page

A summary of Ajax advantages would most certainly include this description: "changes a section of a web page without performing a postback." In previous chapters, you learned how to do this by retrieving data from the server and then using JavaScript and the DOM to use this data to populate an element on the page.

One very neat feature of ASP.NET AJAX is its ability to perform partial page updates. That means that one section of a page is updated, as with a page reload, but without a complete page postback/refresh. As an added bonus, no JavaScript is required (from the developer); ASP.NET AJAX takes care of that.

All of this magic is made possible by the ASP.NET AJAX UpdatePanel control, which lets you confine postbacks to a particular area of a page, such as the input fields of a form. The UpdatePanel control can, for instance, get data from a web service—such as a stock ticker or weather service—and periodically update results.

In addition to saving you a great deal of frustration, using this control can save you a lot of coding, testing, and debugging time as well. It is perhaps one of the most exciting features of the ASP.NET AJAX framework.

In this chapter, you'll learn how you can use the UpdatePanel control to cut down on postbacks of an entire page and improve the responsiveness of your application.

Making a Page Region Updatable

Not surprisingly, the ASP.NET AJAX control UpdatePanel is the main theme of this chapter. Everything inside an update panel operates like a page within a page. The contents of the panel are refreshed from the server (using XMLHttpRequest under the covers, of course). However, from the perspective of server page programming, it looks like a typical page refresh. If you are accessing Page.IsPostBack, this carries the value true when an portion of a page that can be updated is refreshed from the server. All other events that are raised during ordinary postbacks are also raised for update panel refreshes.

You can think of an UpdatePanel as an *iframe* (an internal frame in a web site, using the `<iframe>` HTML element) within a page. This section is reloaded and refreshed on its own. However, the main advantage in comparison to using a conventional iframe is that the ASP.NET page life cycle events are still raised, so programmatically, you only have one page, not two. This makes coding much easier and the architecture much less complex.

Updating a Section

The UpdatePanel control contains a content template (`<ContentTemplate>`), which, in turn, contains the controls and elements that make up the panel. A good demonstration is the ASP.NET 2.0 GridView element (the successor to the DataGrid element in ASP.NET 1.0). It's easy to configure a GridView control with sorting and editing using ASP.NET 2.0 and Visual Studio 2005 (including Visual Web Developer Express Edition). However, whenever you do anything with the grid—sorting, paging, changing into edit mode and back—a postback to the server occurs, including the mandatory page refresh. Placing a GridView control within the `<ContentTemplate>` section of UpdatePanel provides the same functionality without the page reloads. XMLHttpRequest and ASP.NET AJAX do the required magic. (In fact, GridView supports the EnableSortingAndPagingCallbacks property, which implements a similar behavior. But you will discover how little code you actually need to add to avoid page refreshes for any ASP.NET control.)

Technically, ASP.NET AJAX embeds the contents of `<ContentTemplate>` in a `<div>` element. If you would like to use an inline HTML element (`<span>`) instead of a block element (`<div>`), set the RenderMode property of UpdatePanel to "Inline" (the property defaults to "Block").

Here is the GridView control within an UpdatePanel control (again assuming the *AdventureWorks* database). Note that this markup requires that the connection string for accessing the *AdventureWorks* database is stored in *Web.config*. Visual Studio and Visual Web Developer automatically take care of that for you if you drag and drop a table from Database Explorer (Server Explorer in Visual Studio) to the page in Design view. Note in this example Database Explorer displays Purchasing.Vendor as Vendor (Purchasing).

```
<asp:UpdatePanel id="UpdatePanel1" runat="server">
  <ContentTemplate>
    <asp:GridView ID="GridView1" runat="server"
      AllowPaging="True"
      AllowSorting="True"
      AutoGenerateColumns="False"
      DataKeyNames="VendorID" DataSourceID="SqlDataSource1"
      EmptyDataText="There is no data to display.">
```

```
        [...]
      </asp:GridView>
      <asp:SqlDataSource ID="SqlDataSource1"
          runat="server"
          ConnectionString="<%$ ConnectionStrings:AdventureWorksConnectionString1 %>"...
>
        [...]
      </asp:SqlDataSource>
    </ContentTemplate>
  </asp:UpdatePanel>
```

Once you provide an ID for the UpdatePanel control, you can even take advantage of SmartTag support in Design view. However, the only SmartTag action currently available is adding the ScriptManager to the page. The real convenience lies in the ability to drag a data table from Database Explorer into the UpdatePanel control. Figure 6-1 shows the UpdatePanel control in Design view.

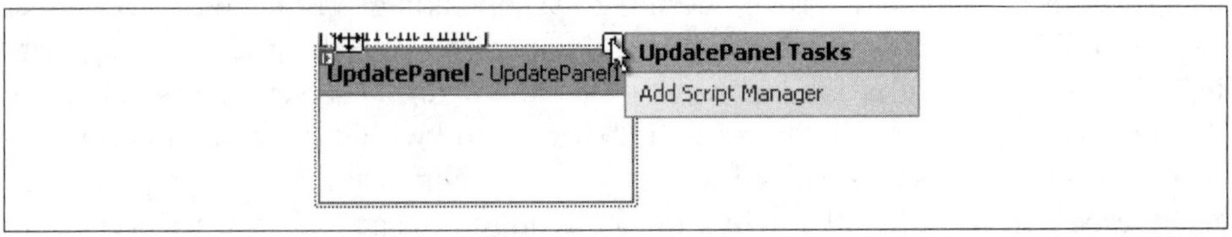

Figure 6-1. The UpdatePanel control in Design view

To demonstrate that there is really no full-page refresh, we'll add a Label control to the page.

```
      <asp:Label ID="CurrentTime" runat="server" />
```

This control will display the current time on the server. If there is a page refresh, code such as the following will update the Label control.

```
      protected void Page_Load(object sender, EventArgs e)
      {
        CurrentTime.Text = DateTime.Now.ToLongTimeString();
      }
```

Example 6-1 shows the complete code for this example.

Example 6-1. A GridView control that is updated without a page refresh

UpdatePanel.aspx

```
<%@ Page Language="C#" %>

<!DOCTYPE html PUBLIC "-//W3C//DTD XHTML 1.0 Transitional//EN"
"http://www.w3.org/TR/xhtml1/DTD/xhtml1-transitional.dtd">

<script runat="server">

  protected void Page_Load(object sender, EventArgs e)
  {
```

Example 6-1. A GridView control that is updated without a page refresh (continued)

```
    CurrentTime.Text = DateTime.Now.ToLongTimeString( );
  }
</script>

<html xmlns="http://www.w3.org/1999/xhtml">
<head runat="server">
  <title>ASP.NET AJAX</title>
</head>
<body>
  <form id="form1" runat="server">
    <asp:ScriptManager ID="ScriptManager1" runat="server">
    </asp:ScriptManager>
    <asp:Label ID="CurrentTime" runat="server" />
    <asp:UpdatePanel ID="UpdatePanel1" runat="server">
      <ContentTemplate>
        <asp:GridView ID="GridView1" runat="server" AllowPaging="True"
AllowSorting="True"
          AutoGenerateColumns="False" DataKeyNames="VendorID"
DataSourceID="SqlDataSource1"
          EmptyDataText="there is no data to display.">
          <Columns>
            <asp:CommandField ShowEditButton="True" />
            <asp:BoundField DataField="VendorID" HeaderText="VendorID"
ReadOnly="True" SortExpression="VendorID" />
            <asp:BoundField DataField="AccountNumber" HeaderText="AccountNumber"
SortExpression="AccountNumber" />
            <asp:BoundField DataField="Name" HeaderText="Name" SortExpression="Name"/>
            <asp:BoundField DataField="CreditRating" HeaderText="CreditRating"
SortExpression="CreditRating" />
            <asp:CheckBoxField DataField="PreferredVendorStatus"
HeaderText="PreferredVendorStatus"
              SortExpression="PreferredVendorStatus" />
            <asp:CheckBoxField DataField="ActiveFlag" HeaderText="ActiveFlag"
SortExpression="ActiveFlag" />
            <asp:BoundField DataField="PurchasingWebServiceURL"
HeaderText="PurchasingWebServiceURL"
              SortExpression="PurchasingWebServiceURL" />
            <asp:BoundField DataField="ModifiedDate" HeaderText="ModifiedDate"
SortExpression="ModifiedDate" />
          </Columns>
        </asp:GridView>
        <asp:SqlDataSource ID="SqlDataSource1" runat="server" ConnectionString="<%$
ConnectionStrings:AdventureWorksConnectionString1 %>"
          DeleteCommand="DELETE FROM [Purchasing].[Vendor] WHERE [VendorID] =
@VendorID"
          ProviderName="<%$ ConnectionStrings:AdventureWorksConnectionString1
.ProviderName %>"
          SelectCommand="SELECT [VendorID], [AccountNumber], [Name], [CreditRating],
[PreferredVendorStatus], [ActiveFlag], [PurchasingWebServiceURL], [ModifiedDate]
FROM [Purchasing].[Vendor]"
          UpdateCommand="UPDATE [Purchasing].[Vendor] SET [AccountNumber] =
@AccountNumber, [Name] = @Name, [CreditRating] = @CreditRating,
```

Example 6-1. A GridView control that is updated without a page refresh (continued)

```
[PreferredVendorStatus] = @PreferredVendorStatus, [ActiveFlag] = @ActiveFlag,
[PurchasingWebServiceURL] = @PurchasingWebServiceURL, [ModifiedDate] =
@ModifiedDate WHERE [VendorID] = @VendorID">
        <UpdateParameters>
          <asp:Parameter Name="AccountNumber" Type="String" />
          <asp:Parameter Name="Name" Type="String" />
          <asp:Parameter Name="CreditRating" Type="Byte" />
          <asp:Parameter Name="PreferredVendorStatus" Type="Boolean" />
          <asp:Parameter Name="ActiveFlag" Type="Boolean" />
          <asp:Parameter Name="PurchasingWebServiceURL" Type="String" />
          <asp:Parameter Name="ModifiedDate" Type="DateTime" />
          <asp:Parameter Name="VendorID" Type="Int32" />
        </UpdateParameters>
        <DeleteParameters>
          <asp:Parameter Name="VendorID" Type="Int32" />
        </DeleteParameters>
      </asp:SqlDataSource>
    </ContentTemplate>
    </asp:UpdatePanel>
  </form>
</body>
</html>
```

> The previous example expects you to have the AdventureWorks connection string saved in *Web.config*, under the name `AdventureWorksConnectionString1`. This is the name Visual Studio automatically uses when dropping a table from AdventureWorks into the page, and this connection string is also embedded into the *Web.config* from the sample downloads for this book. However, you might want to check whether exactly this name is used when you try this example on your own.

As Figures 6-2 and 6-3 show, the `GridView` control functioned just as you'd expect, but the timestamped `Label` control does not change. This proves that indeed, all communication happens in the background.

> When you use the drag-and-drop feature of Visual Studio and drop the Vendor table onto the page in Design view, you may get an ASP.NET error message in the browser (especially when using a pre-SP1 version of Visual Studio or VWD). In spite of Vendor being a unique table name, it is defined with a namespace in the database. The correct name is `Purchasing.Vendor`. Therefore, you may need to go through the automatically generated code and change all occurrences of `[Vendor]` with `[Purchasing].[Vendor]`.

Use these effects carefully, and always be aware of potential side effects. For instance, file uploads are problematic when done within an `UpdatePanel` control.

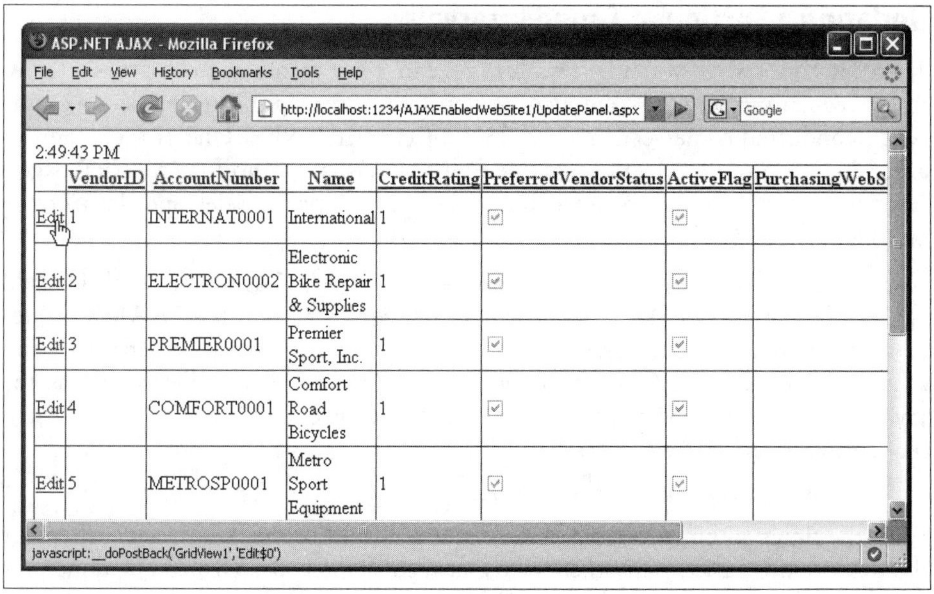

Figure 6-2. Triggering a postback of the GridView control

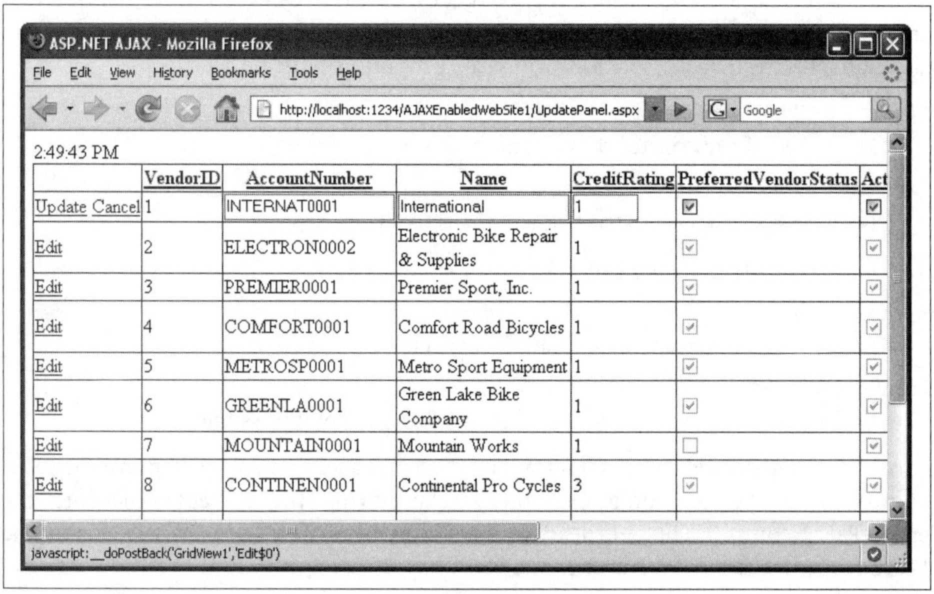

Figure 6-3. Triggering the postback does not change the timestamp on top

If a regular `<iframe>` HTML element suffices, you do not need to rely on ASP.NET AJAX which makes your application a bit harder to debug if something goes wrong. See the "For Further Reading" section at the end of this chapter for pointers to a list of incompatible UpdatePanel controls.

Updating a Section at Timed Intervals

There are times when you might want to refresh the contents of an UpdatePanel control at regular intervals, not simply in response to a user input. I remember an online chat I conducted some years ago on the subject of ASP.NET. One of the attendees asked how to use the Timer control he found in Visual Studio for ASP.NET pages. I answered the question by explaining the client-server model and JavaScript's options for time delays.

Now, with the benefit of a few years and ASP.NET AJAX at my disposal, I would give a different answer. The Timer element that comes with ASP.NET AJAX creates an abstraction layer for the associated JavaScript methods, window.setTimeout() and window.setInterval(). You provide an interval (measured in milliseconds) as the JavaScript methods expect, after which a Tick event occurs. Here is a Timer element that creates a new Tick event every five seconds:

```
<asp:Timer Interval="5000" runat="server" />
```

With the timer control, you can now trigger a refresh of the UpdatePanel whenever the tick event is raised—in other words, at regular intervals. This can be done programmatically, but as usual, there is a declarative way as well.

Within the UpdatePanel control, the <Triggers> element can be used to define event triggers. UpdatePanel. Whenever the trigger event occurs, the UpdatePanel runs through its refresh cycle. The following two properties must be set:

ControlID
> The name of the control that raises the event

EventName
> The name of the event that triggers the refresh

There are two kinds of triggers:

AsyncPostBackTrigger
> Trigger working asynchronously—the preferred choice

PostBackTrigger
> Trigger working synchronously—avoid this choice, if possible

To demonstrate the use of the timer with the UpdatePanel control, we'll move the Label control from the preceding example for displaying the current time into the UpdatePanel control. This will lead to the following: when the page first loads, the Label control is set to the current time.

Every five seconds, the Tick event in the TimerControl occurs, which updates the contents of the UpdatePanel control (this is handled automatically by ASP.NET AJAX).

Example 6-2 shows the complete code for this example.

Example 6-2. Updating a panel at specific time intervals

UpdatePanelTimer.aspx

```
<%@ Page Language="C#" %>

<!DOCTYPE html PUBLIC "-//W3C//DTD XHTML 1.0 Transitional//EN"
"http://www.w3.org/TR/xhtml1/DTD/xhtml1-transitional.dtd">

<script runat="server">

  protected void Page_Load(object sender, EventArgs e)
  {
    CurrentTime.Text = DateTime.Now.ToLongTimeString();
  }
</script>

<html xmlns="http://www.w3.org/1999/xhtml">
<head runat="server">
  <title>ASP.NET AJAX</title>
</head>
<body>
  <form id="form1" runat="server">
    <asp:ScriptManager ID="ScriptManager1" runat="server">
    </asp:ScriptManager>
    <asp:Timer ID="FiveSeconds" Interval="5000" runat="server" />
    <asp:UpdatePanel ID="UpdatePanel1" runat="server">
      <ContentTemplate>
        <asp:Label ID="CurrentTime" runat="server" />
      </ContentTemplate>
      <Triggers>
        <asp:AsyncPostBackTrigger ControlID="FiveSeconds" EventName="Tick" />
      </Triggers>
    </asp:UpdatePanel>
  </form>
</body>
</html>
```

Figure 6-4 shows the results displayed when you load the page and allow it to update at intervals.

Programmatically Updating a Section at Timed Intervals

The most important method exposed by the UpdatePanel control is Update( ). As is fairly self-evident, it updates the panel. One way to use this method is to handle the TimerControl element's Tick event:

```
<asp:Timer ID="FiveSeconds" Interval="5000"
  OnTick="UpdateContents"
  runat="server" />
```

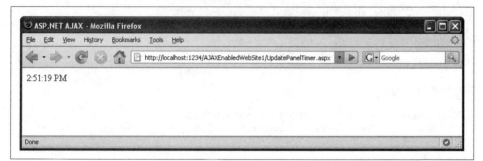

Figure 6-4. The timestamp is updated every five seconds

Then, on the server side, you can write an ordinary ASP.NET event handler that calls the UpdatePanel control's Update method:

```
protected void UpdateContents(object o, EventArgs e)
{
  if (new Random( ).Next(0, 4) == 1) {
    UpdatePanel1.Update( );
  }
}
```

This code updates the panel (and by extension the display that the user sees) on average every fourth request. The Timer control causes a refresh call every five seconds. The code then randomly decides whether the current refresh call should update the panel. In the real world, you would probably check whether some data has changed (in the database, in a file), then trigger the update, if necessary.

The ASP.NET AJAX UpdatePanel control supports two modes, which you set in the UpdateMode attribute of the control:

Always
> The contents of the UpdatePanel control are refreshed whenever a postback occurs (default behavior).

Conditional
> The contents of the UpdatePanel control are only refreshed when a trigger is used, the UpdatePanel's Update( ) method is called (as in this example), or when the parent panel of a nested UpdatePanel control is updated.

Generally, the Conditional mode transfers less data between client and server, optimizing the UpdatePanel control's performance. So, whenever possible (i.e., if you use triggers or Update( )), use UpdateMode="Conditional".

Example 6-3 shows the complete code for an UpdatePanel control being refreshed at a random interval, with changes in vold.

Example 6-3. Programmatically updating a panel

UpdatePanelTimerCode.aspx

```
<%@ Page Language="C#" %>

<!DOCTYPE html PUBLIC "-//W3C//DTD XHTML 1.0 Transitional//EN"
"http://www.w3.org/TR/xhtml1/DTD/xhtml1-transitional.dtd">

<script runat="server">
  private void UpdateContents(object o, EventArgs e)
  {
    if (new Random( ).Next(0, 4) == 1)
    {
      UpdatePanel1.Update( );
    }
  }

  protected void Page_Load(object sender, EventArgs e)
  {
    CurrentTime.Text = DateTime.Now.ToLongTimeString( );
  }
</script>

<html xmlns="http://www.w3.org/1999/xhtml">
<head id="Head1" runat="server">
  <title>ASP.NET AJAX</title>
</head>
<body>
  <form id="form1" runat="server">
    <asp:ScriptManager ID="ScriptManager1" runat="server">
    </asp:ScriptManager>
    <asp:UpdatePanel ID="UpdatePanel1" runat="server"
      UpdateMode="Conditional">
      <ContentTemplate>
        <asp:Timer ID="FiveSeconds" Interval="5000"
          OnTick="UpdateContents"
          runat="server" />
        <asp:Label ID="CurrentTime" runat="server" />
      </ContentTemplate>
    </asp:UpdatePanel>
  </form>
</body>
</html>
```

 Remember that every Tick event leads to network traffic, which might dramatically increase the load of your server. This is one of the differences between the ASP.NET AJAX Timer control and the WinForms Timer control. So use <asp:Timer> judiciously, but as often as necessary.

Displaying a Wait Screen

Another nice feature of UpdatePanel is its ability to display a wait screen while new data in the panel is loaded from the server—particularly if generating this data on the server takes a lot of time (consider complex database operations, for instance). A simple "loading" banner tells the user that his request is being processed and may hinder repeated form submissions.

In the following example, we emulate a slow server script that causes ASP.NET AJAX to display a wait screen while the server script is executed.

First, the slow server script is written. Basically, all this script does is wait five seconds.

```
void WaitFiveSeconds(object o, EventArgs e)
{
  System.Threading.Thread.Sleep(5000);
}
```

The script is triggered by a button within an UpdatePanel control. When the button is clicked, the server script runs for five seconds.

```
<asp:UpdatePanel ID="UpdatePanel1" runat="server">
  <ContentTemplate>
    <asp:Button ID="Button1" runat="server"
      Text="Do something" OnClick="WaitFiveSeconds" />
  </ContentTemplate>
</asp:UpdatePanel>
```

Finally, the wait screen is implemented. For this task, ASP.NET AJAX provides the UpdateProgress control. Within this control, the <ProgressTemplate> element expects HTML (or ASP.NET) markup. Whenever the UpdatePanel on the page is refreshed, the contents of the UpdateProgress control's <ProgressTemplate> template is shown. After the UpdatePanel has been refreshed, the content from <ProgressTemplate> is made invisible again. Some web sites use an hourglass image in their waiting screens; others just display text such as "loading…".

```
<asp:UpdateProgress ID="UpdateProgress1" runat="server">
  <ProgressTemplate>
    <div style="position: absolute; left: 200px; top: 150px; border: solid 2px
black;">
      Loading ... Please stand by ...
    </div>
  </ProgressTemplate>
</asp:UpdateProgress>
```

You need to link UpdatePanel and UpdateProgress; the latter control exposes the AssociatedUpdatePanelID property for this task. Example 6-4 contains the complete code for this example. Figure 6-5 shows the output when the page is run and the button is clicked, causing a five-second-long refresh within the UpdatePanel.

Example 6-4. A wait screen for the UpdatePanel

UpdateProgress.aspx

```
<%@ Page Language="C#" %>

<!DOCTYPE html PUBLIC "-//W3C//DTD XHTML 1.0 Transitional//EN"
"http://www.w3.org/TR/xhtml1/DTD/xhtml1-transitional.dtd">

<script runat="server">
  void WaitFiveSeconds(object o, EventArgs e)
  {
    System.Threading.Thread.Sleep(5000);
    Label1.Text = DateTime.Now.ToLongTimeString();
  }
</script>

<html xmlns="http://www.w3.org/1999/xhtml">
<head runat="server">
  <title>ASP.NET AJAX</title>
</head>
<body>
  <form id="form1" runat="server">
    <asp:ScriptManager ID="ScriptManager1" runat="server" />
    <asp:UpdatePanel ID="UpdatePanel1" runat="server">
      <ContentTemplate>
        <asp:Button ID="Button1" runat="server"
          Text="Do something" OnClick="WaitFiveSeconds" /><br />
        <asp:Label ID="Label1" runat="server" />
      </ContentTemplate>
    </asp:UpdatePanel>
    <asp:UpdateProgress ID="UpdateProgress1" runat="server"
      AssociatedUpdatePanelID="UpdatePanel1">
      <ProgressTemplate>
        <div style="position: absolute; left: 200px; top: 150px; border: solid 2px
black; padding:4px;">
        Loading, please stand by ...
        </div>
      </ProgressTemplate>
    </asp:UpdateProgress>
  </form>
</body>
</html>
```

 When the asynchronous postbacks take very little time, the UpdateProgress control is displayed very briefly, creating an irritating flashing effect. In that case you might want to use the DisplayAfter property of UpdateProgress. This property waits a predefined number of milliseconds before displaying the contents of the UpdateProgress' <ContentTemplate>. Set this to a reasonable delay—for instance, one second—to avoid the flashing effect. The default value is 500 milliseconds.

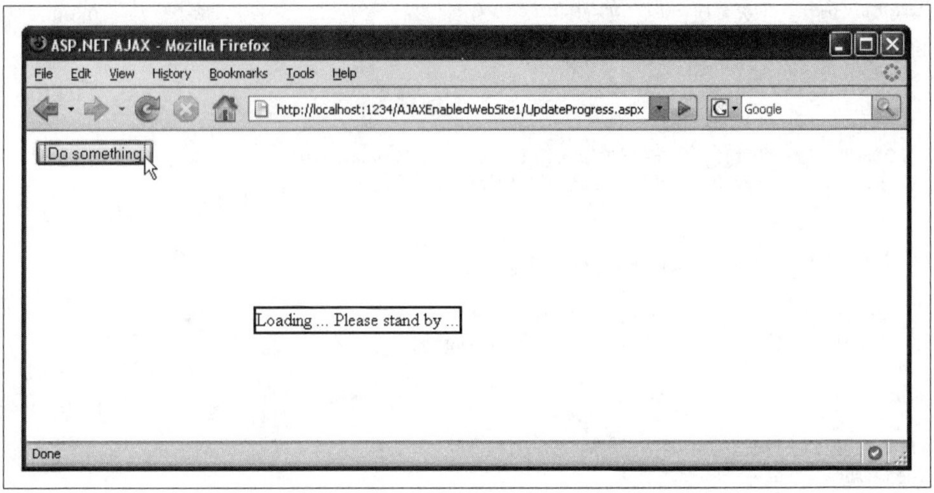

Figure 6-5. *The wait screen appears while the contents of the UpdatePanel control are refreshed*

Managing the Asynchronous Requests

The `PageRequestManager` class is responsible for handling the asynchronous requests ASP.NET AJAX is managing when using the `UpdatePanel` control. The most important feature is to abort a pending HTTP postback request. Remember the `UpdateProgress` control from the previous section? A waiting screen is always a good idea, but if the request times out or just takes too long, you need to react after a certain amount of time.

In order to abort a request, you first need to access the appropriate `PageRequestManager` instance. There is only once such instance per page. To retrieve it, use the following JavaScript code:

```
Sys.WebForms.PageRequestManager.getInstance();
```

You can attach event handlers to the `PageRequestManager` instance. The following events are supported:

`beginRequest`
Before the postback request is sent to the server.

`endRequest`
After the postback request has been completed.

`initializeRequest`
The request is initialized.

`pageLoaded`
The page has been refreshed due to a postback.

`pageLoading`
The postback data has been received, but the page has not been updated yet.

These events occur in the following order: initializeRequest, beginRequest, pageLoading, pageLoaded, and endRequest.

The following example will allow the user to cancel a pending postback by clicking a button. The button itself will also create a postback on its own. Therefore, the previous postback must be aborted when the new postback is about to be initialized. In order to do that, some code must be executed when the initializeRequest event occurs:

```
var manager = Sys.WebForms.PageRequestManager.getInstance();
manager.add_initializeRequest(abortPendingPostback);
```

The JavaScript function, abortPendingPostback( ), automatically gets two arguments (similar to event handler methods in .NET): the object that fired the event, and additional arguments, if applicable. In the case of the PageRequestManager, the additional arguments are of great importance. You can use the get_postBackElement( ) method to access the element that causes the current postback.

In addition, these two PageRequestManager instance methods come in handy:

abortPostback( )
  Aborts the postback

get_isInAsyncPostBack( )
  Checks whether the PageRequestManager is currently working on an asynchronous postback

This makes canceling a pending postback possible. Use the code from Example 6-4 as a start, and add a new button to cancel the postback:

```
<asp:Button ID="Button2" runat="server"
  Text="Abort postback" Style="display:none;" />
```

When the button that actually runs the server code is clicked, this abort button is made visible:

```
<asp:Button ID="Button1" runat="server"
  Text="Do something" OnClick="WaitFiveSeconds"
  OnClientClick="$get('Button2').style.display='';" />
```

Now, the JavaScript logic sets in. The abortPendingPostback( ) function first determines whether PageRequestManager is currently working on a postback. Then, it has a look at the sender's id attribute to determine which button was clicked. (The abortPendingPostback( ) method is called when any of the two buttons is clicked, since both trigger a postback.)

If the "abort" button is clicked, the pending request is aborted:

```
function abortPendingPostback(sender, eventArgs) {
  var manager = Sys.WebForms.PageRequestManager.getInstance();
  if (manager.get_isInAsyncPostBack() &&
    eventArgs.get_postBackElement().getAttribute("id") == "Button2") {
    manager.abortPostBack();
  }
}
```

The only thing left to do is to make the second button disappear when the request actually runs through:

```
Button2.Style["display"] = "none";
```

Refer to Example 6-5 for the complete code for the cancelable asynchronous HTTP request. Figure 6-6 shows how that looks in a browser.

Example 6-5. A cancelable wait screen for the UpdatePanel

UpdateProgressAbort.aspx

```
<%@ Page Language="C#" %>

<!DOCTYPE html PUBLIC "-//W3C//DTD XHTML 1.0 Transitional//EN"
"http://www.w3.org/TR/xhtml1/DTD/xhtml1-transitional.dtd">

<script runat="server">
  void WaitFiveSeconds(object o, EventArgs e)
  {
    System.Threading.Thread.Sleep(5000);
    Label1.Text = DateTime.Now.ToLongTimeString();
    Button2.Style["display"] = "none";
  }
</script>

<html xmlns="http://www.w3.org/1999/xhtml">
<head id="Head1" runat="server">
  <title>ASP.NET AJAX</title>
  <script type="text/javascript">
  function pageLoad() {
    var manager = Sys.WebForms.PageRequestManager.getInstance();
    manager.add_initializeRequest(abortPendingPostback);
  }

  function abortPendingPostback(sender, eventArgs) {
    var manager = Sys.WebForms.PageRequestManager.getInstance();
    if (manager.get_isInAsyncPostBack() &&
      eventArgs.get_postBackElement().getAttribute("id") == "Button2") {
      manager.abortPostBack();
    }
  }
  </script>
</head>
<body>
  <form id="form1" runat="server">
    <asp:ScriptManager ID="ScriptManager1" runat="server" />
    <asp:UpdatePanel ID="UpdatePanel1" runat="server">
      <ContentTemplate>
        <asp:Button ID="Button1" runat="server"
          Text="Do something" OnClick="WaitFiveSeconds"
          OnClientClick="$get('Button2').style.display='';" /><br />
```

Example 6-5. A cancelable wait screen for the UpdatePanel (continued)

```
        <asp:Button ID="Button2" runat="server"
          Text="Abort postback" Style="display:none;" />
        <asp:Label ID="Label1" runat="server" />
      </ContentTemplate>
    </asp:UpdatePanel>
    <asp:UpdateProgress ID="UpdateProgress1" runat="server"
      AssociatedUpdatePanelID="UpdatePanel1">
      <ProgressTemplate>
        <div style="position: absolute; left: 200px; top: 150px; border: solid 2px
black; padding: 4px;">
        Loading, please stand by ...<br />
        </div>
      </ProgressTemplate>
    </asp:UpdateProgress>
  </form>
</body>
</html>
```

Figure 6-6. The request can now be aborted by clicking the button

Summary

This chapter introduced one of the most valuable features of ASP.NET AJAX: the
UpdatePanel control. It also covered the related controls, Timer and UpdateProgress,
the latter of which implements a wait screen that is a commonly used effect in Ajax
applications.

For Further Reading

Gibbs, Matt and Bertrand LeRoy. ASP.NET AJAX UpdatePanel Control (O'Reilly)
More detail about the UpdatePanel control.

http://ajax.asp.net/docs/overview/UpdatePanelOverview.aspx
Microsoft documentation on UpdatePanel; look under "Controls that Are Not Compatible with UpdatePanel Controls" for a list of controls that do not work with UpdatePanel.

CHAPTER 7

Using the ASP.NET AJAX Profile Service

User profiles are storage mechanisms that can store data for both known (authenticated) and unknown (anonymous) users on the server. ASP.NET 2.0 comes with support for user profiles utilizing a type-safe API that provides easy read and write access to this server-side data.

Of course, user profiles are neither a new idea nor something particularly special. HTTP cookies, for example, provide a means to maintain data on the client. For performance reasons though, most profile schemes do not store the full complement of user information on the client, but only use a unique identifier (ID). This ID is then sent back and forth between client and server. The ID serves as (primary) key for a data store to retrieve the actual information. Microsoft began providing mechanisms to facilitate this starting with Windows NT and ASP (Active Server Pages). But the ASP.NET 2.0 implementation incorporates several advantages over previous offerings, including the aforementioned type-safe access.

ASP.NET AJAX comes with a JavaScript API that allows client-side code to access server-side profile data. As a result, JavaScript can read and write profile data, enabling it to create dynamic, profile-driven web pages while using as few page refresh cycles as possible. In the background, the JavaScript code uses the web services support of ASP.NET AJAX to call a server component, which then accesses the profile data. As with many other components of ASP.NET AJAX, this is not a technical revolution, but it does represent a big savings in development time. Apart from using the profile service, ASP.NET AJAX also provides access to other server application services, such as the ASP.NET Membership API (see Chapter 8) and ASP.NET web services (see Chapter 5).

Preparing the Web Site

To take advantage of ASP.NET AJAX profile support, it must first be enabled. To enable it, the *Web.config* file must have additional elements defined. Within the `<system.web>` node (available in the default *Web.config* file of ASP.NET AJAX web sites based on the Visual Studio template), the `<profile>` element is used to define a set of properties you would like to use in your application. This is, by the way, not an ASP.NET AJAX feature, but a part of ASP.NET 2.0.

By default, profile support in ASP.NET 2.0 works only for authenticated users. However, by using the `<anonymousIdentification>` element, you can generate a unique token for unauthenticated users to identify their server-side profile data:

```
<configuration>
  [...]
  <system.web>
    <anonymousIdentification enabled="true" />
```

For the actual profile data, you can define properties in two ways, individually or as groups. The following code snippet shows both an individual username property and a grouped UserData property. The UserData property consists of myUserName and myPassword.

```
<profile>
  <properties>
    <add name="userName" allowAnonymous="true" />
    <group name="UserData">
      <add name="myUserName" allowAnonymous="true" />
      <add name="myPassword" allowAnonymous="true" />
    </group>
  </properties>
</profile>
[...]
</system.web>
[...]
```

> The userName property attribute, allowAnonymous, enables unauthenticated users to utilize this property. This setting is not available, however, for groups as a whole (`<group>` element)—you have to set this property for every individual group element.

Finally, you have to enable the component that grants JavaScript access to the profile information. Add the `<system.web.extensions>` element (specific to ASP.NET AJAX!) to the end of the *Web.config* file, just above the closing `</configuration>` tag, and configure it as shown here:

```
<system.web.extensions>
  <scripting>
    <webServices>
      <profileService
        enabled="true"
        readAccessProperties="userName,UserData.myUserName,UserData.myPassword"
        writeAccessProperties="userName,UserData.myUserName,UserData.myPassword" />
    </webServices>
  </scripting>
</system.web.extensions>
</configuration>
```

In the `<profileService>` property, a list must be provided defining all properties from which the application can read and to which it can write. The properties that you expose to client script can be a subset of all the profile properties defined in the application. In addition, for client-script access, ASP.NET distinguishes between read and write access. Note the dot syntax (*<group>*.*<property>*) for profile information in groups.

Now you are ready and can read and write profile information using JavaScript.

Accessing Profile Data

Profile-related ASP.NET AJAX functionality is defined in the client `Sys.Services.ProfileService` class. The first step for every application using profile support is to load profile information by using the `Sys.Services.ProfileService.load( )` method, which expects four parameters:

propertyNames
> The properties to be loaded. If set to null or to an empty string, all exposed profile properties are retrieved from the server.

loadCompletedCallback
> The method to call when the profile loading succeeds.

failedCallback
> The method to call if profile loading fails (similar to the error callback for web service calls).

userContext
> Optional information that is submitted as an argument to the callback functions.

After loading the profile information, accessing properties is easy. Using `Sys.Services.ProfileService.properties.`*<property name>*, you have read *and* write access to a property—as long as the *Web.config* configuration allows it. In our example, the following expression accesses the `userName` profile property:

```
Sys.Services.ProfileService.properties.userName
```

However, setting a profile property does not actually save this information on the server; it only makes it available to the current script. In order to persist this information, the save( ) method must be called. It expects four arguments, just as load( ) does:

propertyNames
> The properties to be saved. If set to null or to an empty string, all properties available to client script are sent to the server.

saveCompletedCallback
> The method to call when the profile saving succeeds.

`failedCallback`

The method to call in the event the profile saving fails.

`userContext`

Optional information that is submitted as an argument to the callback functions.

The following is an example of how to use this API.

A login form where the user name (and possibly also the password) is persisted (maintained). As usual, the script begins with a `ScriptManager`:

```
<asp:ScriptManager ID="ScriptManager1" runat="server" />
```

Next, we need a login form consisting of the three typical login elements; user name text field, password text field, and a button. Also, an HTML label is used to output status information from our JavaScript profile calls:

```
User name: <input type="text" id="txtUsername" runat="server" /><br />
Password: <input type="password" id="txtPassword" runat="server" /><br />
<input type="button" id="Button1" runat="server" value="Login"
  onclick="alert('not implemented!');" /><br />
<span id="statusText" runat="server"> </span>
```

Now, the client script functionality is implemented. When the page and the ASP.NET AJAX libraries have been fully loaded, all profile data is retrieved from the server, using the load( ) method:

```
function pageLoad( ) {
  Sys.Services.ProfileService.load(
    "",
    profileLoaded,
    profileError,
    "load");
}
```

The `profileLoadedError( )` function just outputs an error message in the status label, providing (hopefully) helpful information:

```
function profileError(result, context) {
  $get("statusText").firstChild.nodeValue =
    "Could not "+ context + " profile (" +
    result.get_message( ) +
    "). Check the configuration in web.config!";
}
```

Note how the user context from the load( ) call is used in the callback function so that the error message will start with *Could not load profile.* As you've probably already guessed, this flexibility allows the `profileError( )` method to be reused later as error handling for profile saving, but with a different context argument.

If the profile information has been successfully loaded, a user name is available. This data is then written into the text field:

```
function profileLoaded( ) {
  $get("statusText").firstChild.nodeValue = "Profile data loaded.";
  if (Sys.Services.ProfileService.properties.userName != null) {
    $get("txtUsername").value = Sys.Services.ProfileService.properties.userName;
  }
}
```

At this point, the path back is still missing. When the user enters another user name into the form, this data needs to be returned to the server and saved in the profile. The saveProfile( ) function starts this process:

```
function saveProfile( ) {
  Sys.Services.ProfileService.properties.userName = $get("txtUsername").value;
  Sys.Services.ProfileService.save(
    null,
    profileSaved,
    profileError,
    "save");
}
```

The profileError( ) function is reused, but the profileSaved( ) function is new. Its purpose is to output the new status information:

```
function profileSaved( ) {
  $get("statusText").firstChild.nodeValue = "Profile data saved.";
}
```

All that remains missing from the application is the saveProfile( ) function. This function must be called when the user changes the user name—that is, by handling an event for the text box's changed event. (You could also consider other scenarios, e.g., only saving the user name when the login button is clicked.) It is easy to wire up this behavior with JavaScript. One way might be to use the $addHandler( ) method ASP.NET AJAX provides:

```
$addHandler(
  $get("txtUsername"),
  "change",
  saveProfile);
```

Example 7-1 presents the complete code. Remember, you must add the elements described earlier to the *Web.config* file so that profile properties are enabled and exposed to client applications.

Example 7-1. Reading and writing profile data

Profile.aspx

```
<%@ Page Language="C#" %>

<!DOCTYPE html PUBLIC "-//W3C//DTD XHTML 1.0 Transitional//EN"
"http://www.w3.org/TR/xhtml1/DTD/xhtml1-transitional.dtd">
```

Example 7-1. Reading and writing profile data (continued)

```html
<html xmlns="http://www.w3.org/1999/xhtml">
<head runat="server">
  <title>ASP.NET AJAX</title>
  <script type="text/javascript">
   function pageLoad( ) {
     $addHandler(
       $get("txtUsername"),
       "change",
       saveProfile);
     Sys.Services.ProfileService.load(
       null,
       profileLoaded,
       profileError,
       "load");
   }

   function profileLoaded( ) {
     $get("statusText").firstChild.nodeValue = "Profile data loaded.";
     if (Sys.Services.ProfileService.properties.userName != null) {
       $get("txtUsername").value = Sys.Services.ProfileService.properties.userName;
     }
   }

   function profileError(result, context) {
     $get("statusText").firstChild.nodeValue =
       "Could not " + context + " profile (" +
       result.get_message( ) +
       "). Check the configuration in web.config!";
   }

   function saveProfile( ) {
     Sys.Services.ProfileService.properties.userName = $get("txtUsername").value;
     Sys.Services.ProfileService.save(
       null,
       profileSaved,
       profileError,
       "save");
   }

   function profileSaved( ) {
     $get("statusText").firstChild.nodeValue = "Profile data saved.";
   }

  </script>
</head>
<body>
  <form id="form1" runat="server">
    <asp:ScriptManager ID="ScriptManager1" runat="server" />
    <div>
```

Example 7-1. Reading and writing profile data (continued)

```
        User name: <input type="text" id="txtUsername" runat="server" /><br />
        Password: <input type="password" id="txtPassword" runat="server" /><br />
        <input type="button" id="Button1" runat="server" value="Login"
          onclick="alert('not implemented!');" /><br />
        <span id="statusText" runat="server"> </span>
      </div>
    </form>
  </body>
</html>
```

When this example is run, the login form is initially empty. (The very first time you run the example you might notice a longer than normal delay; this is because ASP.NET is setting up the profile database.) When you enter a user name and press Tab, the name you enter is saved. From then on, any time you load the page (by refreshing the browser or even closing the browser and then rerunning the example), the user name you entered is preloaded into the User name text box, as Figure 7-1 shows.

Figure 7-1. The User name text field is now prefilled

After running this example, look in the App_Data directory of your web site. There, the profile database has been created as the file *ASPNETDB.MDF*. If you open it, you will see that in the *aspnet_Profile* database there is an entry for the user name (see Figure 7-2).

Accessing Profile Group Data

When you use grouped profile data, accessing this information differs only a little from individual profile properties. Use a dot to separate the group name from the property name:

```
    Sys.Services.ProfileService.properties.<group name>.<property name>
```

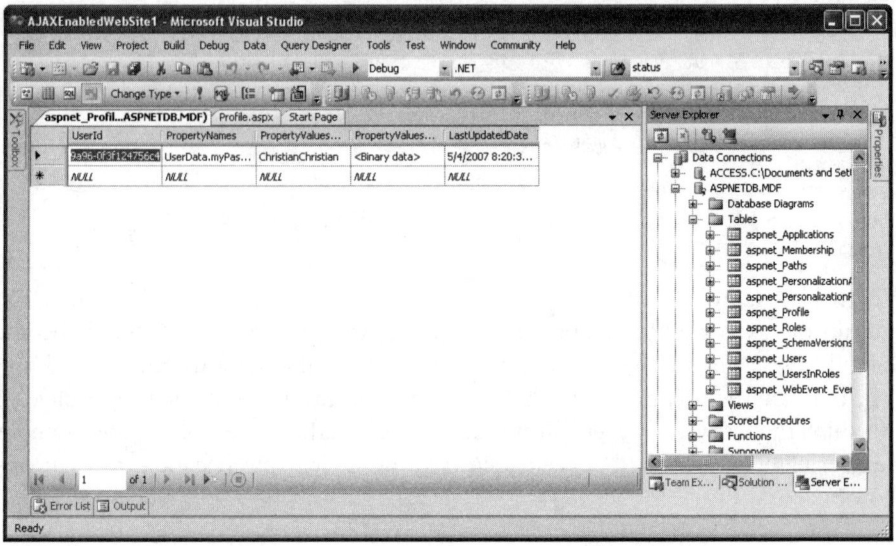

Figure 7-2. The MDF file contains the profile data

Profiles with ASP.NET AJAX: Under the Hood

If you watch the HTTP traffic closely while running the example, you can monitor ASP.NET AJAX as it calls a web service in the background to retrieve the profile information and to write it back to the server. Figure 7-3 shows the typical HTTP traffic using the popular Firebug plugin for Firefox browsers (*http://www.getfirebug.com/*).

Also recall you cannot make a whole profile group readable or writable in *Web.config*, but that you have to provide all group elements individually:

```
<profileService
  enabled="true"
  readAccessProperties="UserData.myUserName,UserData.myPassword"
  writeAccessProperties="UserData.myUserName,UserData.myPassword" />
```

We can now expand Example 7-1 to include saving the password alongside the user name in the profile. It requires only a little extra code—specifically two save functions, one for each property.

```
function saveProfile1() {
  Sys.Services.ProfileService.properties.UserData.myUserName =
$get("txtUsername").value;
  Sys.Services.ProfileService.save(
    null,
```

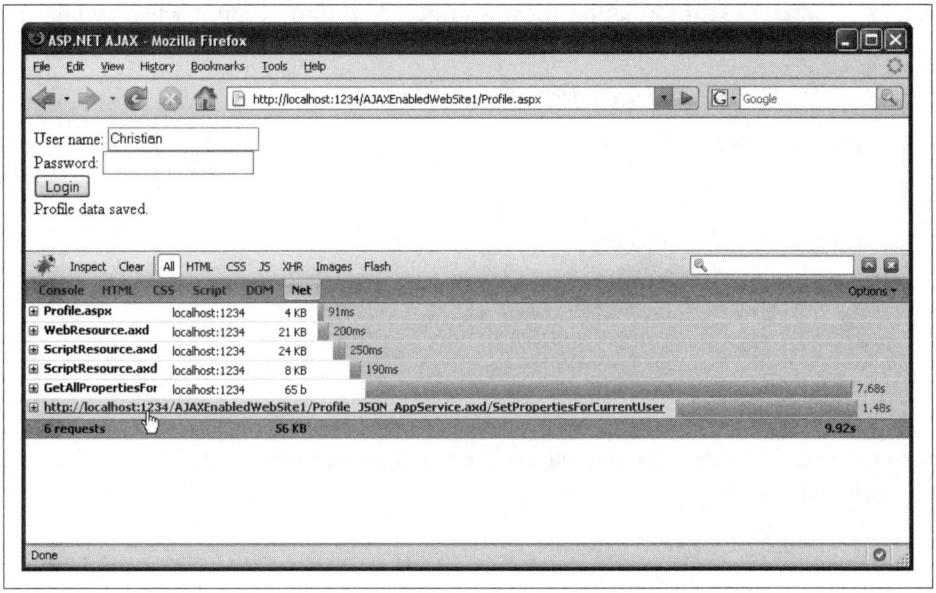

Figure 7-3. ASP.NET AJAX uses its own web services support to access profile data

```
        profileSaved,
        profileError,
        {"operation": "save", "property": "username"});
}

function saveProfile2() {
   Sys.Services.ProfileService.properties.UserData.myPassword =
$get("txtPassword").value;
   Sys.Services.ProfileService.save(
      null,
      profileSaved,
      profileError,
      {"operation": "save", "property": "password"});
}
```

As you can see, the context is once again used, but this time we're using an object instead of a simple string. The object's operation property contains either "save" or "load" (in the save functions, of course, only the former value), and the property member is used to transmit which profile information has been saved. This serves two purposes: only one error handling function is required, and also only one handling function is required to respond to a successful save. Let's first have a look at the latter handler:

```
function profileSaved(success, context) {
   $get("statusText").firstChild.nodeValue =
      "Profile data (" + context.property + ") saved.";
}
```

The special context information must also be taken into account when calling the
load( ) method:

```
Sys.Services.ProfileService.load(
  "",
  profileLoaded,
  profileError,
  {"operation": "load"});
```

Finally, the profileError( ) function must be altered:

```
function profileError(result, context) {
  $get("statusText").firstChild.nodeValue =
    "Could not " + context.operation + " profile (" +
    result.get_message() +
    "). Check the configuration in web.config!";
}
```

Example 7-2 contains the complete code for this application, while Figure 7-4 shows
a possible output.

Example 7-2. Reading and writing profile group data

ProfileGroup.aspx

```
<%@ Page Language="C#" %>

<!DOCTYPE html PUBLIC "-//W3C//DTD XHTML 1.0 Transitional//EN" "http://www.w3.org/TR/
xhtml1/DTD/xhtml1-transitional.dtd">

<html xmlns="http://www.w3.org/1999/xhtml">
<head id="Head1" runat="server">
  <title>ASP.NET AJAX</title>
  <script type="text/javascript">
   function pageLoad() {
     $addHandler(
       $get("txtUsername"),
       "change",
       saveProfile1);
     $addHandler(
       $get("txtPassword"),
       "change",
       saveProfile2);
     Sys.Services.ProfileService.load(
       null,
       profileLoaded,
       profileError,
       {"operation": "load"});
   }

   function profileLoaded() {
     if (Sys.Services.ProfileService.properties.UserData != null) {
       $get("statusText").firstChild.nodeValue = "Profile data loaded.";
       $get("txtUsername").value =
Sys.Services.ProfileService.properties.UserData.myUserName;
       $get("txtPassword").value =
```

Example 7-2. Reading and writing profile group data (continued)

```
Sys.Services.ProfileService.properties.UserData.myPassword;
    } else {
      $get("statusText").firstChild.nodeValue = "No data available.";
    }
  }

  function profileError(result, context) {
    $get("statusText").firstChild.nodeValue =
      "Could not " + context.operation + " profile (" +
      result.get_message() +
      "). Check the configuration in web.config!";
  }

  function saveProfile1() {
    Sys.Services.ProfileService.properties.UserData.myUserName =
$get("txtUsername").value;
    Sys.Services.ProfileService.save(
      null,
      profileSaved,
      profileError,
      {"operation": "save", "property": "username"});
  }

  function saveProfile2() {
    Sys.Services.ProfileService.properties.UserData.myPassword =
$get("txtPassword").value;
    Sys.Services.ProfileService.save(
      null,
      profileSaved,
      profileError,
      {"operation": "save", "property": "password"});
  }

  function profileSaved(success, context) {
    $get("statusText").firstChild.nodeValue = "Profile data (" + context.property
+ ") saved.";
  }

  </script>
</head>
<body>
  <form id="form1" runat="server">
    <asp:ScriptManager ID="ScriptManager1" runat="server" />
    <div>
      User name: <input type="text" id="txtUsername" runat="server" /><br />
      Password: <input type="password" id="txtPassword" runat="server" /><br />
      <input type="button" id="Button1" runat="server" value="Login"
        onclick="alert('not implemented!');" /><br />
      <span id="statusText" runat="server"> </span>
    </div>
  </form>
</body>
</html>
```

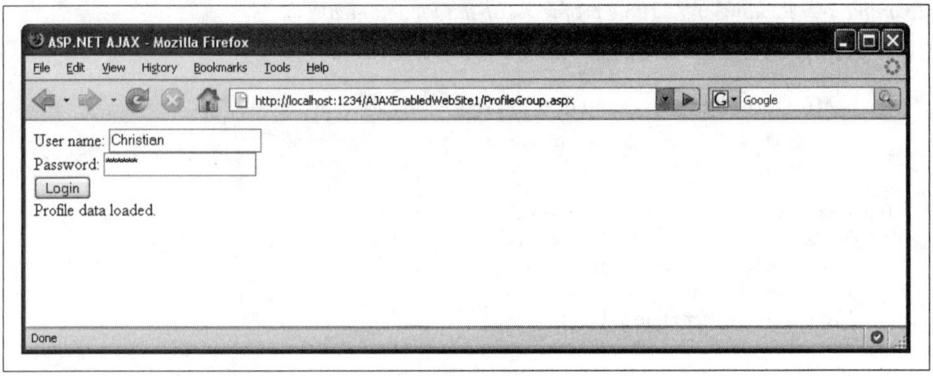

![Browser window screenshot showing ASP.NET AJAX - Mozilla Firefox. URL: http://localhost:1234/AJAXEnabledWebSite1/ProfileGroup.aspx. Form contains User name: Christian, Password field, Login button, and text "Profile data loaded."]

Figure 7-4. Now both the user name and password are persisted

Note that passwords should never be saved in clear text. The ASP.NET 2.0 authentication mechanism (which will be covered in the next chapter), for instance, stores passwords in an encrypted form by default. And although the passwords are not retained in clear text on the client, they are unprotected on the server. Using HTTPS makes at least the transmission of the passwords secure.

Summary

This chapter used the ASP.NET 2.0 Profile Service, but without any server code. Instead, we used the JavaScript API provided by ASP.NET AJAX, accessing profile data with only client code.

For Further Reading

http://ajax.asp.net/docs/tutorials/UsingProfileInformationTutorial.aspx
   The JavaScript Profile API in the Microsoft ASP.NET AJAX documentation

http://www.ondotnet.com/pub/a/dotnet/2004/10/25/libertyonwhidbey.html
   Online article on ASP.NET 2.0 profiles

CHAPTER 8

Using the ASP.NET AJAX Authentication Service

One of the design goals of ASP.NET 2.0 was to reduce the time required to implement common web site tasks. Among these tasks are user and access management operations, including user login, terminating user sessions, creating roles, and so on. Actually, creating a protected web site based on ASP.NET 2.0 is very simple: create users and employ the ASP.NET web controls such as Login, and you are more or less done.

Some of these access-management features can also be implemented from JavaScript, thanks to the ASP.NET AJAX authentication service. The list of these supported features is rather short, but nevertheless, very convenient. ASP.NET AJAX supports ASP.NET 2.0 forms authentication. As a result, JavaScript code can validate user credentials. However, actual content protection *must* be done on the server. Always remember that JavaScript can be deactivated, which renders it insufficient to secure sensitive data.

Preparing the Application

In order to use the ASP.NET AJAX authentication service, you need users within your application. The ASP.NET Web Application Administration Tool that comes with Visual Studio and Visual Web Developer provides a very easy way to create users. First, run the tool using the ASP.NET Configuration command in the Web Site menu (see Figure 8-1).

Click the Security link, then, on the next page, click "Select authentication type." There, change the current authentication type by selecting "From the internet" (see Figure 8-2), which basically means ASP.NET forms authentication instead of Windows authentication. When you're done, click Done.

Next, click on the "Create user" link and enter the credentials for at least one new user (see Figure 8-3).

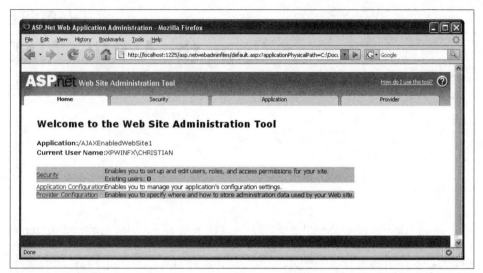

Figure 8-1. The ASP.NET Configuration Tool (looks better in Internet Explorer, though)

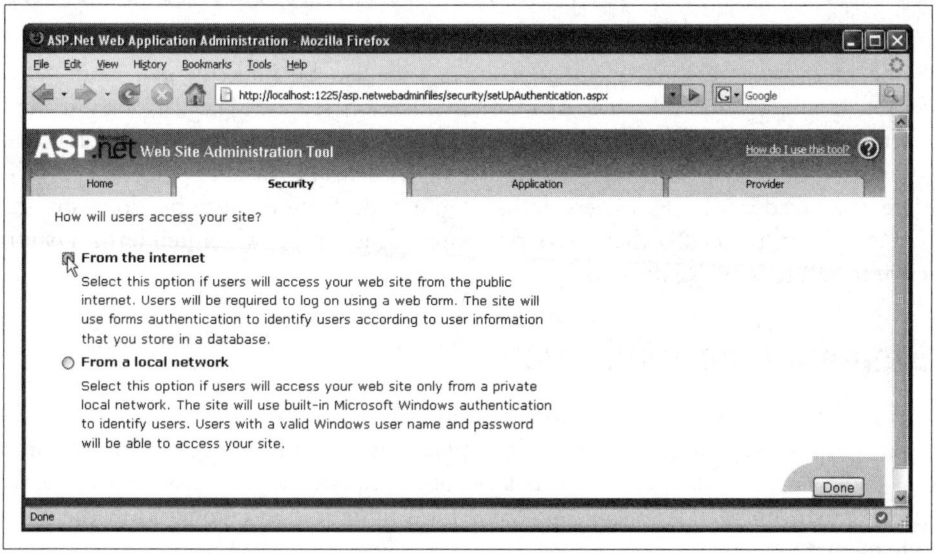

Figure 8-2. Set the correct authentication type

If you happen to have *Web.config* open in your IDE before running the ASP.NET configuration tool, Visual Studio (or Visual Web Developer) will prompt you to reload the file. This is because your actions in the tool prompted the addition of the following line in *Web.config*, within the `<system.web>` node:

```
<authentication mode="Forms" />
```

ASP.net Web Site Administration Tool   How do I use this tool?

| Home | Security | Application | Provider |

Add a user by entering the user's ID, password, and e-mail address on this page.

Create User

Sign Up for Your New Account

User Name:

Password:

Confirm Password:

E-mail:

Security Question:

Security Answer:

[Create User]

Roles

Roles are not enabled.

Done

Figure 8-3. Create a new user (or two or three)

There is one more configuration setting that you need to add to *Web.config*. This one, unfortunately, must be done without the help of a GUI tool. In the previous chapter, the <system.web.extensions> node was added to *Web.config*. Within this node, add an <authenticationService> element and set its enabled attribute to true, which gives you the following result:

```
<configuration
  [...]
  <system.web.extensions>
    <scripting>
      <webServices>
        <profileService
          enabled="true"
          readAccessProperties="userName,UserData.myUserName,UserData.myPassword"
          writeAccessProperties="userName,UserData.myUserName,UserData.myPassword" />
        <authenticationService enabled="true" />
      </webServices>
    </scripting>
  </system.web.extensions>

</configuration>
```

This sets up the necessary JavaScript code that connects the client to the server API.

Make sure that you configure your application according to the instructions presented at the beginning or this chapter and in the previous chapter, so that both the profile API and the authentication API are supported and the used profile properties are supported.

Login and Logout

The `Sys.Services.AuthenticationService` class contains two methods to support ASP.NET AJAX Forms Authentication: `login( )` and `logout( )`. Let's start with user login. This method allows no fewer than eight arguments:

userName
> The user name

password
> The associated password

isPersistent
> Whether to log the user in permanently using a persistent cookie (defaults to `false`)

redirectUrl
> The URL to which to redirect the browser after logging the user in, or `null` for no redirection (default)

customInfo
> Currently not used

loginCompletedCallback
> Function to call after successful login

failedCallback
> Function to call after unsuccessful login

userContext
> Data to pass to the callback functions

There are two choices for implementing the authentication:

1. Call `login( )` and let JavaScript redirect to another page by setting `redirectUrl`.
2. Call `login( )` and use the `loginCompletedCallback` and `failedCallback` callback functions to handle the authentication result.

Quite often, the latter option is the preferred one. A redirection hints at data protection by JavaScript, which, as mentioned earlier, is not a very secure approach.

Logging out is done with the `logout( )` method. It supports "only" four arguments:

redirectUrl
> The URL to which to redirect the browser after logging the user out, or `null` for no redirection (default)

logoutCompletedCallback
> Function to call after successful logout

failedCallback
> Function to call after unsuccessful logout

userContext
> Data to be passed to the callback functions

These two functions will now be added to the *ProfileGroup.aspx* file presented in Chapter 7, creating a new file, *Authentication.aspx*. As you recall, the *ProfileGroup.aspx* page provides the user with a login form and stores the user name and password in profile variables. To that point, the login form's button element did not contain any functionality. We will now add that functionality. First we need to strip the dummy JavaScript code associated with the button so the following markup remains:

```
<input type="button" id="Button1" runat="server" value="Login" />
```

In the pageLoad( ) function, a click event handler is provided for the button:

```
$addHandler(
  $get("Button1"),
  "click",
  doClick);
```

The doClick( ) function referenced in the above code snippet then checks the status of the button caption. If it is "Login", the application tries to log the user in; if it is "Logout", it attempts to log the user out.

The main challenge now is to set the appropriate arguments for the login( ) and logout( ) methods. Since the user credentials are stored in the profile anyway, no persistent login is necessary. We also do not want to redirect the user after logging her in or out. Finally, we will apply the trick learned in Chapter 7 and set the userContext argument to values that will allow us to use the same callback functions for both login and logout.

```
function doClick( ) {
  switch ($get("Button1").value) {
    case "Login":
      Sys.Services.AuthenticationService.login(
        $get("txtUsername").value,
        $get("txtPassword").value,
        false,
        null,
        null,
        loginComplete,
        loginError,
        "login");
      break;
    case "Logout":
      Sys.Services.AuthenticationService.logout(
        null,
        loginComplete,
        loginError,
        "logout");
      break;
  }
}
```

The `loginError()` function handles unsuccessful login and logout attempts, such as invalid credentials, missing user name, or an incorrect server configuration. An appropriate error message is shown in the HTML label:

```
function loginError(result, context) {
  $get("statusText").firstChild.nodeValue =
    "Could not " + context + " (" +
    result.get_message() + ").";
}
```

Finally, the `loginComplete()` function prints out a status message. Additionally, it changes the login form. After the user has successfully logged in, both text fields are disabled and the caption of the button is changed from "Login" to "Logout". Once the user logs out, the button's caption goes back to "Login" and the two text fields are again active.

```
function loginComplete(result, context) {
  switch (context) {
    case "login":
      if (result == true) {
        $get("txtUsername").disabled = true;
        $get("txtPassword").disabled = true;
        $get("Button1").value = "Logout";
        $get("statusText").firstChild.nodeValue = "Logged in";
      } else {
        $get("statusText").firstChild.nodeValue = "Login failed";
      }

      break;
    case "logout":
      $get("txtUsername").disabled = false;
      $get("txtPassword").disabled = false;
      $get("Button1").value = "Login";
      $get("statusText").firstChild.nodeValue = "Logged out";
      break;
  }
}
```

Example 8-1 shows the complete code for this example. Remember to make the appropriate changes to the *Web.config* file before you try to run this example.

Example 8-1. Authentication users with JavaScript

```
Authentication.aspx

<%@ Page Language="C#" %>

<!DOCTYPE html PUBLIC "-//W3C//DTD XHTML 1.0 Transitional//EN" "http://www.w3.org/TR/
xhtml1/DTD/xhtml1-transitional.dtd">

<html xmlns="http://www.w3.org/1999/xhtml">
<head id="Head1" runat="server">
  <title>ASP.NET AJAX</title>
```

Example 8-1. Authentication users with JavaScript (continued)

```
<script type="text/javascript">
function pageLoad( ) {
  $addHandler(
    $get("Button1"),
    "click",
    doClick);
  $addHandler(
    $get("txtUsername"),
    "change",
    saveProfile1);
  $addHandler(
    $get("txtPassword"),
    "change",
    saveProfile2);
  Sys.Services.ProfileService.load(
    "",
    profileLoaded,
    profileError,
    {"operation": "load"});
}

function profileLoaded( ) {
  if (Sys.Services.ProfileService.properties.UserData != null) {
    $get("statusText").firstChild.nodeValue = "Profile data loaded.";
    $get("txtUsername").value =
Sys.Services.ProfileService.properties.UserData.myUserName;
    $get("txtPassword").value =
Sys.Services.ProfileService.properties.UserData.myPassword;
  } else {
    $get("statusText").firstChild.nodeValue = "No data available.";
  }
}

function profileError(result, context) {
  $get("statusText").firstChild.nodeValue =
    "Could not " + context.operation + " profile (" +
    result.get_message( ) +
    ". Check the configuration in web.config!";
}

function saveProfile1( ) {
  Sys.Services.ProfileService.properties.UserData.myUserName =
$get("txtUsername").value;
  Sys.Services.ProfileService.save(
    null,
    profileSaved,
    profileError,
    {"operation": "save", "property": "username"});
}

function saveProfile2( ) {
  Sys.Services.ProfileService.properties.UserData.myPassword =
```

Example 8-1. Authentication users with JavaScript (continued)

```javascript
$get("txtPassword").value;
    Sys.Services.ProfileService.save(
      null,
      profileSaved,
      profileError,
      {"operation": "save", "property": "password"});
  }

  function profileSaved(success, context) {
    $get("statusText").firstChild.nodeValue = "Profile data (" + context.property
+ ") saved.";
  }

  function doClick( ) {
    switch ($get("Button1").value) {
      case "Login":
        Sys.Services.AuthenticationService.login(
          $get("txtUsername").value,
          $get("txtPassword").value,
          false,
          null,
          null,
          loginComplete,
          loginError,
          "login");
        break;
      case "Logout":
        Sys.Services.AuthenticationService.logout(
          null,
          loginComplete,
          loginError,
          "logout");
        break;
    }
  }

  function loginComplete(result, context) {
    switch (context) {
      case "login":
        if (result == true) {
          $get("txtUsername").disabled = true;
          $get("txtPassword").disabled = true;
          $get("Button1").value = "Logout";
          $get("statusText").firstChild.nodeValue = "Logged in";
        } else {
          $get("statusText").firstChild.nodeValue = "Login failed";
        }
        break;
      case "logout":
```

Example 8-1. Authentication users with JavaScript (continued)

```
            $get("txtUsername").disabled = false;
            $get("txtPassword").disabled = false;
            $get("Button1").value = "Login";
            $get("statusText").firstChild.nodeValue = "Logged out";
            break;
      }
   }

   function loginError(result, context) {
      $get("statusText").firstChild.nodeValue =
         "Could not " + context + " (" +
         result.get_message() + ").";
   }

    </script>
</head>
<body>
   <form id="form1" runat="server">
      <asp:ScriptManager ID="ScriptManager1" runat="server" />
      <div>
         User name: <input type="text" id="txtUsername" runat="server" /><br />
         Password: <input type="password" id="txtPassword" runat="server" /><br />
         <input type="button" id="Button1" runat="server" value="Login" /><br />
         <span id="statusText" runat="server"> </span>
      </div>
   </form>
</body>
</html>
```

Figure 8-4 shows the form before the user logs in. Figure 8-5 displays the inactive text fields and the changed button resulting from a successful login.

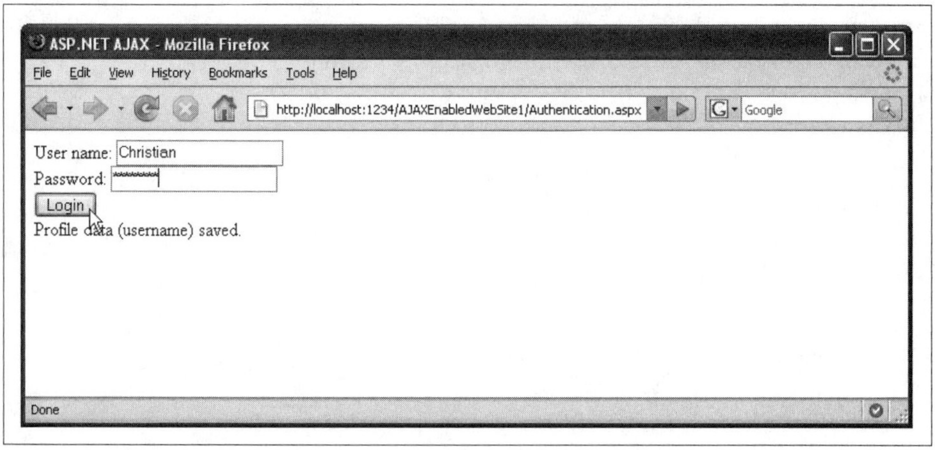

Figure 8-4. Before logging in

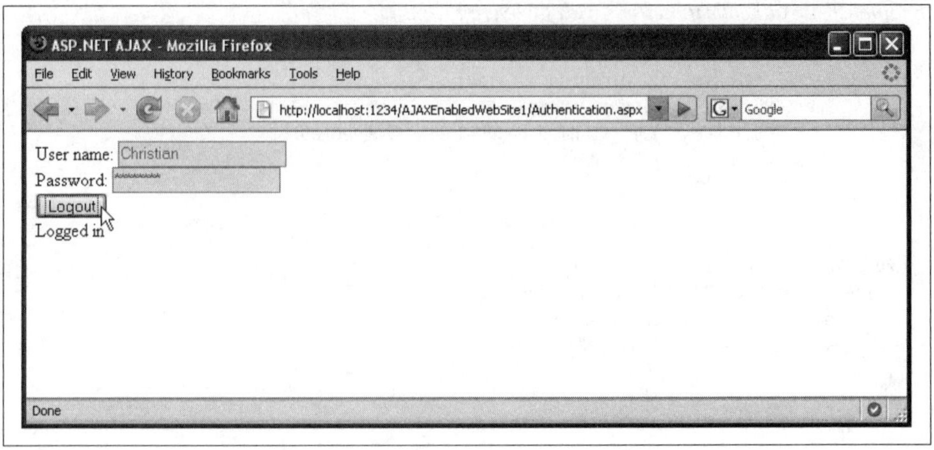

Figure 8-5. Before logging out

Summary

This chapter used ASP.NET 2.0 forms authentication without the assistance of any server code. JavaScript and ASP.NET AJAX was all that has been used. This allows, among other things, logging users in without a page refresh.

For Further Reading

http://ajax.asp.net/docs/tutorials/UsingFormsAuthenticationTutorial.aspx
> Information on the Forms Authentication JavaScript API in the Microsoft ASP.NET AJAX documentation

http://msdn2.microsoft.com/en-us/library/ms998310.aspx
> MSDN article on ASP.NET 2.0 Forms Authentication

CHAPTER 9

Localizing and Globalizing Applications

Let me tell you an embarrassing story...

When the publisher sends me complimentary copies of one of my books, I usually give them to friends, or raffle them away in my blog, or just put them in the basement archives. To be clear, I do not have a fetish for collecting my own books. However, there is one notable exception: I am extremely fond of acquiring foreign language editions of my books. But publishers don't always get copies of translated books. Needless to say, if they're not available to the publisher, I'm not going to get a complimentary copy. And even if they do have some to give out, it seems to take an eternity to get one. So, whenever I hear that one of my books has been translated, I fire up my web browser and go hunting.

Usually, I surf to some online bookstore in a language I do not understand and try my best to provide my address and credit card information to the appropriate fields. I consider myself lucky, as my personal data has not yet been stolen (I have a special card just for "obscure orders," as I call them), and from time to time I get a shipment that went through quite a trek to get to me.

But why do I have to struggle anyway? In a globalized world, web site owners will most certainly get visitors that do not share their language, or that of the web site itself. In my opinion, there are two reasons why most web sites are monolingual. First, translating a site is quite expensive and—depending on the target audience of the site—is often not worth the gain. Second, there are technical obstacles. If you want to avoid using the copy-and-paste "design method" to create multilingual sites, you need automation that allows you to translate a site with little effort. Thanks to the growing importance and proliferation of JavaScript and Ajax applications, translation features are also becoming both more important and common.

As always, it is possible to create home-grown solutions for these scenarios, but ASP.NET AJAX comes with some support for localization and globalization. This allows you to use various languages in your ASP.NET AJAX-enabled web sites and to create web sites that can react according to the user's browser language setting.

(In case you weren't aware, the browser can pass a list of preferred languages to the web server. You will read more about this later in the chapter.)

Localization

Web site localization is the process of adapting the content to a locale (language and region settings of a system), most often to the locale of the user. A quite common abbreviation for localization is l10n, which stands for "*l*, then 10 letters, then *n*" (a so-called *numeronym*).

A web site provides different spots that might be localized. There is the actual text on the site; in addition, the currency, time, and date formats are candidates for localization. ASP.NET provides several localization features (see "For Further Reading" at the end of this chapter). ASP.NET AJAX uses some of these features to enable localization for JavaScript code, as well.

Localizing Scripts

An easy approach to localization is to write script custom tailored for the task. For example, you would need to determine the locale, and then load a specific script library depending on that locale. ASP.NET can handle one half of this task, and ASP.NET AJAX can take care of the rest.

The following brief sample script uses JavaScript to output the current date in a localized format. The JavaScript file *Dayname.js* defines two variables:

dateformat
> String with a (local) format for a date, using the placeholders ss (day of week), dd (day), mm (month), and yyyy (year)

daynames
> Array with localized name of the seven days of the week

Example 9-1 shows the contents of the *Dayname.js* file.

Example 9-1. Localized English date information

Dayname.js

```
var dateformat = "ss, yyyy-mm-dd";

var daynames = ["Sunday", "Monday", "Tuesday", "Wednesday", "Thursday", "Friday",
"Saturday"];
```

This file can be easily translated. Example 9-2 shows the same file, but this time with German date information. Both the date format and the day names are different.

Example 9-2. Localized German date information

Dayname.de-DE.js

```
var dateformat = "ss, dd.mm.yyyy";

var daynames = ["Sonntag", "Montag", "Dienstag", "Mittwoch", "Donnerstag", "Freitag",
"Samstag"];
```

The important thing is the filename for the localized file. Right before the file extension (*.js*), you add the language and optionally the locale in the format lang-loc, where lang is a two-letter language code and loc is a two-letter locale code. Language, of course, specifies in what language the text appears. The locale is used to determine how to format (Different speakers of the same language might have different conventions for formatting—i.e., between the United States and the United Kingdom.) For example, American English is en-US, British English is en-UK, German (Germany) is de-DE, German (Austria) is de-AT, and so on. The codes are established by the ISO, and by convention, the language code is lowercase and the locale code is uppercase. The file in Example 9-2 is called *Dayname.de-DE.js*, indicating that it pertains to German and Germany.

Now let's create a new *.aspx* page that uses these localized files. To begin, the page contains a <span> element, which will be used to dynamically output the localized date. Notice the nonbreaking space character ( ) within the <span> element; it is important for the JavaScript code. A regular space would not work due to an Internet Explorer behavior.

```
<span id="date"> </span>
```

We can now add some JavaScript code that uses the dateformat and daynames variables defined in the external JavaScript file to create a localized date representation:

```
<script type="text/javascript">
  function pageLoad( ) {
    var d = new Date( );
    var datestring = dateformat.replace("ss", daynames[d.getDay( )])
                               .replace("dd", d.getDate( ))
                               .replace("mm", d.getMonth( ) + 1)
                               .replace("yyyy", d.getFullYear( ));
    $get("date").firstChild.nodeValue = datestring;
  }
</script>
```

So far, we have seen nothing special. But now both ASP.NET and ASP.NET AJAX will do their magic. First, ASP.NET AJAX loads the external JavaScript file, and then (this is the magic) it finds the appropriate one for the current language and locale, based on the filename. Within the ScriptManager control, use the <Scripts> element to load the *Dayname.js* file. Two attributes take care of most of the rest:

`ResourceUICultures` *(attribute of* `<asp:ScriptReference>`*)*

Provides a comma-delimited list of all supported cultures where translations exist.

`EnableScriptLocalization` *(attribute of* `<asp:ScriptManager>`*)*

If set to true, activates the ASP.NET AJAX localization support on the current page:

```
<asp:ScriptManager ID="ScriptManager1" runat="server"
  EnableScriptLocalization="true">
  <Scripts>
    <asp:ScriptReference Path="Dayname.js" ResourceUICultures="de-DE,fr-FR" />
  </Scripts>
</asp:ScriptManager>
```

The default (fallback) file is *Dayname.js*; however if one of the cultures referred to in `ResourceUICultures` is used (i.e., the browser requests one of the cultures based on its settings), the appropriate localized file would be loaded.

So far the page does not set its culture according to the client browser. This is where ASP.NET comes in. The following `Page` directive automatically sets the correct UI culture according to browser preferences:

```
<%@ Page Language="C#" UICulture="auto" %>
```

A browser set to use French would load the *Dayname.fr-FR.js* file; a browser set to Italian, on the other hand, would load *Dayname.js*, as no localized Italian JavaScript file has been provided. That is, *Dayname.js* is the fallback file for situations where no matching language can be found.

Example 9-3 contains the complete code for a page that uses the ASP.NET AJAX localization you've just seen. To run the example, you must add at least the *Dayname.js* file to the root of your web site.

Figure 9-1 shows the result of displaying the page in a browser set to use English. Figure 9-2 depicts a browser set to German that displays a typical German date format.

Example 9-3. Localizing a script

```
Localization-Inline.aspx

<%@ Page Language="C#" UICulture="auto" %>

<!DOCTYPE html PUBLIC "-//W3C//DTD XHTML 1.0 Transitional//EN"
"http://www.w3.org/TR/xhtml1/DTD/xhtml1-transitional.dtd">

<script runat="server">
</script>

<html xmlns="http://www.w3.org/1999/xhtml">
<head runat="server">
  <title>ASP.NET AJAX</title>
  <script type="text/javascript">
```

Example 9-3. Localizing a script (continued)

```
  function pageLoad( ) {
    var d = new Date( );
    var datestring = dateformat.replace("ss", daynames[d.getDay( )])
                               .replace("dd", d.getDate( ))
                               .replace("mm", d.getMonth( ) + 1)
                               .replace("yyyy", d.getFullYear( ));
    $get("date").firstChild.nodeValue = datestring;
  }
  </script>
</head>
<body>
  <form id="form1" runat="server">
    <asp:ScriptManager ID="ScriptManager1" runat="server"
      EnableScriptLocalization="true">
      <Scripts>
        <asp:ScriptReference Path="Dayname.js" ResourceUICultures="de-DE,fr-FR" />
      </Scripts>
    </asp:ScriptManager>
    <div>
      <span id="date"> </span>
    </div>
  </form>
</body>
</html>
```

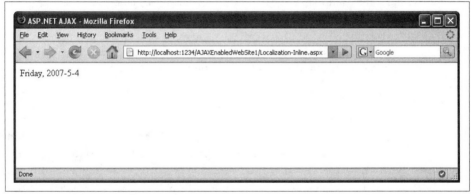

Figure 9-1. The page in English

Using Satellite Resources from ASP.NET AJAX

Another way of localizing an ASP.NET application is to use so-called *satellite resources* (sometimes referred to as *satellite assemblies*). This refers to a compiled external resource file that will only be loaded if it is required for the current culture. ASP.NET AJAX enables web sites to put JavaScript (*.js*) files into these satellite assemblies as resources, and the Ajax framework provides a mechanism to use the resource data from JavaScript code.

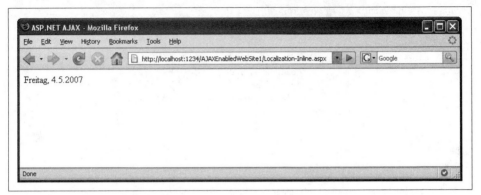

Figure 9-2. The page in German

Setting the Culture with ASP.NET

Example 9-1 employed automatic detection to determine the culture to be used. However, ASP.NET AJAX provides other means to set this culture dynamically. You can provide the user with an interface to change the culture, such as via LinkButton elements or by providing a drop-down list. (The often-used country flags are not considered good programming practice, since many languages are spoken in more than one country, and some countries even have more than one official language.)

To set the UI culture of the current page, use System.Threading.Thread.CurrentThread. CurrentUICulture. The System.Globalization namespace contains helper methods to create a suitable culture for the CurrentUICulture property of the current thread. Refer to "For Further Reading," at the end of this chapter, for more information about this ASP.NET feature.

Example 9-4 uses the localization feature of ASP.NET AJAX as part of a custom ASP.NET control that you can use in an ASP.NET web page. The control illustrates two tasks. First, ASP.NET AJAX will be used so the correct satellite assembly will be loaded. Then the script code within the assembly will access the correct localized data and output text in the language of the user's browser.

Creating the control requires Visual Studio 2005, because you need to be able to create a compiled assembly. If you are using Visual Web Developer Express Edition, you cannot create the assembly in the IDE. However, you can install Visual C# Express Edition (another free download) and use that.

To begin, create a new project (see Figure 9-3). Name the project LocalizedDate. The name is generally not mandatory, but as it will be used throughout this example, you need to use it as well to follow along.

When using Visual C# Express Edition, create a new project from scratch. Users of Visual Studio 2005 just need to add a new project to an existing ASP.NET AJAX web site. In either case, the project type must be a class library project, as Figure 9-3 illustrates.

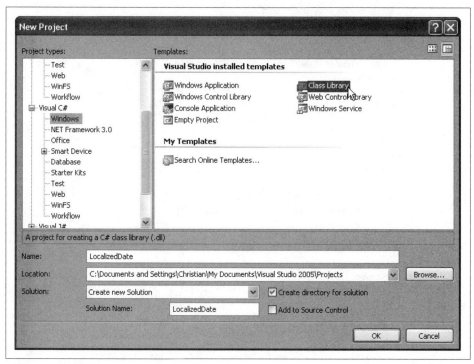

Figure 9-3. Create a new class library project

First, add references to `System.Web` and `System.Web.Extensions` to the project. Then, add some resource files to the project. As shown in Figure 9-4, you start with the file *DateResources.resx*, which is in English (the fallback). Actually, Figure 9-4 shows only the GUI for editing the *DateResources.resx* file. Internally, resource files are in XML format. Example 9-4 shows the (shortened) XML markup for the German resource file. As you can see, using the GUI is much more convenient and much less error prone. (To edit the XML of a resource file, go to the Visual Studio Solution Explorer, right-click the file and then click View Code.) Create the German version of the resource file and name it *DateResources.de.resx*.

Example 9-4. The German resource file

DateResources.de.resx

```
<?xml version="1.0" encoding="utf-8"?>
<root>
```

Example 9-4. The German resource file (continued)

```
<xsd:schema id="root" xmlns="" xmlns:xsd="http://www.w3.org/2001/XMLSchema"
xmlns:msdata="urn:schemas-microsoft-com:xml-msdata">
  <xsd:import namespace="http://www.w3.org/XML/1998/namespace" />
  <xsd:element name="root" msdata:IsDataSet="true">
    <xsd:complexType>
      <xsd:choice maxOccurs="unbounded">
        <xsd:element name="metadata">
          <xsd:complexType>
            <xsd:sequence>
              <xsd:element name="value" type="xsd:string" minOccurs="0" />
            </xsd:sequence>
            <xsd:attribute name="name" use="required" type="xsd:string" />
            <xsd:attribute name="type" type="xsd:string" />
            <xsd:attribute name="mimetype" type="xsd:string" />
            <xsd:attribute ref="xml:space" />
          </xsd:complexType>
        </xsd:element>
        <xsd:element name="assembly">
          <xsd:complexType>
            <xsd:attribute name="alias" type="xsd:string" />
            <xsd:attribute name="name" type="xsd:string" />
          </xsd:complexType>
        </xsd:element>
        <xsd:element name="data">
          <xsd:complexType>
            <xsd:sequence>
              <xsd:element name="value" type="xsd:string" minOccurs="0"
msdata:Ordinal="1" />
              <xsd:element name="comment" type="xsd:string" minOccurs="0"
msdata:Ordinal="2" />
            </xsd:sequence>
            <xsd:attribute name="name" type="xsd:string" use="required"
msdata:Ordinal="1" />
            <xsd:attribute name="type" type="xsd:string" msdata:Ordinal="3" />
            <xsd:attribute name="mimetype" type="xsd:string" msdata:Ordinal="4" />
            <xsd:attribute ref="xml:space" />
          </xsd:complexType>
        </xsd:element>
        <xsd:element name="resheader">
          <xsd:complexType>
            <xsd:sequence>
              <xsd:element name="value" type="xsd:string" minOccurs="0"
msdata:Ordinal="1" />
            </xsd:sequence>
            <xsd:attribute name="name" type="xsd:string" use="required" />
          </xsd:complexType>
        </xsd:element>
      </xsd:choice>
    </xsd:complexType>
  </xsd:element>
</xsd:schema>
```

Example 9-4. The German resource file (continued)

```
<resheader name="resmimetype">
  <value>text/microsoft-resx</value>
</resheader>
<resheader name="version">
  <value>2.0</value>
</resheader>
<resheader name="reader">
  <value>System.Resources.ResXResourceReader, System.Windows.Forms,
Version=2.0.0.0, Culture=neutral, PublicKeyToken=b77a5c561934e089</value>
</resheader>
<resheader name="writer">
  <value>System.Resources.ResXResourceWriter, System.Windows.Forms,
Version=2.0.0.0, Culture=neutral, PublicKeyToken=b77a5c561934e089</value>
</resheader>
<data name="dateformat" xml:space="preserve">
  <value>ss, dd.mm.yyyy</value>
</data>
<data name="daynames" xml:space="preserve">
  <value>["Sonntag", "Montag", "Dienstag", "Mittwoch", "Donnerstag", "Freitag",
"Samstag"]</value>
</data>
<data name="loading" xml:space="preserve">
  <value>Lade Datum ...</value>
</data>
</root>
```

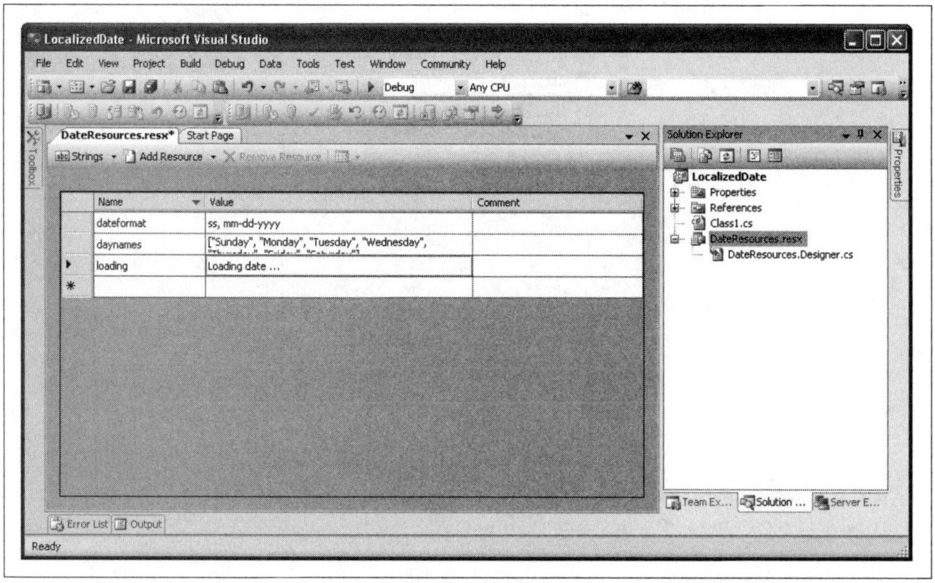

Figure 9-4. The English resource file

What you can also see from the XML is what information is put into the resource files:

dateformat
> The date format, using placeholders

daynames
> The localized names for the days of the week

loading
> The text "Loading date…" translated in the individual languages

Make sure you have at least two resource files (English and German). Feel free to add additional languages at your pleasure. For the day names, use the JSON array syntax to provide the names (see Chapter 3). Be careful to avoid typos, as this application involves server code, JavaScript code, and resources, and is very hard to debug.

In Solution Explorer, open the *Properties* folder of the current project. Inside, you will find the *AssemblyInfo.cs* file that provides further information about the library project. If you do not see that file, click on the Show All Files button as shown in Figure 9-5.

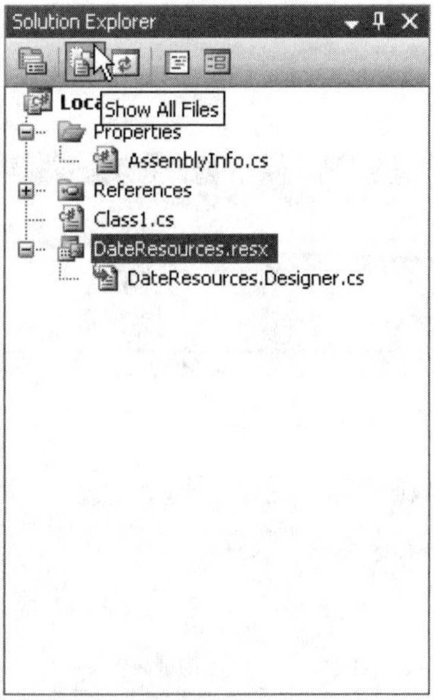

Figure 9-5. This button makes the AssemblyInfo.cs file visible

At the end of *AssemblyInfo.cs*, add the following two lines:

```
[assembly: System.Web.UI.WebResource("LocalizedDate.Dayname.js", "application/x-
javascript")]
[assembly: System.Web.UI.ScriptResource("LocalizedDate.Dayname.js",
"LocalizedDate.DateResources", "LocData")]
```

Note the value LocData in the last argument. This name allows you to access all resource data from JavaScript using the LocData object. The name is arbitrary, but will be used in the following code examples.

The other values in the preceding snippet contain data that is related to the rest of the application. LocalizedDate is the name of the project, *Dayname.js* is the Java-Script file we will create in the next step, and DateResources will also be used in a later step to access resource data (from C#).

The file *Dayname.js* contains JavaScript code that determines the current date and formats it according to the current locale. As mentioned, LocData grants JavaScript access to the resource information. LocData.dateformat contains the date format string, and LocData.daynames contains the array of day names. The latter value is in JSON format (see Chapter 3), so we need an eval( ) call to convert this string into a JavaScript object:

```
var daynames = eval("(" + LocData.daynames + ")");
```

Similar to the JavaScript code in Example 9-3, the code in *Dayname.js* replaces the placeholders in the dateformat string and displays it in the browser. Note a one second delay has been added (to more clearly see the effect). Example 9-5 contains the complete code for the JavaScript file. Add this code to your project.

Example 9-5. The JavaScript code in the class library

Dayname.js

```
Sys.Application.add_load(function( ) {
    var d = new Date( );
    var daynames = eval("(" + LocData.daynames + ")");
    var datestring = LocData.dateformat.replace("ss", daynames[d.getDay( )])
                            .replace("dd", d.getDate( ))
                            .replace("mm", d.getMonth( ) + 1)
                            .replace("yyyy", d.getFullYear( ));
    setTimeout('$get("date").firstChild.nodeValue = "' + datestring + '"', 1000);
});
```

Finally, you have to make sure that the *Dayname.js* file will be embedded in the assembly. Click on the filename in Solution Explorer. In the Properties window, set Build Action to Embedded Resource (see Figure 9-6). This will later compile the JavaScript file directly into the DLL.

You may have noticed that the *Dayname.js* code uses the $get( ) function to access an as yet undefined element called "date". This element will be defined as part of the control code in the C# class file.

In Solution Explorer, rename the *Class1.cs* file to *LocDateControl.cs* (right-click the filename, then click Rename). Choose the option to update all references. This will be the C# code for the ASP.NET custom control. Our control will inherit from the .NET Sys.Web.UI.Control class.

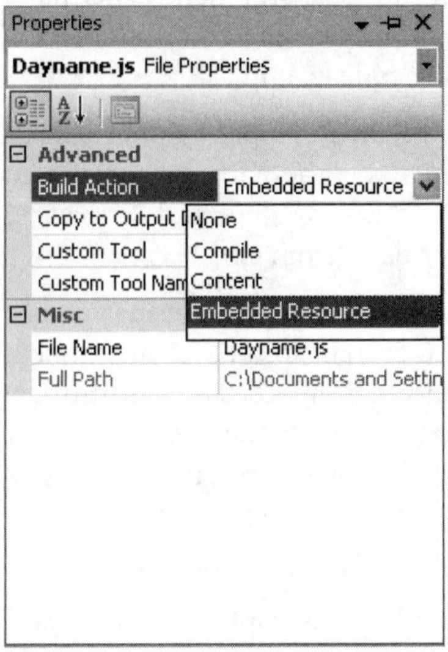

Figure 9-6. The JavaScript file will be embedded

In the `LocDateControl` class, we overwrite the control's base `CreateChildControls( )` method and add our own HTML element, a <span> label called "date":

```
hgc = new HtmlGenericControl( );
hgc.TagName = "span";
hgc.ID = "date";
```

The text in this <span> element is "Loading data..." or whatever is defined in the language of choice. The control must query the embedded resources to get the correct string. The following code takes care of this:

```
System.Resources.ResourceManager r = new System.Resources.ResourceManager(
  "LocalizedDate.DateResources",
  this.GetType( ).Assembly);
hgc.InnerHtml = r.GetString("loading");
```

Finally, the new control with localized text is added to the page:

```
Controls.Add(hgc);
```

Example 9-6 contains the complete code for the class library file.

Example 9-6. The code for the class library

LocDateControl.cs

```
using System;
using System.Collections.Generic;
using System.Text;
using System.Web.UI;
using System.Web.UI.HtmlControls;
```

Example 9-6. The code for the class library (continued)

```
namespace LocalizedDate
{
    public class LocDateControl : Control
    {
        private HtmlGenericControl hgc;

        protected override void CreateChildControls()
        {
            base.CreateChildControls();

            hgc = new HtmlGenericControl();
            hgc.TagName = "span";
            hgc.ID = "date";

            System.Resources.ResourceManager r = new
            System.Resources.ResourceManager(
                "LocalizedDate.DateResources",
                this.GetType().Assembly);
            hgc.InnerHtml = r.GetString("loading");

            Controls.Add(hgc);
        }
    }
}
```

Now it is time to build the class library project. This will generate a pair of files. *LocalizedDate.dll* contains the control implemented in the class library and an assembly that contains the default resource file (from *DateResources.resx*). For each additional language, a folder with a satellite assembly has been created. For instance, the German translation resides in a folder called *de* and contains the assembly *LocalizedDate.resources.dll*.

When using Visual Studio 2005, the new assemblies are usually immediately available in your ASP.NET AJAX applications (if not, reference the class library explicitly in the web site). If you are using Visual Web Developer Express and Visual C# Express Edition, in Visual Web Developer create a *Bin* folder in the ASP.NET AJAX application, then in this folder, place a copy of both the *LocalizedDate.dll* file and all subdirectories (*de,...*).

Now you can import the control on any ASP.NET page with the following directive:

```
<%@ Register TagPrefix="OReilly" Assembly="LocalizedDate" Namespace="LocalizedDate"
%>
```

Since the control does not expose any public properties, it can be included on a page with very little effort:

```
<OReilly:LocDateControl ID="ldc1" runat="server" />
```

The control contains all the JavaScript code required to both display the waiting screen ("Loading data...") and to display the localized date. All there is left for ASP.NET

AJAX to do is to be sure to load the assembly in the ScriptManager control. Both the assembly name (LocalizedDate) and the canonical embedded JavaScript name (LocalizedDate.Dayname.js) must be provided in the ScriptReference element. Do not forget the EnableScriptLocalization attribute of the ScriptManager!

```
<asp:ScriptManager ID="ScriptManager1" runat="server"
  EnableScriptLocalization="true">
  <Scripts>
    <asp:ScriptReference Assembly="LocalizedDate" Name="LocalizedDate.Dayname.js" />
  </Scripts>
</asp:ScriptManager>
```

Finally, set the page to automatically determine the correct culture:

```
<%@ Page Language="C#" UICulture="auto" %>
```

Example 9-7 contains the complete code for the *.aspx* page. Figures 9-7 and 9-8 show the various states of the application, from wait screen to final result.

Example 9-7. Using a satellite assembly with ASP.NET AJAX

Localization-Satellite.aspx

```
<%@ Page Language="C#" UICulture="auto" %>

<%@ Register TagPrefix="OReilly" Assembly="LocalizedDate" Namespace="LocalizedDate" %>

<!DOCTYPE html PUBLIC "-//W3C//DTD XHTML 1.0 Transitional//EN"
"http://www.w3.org/TR/xhtml1/DTD/xhtml1-transitional.dtd">

<script runat="server">
</script>

<html xmlns="http://www.w3.org/1999/xhtml">
<head id="Head1" runat="server">
  <title>ASP.NET AJAX</title>
</head>
<body>
  <form id="form1" runat="server">
    <asp:ScriptManager ID="ScriptManager1" runat="server"
      EnableScriptLocalization="true">
      <Scripts>
        <asp:ScriptReference Assembly="LocalizedDate"
Name="LocalizedDate.Dayname.js" />
      </Scripts>
    </asp:ScriptManager>
    <div>
      <OReilly:LocDateControl ID="ldc1" runat="server" />
    </div>
  </form>
</body>
</html>
```

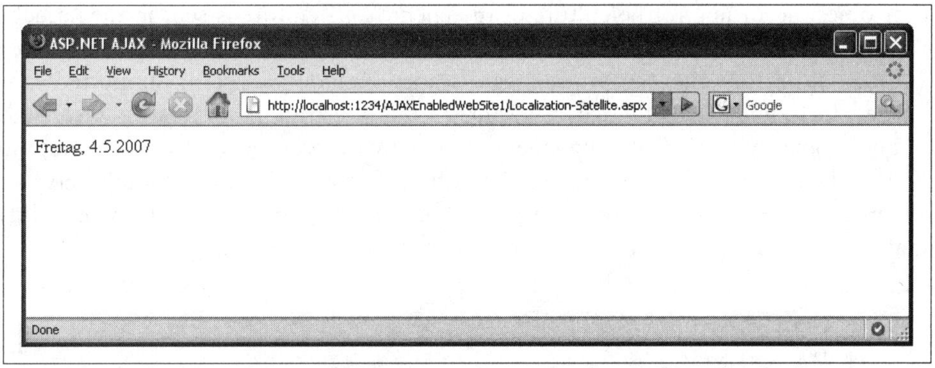

Figure 9-7. The localized German page

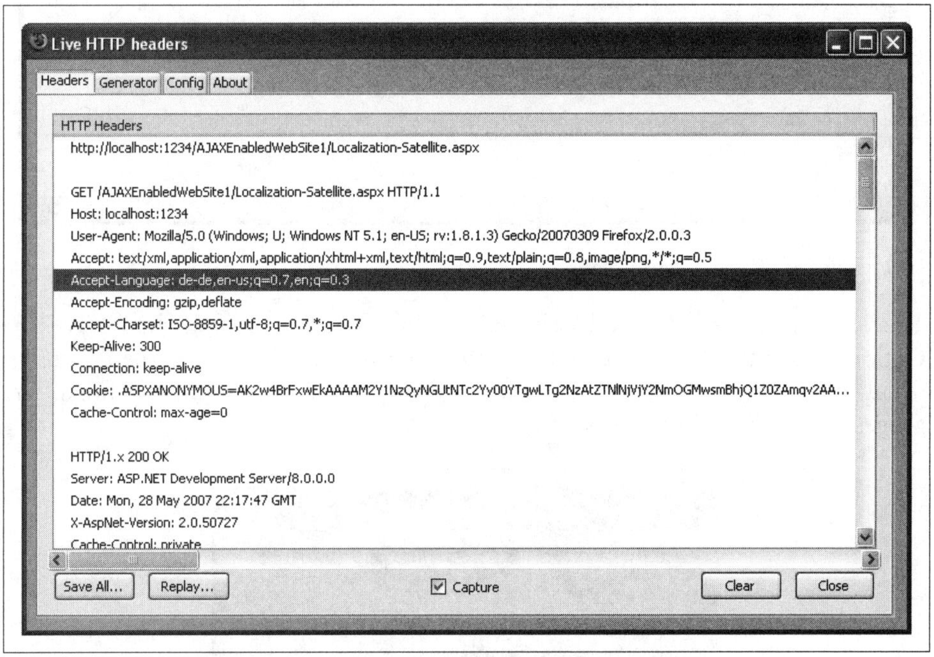

Figure 9-8. Typical HTTP headers, with Accept-Language highlighted

Globalization and Internationalization

In addition to providing support for localization, ASP.NET AJAX supports globalization, which is sometimes referred to as internationalization (or i18n, if you are fond of numeronyms). The ScriptManager control supports the EnableScriptGlobalization property. If this property is set to true, ASP.NET AJAX is capable of automatically localizing date values. For this to work, the Ajax library extends JavaScript's Date object (and other objects—refer to Chapter 4 and Appendix D for more information) so that it supports a new method called localeFormat( ). This method formats a

Date object according to the culture of the client. This culture is sent in the Accept-Language HTTP header. Figure 9-9 shows HTTP headers sent by a German version of Firefox. Note that the Accept-Language header includes a list of supported languages, including their preference weight. In this illustration, German is preferred, English comes next. English-language browsers, by the way, generally only prefer the English language in their default configuration, sometimes differentiating between American, British, and Canadian English. Of course, the language the browser sends may not be reliable, so the best option is still to let users choose explicitly.

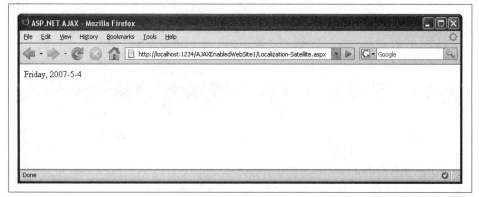

Figure 9-9. The original English page

This language preference can be changed by the user. For Firefox, choose Tools → Options, select the Advanced tab and click on the Choose button. In the Languages dialog box (Figure 9-10), you can rearrange preference order, add additional languages, or remove existing ones.

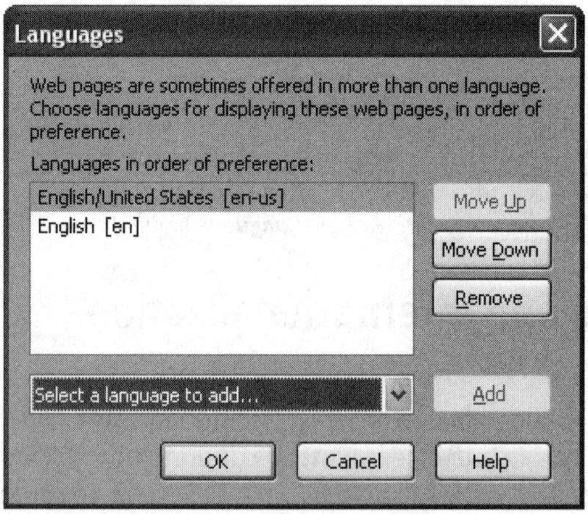

Figure 9-10. Changing the preferred languages in Firefox

When using the Internet Explorer, choose Tools › Internet Options, select the General tab and click on the Language button to get the dialog shown in Figure 9-11.

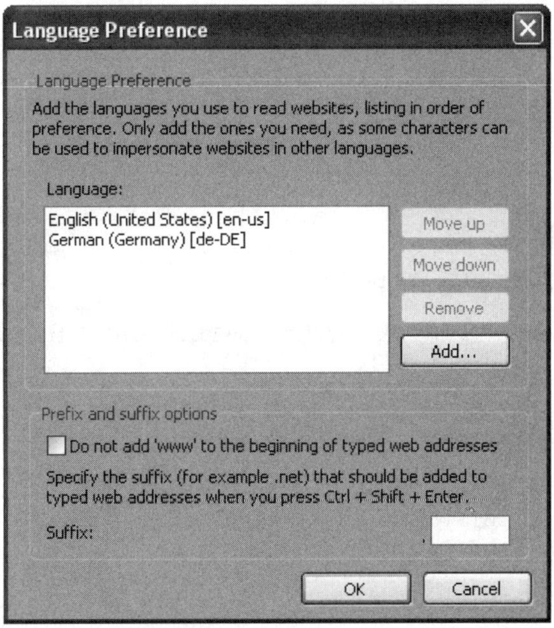

Figure 9-11. Changing the preferred languages in Internet Explorer

Other browsers provide similar means to adapt their own language behavior.

But back to the topic of ASP.NET AJAX and date globalization. The `Date.localFormat()` method uses placeholders and replaces them with localized names for weekdays and months. The following code outputs something similar to "Wednesday, 1. May 2007", depending on the current browser language setting:

```
<script type="text/javascript">
  function pageLoad() {
    $get("date").firstChild.nodeValue =
      (new Date()).localeFormat("dddd, dd. MMMM yyyy");
  }
</script>
```

However, one more step is necessary. The ASP.NET application must set the correct culture. The culture can be set in *Web.config*, programmatically, and via markup in the page. Refer to "For Further Reading," at the end of this chapter, for more information about the available options.

In the following sample, the culture is set using the @ Page directive. We could provide a specific culture, but we prefer to let ASP.NET AJAX figure out the correct setting depending on the Accept-Language HTTP header. The following declaration takes care of this:

```
<%@ Page Language="C#" Culture="auto" %>
```

And that's it—Example 9-8 shows the complete code, which is conveniently short this time.

Example 9-8. Globalizing a date

Globalization.aspx

```
<%@ Page Language="C#" Culture="auto" %>

<!DOCTYPE html PUBLIC "-//W3C//DTD XHTML 1.0 Transitional//EN" "http://www.w3.org/TR/
xhtml1/DTD/xhtml1-transitional.dtd">
<html xmlns="http://www.w3.org/1999/xhtml">
<head runat="server">
  <title>ASP.NET AJAX</title>
  <script type="text/javascript">
  function pageLoad( ) {
    $get("date").firstChild.nodeValue =
      (new Date( )).localeFormat("dddd, dd. MMMM yyyy");
  }
  </script>
</head>
<body>
  <form id="form1" runat="server">
    <asp:ScriptManager ID="ScriptManager1" runat="server"
      EnableScriptGlobalization="true">
    </asp:ScriptManager>
    <div>
      <span id="date"> </span>
    </div>
  </form>
</body>
</html>
```

Figure 9-12 shows the result in German, while Figure 9-13 displays the result in French. Both results have been created by setting the appropriate language preferences in the browser. You will note that both the day name (place holder dddd) and the month name (MMMM) have been translated. However, the date format is not fully localized: the period after the day is common in German, but not in French. To get around this type of problem, you have to manually localize date information, as was illustrated in Examples 9-3 and 9-7.

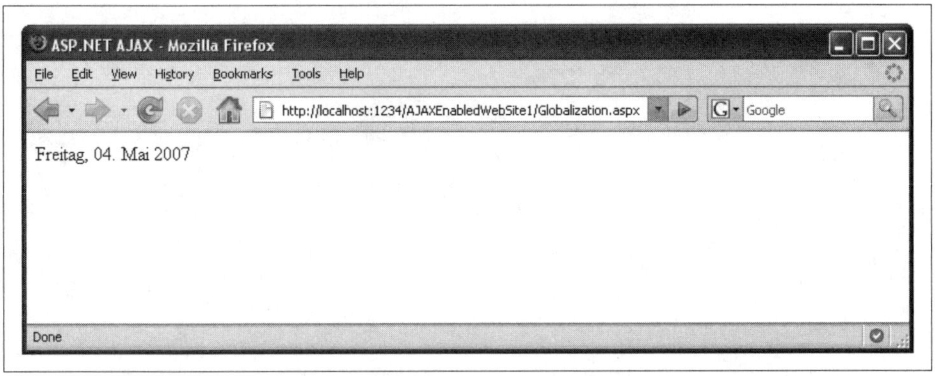

Figure 9-12. The date in German

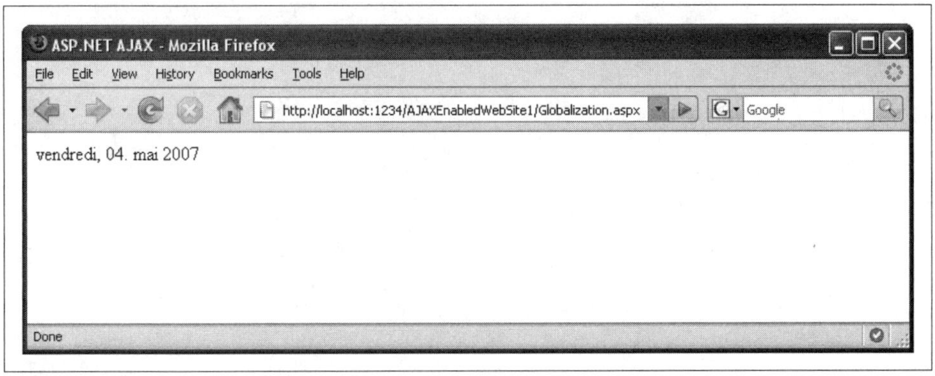

Figure 9-13. The date in French

Summary

In a globalized world, web sites should expect to interact with users from many different countries, who speak many different languages. This chapter showed you several techniques to make a web site multilingual and multicultural, courtesy of ASP.NET AJAX.

For Further Reading

http://msdn2.microsoft.com/en-us/library/76091f86-f967-4687-a40f-de87bd8cc9a0.aspx

   MSDN information about setting the culture and UI culture from ASP.NET

http://ajax.asp.net/docs/tutorials/GlobalizingDateUsingClientScript.aspx

   A globalization tutorial in the Microsoft documentation for ASP.NET AJAX

ASP.NET AJAX Control Toolkit

CHAPTER 10

Using the Control Toolkit

Some critics of ASP.NET 2.0 AJAX say it is nothing more than the UpdatePanel control plus a couple of JavaScript APIs. Indeed, in order to keep the size of the ASP.NET AJAX library as small as possible (to make it more acceptable for use by large sites), functionality that existed in Atlas (the pre-release version of ASP.NET AJAX) was stripped out of the release version. Of course, not all of it was stripped, so ASP.NET AJAX alone is still an excellent choice.

The ASP.NET AJAX Control Toolkit was created to allow both Microsoft and the ASP.NET community to easily add noncore functionality to the framework, independent of the ASP.NET AJAX update cycle and outside of official Microsoft support. The software, including source code, has been released under a shared source license (the Microsoft Permissive License, also known as MS-PL). Microsoft has also created a site where company developers and community members can add new functionality. (See the section "For Further Reading" at the end of this chapter.)

This chapter shows how to install and use the ASP.NET AJAX Control Toolkit, and it introduces you to some of the more useful controls the toolkit contains. However, because the toolkit continues to evolve with new controls and functionality being added on a monthly basis, the information here can change quite quickly. You should always check the ASP.NET AJAX Controls Toolkit site for the latest updates and information (See the section "For Further Reading" at the end of this chapter.)

Installing the Control Toolkit

Before you can use ASP.NET AJAX controls, you need to add the Toolkit controls to your development environment. You can download it from the ASP.NET AJAX home page at *http://ajax.asp.net/toolkit/default.aspx?tabid=47*. Up-to-date documentation can be found at *http://ajax.asp.net/ajaxtoolkit*. The toolkit is hosted on CodePlex web site (*http://www.codeplex.com/AtlasControlToolkit/*) and is provided in the form of a ZIP archive. Actually, two archives: one contains the toolkit plus source code; the other, smaller archive, does not come with the sources. To simply use the toolkit, the "NoSource" option will suffice to get you going. If you would like to see how the components are actually implemented, select the ZIP archive with the source code.

Figure 10-1 shows the contents of the "NoSource" ZIP archive.

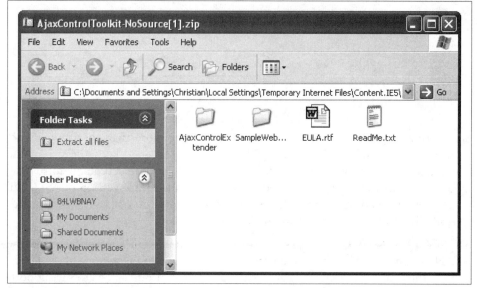

Figure 10-1. The ASP.NET AJAX Control Toolkit ZIP archive

In addition to the EULA and a README file, the ZIP archive contains two folders:

SampleWebSite
An ASP.NET web site that showcases all controls in the toolkit, and the toolkit documentation

AjaxControlExtender
A VSI (Visual Studio Integration) installer that provides several Toolkit-related templates for Visual Studio

The sample web site provided with the toolkit also serves as its documentation. The site is based on ASP.NET 2.0, which makes it possible to see the sample controls in action. Figure 10-2 shows the documentation web site in the browser. It not only provides you with a list of controls, their properties, and usage information, but it also demonstrates each one in action.

Before browsing the site, take a minute to run the *AjaxControlExtender.vsi* installer. As Figure 10-3 shows, it can install up to six templates. Of those templates, only the last two are absolutely necessary to run controls from the Toolkit. Go ahead and install the entire set though, as you will use them later in Chapter 14. You can ignore the warning that the templates are not digitally signed.

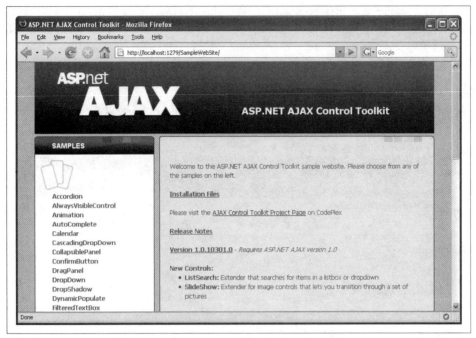

Figure 10-2. The local ASP.NET AJAX Control Toolkit documentation

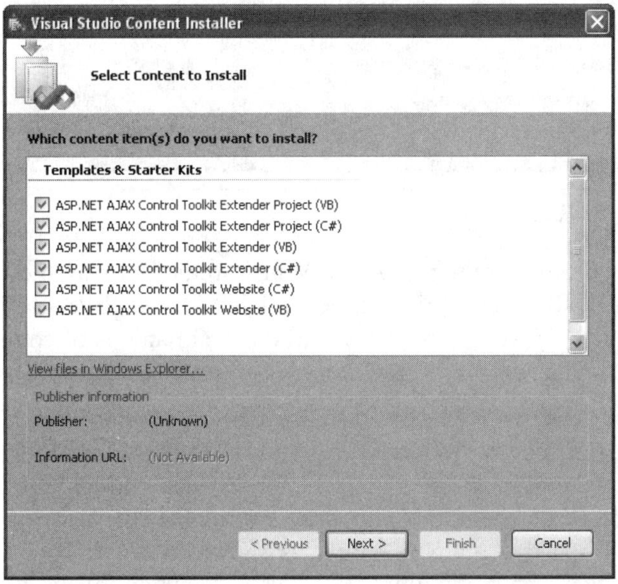

Figure 10-3. The VSI Installer for the Toolkit

The VSI installer provides you with a web site template that generates a suitable *Web.config* file for a Toolkit-driven site, similar to the ASP.NET AJAX and ASP.NET AJAX Futures templates.

The first four templates set up the infrastructure for creating custom controls for the toolkit. Chapter 14 will provide more details about how this can be done.

Now create a new web site in Visual Studio or Visual Web Developer Express Edition, using the AJAX Control Toolkit Web Site template (see Figure 10-4).

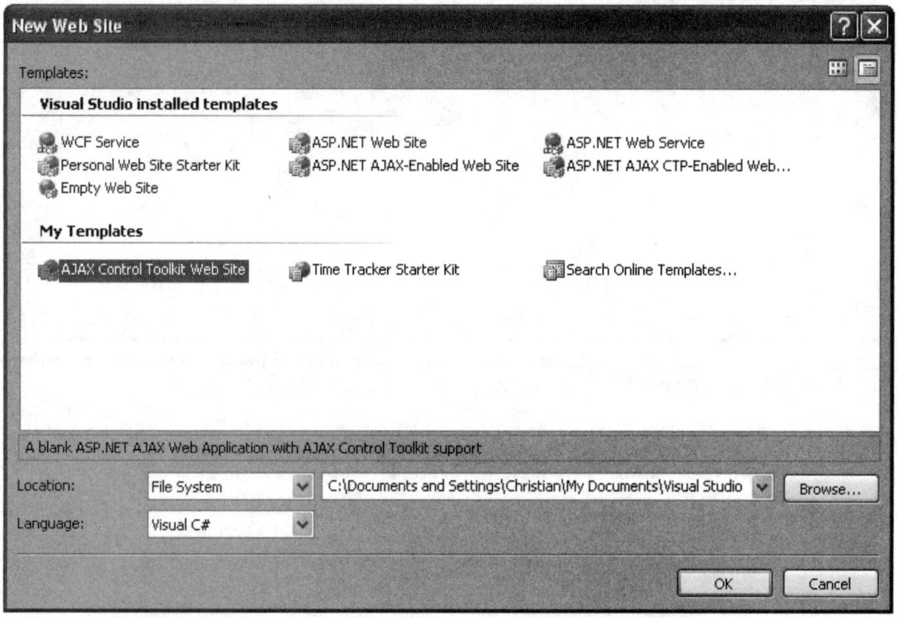

Figure 10-4. The Toolkit template

Next, add the controls to the toolbox in Visual Studio. Display the Toolbox in the Design view of the IDE. Then, right-click the Toolbox and click Add Tab. Name the new tab *ASP.NET AJAX Control Toolkit* (the actual name is of course not mandatory; any name will do).

Right-click the newly created tab and click Choose Toolbox Items (displayed as Choose Items in Visual Web Developer). Add the ASP.NET AJAX Control Toolkit assembly, *AjaxControlToolkit.dll*. The assembly resides in the *Bin* folder of the current web site based on the ASP.NET AJAX Control Toolkit Web Site template. The Toolbox now displays some new entries as shown in Figure 10-5. (Note that the toolbox items won't be visible until you have a document open, like an ASP.NET page, where you can use them.)

The toolkit is now ready to use (see Chapters 12 and 13). You can even contribute to it yourself (see Chapter 14)!

Figure 10-5. The new Toolbox items

Using the Control Toolkit

Once you've added the toolkit to the project, you can use its controls in your web site. Let's demonstrate how it works by adding one of its more simple controls to a web page, the ConfirmButton control. ConfirmButton displays a JavaScript confirmation dialog box (using the window.prompt( ) method, of course), which asks the user whether or not to continue the current operation. If the user clicks No, the action is cancelled. This is useful when an online form is posted by clicking on a LinkButton or a regular button: if No is clicked, JavaScript is able to cancel the click on the button, preventing the form from being submitted.

Before you can use any toolkit controls on a page, you have to register the toolkit by adding the following markup to the page. You can save yourself a little typing though, as this will be done for you automatically if you drag a toolkit component on the page in either Design or Code view.

```
<%@ Register Assembly="AkaxControlToolkit" Namespace="AjaxControlToolkit"
TagPrefix="aajaxToolkit" %>
```

Use the name that you assign to the TagPrefix property each time you reference a control in the toolkit. If you don't assign a TagPrefix value, whenever you drag an extender from the IDE Toolbox to the design surface, the IDE assigns the prefix cc1 by default. The ajaxToolkit prefix is more descriptive. You'll also need to add a ScriptManager control to the page for the toolkit controls to work.

Most controls in the ASP.NET AJAX Control Toolkit provide their functionality by extending the functionality of other controls on the page. (See Chapter 1 for a discussion of the extenders that ship with ASP.NET AJAX.) The specific properties available for an extender depend on which toolkit control you use, but the overall approach is the same: you add a control to the page, then add the extender and set the TargetControlID property with the ID of the target HTML element or ASP.NET control.

The ConfirmButton control has one additional property called the ConfirmText value. This contains the text of the message that is displayed when you click the LinkButton control.

Run the page and click the control with which the ConfirmButton extender is associated. You'll be asked if you want to continue. If you choose Yes, the action of the LinkButton control is executed, meaning the LinkButton link is followed and the form is submitted. A text is then displayed to confirm that a postback has occurred. Clicking No, on the other hand, cancels the action. Example 10-1 contains the complete code for this example.

Example 10-1. Using the ConfirmButton extender control

```
ConfirmButton.aspx

<%@ Page Language="C#" %>

<%@ Register Assembly="AjaxControlToolkit" Namespace="AjaxControlToolkit"
TagPrefix="ajaxToolkit" %>

<script runat="server">
  void Page_Load( )
  {
    if (Page.IsPostBack)
    {
      Label1.Text = "You have been warned!";
    }
  }
</script>
```

Example 10-1. Using the ConfirmButton extender control (continued)

```
<!DOCTYPE html PUBLIC "-//W3C//DTD XHTML 1.0 Transitional//EN"
"http://www.w3.org/TR/xhtml1/DTD/xhtml1-transitional.dtd">
<html xmlns="http://www.w3.org/1999/xhtml">
<head id="Head1" runat="server">
  <title>ASP.NET AJAX</title>
</head>
<body>
  <form id="form1" runat="server">
    <asp:ScriptManager ID="ScriptManager1" runat="server" />
    <div>
      <asp:LinkButton ID="LinkButton1" runat="server">LinkButton</asp:LinkButton>
      <ajaxToolkit:ConfirmButtonExtender ID="ConfirmButtonExtender1" runat="server"
ConfirmText="Are you sure?! "
        TargetControlID="LinkButton1" />
      <br />
      <asp:Label ID="Label1" runat="server" />
    </div>
  </form>
</body>
</html>
```

Figure 10-6 shows the result displayed in the browser. When the LinkButton control is clicked, the pop-up window appears. If No is clicked, the form is not posted to the server.

Figure 10-6. The Confirm text that is displayed when the button is clicked

The other toolkit extenders work in a similar fashion. Just add the extender control (create an <ajaxToolkit:*control*Extender> element) to the page and set the extender's properties.

From a JavaScript point of view, the effect that the ConfirmButtonExtender provides is trivial. The following JavaScript code is all you need to add a prompt to a regular HTML hyperlink (something the ConfirmButtonExtender control yet cannot do):

```
<a href="http://atlas.asp.net/"
    onclick="return window.confirm('Are you
sure?!');">Go to the ASP.NET AJAX homepage</a>
```

This extender shows that ASP.NET AJAX is more than just an Ajax toolkit—thanks to the Control Toolkit, it is also becoming a Java-Script toolkit.

Summary

This chapter introduced the ASP.NET AJAX Control Toolkit, installed the package, and also provided a first example. Be sure to read the following chapters, which will feature many of the exciting controls and features provided by this open source project.

For Further Reading

http://www.codeplex.com/AtlasControlToolkit
ASP.NET AJAX Control Toolkit home page on CodePlex

http://ajax.asp.net/ajaxtoolkit/
Live version of the Control Toolkit

CHAPTER 11

Adding Animation to a Web Page

One key component of the ASP.NET AJAX Control Toolkit is a powerful animation framework that provides several means to create complex animations without the need for extensive JavaScript coding. This chapter will examine how to take advantage of that framework. We'll also touch on a related feature of the Control Toolkit—drag-and-drop support.

Note, the examples in this chapter require you to have installed the ASP.NET AJAX Control Toolkit. You will also need to have a web site configured to use the toolkit. For details on the Control Toolkit, see Chapter 10.

Animation Framework

ASP.NET AJAX offers two choices to create animations with very little effort (both unsupported). You may choose either ASP.NET AJAX Futures, which provides several animation options (refer to Chapter 20 for an in-depth discussion), or you can use the ASP.NET AJAX Control Toolkit. Equipped with more than just some web controls for Ajax-y animation effects, the toolkit comes with an entire animation framework that we will explore through the examples in this chapter. It is hard to say which option will "win" in the end, but I would personally bet on the Control Toolkit, since this is more community-driven than Futures. Time will tell.

Animation Basics

The Control Toolkit animation framework provides web control the `AnimationExtender` element. First though, you need the property, `TargetControlID`, which must contain the ID of the element to be animated:

```
<ajaxToolkit:AnimationExtender ID="AnimationExtender1" runat="server"
  TargetControlID="myTargetElement">
  <!-- ... -->
</ajaxToolkit:AnimationExtender>
```

However, the actual animation is defined within the `AnimationExtender` element. There you can place XML markup which controls the animation. The root node of this markup is `<Animations>`. Within this node you need to provide the following information:

Events

> When to start an animation—that is, a trigger

Animation types and properties

> Which animations to use, which includes fades, movement, resizing, and so on (more on these in a moment)

Example 11-1 demonstrates an animation. Within the `<Animations>` node, the `<OnLoad>` node represents animation(s) that will run when the page has been fully loaded. There is only one animation within `<OnLoad>`, in this case, the `<FadeOut>` element. So, the target element fades out, within three seconds (`Duration` attribute), using 25 animation steps (`Fps` attribute, [frames per second]). Figure 11-1 shows the browser midway through that animation.

Example 11-1. A simple fade-out animation

AnimationFade.aspx

```
<%@ Page Language="C#" %>

<!DOCTYPE html PUBLIC "-//W3C//DTD XHTML 1.0 Transitional//EN"
"http://www.w3.org/TR/xhtml1/DTD/xhtml1-transitional.dtd">

<html xmlns="http://www.w3.org/1999/xhtml">
<head runat="server">
  <title>ASP.NET AJAX</title>
</head>
<body>
  <form id="form1" runat="server">
    <asp:ScriptManager ID="ScriptManager1" runat="server" />
    <div>
      <asp:Label ID="Label1" runat="server" Text="See me fading ..."
        Style="display: inline-block; background-color: Red;" />
    </div>
    <ajaxToolkit:AnimationExtender ID="AnimationExtender1" runat="server"
      TargetControlID="Label1">
      <Animations>
        <OnLoad>
          <FadeOut Duration="3" Fps="25" />
        </OnLoad>
      </Animations>
    </ajaxToolkit:AnimationExtender>
  </form>
</body>
</html>
```

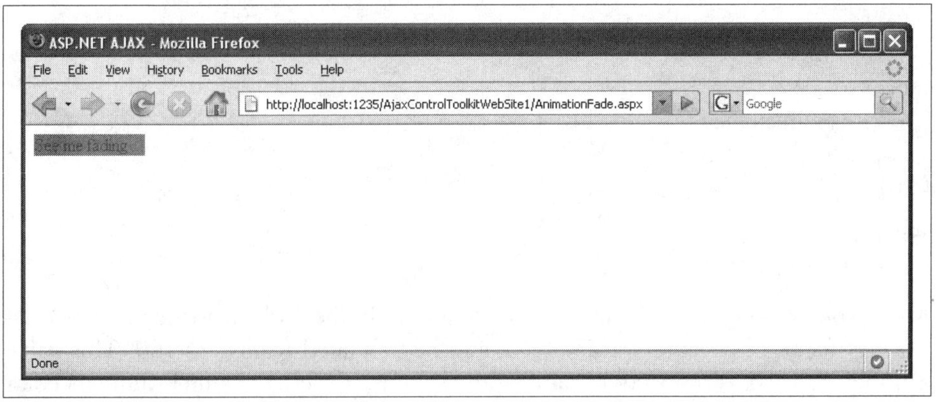

Figure 11-1. The element is fading out

Animation events

There are several more triggers in addition to <OnLoad>:

<OnClick>
> The user clicks on an element to start the animation.

<OnHoverOut>
> The animation starts when the mouse pointer leaves an element.

<OnHoverOver>
> The animation starts when the mouse pointer enters an element. (This stops any <OnHoverOut> animation for the same element.)

<OnMouseOut>
> The animation starts when the mouse pointer leaves an element.

<OnMouseOver>
> The animation starts when the mouse pointer enters an element. This does *not* stop any <OnMouseOut> animation for the same element.

Animation types

The animation framework supports an impressive set of animations:

<Fade>
> Fades an element in or out

<FadeIn>
> Fades an element in

<FadeOut>
> Fades an element out

<Pulse>
> Pulsates an element (by fading it in and out repeatedly)

`<Color>`

   Changes the color of an element between two values

`<Move>`

   Moves an element

`<Resize>`

   Changes the size of an element

`<Scale>`

   Scales an element

Apart from these visual animations, the animation framework is also capable of "animating" values. For instance, a value could be animated from 1 to 100. This value can then be used as the x coordinate of an element, its alpha channel value, its color code, or as its width (there are even more possibilities). Here are just some of these animations:

`<Discrete>`

   Animates a value based on a list of given target values

`<Interpolated>`

   Animates a value using equal steps within a given interval

`<Length>`

   Animates a value using equal steps within a given interval, but appends a unit string (e.g., "px" or "em") to each value

A special case of animation is a so-called *action*. Actions defined by the animation framework are executed immediately, not gradually such as the aforementioned animations. Here are some typical actions:

`<EnableAction>`

   Enables or disables an element

`<HideAction>`

   Hides an element (by using the CSS property `display:none`)

`<StyleAction>`

   Sets a CSS style property of an element

`<OpacityAction>`

   Sets the opacity of an element

Complex Animations

The implementation of the animation framework only allows one animation within each animation event node (`<OnLoad>`, `<OnClick>`, etc. However, it is possible to join several relatively simple animations together into one, increasingly complex animation. This can then be used within `<OnLoad>` and the other event nodes. Depending on how the individual animation within an animation group runs, there are different types of these aggregating animations:

`<Case>`

Runs one of a set of animations depending on a condition (comparable to switch( ) in C# and Select Case in Visual Basic)

`<Condition>`

Runs one of animations depending on a condition (comparable to the C# ? operator)

`<Parallel>`

Runs all animations at the same time

`<Sequence>`

Runs all animations sequentially, one at a time

Example 11-2 uses several animations at once. Two animations are run at the same time (`<Parallel>` element). The first one is the `<FadeOut>` animation that you already know, the second, a `<Condition>` animation. The condition is Math.random( ) < 0.5, which should statistically evaluate to true every other time. Depending on the value of Math.random( ) (a random number between 0 and 1), either the style.top or the style.left property of the element is animated from 0px to 250px. Figure 11-2 shows a possible outcome. (When you run the example, refresh the browser several times to see the two possible animations.)

Example 11-2. Running several animations at once

AnimationGroup.aspx

```
<%@ Page Language="C#" %>

<!DOCTYPE html PUBLIC "-//W3C//DTD XHTML 1.0 Transitional//EN"
"http://www.w3.org/TR/xhtml1/DTD/xhtml1-transitional.dtd">

<html xmlns="http://www.w3.org/1999/xhtml">
<head id="Head1" runat="server">
  <title>ASP.NET AJAX</title>
</head>
<body>
  <form id="form1" runat="server">
    <asp:ScriptManager ID="ScriptManager1" runat="server" />
    <div>
      <asp:Label ID="Label1" runat="server" Text="See me fading ..."
        Style="display: inline-block; background-color: Red; position: relative;
left: 8px; top: 8px;" />
    </div>
    <ajaxToolkit:AnimationExtender ID="AnimationExtender1" runat="server"
      TargetControlID="Label1">
      <Animations>
        <OnLoad>
          <Parallel>
            <FadeOut Duration="3" Fps="25" />
            <Condition ConditionScript="(Math.random() &lt; 0.5)">
              <Length StartValue="0" EndValue="250" Unit="px"
```

Example 11-2. Running several animations at once (continued)

```
            Property="style" PropertyKey="left" />
          <Length StartValue="0" EndValue="250" Unit="px"
            Property="style" PropertyKey="top" />
        </Condition>
      </Parallel>
    </OnLoad>
  </Animations>
</ajaxToolkit:AnimationExtender>
</form>
</body>
</html>
```

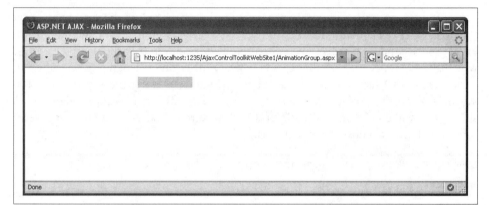

Figure 11-2. Two animations at once

 Be careful to use valid XML. In the previous example, the condition `Math.random() < 0.5` must first be properly escaped as the opening angle bracket has a special meaning within XML. Therefore, the correct condition is actually `Math.random() &lt; 0.5`, (as the syntax in Example 11-2 properly displayed).

Programming Animations

All animations can also be programmatically set. As of time of writing, there is no full-blown API available that would allow you to add and remove individual animations at will, but you can assign XML (server code) or JSON (client code) to an `AnimationExtender` control.

Let's start with the server side. The `AnimationExtender` control exposes the `Animations` property. You can assign an XML string with the animation information. Just make sure you omit the `<Animations>` node and start right off with the first event, as Example 11-3 illustrates. This example has the same effect as the previous one, but adds the animation information to the extender using C# code.

Example 11-3. Setting animations on the server side

AnimationServer.aspx

```
<%@ Page Language="C#" %>

<!DOCTYPE html PUBLIC "-//W3C//DTD XHTML 1.0 Transitional//EN"
"http://www.w3.org/TR/xhtml1/DTD/xhtml1-transitional.dtd">

<script runat="server">

  protected void Page_Load(object sender, EventArgs e)
  {
    string animations = "<OnLoad><Parallel><FadeOut Duration='3' Fps='25'
/><Condition ConditionScript='(Math.random( ) &lt; 0.5)'><Length StartValue='0'
EndValue='250' Unit='px' Property='style' PropertyKey='left' />
<Length StartValue='0' EndValue='250' Unit='px' Property='style'
PropertyKey='top' /></Condition></Parallel></OnLoad>";
    AnimationExtender1.Animations = animations;
  }
</script>

<html xmlns="http://www.w3.org/1999/xhtml">
<head id="Head1" runat="server">
  <title>ASP.NET AJAX</title>
</head>
<body>
  <form id="form1" runat="server">
    <asp:ScriptManager ID="ScriptManager1" runat="server" />
    <div>
      <asp:Label ID="Label1" runat="server" Text="See me fading ..."
        Style="display: inline-block; background-color: Red; position: relative;
left: 8px; top: 8px;" />
    </div>
    <ajaxToolkit:AnimationExtender ID="AnimationExtender1" runat="server"
      TargetControlID="Label1" />
  </form>
</body>
</html>
```

This is possible from JavaScript, as well. The only thing that changes here is the format of the animation configuration. Instead of an XML string, you need to provide a JSON string. The object signified by this JSON string contains all animation information. Use the AnimationName property to provide the name of the animation (which is identical to the name of the corresponding XML element). The elements within an XML element are provided as an array in the AnimationChildren property. The following is just such a JSON string, broken up into multiple lines for better legibility:

```
{
  'AnimationName':'Parallel',
  'AnimationChildren':
  [
    {
```

```
    'AnimationName':'FadeOut',
    'Duration':'3',
    'Fps':'25'
  },
  {
   'AnimationName':'Condition',
   'ConditionScript':'(Math.random() < 0.5)',
   'AnimationChildren':
   [
    {
     'AnimationName':'Length',
     'StartValue':'0',
     'EndValue':'250',
     'Unit':'px',
     'Property':'style',
     'PropertyKey':'left'
    },
    {
     'AnimationName':'Length',
     'StartValue':'0',
     'EndValue':'250',
     'Unit':'px',
     'Property':'style',
     'PropertyKey':'top'
    }
   ]
  }
 ]
}
```

You also need a way to access the control on the page, as the `AnimationExtender` itself does not have a visual representation. For all elements, ASP.NET AJAX provides the `$find()` helper function which lets you access these controls. Once you have a reference to the control, you can assign the JSON string to one of its animation events. For example, the `set_OnClick()` method sets the animation to start when the target element of the animation is clicked.

Example 11-4 shows the complete code. Again, the result is the same as Examples 11-2 and 11-3, but this time the animation is defined in client script.

Example 11-4. Setting animations on the client side

AnimationClient.aspx

```
<%@ Page Language="C#" %>

<!DOCTYPE html PUBLIC "-//W3C//DTD XHTML 1.0 Transitional//EN"
"http://www.w3.org/TR/xhtml1/DTD/xhtml1-transitional.dtd">

<html xmlns="http://www.w3.org/1999/xhtml">
<head id="Head1" runat="server">
```

Example 11-4. Setting animations on the client side (continued)

```
<title>ASP.NET AJAX</title>
<script type="text/javascript">
function pageLoad( ) {
  var animations =
"{'AnimationName':'Parallel','AnimationChildren':
[{'AnimationName':'FadeOut','Duration':'3','Fps':'25'},
{'AnimationName':'Condition','ConditionScript':
'(Math.random( ) < 0.5)','AnimationChildren':
[{'AnimationName':'Length','StartValue':'0','EndValue':'250','Unit':'px','Property'
:'style','PropertyKey':'left'},
{'AnimationName':'Length','StartValue':'0','EndValue':'250','Unit':'px','Property':
'style','PropertyKey':'top'}]}]}";
  var extender = $find("AnimationExtender1");
  extender.set_OnLoad(animations);
}
</script>
</head>
<body>
  <form id="form1" runat="server">
    <asp:ScriptManager ID="ScriptManager1" runat="server" />
    <div>
      <asp:Label ID="Label1" runat="server" Text="See me fading ..."
        Style="display: inline-block; background-color: Red; position: relative;
left: 8px; top: 8px;" />
    </div>
    <ajaxToolkit:AnimationExtender ID="AnimationExtender1" runat="server"
      TargetControlID="Label1" />
  </form>
</body>
</html>
```

There is much more to the animation framework. In addition to the features demonstrated in this chapter, it is also extendable, providing a great deal of flexibility and taking at least some JavaScript burden off developers' backs. If you are interested in more documentation, the ASP.NET AJAX Control Toolkit sample web site (called *SampleWebsite*) contains a reference as well as a walkthrough.

Drag-and-Drop

Drag-and-drop is considered one of the most difficult tasks for JavaScript developers. All browsers provide drag-and-drop support, but the subtle differences in implementations among different browsers are profound. Fortunately, the ASP.NET AJAX Control Toolkit comes with the DragPanel extender that makes ASP.NET Panel controls "draggable." To drag-and-drop elements, simply put them into an <asp:Panel> element then add the DragPanelExtender control to the page. Next, set the following properties of the extender:

TargetControlID
> The ID of the panel

DragHandleID
> The ID of an element that serves as the drag handle (should ideally be placed within the panel to be dragged)

Example 11-5 contains two panels: one contains dummy text, the other contains an inbox with a random number of new emails. This box can be dragged thanks to the DragPanelExtender control. Figure 11-3 shows the result.

Example 11-5. Making a panel "draggable"

DragPanel.aspx

```
<%@ Page Language="C#" %>

<!DOCTYPE html PUBLIC "-//W3C//DTD XHTML 1.0 Transitional//EN"
"http://www.w3.org/TR/xhtml1/DTD/xhtml1-transitional.dtd">

<script runat="server">
  protected void Page_Load(object sender, EventArgs e)
  {
    inbox.Text = new Random().Next(0, 100).ToString();
  }
</script>

<html xmlns="http://www.w3.org/1999/xhtml">
<head id="Head1" runat="server">
  <title>ASP.NET AJAX</title>
  <style type="text/css">
  .box { border: solid 2px black; }
  .mailbox { border: solid 2px black; width: 150px; background-color: white;}
  .mailboxHeader {border: solid 2px black; background-color: blue; font-weight:
bold; cursor: move;}
  </style>
</head>
<body>
  <form id="form1" runat="server">
    <asp:ScriptManager ID="ScriptManager1" runat="server">
    </asp:ScriptManager>
    <div style="height: 400px; background-color: purple">
      <asp:Panel ID="ContentPanel" CssClass="box" runat="server">
        <h1>My Portal</h1>
        <p>
          Welcome to your personal portal, powered by Microsoft ASP.NET AJAX.
          The mail status window is freely draggable. Welcome to your personal
portal, powered by Microsoft ASP.NET AJAX.
          The mail status window is freely draggable. Welcome to your personal
portal, powered by Microsoft ASP.NET AJAX.
          The mail status window is freely draggable.
```

Example 11-5. Making a panel "draggable" (continued)

```
    </p>
    <p>
        Welcome to your personal portal, powered by Microsoft ASP.NET AJAX.
        The mail status window is freely draggable. Welcome to your personal
portal, powered by Microsoft ASP.NET AJAX.
        The mail status window is freely draggable. Welcome to your personal
portal, powered by Microsoft ASP.NET AJAX.
        The mail status window is freely draggable.
    </p>
    <p>
        Welcome to your personal portal, powered by Microsoft ASP.NET AJAX.
        The mail status window is freely draggable. Welcome to your personal
portal, powered by Microsoft ASP.NET AJAX.
        The mail status window is freely draggable. Welcome to your personal
portal, powered by Microsoft ASP.NET AJAX.
        The mail status window is freely draggable.
    </p>
  </asp:Panel>
  <asp:Panel CssClass="mailbox" ID="DragPanel" runat="server">
    <div id="DragPanelHandle" runat="server" class="mailboxHeader">New
mail!</div>
    <p>
        You currently have <asp:Label id="inbox" runat="server"></asp:Label>
        mails in your <a href="http://www.hotmail.com/">inbox</a>.
    </p>
  </asp:Panel>
  <ajaxToolkit:DragPanelExtender ID="DragPanelExtender1" runat="server"
    TargetControlID="DragPanel" DragHandleID="DragPanelHandle" />
  </div>
  </form>
</body>
</html>
```

> Note the purple area within the page. The `DragPanelExtender` uses the
> current block element in which it resides as the drop zone (the area
> where the panel may be dropped). In this case, a `<div>` element with a
> height of 400 pixels is used to create such a drop zone; the purple
> background shows where the zone is.

Summary

Not every web application gets better when you add animations. However if you do
need them, try the `Animation` framework in the ASP.NET AJAX Control Toolkit. And
if drag-and-drop functionality is required, have a look at the `DragPanel` extender.

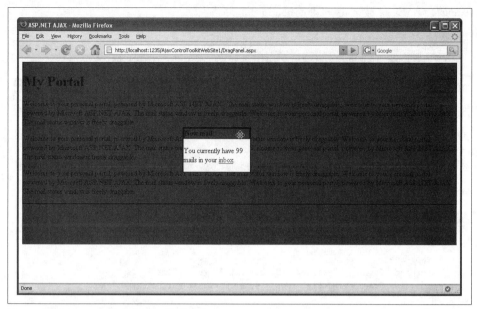

Figure 11-3. A panel with drag-and-drop features

For Further Reading

http://ajax.asp.net/ajaxtoolkit/Animation/Animation.aspx
    Documentation for the Animation framework

http://ajax.asp.net/ajaxtoolkit/DragPanel/DragPanel.aspx
    Documentation for the DragPanel extender

CHAPTER 12

Autocompleting User Input, Fighting Spam, and More

The ASP.NET AJAX Control Toolkit contains an incredible number of controls—too many, in fact, to list here. And while the project is ultimately controlled by Microsoft and does receive support from individual members of the Microsoft AJAX team, there is no guarantee that APIs and functionality will remain the same. After all, the company provides no customer support and does accept (in fact encourages) contributions from third parties. Meanwhile, a printed book can only provide a snapshot of conditions as they existed at the time of production. So, this chapter will demonstrate a few of my favorite controls as they were at the time of printing.

 The ASP.NET AJAX Control Toolkit is a very dynamic project. All of it is subject to change at one point or another. However, the Control Toolkit team strives to keep APIs stable unless there are very good reasons to change them, so you should not expect to come across too many surprises. This chapter will restrict itself to introductory examples of the most important (arguably) of these controls. Updates to these listings will be posted on the web site for this book (see the Preface).

Creating an Accordion Pane

Many usability studies suggest that users do not like scrolling. With the addition of a little bit of JavaScript, scrolling may be avoided. The ASP.NET AJAX Control Toolkit's Accordion control coordinates the presentation of several panes simultaneously but with only one being visible at a time. Using an animation effect, clicking on a pane displays its contents while hiding the contents of all other panes.

The Accordion control consists of two parts: a header that displays a title that is always visible, and a content area that can be hidden or displayed as part of the accordion effect. To implement accordion behavior in a pane, we start by defining two CSS classes in a new *.aspx* file, one for the header and one for content.

These classes define the appearance of the control (and a little bit of its behavior) and will be used later for the panes and for the content of those panes.

```
<style type="text/css">
  .accordionHeader { background-color: blue; border: solid; cursor: pointer; }
  .accordionContent { fbackground-color: white; border: solid; }
</style>
```

 The cursor: pointer CSS style is used for the header. When the mouse pointer hovers over an accordion pane that is using the accordionHeader CSS class, it changes to a pointing hand, as it would do over a hyperlink. This informs users that the panes can be clicked.

In the actual Accordion control, these two CSS classes are referenced:

```
<ajaxToolkit:Accordion ID="Accordion1" runat="server"
  ContentCssClass="accordionContent" HeaderCssClass="accordionHeader">
```

Within the Accordion control, the <Panes> element holds a list of accordion panes, represented by AccordionPane controls. Each AccordionPane control expects these two subelements:

<Header>
    The pane's header

<Content>
    The pane's content

Thanks to IntelliSense, you almost can't go wrong when you create a page with an Accordion control. Example 12-1 shows a complete example and Figure 12-1 its output in the browser.

Example 12-1. Using the Accordion control

Accordion.aspx

```
<%@ Page Language="C#" %>

<!DOCTYPE html PUBLIC "-//W3C//DTD XHTML 1.0 Transitional//EN"
"http://www.w3.org/TR/xhtml1/DTD/xhtml1-transitional.dtd">

<html xmlns="http://www.w3.org/1999/xhtml">
<head runat="server">
  <title>ASP.NET AJAX</title>
  <style type="text/css">
    .accordionHeader { background-color: blue; border: solid; cursor: pointer; }
    .accordionContent { background-color: white; border: solid; }
  </style>
</head>
<body>
  <form id="form1" runat="server">
    <asp:ScriptManager ID="ScriptManager1" runat="server" />
    <div>
```

Example 12-1. Using the Accordion control (continued)

```
        <ajaxToolkit:Accordion ID="Accordion1" runat="server"
          ContentCssClass="accordionContent" HeaderCssClass="accordionHeader">
          <Panes>
            <ajaxToolkit:AccordionPane ID="AccordionPane1" runat="server">
              <Header>ASP.NET AJAX, Ajax, and ASP.NET</Header>
              <Content>Chapter 1 gives a high-level overview of Ajax and the ASP.NET AJAX
framework and then covers the installation of ASP.NET AJAX,
a review of its structure, and a first simple example.</Content>
            </ajaxToolkit:AccordionPane>
            <ajaxToolkit:AccordionPane ID="AccordionPane2" runat="server">
              <Header>JavaScript</Header>
              <Content>Chapter 2 is a concise introduction to JavaScript. Although
ASP.NET AJAX does its best to hide the details from ASP.NET programmers,
a certain knowledge of JavaScript is required to really master ASP.NET AJAX.</Content>
            </ajaxToolkit:AccordionPane>
            <ajaxToolkit:AccordionPane ID="AccordionPane3" runat="server">
              <Header>Ajax</Header>
              <Content>Chapter 3 explains the technologies beyond the hype.
You learn what happens in the background, how Ajax works, and what it really is all about,
in fewer than 20 pages.</Content>
            </ajaxToolkit:AccordionPane>
          </Panes>
        </ajaxToolkit:Accordion>
      </div>
    </form>
  </body>
</html>
```

Figure 12-1. Creating an accordion effect without any code

Maintaining the Relative Position of an Element

CSS allows you to position HTML elements anywhere on a page using x-y coordinates. However, the position of a control can change as the user scrolls the page. With a bit of JavaScript, you can maintain the element's position, so that it appears at the same relative position in the browser no matter where the user scrolls.

As you might probably expect, the ASP.NET AJAX Control Toolkit offers a solution for this task, the AlwaysVisibleControlExtender control. This extender can be attached to any control and enables positioning relative to the browser borders. For instance, the HorizontalSide property of the extender can be set to Center, Left, and Right; the VerticalSide property can be set to Top, Middle, or Bottom. You can also provide offset values to the left and top border of the browser in the HorizontalOffset and VerticalOffset properties. Here is some sample markup for the extender that positions an HTML element in the top-left corner of the browser:

```
<ajaxToolkit:AlwaysVisibleControlExtender ID="AlwaysVisibleControlExtender1"
runat="server" TargetControlID="banner" HorizontalSide="Left" VerticalSide="Top" />
```

Example 12-2 contains a complete listing with the output shown in Figure 12-2. The figure illustrates how the banner remains in the top-left corner as you scroll the page.

Example 12-2. Using the AlwaysVisibleControlExtender

AlwaysVisible.aspx

```
<%@ Page Language="C#" %>

<!DOCTYPE html PUBLIC "-//W3C//DTD XHTML 1.0 Transitional//EN"
"http://www.w3.org/TR/xhtml1/DTD/xhtml1-transitional.dtd">

<html xmlns="http://www.w3.org/1999/xhtml">
<head runat="server">
  <title>ASP.NET AJAX</title>
</head>
<body>
  <form id="form1" runat="server">
    <asp:ScriptManager ID="ScriptManager1" runat="server" />
    <div id="banner" style="background-color: white; border: solid; width: 240px;
height: 80px;" runat="server">
      <h2>And here is from our sponsors ...</h2>
    </div>
    <ajaxToolkit:AlwaysVisibleControlExtender ID="AlwaysVisibleControlExtender1"
runat="server"
      TargetControlID="banner" HorizontalSide="Left" VerticalSide="Top" />
    <p>Welcome to the ASP.NET AJAX Control Toolkit sample website. </p>
    <p>Welcome to the ASP.NET AJAX Control Toolkit sample website. </p>
    <p>Welcome to the ASP.NET AJAX Control Toolkit sample website. </p>
    <p>Welcome to the ASP.NET AJAX Control Toolkit sample website. </p>
    <p>Welcome to the ASP.NET AJAX Control Toolkit sample website. </p>
    <p>Welcome to the ASP.NET AJAX Control Toolkit sample website. </p>
    <p>Welcome to the ASP.NET AJAX Control Toolkit sample website. </p>
    <p>Welcome to the ASP.NET AJAX Control Toolkit sample website. </p>
    <p>Welcome to the ASP.NET AJAX Control Toolkit sample website. </p>
    <p>Welcome to the ASP.NET AJAX Control Toolkit sample website. </p>
  </form>
</body>
</html>
```

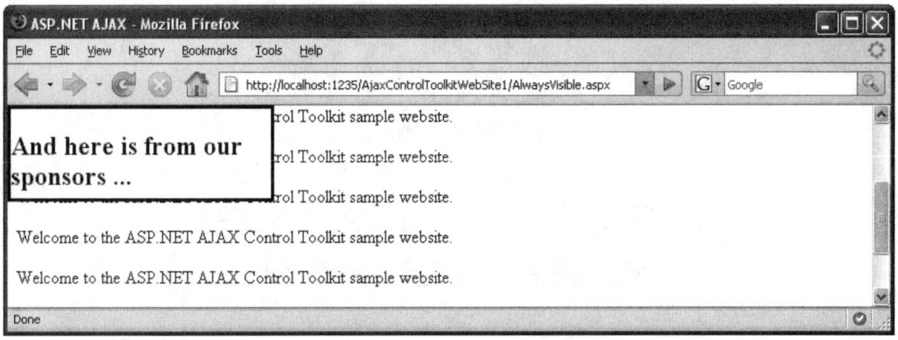

Figure 12-2. The banner appears at the top-left corner, even after scrolling

Adding Autocomplete Behavior to a TextBox Control

The use of Ajax technologies has made it possible for web applications to become more and more like desktop applications. One feature some desktop applications have, but web sites often lack is autocomplete. When entering information in a text box, the application looks up data suitable for the field (within most browsers for instance, a list of previously entered data in similar fields) and offers to fill in the field for you.

One of the first well-known web applications to support this feature was Google Suggest (*http://www.google.com/webhp?complete=1&hl=en*). When you start typing in the text field, the web page suggests popular search terms. It also shows approximately how many results this search may turn up, as shown in Figure 12-3. By now you know how this is done; an `XMLHttpRequest` is sent to a web service, which returns search terms and the estimated number of results.

ASP.NET AJAX provides a control extender called `AutoCompleteExtender` that serves just this purpose; searching data in the background, then presenting the results of that search as data for a form element. This task involves coding the CSS and Java-Script necessary to display the suggestions and make them keyboard-navigable. With an extender from the Control Toolkit, this work has already been done, and you simply need to apply this feature and create a web service that can return the data. Note however, that some of the more tricky bits of Google Suggest (including the keyboard navigation) are not fully implemented in the extender.

From the point of view of web control, the only element for which autocompletion ultimately makes sense is `TextBox`. Following is a snippet demonstrating the element:

```
<asp:TextBox ID="vendor" runat="server"></asp:TextBox>
```

Figure 12-3. Google Suggest

Next, the `AutoCompleteExtender` control must be included. Within this element, several properties can be used to configure the autocompletion effect. The following element attributes are the most important ones:

`TargetControlID`
> The ID of the control you want to perform autocompletion

`ServicePath`
> The path to the web service that generates the autocompletion data

`ServiceMethod`
> The method of the web service that you call to get autocompletion data

Here is some sample markup for the extender:

```
<ajaxToolkit:AutoCompleteExtender runat="server"
    ServicePath="Vendors.asmx" ServiceMethod="GetVendors"
    TargetControlID="vendor" />
```

Example 12-3 shows how to create an ASP.NET page with a text box that supports autocompletion behavior.

Example 12-3. Adding autocompletion behavior to a text box

`AutoComplete.aspx`

```
<%@ Page Language="C#" %>

<%@ Register Assembly="AjaxControlToolkit" Namespace="AjaxControlToolkit"
TagPrefix="ajaxToolkit" %>
<!DOCTYPE html PUBLIC "-//W3C//DTD XHTML 1.0 Transitional//EN"
```

Example 12-3. Adding autocompletion behavior to a text box (continued)

```
"http://www.w3.org/TR/xhtml1/DTD/xhtml1-transitional.dtd">
<html xmlns="http://www.w3.org/1999/xhtml">
<head id="Head1" runat="server">
  <title>ASP.NET AJAX</title>
</head>
<body>
  <form id="form1" runat="server">
    <asp:ScriptManager ID="ScriptManager1" runat="server">
    </asp:ScriptManager>
    <asp:TextBox ID="vendor" runat="server"></asp:TextBox>
    <input type="button" value="Display Information"
           onclick="window.alert('not implemented!');" />
    <ajaxToolkit:AutoCompleteExtender runat="server"
        ServicePath="Vendors.asmx" ServiceMethod="GetVendors"
        TargetControlID="vendor" />
  </form>
</body>
</html>
```

You must also implement a web service that retrieves the data. The web service must include a method the extender can call, which requires a specific signature. Here is the signature:

```
public string[] <MethodName>(string prefixText, int count)
```

The method takes two parameters with rather obvious meanings:

prefixText
> The text that the user enters into the text field, which must be the prefix of all matches

count
> The maximum number of results to be returned

The return data must be an array of string, so unfortunately, you cannot use a dataset or something similar.

Exploring Data Sent by ASP.NET AJAX

Sniffing the XMLHttpRequest call can help you to find out what data ASP.NET AJAX sends to the server. And as you can see in Figure 12-4, it is also a helpful measure in further exploring the inner workings of ASP.NET AJAX when working with server components.

In the example web service, the *AdventureWorks* database is queried for the auto-completion data. The company names of all vendors are returned. As usual, you may

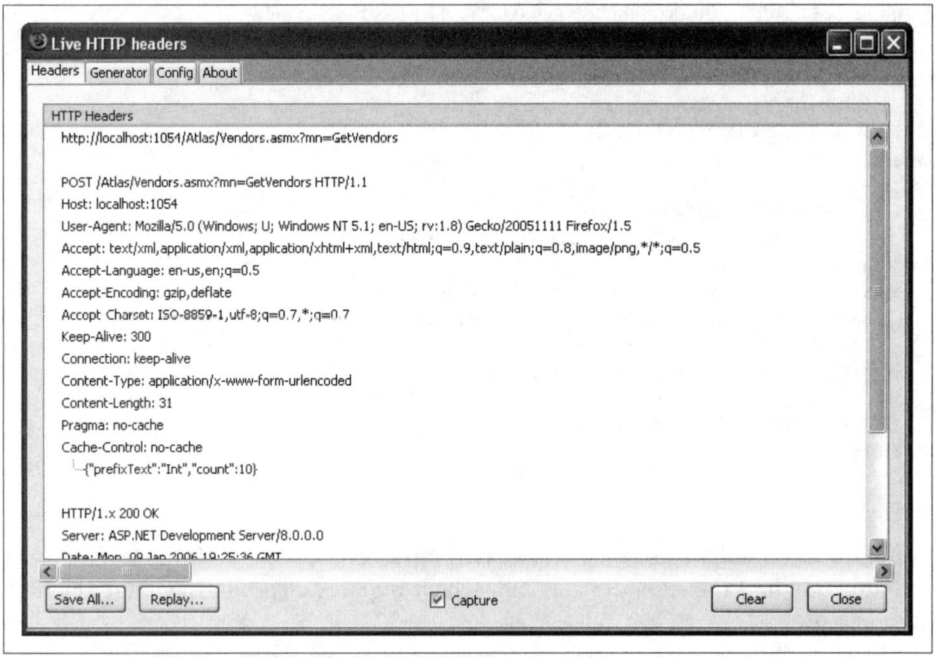

Figure 12-4. Tools such as Live HTTP headers reveal the signature

have to adapt the connection string to your local system—in the code, we assume that the SQL Server 2005 Express Edition is available using Windows authentication at (local)\SQLEXPRESS.

To begin, the web service code checks the search term. For the sake of simplicity, only letters from a to z (both upper- and lowercase) are allowed. This data check is mandatory to avoid SQL injection, because the code must execute a search query with LIKE (see the upcoming sidebar, "Security Alert: Avoiding SQL Injection"). As an alternative, you could use a parameterized query.

If you use a regular expression to validate input data, consider allowing foreign-language characters such as German umlauted letters or French accented letters. The "dangerous" characters from a security standpoint that you do not want to accept are single quotes, double quotes, square brackets, underscore characters, double hyphens, semicolons, and percent characters. These characters (and their encoded versions) all have a special meaning within the query. That's why it's better to validate user input using a *whitelist* approach (allow a predefined set of valid input) rather than a *blacklist* approach (disallow a predefined set of invalid input).

The web service also checks the count parameter provided to the method to make sure it is a positive number and not greater than 100 (to avoid providing an easy way to launch denial-of-service [DoS] attacks).

Security Alert: Avoiding SQL Injection

SQL injection is one of the most dangerous security vulnerabilities in web applications today. The issue arises when dynamic data from the user is employed to construct a SQL query. For example, have a look at the string concatenation in the vendor's web service that generates the SQL command:

```
SqlCommand comm = new SqlCommand(
  "SELECT TOP " +
    count +
    " Name FROM Purchasing.Vendor WHERE Name LIKE '" +
    PrefixText +
    "%'",
  conn);
```

Now consider count a string, not an integer, or that prefixText is not being checked for "dangerous" values. This code could turn out dangerous. There are several possibilities to exploit this, but look at the following value for prefixText:

```
' OR 2>1 --
```

Then, the SQL command will look similar to this:

```
SELECT TOP 10 Name FROM Purchasing.Vendor WHERE Name LIKE '' OR 2 > 1 -- %'
```

This would return the first 10 entries of the table, not just the first 10 that match some specific letter. There are still other, far more dangerous exploits.

Usually, you can prevent this attack by using prepared statements: use placeholders for all user-supplied values in the WHERE clause, then later fill the placeholders with user-supplied data. Unfortunately, this does not work with our specific query because we have to append the % wildcard character to the user data. As an alternative, use a prepared statement and append the % wildcard character to the value of the placeholder (remember to check the placeholder data for special characters like percents [%] and underscores [_]). Therefore, the code first checks prefixText and exits when any characters are found that are not allowed.

This is what the web service code that performs these validations looks like:

```
using System.Text.RegularExpressions;
...
[WebMethod]
public string[] GetVendors(string prefixText, int count)
{
  Regex regex = new Regex("^[a-zA-Z ]*$");
  if (!regex.IsMatch(prefixText) || count < 1 || count > 100)
  {
    return null;
  }
```

After the data is validated, the SQL query is dynamically assembled and sent to the database. A typical query would look like this:

```
SELECT TOP 10 Name FROM Purchasing.Vendor WHERE NAME LIKE 'Int%'
```

This assumes that count has the value 10 (which is, in fact, the value ASP.NET AJAX sends by default) and the user typed Int into the text field. Here is the complete code for the database query, including returning the results into a dataset:

```
SqlConnection conn = new SqlConnection(
   "server=(local)\\SQLEXPRESS; Integrated Security=true; Initial
Catalog=AdventureWorks");
conn.Open( );
SqlCommand comm = new SqlCommand(
   "SELECT TOP " +
     count +
     " Name FROM Purchasing.Vendor WHERE Name LIKE '" +
     prefixText +
     "%'",
   conn);
SqlDataAdapter adap = new SqlDataAdapter(comm);
DataSet ds = new DataSet( );
adap.Fill(ds);
```

Then the data must be transformed into a string array. This array must contain no more than count elements (a call to Math.Min( ) will ensure that only count elements are returned even if the database contains more elements).

This can easily be achieved using a for loop:

```
string[] vendors = new string[Math.Min(count, ds.Tables[0].Rows.Count)];
for (int i = 0; i < Math.Min(count, ds.Tables[0].Rows.Count); i++)
{
  vendors[i] = ds.Tables[0].Rows[i].ItemArray[0].ToString( );
}
return vendors;
}
```

Example 12-4 shows the complete code for implementing this web service. Recall from Chapters 1 and 5 that you need the [ScriptService] attribute in order for ASP.NET AJAX to create the JavaScript proxy for the service.

Example 12-4. A web service that retrieves possible matches

Vendors.asmx

```
<%@ WebService Language="C#" Class="Vendors" %>

using System;
using System.Web;
using System.Web.Services;
```

Example 12-4. A web service that retrieves possible matches (continued)

```
using System.Web.Services.Protocols;
using System.Data;
using System.Data.SqlClient;
using System.Text.RegularExpressions;

[WebService(Namespace = "http://hauser-wenz.de/")]
[WebServiceBinding(ConformsTo = WsiProfiles.BasicProfile1_1)]
[System.Web.Script.Services.ScriptService]
public class Vendors : System.Web.Services.WebService
{

  [WebMethod]
  public string[] GetVendors(string prefixText, int count)
  {
    Regex regex = new Regex("^[a-zA-Z ]*$");
    if (!regex.IsMatch(prefixText) || count < 1 || count > 100)
    {
      return null;
    }
    SqlConnection conn = new SqlConnection(
      "server=(local)\\SQLEXPRESS; Integrated Security=true; Initial
Catalog=AdventureWorks");
    conn.Open( );
    SqlCommand comm = new SqlCommand(
      "SELECT TOP " +
        count +
        " Name FROM Purchasing.Vendor WHERE Name LIKE '" +
        prefixText +
        "%'",
      conn);
    SqlDataAdapter adap = new SqlDataAdapter(comm);
    DataSet ds = new DataSet( );
    adap.Fill(ds);

    string[] vendors = new string[Math.Min(count, ds.Tables[0].Rows.Count)];
    for (int i = 0; i < Math.Min(count, ds.Tables[0].Rows.Count); i++)
    {
      vendors[i] = ds.Tables[0].Rows[i].ItemArray[0].ToString( );
    }
    return vendors;
  }

}
```

Let's take a look at the results in the browser. Load the page and enter a few letters—
at least three (ASP.NET AJAX does not issue a web service call for fewer than three
characters). If some matches are found, they are displayed with a slight delay in the
text box.

With the web service outlined in Example 12-4, caching may be of great use, especially when the same terms are searched over and over again. In set caching, simply change the `WebMethod` attribute of `GetVendors()` to include a cache duration value:

```
[WebMethod(CacheDuration = 60)]
```

The `CacheDuration` value is measured in seconds, so the preceding attribute would cache the web service's results for one minute.

If you are using Microsoft SQL Server as the database backend (as in this example), you can also create a `SqlCacheDependency` on the `DataSet` objects (for further details, consult the recommended resources in the "For Further Reading" section at the end of this chapter).

If you do not get any results, try this: there are several companies whose names begins with the word "International" so entering that word should net a number of matches. Figure 12-5 shows you some typical results.

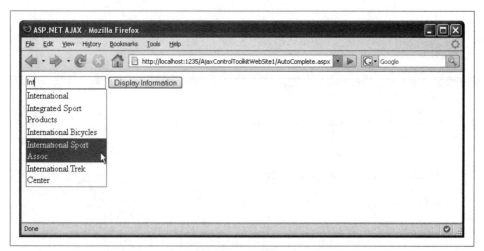

Figure 12-5. ASP.NET AJAX is suggesting vendor names

Attaching a Calendar to a Text Field

Whether it is hotel booking sites, flight booking sites, or rental car booking sites, any page where users make reservations needs to provide a text box to enter a date (the date of arrival and departure for a hotel visit or airline flight itinerary). For convenience, most of those web sites provide a calendar in some fashion or another from which users may choose a date.

You can implement a calendar for your site using the `UpdatePanel` and the ASP.NET `Calendar` control, but the `CalendarExtender` in the ASP.NET AJAX Control Toolkit is more convenient and provides extra features like localization. As you can gather from the name, `CalendarExtender` is indeed, an extender, so it must be attached to a control (generally a text box). Have a look at Example 12-5 to see how little code is necessary to create the effect shown in Figure 12-6. When the user clicks on the text box, the calendar appears. If the user selects a date, the date is automatically entered into the text field. When the text box loses focus, the calendar disappears.

Example 12-5. Using the CalendarExtender

Calendar.aspx

```
<%@ Page Language="C#" %>

<!DOCTYPE html PUBLIC "-//W3C//DTD XHTML 1.0 Transitional//EN"
"http://www.w3.org/TR/xhtml1/DTD/xhtml1-transitional.dtd">

<script runat="server">

</script>

<html xmlns="http://www.w3.org/1999/xhtml">
<head runat="server">
  <title>ASP.NET AJAX</title>
</head>
<body>
  <form id="form1" runat="server">
    <asp:ScriptManager ID="ScriptManager1" runat="server" />
    <div>
      <asp:TextBox ID="TextBox1" runat="server" />
    </div>
    <ajaxToolkit:CalendarExtender ID="CalendarExtender1" runat="server"
      TargetControlID="TextBox1" />
  </form>
</body>
</html>
```

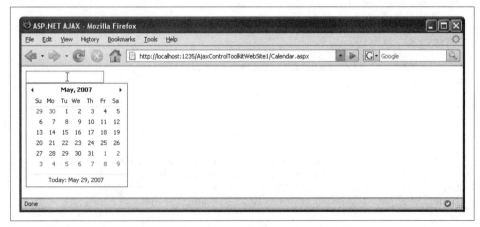

Figure 12-6. The calendar appears when the user clicks into the text field

Dynamically Collapsing a Single Panel

The section "Creating an Accordion Pane," earlier in this chapter, showed how to create an accordion consisting of several panes. Now let's consider that you only have one pane. If this pane is represented in an ASP.NET Panel control, the CollapsiblePanelExtender of the ASP.NET AJAX Control Toolkit can implement the type of behavior that the Accordion extender creates for multiple panes. In the CollapsiblePanelExtender, you need to set the following properties:

CollapseControlID
> The control that collapses the panel

ExpandControlID
> The control that expands the panel

TargetControlID
> The control (pane) that will be collapsed and expanded

Usually, the CollapseControlID and ExpandControlID properties have the same values and point to the header of the panel to expand or collapse. Example 12-6 shows a complete example, using the cursor: pointer CSS style that you saw earlier in the Accordion example. In Figure 12-7, you see the animation that expands the panel. (Of course, a still picture can never capture the real effect!)

Example 12-6. Using the CollapsiblePanelExtender

CollapsiblePanel.aspx

```
<%@ Page Language="C#" %>

<!DOCTYPE html PUBLIC "-//W3C//DTD XHTML 1.0 Transitional//EN"
"http://www.w3.org/TR/xhtml1/DTD/xhtml1-transitional.dtd">

<html xmlns="http://www.w3.org/1999/xhtml">
<head runat="server">
  <title>ASP.NET AJAX</title>
  <style type="text/css">
    .panelHeader { background-color: blue; border: solid; cursor: pointer; }
    .panelContent { background-color: white; border: solid; }
  </style>
</head>
<body>
  <form id="form1" runat="server">
    <asp:ScriptManager ID="ScriptManager1" runat="server" />
    <div>
      <asp:Panel ID="Panel1" runat="server" CssClass="panelHeader">Chapter 1</asp:Panel>
      <asp:Panel ID="Panel2" runat="server" CssClass="panelContent">Chapter 1 gives a
high-level overview of Ajax and the ASP.NET AJAX framework and then covers the
installation of ASP.NET AJAX, a review of its structure, and a first
simple example.</asp:Panel>
    </div>
```

Example 12-6. Using the CollapsiblePanelExtender (continued)

```
    <ajaxToolkit:CollapsiblePanelExtender ID="CollapsiblePanelExtender1" runat="server"
    TargetControlID="Panel2" CollapseControlID="Panel1" ExpandControlID="Panel1" />
    </form>
</body>
</html>
```

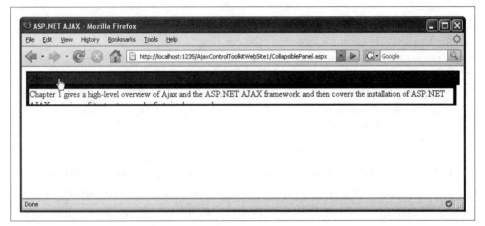

Figure 12-7. The panel expands and collapses upon mouse click

Displaying a Pop Up Over a Page

Modal pop ups were among the first JavaScript effects to be widely adopted by web sites like Google and Amazon who were looking for an interactive edge with their customers. The window.alert( ) method implements the effect, however, the layout of these pop ups could not be changed. Thanks to CSS and the DOM, today you can create better pop ups, without the need to open new windows.

Modal pop ups are commonly generated by creating a new DOM element (usually a <div> container), using JavaScript to display the element, then CSS to style it. To make the pop up modal, you also create a second <div> element that consumes the complete display area of the browser. Then using the z-order CSS property (which sets the virtual z coordinate of an element, effectively placing elements in front of or behind each other), stack both elements over the current content of the page; "100% display area" <div> first, then the pop up <div>. The stacking part is taken care of by ASP.NET AJAX; you just have to provide the rest.

Then, the original content of the page is still visible, but since a 100 percent width, 100 percent height <div> element is placed over it, the user cannot click any links outside the pop up, effectively making the pop up modal.

The first step to implement this is to create the appropriate CSS classes. We need two: one for the pop up, one for the 100 percent display area <div>. For the first class, we just apply a border, a background color, and a width (the height is determined automatically by the browser's rendering engine):

```
.popup {
  border: solid;
  background-color: yellow;
  width: 200px;
}
```

The second CSS class also uses a background color, such as gray, but we also set an opacity value so that the background (the content of the page) is visible through the <div> element. Internet Explorer supports the filter property for this task, and all other browsers use the opacity style.

```
.content {
  background-color: grey;
  filter: alpha(opacity=50);
  opacity: 0.5;
}
```

Next, we need a server control to display the modal pop up. A link is a good choice:

```
<asp:HyperLink ID="HyperLink1" runat="server" Text="More ..." NavigateUrl="#" />
```

Now we create the actual pop up. As shown here, the user could be prompted to log in:

```
<asp:Panel ID="popupPanel" runat="server" CssClass="popup">
  <p>Login to get more information!<br />
    User <input type="text" /> - Password <input type="password" />
    <input type="button" value="Login" id="Button1" runat="server" />
  </p>
</asp:Panel>
```

Finally, the ModalPopupExtender from the ASP.NET AJAX Control Toolkit comes into play. It lets you create a modal pop up that can be put over the current content of the page. This includes a bit of work, both from the toolkit and from you. You will need the following properties for ModalPopupExtender:

BackgroundCssClass
    The CSS class to use to make the page's contents look disabled

PopupControlID
    The ID of the pop up to display

TargetControlID
    The ID of the element that triggers showing the pop up

OKControlID
    The ID of the element that lets the pop up disappear

Refer to Example 12-7 for a complete listing. Figure 12-8 displays the pop up that is positioned over the actual page. (The default position is the center of the page.)

Example 12-7. Using the ModalPopupExtender

ModalPopup.aspx

```
<%@ Page Language="C#" %>

<!DOCTYPE html PUBLIC "-//W3C//DTD XHTML 1.0 Transitional//EN"
"http://www.w3.org/TR/xhtml1/DTD/xhtml1-transitional.dtd">

<html xmlns="http://www.w3.org/1999/xhtml">
<head runat="server">
  <title>ASP.NET AJAX</title>
  <style type="text/css">
  .content {
    background-color: gray;
    filter: alpha(opacity=50);
    opacity: 0.5;
  }
  .popup {
    border: solid;
    background-color: yellow;
    width: 200px;
  }
  </style>
</head>
<body>
  <form id="form1" runat="server">
    <asp:ScriptManager ID="ScriptManager1" runat="server" />
    <asp:Panel ID="contentPanel" runat="server">
      <p>Chapter 1 gives a high-level overview of Ajax and the ASP.NET AJAX
framework and then covers the installation of ASP.NET AJAX, a review of its structure,
and a first simple example.</p>
      <p>Chapter 2 is a concise introduction to JavaScript. Although Atlas does its
 best to hide the details from ASP.NET programmers, a certain knowledge of JavaScript
is required to really master ASP.NET AJAX.</p>
      <p>Chapter 3 explains the technologies beyond the hype. You learn what happens
in the background, how Ajax works, and what it really is all about,
 in fewer than 20 pages.</p>
      <p><asp:HyperLink ID="HyperLink1" runat="server" Text="More ..." NavigateUrl="#" />
</p>
    </asp:Panel>
    <asp:Panel ID="popupPanel" runat="server" CssClass="popup">
      <p>Login to get more information!<br />
        User <input type="text" /> - Password <input type="password" />
        <input type="button" value="Login" id="Button1" runat="server" />
      </p>
    </asp:Panel>
    <ajaxToolkit:ModalPopupExtender ID="ModalPopupExtender1" runat="server"
      PopupControlID="popupPanel" TargetControlID="HyperLink1" OkControlID="Button1"
      BackgroundCssClass="content" />
  </form>
</body>
</html>
```

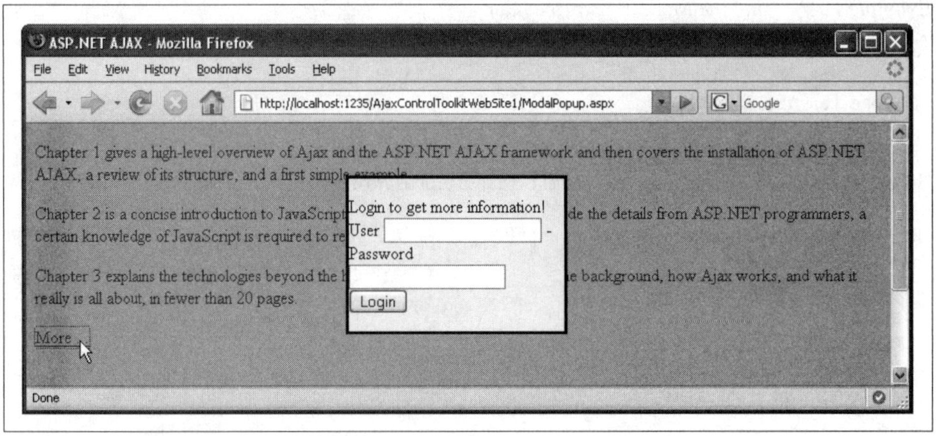

Figure 12-8. The pop up appears; the page's content disappears underneath the gray

Fighting Spam in Blogs and in Other Entry Forms

Anyone who has a blog or a public guestbook knows how annoying and time consuming spammers can be—particularly spammers without a social life who have too much time on their hands. Automated robots surf the Web and try to unload their links, or advertisements, or other undesirable content wherever they find an HTML form.

One common antispam measure in many blogs is a CAPTCHA, for Completely Automated Public Turing test to tell Computers and Humans Apart. When you try to submit a URL to Google, to create a Yahoo! account, or to buy tickets at Ticketmaster, you see an image with some distorted characters. The idea is elegantly simple: only a human can decipher the text—an OCR algorithm will fail. Unfortunately, there are disadvantages: most CAPTCHAs require that the client support images, so accessibility is a key issue. Also, some CAPTCHAs show text that is so distorted that even people with keen visual skills fail to understand it.

The NoBot control in the ASP.NET AJAX Control Toolkit tries to provide a weaker, but more accessible protection for a form. When NoBot is added to a web form, it adds some security checks to the page submission mechanism. For example, it uses ASP.NET session management to determine when the user last submitted the form. If a user repeatedly tries to submit the form without enough time between the HTTP requests, an error message is generated.

This error message is not automatically shown in the browser. Instead, the IsValid( ) method of NoBot checks the form and returns a status message (as an out parameter) if there has been a problem. This data can then be used on the server to provide the appropriate error message to the user. Figure 12-9 shows such an error message created by the code in Example 12-8. In order to create this error message, the form was submitted twice in a two-second interval, which was less than the value specified (for this example, 3) in the ResponseMinimumDelaySeconds property of NoBot.

Example 12-8. Using the NoBot control

AntiSpam.aspx

```
<%@ Page Language="C#" %>

<!DOCTYPE html PUBLIC "-//W3C//DTD XHTML 1.0 Transitional//EN"
"http://www.w3.org/TR/xhtml1/DTD/xhtml1-transitional.dtd">

<script runat="server">

  protected void ProcessData(object sender, EventArgs e)
  {
    NoBotState state;
    if (!NoBot1.IsValid(out state))
    {
      Label1.Text = "Entry refused (" + HttpUtility.HtmlEncode(state.ToString()) + ")!";
    }
    else
    {
      Label1.Text = "Entry accepted!";
    }
  }
</script>

<html xmlns="http://www.w3.org/1999/xhtml">
<head runat="server">
  <title>ASP.NET AJAX</title>
</head>
<body>
  <form id="form1" runat="server">
    <asp:ScriptManager ID="ScriptManager1" runat="server" />
    <div>
      Your blog entry comment:
      <asp:TextBox ID="TextBox1" TextMode="MultiLine" runat="server" />
      <br />
      <asp:Button ID="Button1" runat="server"
        Text="Enter comment" OnClick="ProcessData" />
      <br />
      <asp:Label ID="Label1" runat="server" />
    </div>
    <ajaxToolkit:NoBot ID="NoBot1" runat="server"
      CutoffMaximumInstances="5" CutoffWindowSeconds="30" ResponseMinimumDelaySeconds="3"
/>
  </form>
</body>
</html>
```

The protection provided by NoBot is in no way sufficient for a site that is plagued by loads of spam. However, it can prove quite useful to defeat less sophisticated attacks. It also avoids many of the usability and/or accessibility problems inherent to CAPTCHAs.

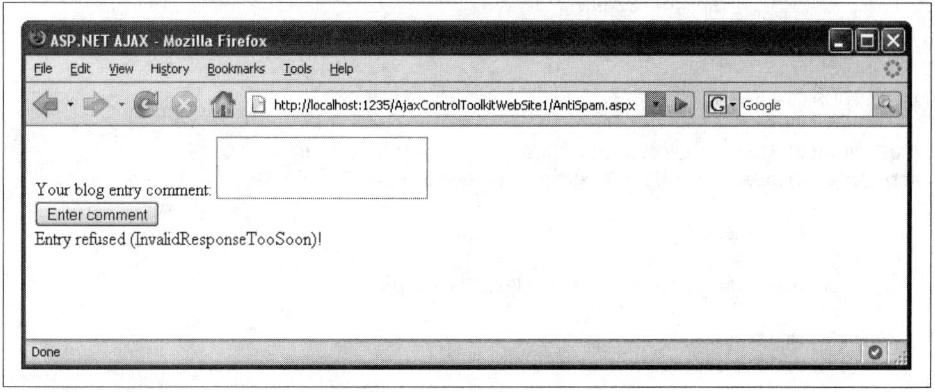

Figure 12-9. The server refuses the data because it was submitted multiple times too quickly

Creating a Tabbed Interface

Most desktop applications and many modern browsers utilize tabbed interfaces. In order to create tabs on a web site, you can use the TabPanel and TabContainer controls in the ASP.NET AJAX Control Toolkit.

Each TabPanel control represents one tab. You can use the HeaderText property to provide a caption for the tab. In a TabPanel child control, the <ContentTemplate> element holds the content of the actual tab, including optional style information:

```
<ajaxToolkit:TabPanel ID="TabPanel1" runat="server" HeaderText="Chapter 1">
   <ContentTemplate>
      Chapter 1 gives a high-level overview of Ajax and the ASP.NET AJAX
framework and then covers the installation of ASP.NET AJAX, a review of its
structure, and a first simple example.
   </ContentTemplate>
</ajaxToolkit:TabPanel>
```

The TabContainer control serves as the container for all TabPanel controls. The ASP.NET AJAX Control Toolkit takes care of the rest. When a user clicks on a tab, its contents automatically appear. See Example 12-9.

Example 12-9. Using the TabContainer and TabPanel controls

Tab.aspx

```
<%@ Page Language="C#" %>

<!DOCTYPE html PUBLIC "-//W3C//DTD XHTML 1.0 Transitional//EN"
"http://www.w3.org/TR/xhtml1/DTD/xhtml1-transitional.dtd">

<html xmlns="http://www.w3.org/1999/xhtml">
```

Example 12-9. Using the TabContainer and TabPanel controls (continued)

```
<head runat="server">
  <title>ASP.NET AJAX</title>
</head>
<body>
  <form id="form1" runat="server">
    <asp:ScriptManager ID="ScriptManager1" runat="server" />
    <div>
      <ajaxToolkit:TabContainer ID="TabContainer1" runat="server">
        <ajaxToolkit:TabPanel ID="TabPanel1" runat="server" HeaderText="Chapter 1">
          <ContentTemplate>
            Chapter 1 gives a high-level overview of Ajax and the ASP.NET AJAX
framework and then covers the installation of ASP.NET AJAX, a review of its structure,
and a first simple example.
          </ContentTemplate>
        </ajaxToolkit:TabPanel>
        <ajaxToolkit:TabPanel ID="TabPanel2" runat="server" HeaderText="Chapter 2">
          <ContentTemplate>
            Chapter 2 is a concise introduction to JavaScript. Although ASP.NET AJAX does
its best to hide the details from ASP.NET programmers, a certain knowledge of JavaScript
is
required to really master ASP.NET AJAX.
          </ContentTemplate>
        </ajaxToolkit:TabPanel>
        <ajaxToolkit:TabPanel ID="TabPanel3" runat="server" HeaderText="Chapter 3">
          <ContentTemplate>
            Chapter 3 explains the technologies beyond the hype. You learn what happens
in the background, how Ajax works, and what it really is all about, in fewer than 20
pages.
          </ContentTemplate>
        </ajaxToolkit:TabPanel>
      </ajaxToolkit:TabContainer>
    </div>
  </form>
</body>
</html>
```

Figure 12-10 illustrates a tabbed interface comprised of three tabs. There is a catch, though—at least for the moment. If you disabled JavaScript in your browser, Example 12-9 will look like Figure 12-11. The reason for that is that the tabs' contents are hidden when the page is loaded; JavaScript then makes the current tab's contents visible. If there is no JavaScript, there are no tabs, either. But who knows, in an upcoming release of the ASP.NET AJAX Control Toolkit, this might work better without scripting support. Enjoy experimenting with the controls!

 Chapter 17 will show you an alternative way to create a tabbed interface, using the ASP.NET AJAX Futures release.

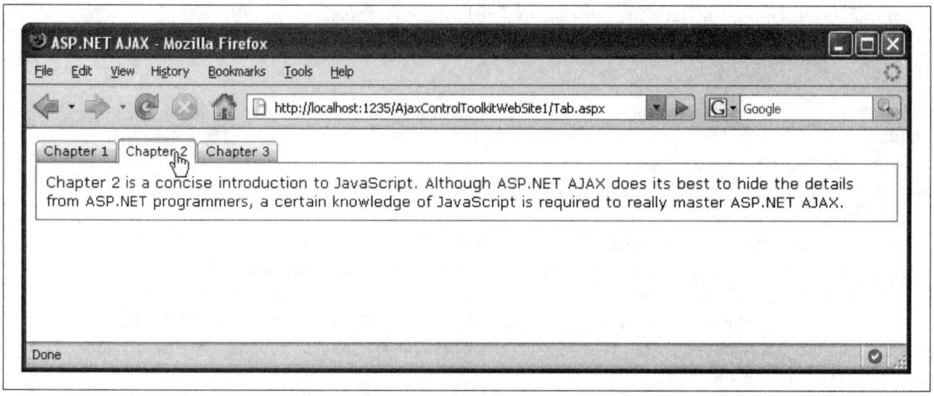

Figure 12-10. A click on the tab displays its contents

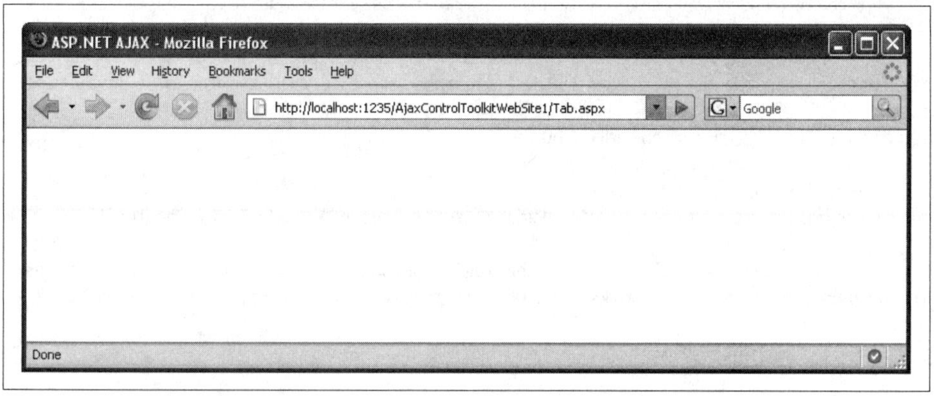

Figure 12-11. No JavaScript, no tabs

Summary

This chapter explained a variety of the controls in the ASP.NET AJAX Control Toolkit. There are many more controls available, and every release brings new features and new controls, so make sure to visit the Toolkit home page often!

For Further Reading

http://ajax.asp.net/ajaxtoolkit/
    Up-to-date live test page for the Control Toolkit

http://www.google.com/webhp?complete=1&hl=en
    Google Suggest

CHAPTER 13

Writing Custom Controls and Contributing to the Community

As you have seen in Chapters 10, 11, and 12, the ASP.NET AJAX Control Toolkit offers a number of valuable controls. This chapter will go one step further by demonstrating how to use the toolkit infrastructure to write your own controls. You will also be introduced to some of the methods to contribute to the Toolkit community at large.

Writing Custom ASP.NET AJAX Controls

The array of controls offered by the ASP.NET AJAX Control Toolkit continues to expand from release to release. Yet in addition to this already impressive list is a framework for creating your own custom controls. If you find yourself using the same JavaScript effects over and over, making them available for reuse via ASP.NET AJAX is a good idea.

In this section, you'll create an extender that restricts input into an HTML text box to a set of predefined characters—functionality not offered by HTML. The ASP.NET AJAX Control Toolkit provides a project template for Visual Studio 2005 to facilitate this work. You begin by installing the template, then modify it and add the logic for the new extender.

As you've seen, the ASP.NET AJAX Control Toolkit comes as one DLL file that contains the complete set of controls. To create a custom control, you will need to compile code. Fortunately, the toolkit is equipped with a Visual Studio template that makes it easy to generate extenders such as the one we are about to create.

In Chapter 10 you were introduced to the VSI installer that created templates for, among other things, the ASP.NET AJAX Toolkit-driven web site. These "other things" were basically C# and VB templates to produce your own custom controls. When you launch Visual Studio and create a new project, note the ASP.NET AJAX Control Project template (see Figure 13-1).

New Project

Project types:
- Test
- Web
- WinFS
- Workflow
- Visual C#
  - Windows
  - NET Framework 3.0
  - Office
  - Smart Device
  - Database
  - Starter Kits
  - Test
  - Web
  - WinFS
  - Workflow
  - Visual J#

Templates:

Visual Studio installed templates

- WinFS Console Application
- WinFS Windows Application
- Class Library
- Windows Control Library
- Device Application
- Outlook Add-in
- ASP.NET Web Service Application
- ASP.NET AJAX CTP Enabled Web A...
- Windows Application
- Windows Application (WPF)
- WCF Service Library
- Console Application
- Excel Workbook
- ASP.NET Web Application
- ASP.NET AJAX-Enabled Web Applic...

My Templates

- "Atlas" Control Project
- Search Online Templates...
- ASP.NET AJAX Control Project

Create new ASP.NET AJAX Control Extenders and Behaviors

Name: TextBoxMask

Location: C:\Documents and Settings\Christian\My Documents\Visual Studio 2005\Projects   Browse...

Solution Name: TextBoxMask   ☑ Create directory for solution

☐ Add to Source Control

OK   Cancel

Figure 13-1. The ASP.NET AJAX Control template

If you are using Visual Web Developer Express Edition, you can install the VSI, but you cannot create a new control extender project. The Express Edition enables you to create only web projects, not custom control projects. However, the project templates work with Microsoft Visual Basic 2005 Express Edition and Microsoft Visual C# 2005 Express Edition. Just as with Visual Web Developer Express Edition, these products are free. If you do not already have one of them installed, visit the Microsoft Express Editions web site (*http://msdn.microsoft.com/vstudio/express*) to download and install one or both. You can then create projects that you can compile to produce .NET assemblies (.*dll* files). Obviously, the most convenient way to use the VSI is with Visual Studio 2005. If you can use Visual Studio 2005, you can create a single solution that contains both the custom extender project as well as the project for the web site that will use the newly created extender.

In the following example, we'll use Visual Studio 2005 and C#. As noted, the example also works with the Express Edition versions of Visual Web Developer, Visual C#, and Visual Basic. However, if you use Visual C# Express Edition or Visual Basic Express Edition, you have to take an extra step during development: every time you make a change to the extender code, you need to recompile it in Visual C# Express Edition or Visual Basic Express Edition, and update the reference.

When you create an extender, you will be extending an existing ASP.NET server control. Therefore, in Visual Studio, open a web site where you can work with the custom extender and an existing ASP.NET control at the same time. Load an ASP.NET AJAX web site in Visual Studio. From the File menu, click Add, then New Project. Choose the ASP.NET AJAX Control Project template, as shown in Figure 13-1. Use TextBoxMask as the project name for this example.

The new template creates a default project, using the project name (therefore, the TextBoxMask extender). It consists initially of four files:

TextBoxMaskBehavior.js
 The JavaScript code that makes up the extender

TextBoxMaskDesigner.cs
 Code used for the Visual Studio designer

TextBoxMaskExtender.cs
 The C# code that makes the extender work with the Visual Studio property inspector at design time, exposing properties so that they can be changed there

Most of your work will go into the most important part of the extender, *TextBoxMaskBehavior.js* where all client-side JavaScript logic resides.

But first let's tweak the two other files for the example. Open the *TextBoxMaskDesigner.cs* file and note that it contains nothing more than an empty class. It looks like the code from Example 13-1.

Example 13-1. The Designer class

```
TextBoxMaskDesigner.cs

using System.Web.UI.WebControls;
using System.Web.UI;

namespace TextBoxMask
{
    class TextBoxMaskDesigner : AjaxControlToolkit.Design.
ExtenderControlBaseDesigner<TextBoxMaskExtender>
    {


    }
}
```

The *TextBoxMaskExtender.cs* file contains designer information about the extender. As you can see in Example 13-2, the code references the *TextBoxMaskBehavior.js* file. The default data type for elements used with this extender is Control. However, as we want to extend a text box, change Control to TextBox.

```
    [TargetControlType(typeof(TextBox))]
```

Further along in the file you will see the one property the template provides: MyProperty. Remove this class member and create a ValidChars string property instead using getter and setter methods. This property will later hold the valid characters that may be entered in the text field.

For these getter and setter methods, use the helper functions GetPropertyValue( ) and SetPropertyValue( ) to access the property value. Also, use the DefaultProperty attribute to make ValidChars the default property for the extender. Example 13-2 contains the complete code.

Example 13-2. The Extender class

TextBoxMaskProperties.cs

```
using System;
using System.Web.UI.WebControls;
using System.Web.UI;
using System.ComponentModel;
using System.ComponentModel.Design;
using AjaxControlToolkit;

[assembly: System.Web.UI.WebResource("TextBoxMask.TextBoxMaskBehavior.js",
"text/javascript")]

namespace TextBoxMask
{
    [Designer(typeof(TextBoxMaskDesigner))]
    [ClientScriptResource("TextBoxMask.TextBoxMaskBehavior",
"TextBoxMask.TextBoxMaskBehavior.js")]
    [TargetControlType(typeof(TextBox))]
    [DefaultProperty("ValidChars")]
    public class TextBoxMaskExtender : ExtenderControlBase
    {
        // TODO: Add your property accessors here.
        //
        [ExtenderControlProperty]
        [DefaultValue("")]
        public string ValidChars
        {
            get
            {
                return GetPropertyValue("ValidChars", "");
            }
            set
            {
                SetPropertyValue("ValidChars", value);
            }
        }
    }
}
```

One property that is available by default and does not have to be registered is `TargetControlID`, which references the control to which the extender is bound.

Finally, you need to create the JavaScript code that extends the functionality of the text boxes to which the control is bound. That code will reside in the file *TextBox-MaskBehavior.js*.

The template *.js* file contains some helpful comments with all the steps you need to take at the places where these steps are required. The first step is to define JavaScript variables for each property of the extender. The syntax convention is to prefix each variable with the underscore (_) character and follow it with a lowercase letter:

```
this._validChars = "";
```

The next step consists of writing getter and setter methods for all properties, if you would like to expose this functionality to JavaScript code. This is a simple task you can carry out mostly with copy and paste. Just keep in mind that JavaScript is case-sensitive, therefore you need to consistent with case for both the JavaScript variables and for the C# property names.

```
get_ValidChars : function() {
  return this._validChars;
},

set_ValidChars : function(value) {
  this._validChars = value;
}
```

The final step covers the initialization code of the extender. This is the where you attach JavaScript code to the control in question. For the example, we're creating an extender that validates user entry into a text box. It will work in the following fashion: the extender exposes a property that enables the page developer to specify a string containing the characters the text box will accept. For example, if the property is set to `"0123456789"`, the text box will accept only numeric characters.

In the example, we want a validation function to be executed when the user presses a key. If the user presses a key that is not one of the permitted characters, the event must be cancelled so that the associated character does not display in the text box.

The event handler must be put in the `initialize()` method of the `TextBoxMaskBehavior` class (the template has already created both the class and the method).

 You may also want to put code in the existing `dispose()` method. This method is called for cleanup purposes. Typically, during the dispose event you release any resources that the control has used, which includes unbinding any event handlers.

We let ASP.NET AJAX scan the browser's capabilities to determine how to look for and handle a user keystroke. The $addhandler() method takes care of most of this work. First, you need to put it in the initialize() method. The code to attach the method to the event looks like this:

```
this._keydownHandler = Function.createDelegate(this, this._onkeydown);
$addHandler(this.get_element(),"keydown", this._keydownHandler);
```

In the dispose() method, you can remove the handler again, this time using the $removehandler() method in the following fashion:

```
$removeHandler(this.get_element(), "keydown", this._keydownHandler);
this._keydownHandler = null;
```

Finally, you must write the actual JavaScript code for the extender. The code first determines which key has been pressed, depending on the browser type. Then the code looks for the key in the list of valid characters. If the key is not in that list, the method ends with return false, which cancels the key event and prevents the character from displaying in the text box. If the key is in the list, the method exits with return true and the key event is propagated.

 The method also returns true when the key codes 8, 9, 16, 35, 36, 37, 38, 39, 40, 45, or 46 are detected—these are the codes for the Backspace key, the Tab key, Shift, Home, End, the four arrow keys, insert, and delete. Another special case is the digits on the numeric keypad (key codes 96 through 105); the JavaScript String.fromCharCode() method does not convert these back to the associated digits. Therefore, any key code between 96 and 105 will be converted into the key code for the appropriate digit key on the regular keyboard.

For Internet Explorer, returning false from a handler method does not suffice to prevent the entered key from displaying in the text box. You must call the preventDefault() method of the key down event.

```
this._onkeydown : function(e) {
  var key = e.rawEvent.keyCode;
  if (key >= 96 && key <= 105) {
    key -= 48;
  }
  if (key == 8 || key == 9 || key == 16
    || (key >= 35 && key <= 40) || key == 45 || key == 46
    || _validChars.indexOf(String.fromCharCode(key)) != -1) {
    return true;
  } else {
    e.preventDefault();
    return false;
  };
}
```

And that's it, as far as JavaScript is concerned. Example 13-3 contains the complete code for your extender. For reference purposes, all comments from the control template remain intact.

Example 13-3. The JavaScript code for the extender

TextBoxMaskBehavior.js

```
// README
//
// There are two steps to adding a property:
//
// 1. Create a member variable to store your property
// 2. Add the get_ and set_ accessors for your property.
//
// Remember that both are case sensitive!
//

Type.registerNamespace('TextBoxMask');

TextBoxMask.TextBoxMaskBehavior = function(element) {

    TextBoxMask.TextBoxMaskBehavior.initializeBase(this, [element]);

    // TODO : (Step 1) Add your property variables here
    //
    this._validChars = null;

}

TextBoxMask.TextBoxMaskBehavior.prototype = {

    initialize : function() {
        TextBoxMask.TextBoxMaskBehavior.callBaseMethod(this, 'initialize');

        // TODO: add your initalization code here
        this._keydownHandler = Function.createDelegate(this, this._onkeydown);
        $addHandler(this.get_element(), "keydown", this._keydownHandler);
    },

    dispose : function() {
        // TODO: add your cleanup code here
        $removeHandler(this.get_element(), "keydown", this._keydownHandler);
        this._keydownHandler = null;

        TextBoxMask.TextBoxMaskBehavior.callBaseMethod(this, 'dispose');
    },


    _onkeydown : function(e) {
      var key = e.rawEvent.keyCode;
      if (key >= 96 && key <= 105) {
```

Example 13-3. The JavaScript code for the extender (continued)

```
        key -= 48;
    }
    if (key == 8 || key == 9 || key == 16
        || (key >= 35 && key <= 40) || key == 45 || key == 46
        || this._validChars.indexOf(String.fromCharCode(key)) != -1) {
        return true;
    } else {
        e.preventDefault( );
        return false;
    }
},


    // TODO: (Step 2) Add your property accessors here
    //
    get_ValidChars : function( ) {
        return this._validChars;
    },

    set_ValidChars : function(value) {
        this._validChars = value;
    }

}

TextBoxMask.TextBoxMaskBehavior.registerClass('TextBoxMask.TextBoxMaskBehavior',
AjaxControlToolkit.BehaviorBase);
```

Now, let's build the project. This will create the *TextBoxMask.dll* file and include the *.js* file as an embedded resource available to the Scriptmanager control at runtime. Usually, the TextBoxMask extender automatically appears in the toolbox. However, you typically need to add this item to your web site project manually. To do this in Solution Explorer, right-click the name of your ASP.NET AJAX web site and choose Add Reference. In the Projects tab, load the *TextBoxMask.dll* assembly. The assembly is then copied automatically to the *Bin* directory.

 If you are using Visual Web Developer Express Edition, you cannot simply reference the custom control project. Rather, you must add a reference to the *TextBoxMask.dll* assembly. In Solution Explorer, right-click the web site name and then click Add Reference. In the Add Reference dialog box, click the Browse button, and then browse to the build folder for your custom control project. A typical location for the project output to reside is as follows:

C:\Documents and Settings\<name>\My Documents\Visual Studio 2005\Projects\TextBoxMask\TextBoxMask\bin\Release

Select the *TextBoxMask.dll* file, then click OK. (If Visual Web Developer prompts you to overwrite existing *.dll*s, click No.)

A reference to the *.dll* file is added to your web project. Whenever you recompile the custom control in Visual C# or Visual Basic, you need to update the reference in Visual Web Developer. To do so, in Solution Explorer, open the *Bin* folder, right-click *TextBoxMask.dll*, and select Update Reference. If you have a page open that uses the control, you may need to close and reopen the page.

 If you are using Visual Studio 2005, rebuilding the C# extender project automatically updates the reference in the web site project.

In the web site project, create a new ASP.NET page. Register a tag prefix for the extender at the top of your ASP.NET page by entering the following markup:

```
<%@ Register Assembly="TextBoxMask" Namespace="TextBoxMask" TagPrefix="cc1"%>
```

Finally, embed the TextBoxMask control on your page—don't forget the ScriptManager control. Add a text box and then bind the extender to its text field by setting the extender's TargetControlID property. The code in Example 13-4 creates a text box that accepts only digits, specified by the string in the ValidChars property. This is a bit tricky to implement with pure JavaScript, so the TextBoxMask extender can really save you time and effort. And as an added benefit, the resulting extender is highly reusable.

Example 13-4. Using the custom extender

TextBoxMask.aspx

```
<%@ Page Language="C#" %>
<%@ Register Assembly="TextBoxMask" Namespace="TextBoxMask" TagPrefix="cc1"%>

<!DOCTYPE html PUBLIC "-//W3C//DTD XHTML 1.1//EN"
"http://www.w3.org/TR/xhtml11/DTD/xhtml11.dtd">
<html xmlns="http://www.w3.org/1999/xhtml">
<head runat="server">
  <title>ASP.NET AJAX</title>
</head>
<body>
  <form id="form1" runat="server">
    <asp:ScriptManager ID="ScriptManager1" runat="server" />
    <cc1:TextBoxMaskExtender ID="TextBoxMaskExtender1" runat="server"
      TargetControlID="TextBox1" ValidChars="1234567890" />
    <div>
      <asp:TextBox ID="TextBox1" runat="server"></asp:TextBox>
    </div>
  </form>
</body>
</html>
```

Figure 13-2 shows how the page looks in a browser. And although you cannot see what happens when you try to press a nondigit key (result: nothing), the screenshot does give you an idea of how this extender can be used to allow only certain content in a page.

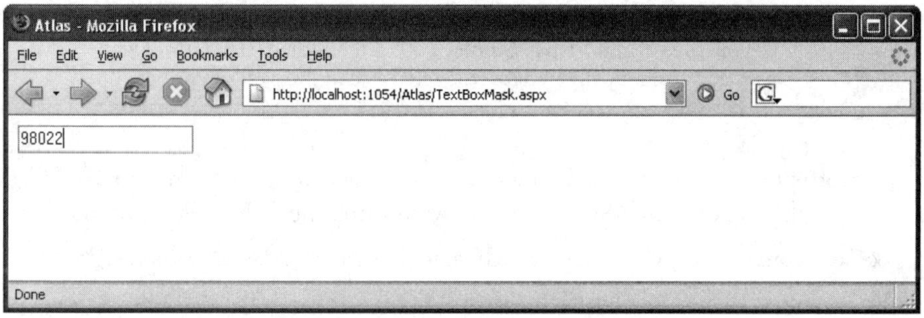

Figure 13-2. The text field now accepts only digits

Additional features you could add to this extender (which implements a whitelist approach) include a blacklist mechanism—all characters are allowed except those that you explicitly exclude. You could also implement an extender that enables you to specify a character mask. The extender could then validate user data against the mask.

Contributing to the Control Toolkit

So far, you have seen how to create a component using the ASP.NET AJAX Control Toolkit infrastructure. From there, you could submit the new extender to be included as a permanent part of the Control Toolkit project. It will be reviewed by the toolkit team and, if crafted well enough, eventually it could be accepted into the toolkit for use by the community at large. However, there are easier ways to contribute to the community effort. For instance, you could provide patches for the toolkit: code snippets that fix a bug or add a new feature. The toolkit team provides you with a convenient tool that allows you to both download the most up to date version, then send in your patches. In this section, we will guide you through that process, actually fixing a feature request that existed at the time of writing (the focus here will be on the process, not on the feature or its code).

First, you need the toolkit patch utility available at *http://ajax.asp.net/ajaxtoolkit/patchtool/*. Be sure to install both the .NET Framework 2.0 and the Visual J# .Net Redistributable Package 2.0 (the utility page has links to each of them). Figure 13-3 shows you the patch utility page.

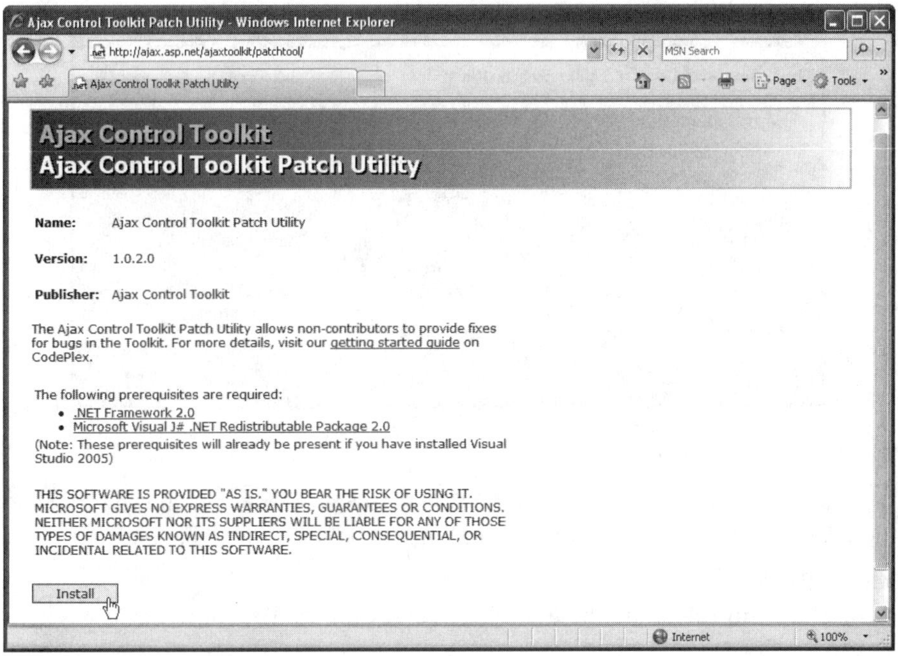

Figure 13-3. The Ajax Control Toolkit Patch Utility page

Click the Install button to begin the process. A screen appears asking you to confirm the installation (Figure 13-4). Upon confirmation, the application and tools are downloaded and installed (Figure 13-5).

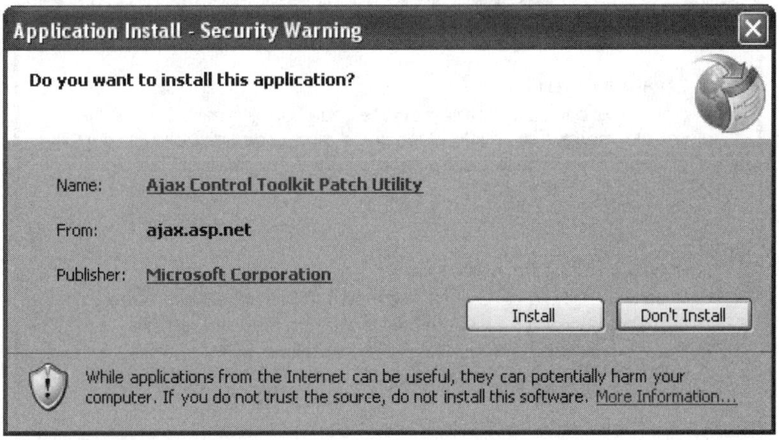

Figure 13-4. The patch utility will be installed

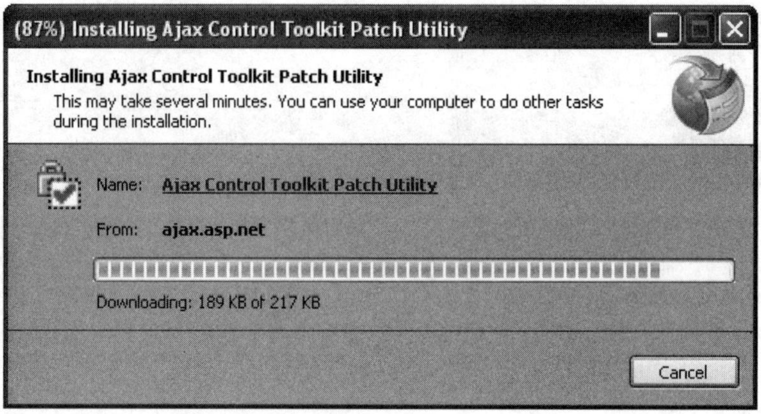

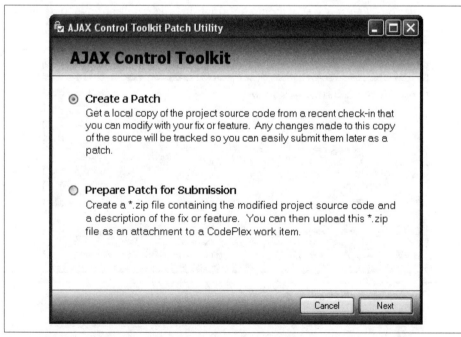

Figure 13-5. The patch utility is being downloaded

The installer adds the patch utility to the Windows Start menu and launches the application. You are then presented with two options in the start dialog (Figure 13-6):

Create a Patch
> Assists in downloading the ASP.NET AJAX Control Toolkit to begin work on a patch

Prepare Patch for Submission
> Bundles a patch to be uploaded to the toolkit project page at CodePlex

Figure 13-6. The start dialog of the patch utility

Choose the Create a Patch option. After a short while, you will receive a list of all available ASP.NET AJAX Control Toolkit versions (Figure 13-7). You could download and use the latest release version, but the best option is to use the most up-to-date code. Otherwise, changes you apply to one file might conflict with other recent changes to the same file. The first download presented is always the most recent one.

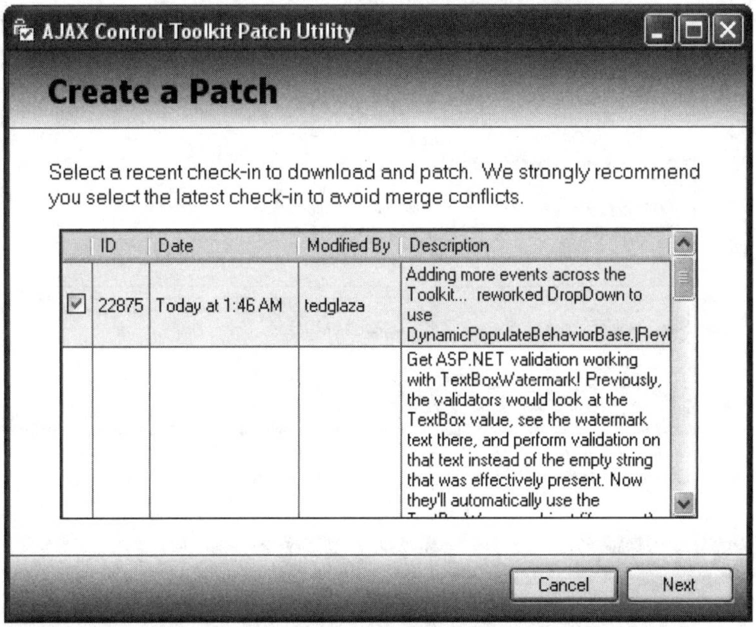

Figure 13-7. Select a toolkit version—the most recent one is recommended

Upon acceptance of the license agreement (Figure 13-8), the selected version is downloaded. The patch utility then prompts you to select a directory in which to unzip the downloaded code. When clicking the "Choose folders to include" link, you will be presented a list of branches to unzip, as shown in Figure 13-9. Select only the Development Branch; the Release Branch and Orcas Branch are, for all intents and purpose, not accessible. Even some control toolkit members are not allowed to check in code for these two branches.

After unzipping the toolkit, the patch utility automatically opens the project in Visual Studio (assuming the default option remained set to "Open the project in Visual Studio upon completion"). Visual Studio might then prompt you with one or two security warnings (as shown in Figure 13-10); use the "Load project normally" option to have full access to the project.

The next step is probably the hardest: creating the patch itself. Open the toolkit source code, add functionality or fix issues, save your changes, rebuild the project, and then test the code.

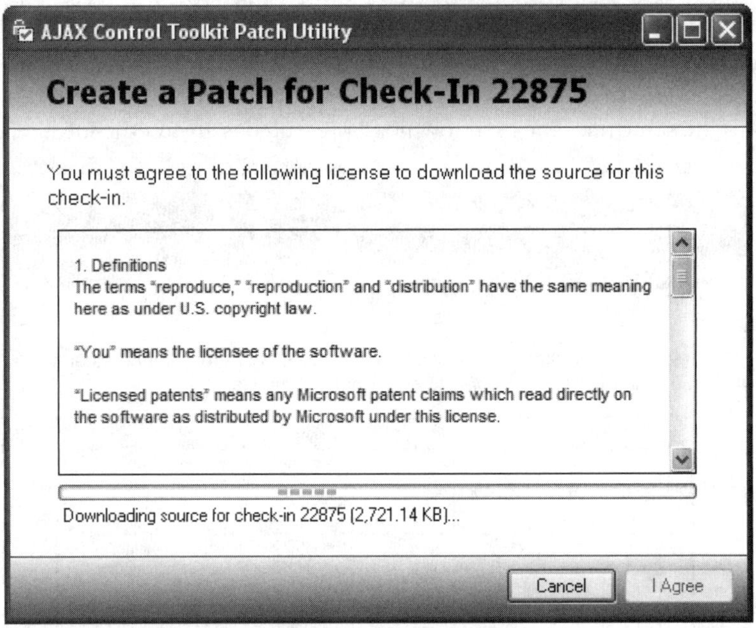

Figure 13-8. Read the license, and then the source code is downloaded

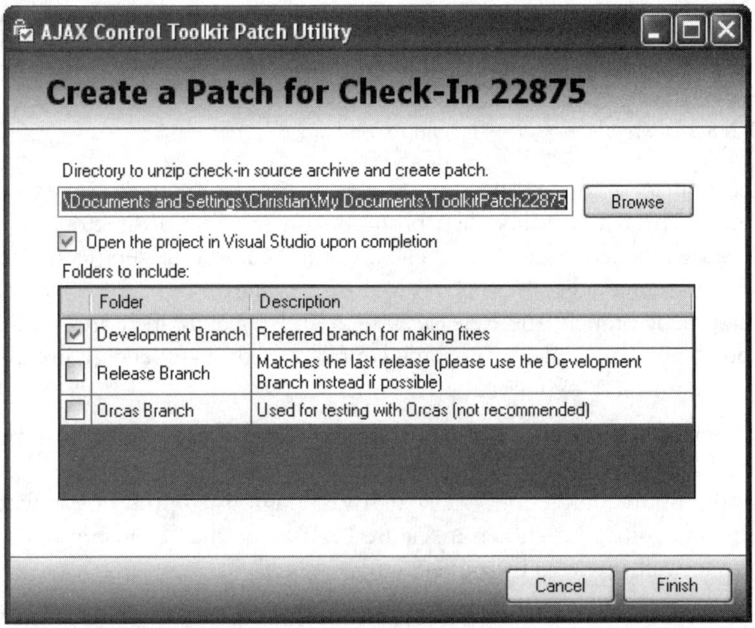

Figure 13-9. You only need to download the Development Branch

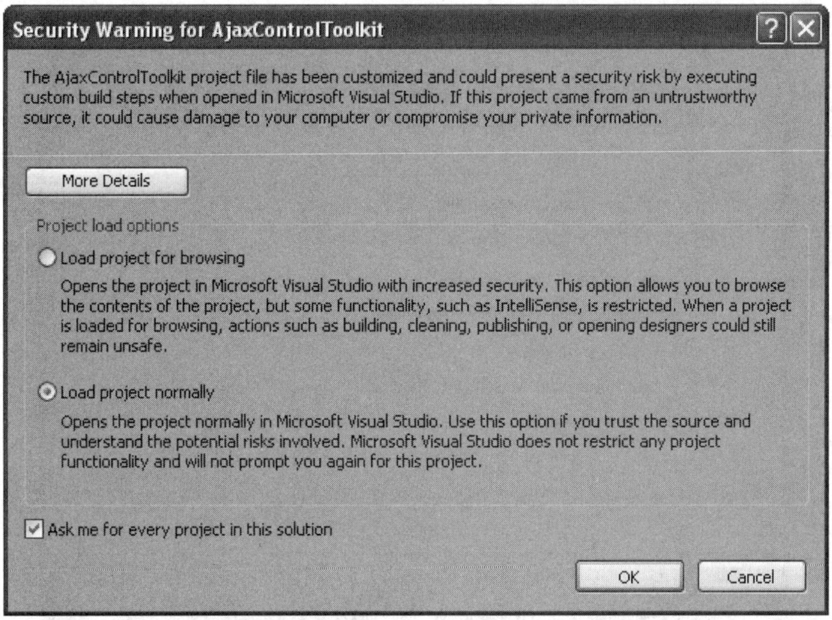

Figure 13-10. You can ignore this warning when opening the project in Visual Studio

When you are finished, start the patch utility again. This time, choose the second option in the start dialog, Prepare Patch for Submission. The utility prompts you to confirm that you did, in fact, test and comment your code (see Figure 13-11). If you added additional functionality, you should provide test results for that as well. Refer to the toolkit test web site to view existing tests and to add new ones.

The next step requires the name of the directory where you previously downloaded the ASP.NET AJAX Control Toolkit. By default, the patch utility chooses the path from the last download (see Figure 13-12).

You will then be presented a list of files that you modified (Figure 13-13). Uncheck all files that are not absolutely necessary—for example, change to the *Web.config* file. Clicking the Diff link next to each file prepares a comparison of your updated file with the original file, and displays a detailed listing of any changes you made (Figure 13-14).

You are nearly there. Now it's time to supply a meaningful description for your patch (Figure 13-15) and provide the toolkit team your contact information in case they want to get in touch with you. Be aware, however, that this information is publicly visible. Finally, click on the Finish button to save the patch in a ZIP file (see Figure 13-16).

One final step: visit the CodePlex page for the ASP.NET AJAX Control Toolkit (*http://www.codeplex.com/AtlasControlToolkit*) and navigate to the work item, which you've modified (entry in the bug tracking system). If no work item exists yet, create one.

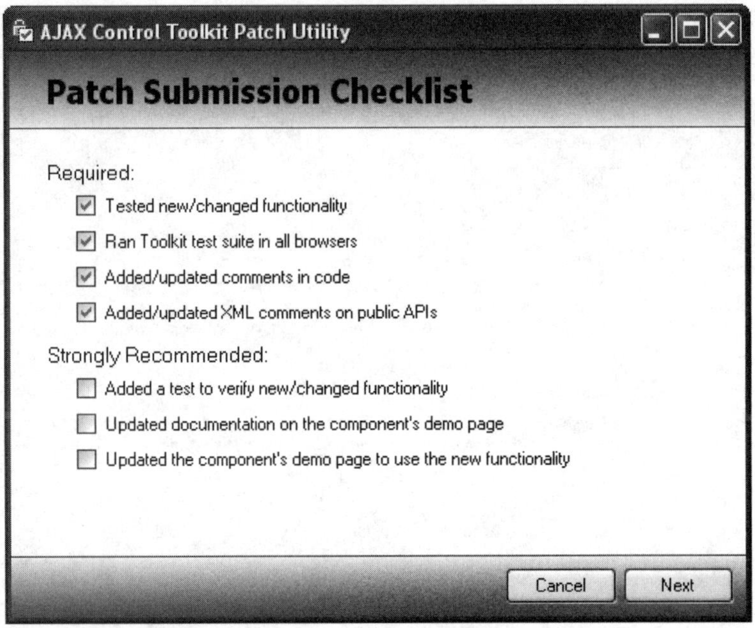

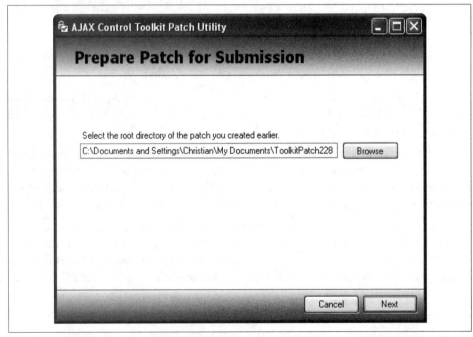

Figure 13-11. A checklist before packaging the patch

Figure 13-12. Where do you want to save the patch?

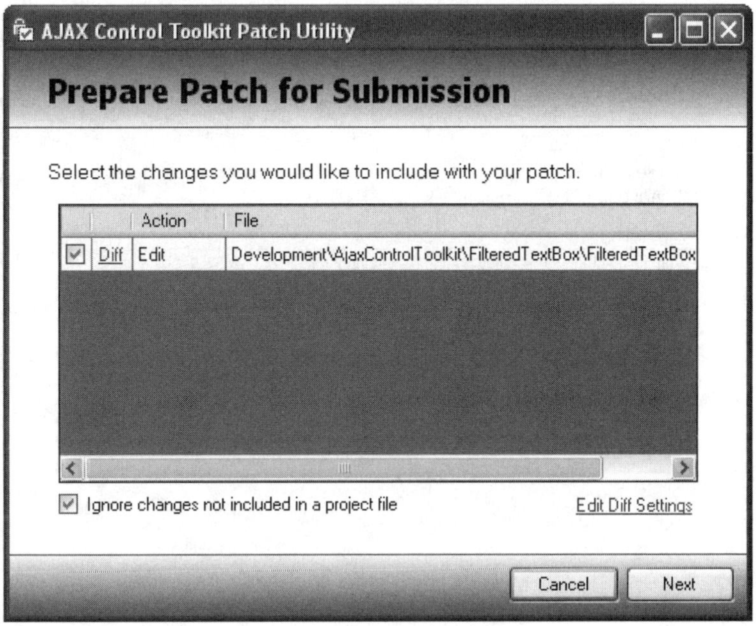

Figure 13-13. A list of files that have been changed

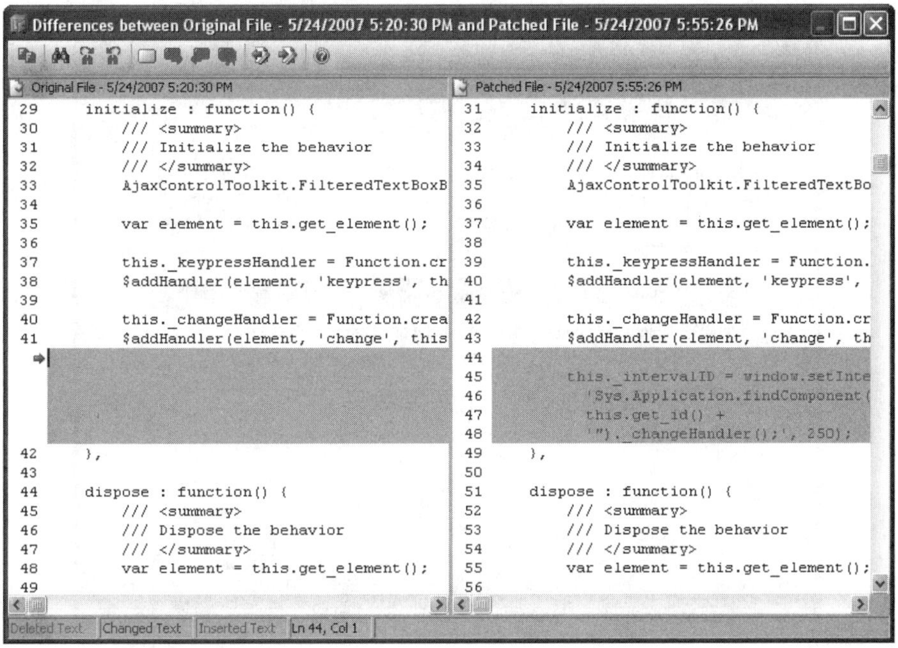

Figure 13-14. The difference between the old and the new file

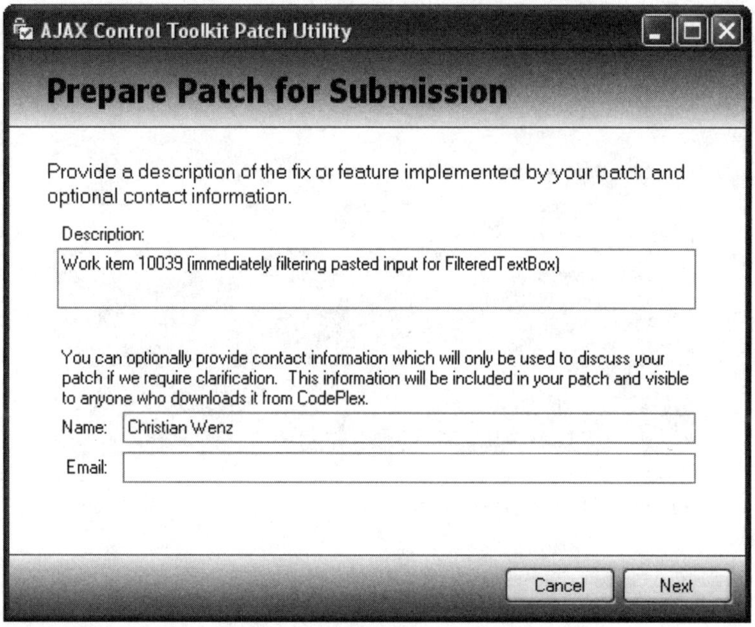

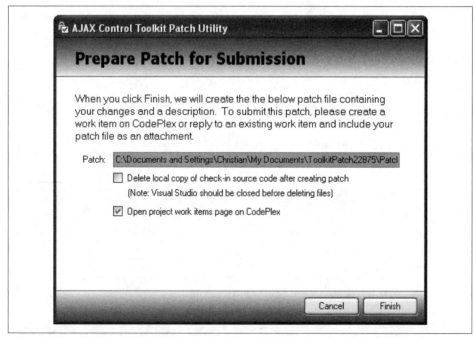

Figure 13-15. Providing information about the patch

Figure 13-16. The final step to package the patch

Then, upload your patch and write a short comment describing it (see Figure 13-17). A member of the ASP.NET AJAX Control Toolkit team will get back to you if any questions arise, or your patch will simply be accepted and applied.

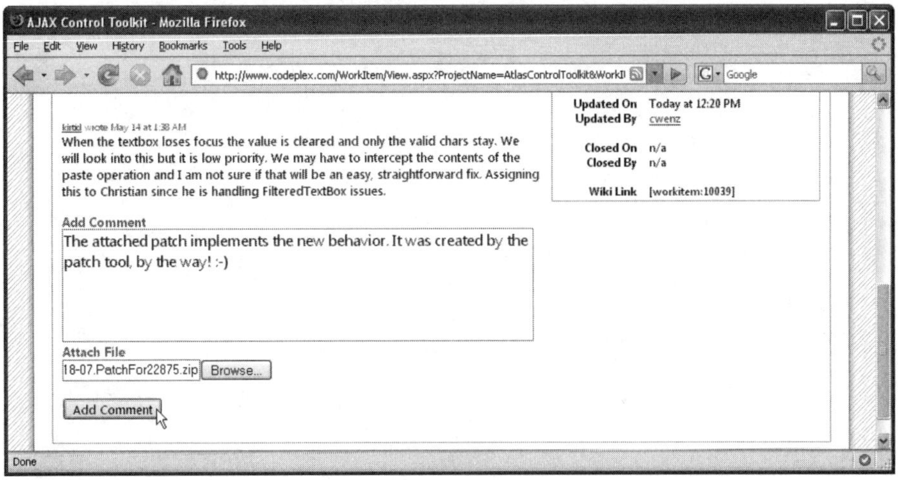

Figure 13-17. Upload the patch to a CodePlex work item

There are more incentives planned for contributors, including points for patches and, for the most active patch developers, invitations to join the toolkit project as an official contributor. Hope to see you in the project soon!

Summary

In this chapter, you learned how to install and use the ASP.NET AJAX Control Toolkit. You also learned how to create your own custom control using the toolkit. A modified and extended version of the example highlighted in this chapter is now part of the toolkit. Look for the FilteredTextBox control and try it out!

For Further Reading

http://ajax.asp.net/default.aspx?tabid=47&subtabid=477
>   The Microsoft site for the ASP.NET AJAX Control Toolkit contains release notes and live demos.

http://www.codeplex.com/Wiki/View.aspx?ProjectName=AtlasControlToolkit
>   The community site for the toolkit is located at the CodePlex site, the new Microsoft site for shared source projects.

http://www.microsoft.com/resources/sharedsource/licensingbasics/sharedsourcelicenses. mspx
>   The Microsoft Permissive License is posted at the toolkit site, but this site explains it and provides an overview of other Microsoft shared source licenses.

ASP.NET AJAX Futures

CHAPTER 14

Client Controls

This chapter covers client-side controls that ship with the ASP.NET AJAX Futures. These controls mimic the behavior of ASP.NET web controls and allow for consistent development on both the server and the client. In addition, they support convenient features, such as data binding, which you'll explore in Chapter 16.

Introducing ASP.NET AJAX Client Controls

The core release of ASP.NET AJAX 1.0 does not include purely client-based controls. However, these controls are found in the Futures release and are implemented in the Sys.Preview.UI namespace. Sys.Preview.UI is the client-side equivalent of the similarly named and well-known Web.UI namespace in ASP.NET.

 In pre-release versions of ASP.NET AJAX, the client-side namespace was named Web.UI and Sys.UI.

Sys.Preview.UI contains a large number of ASP.NET AJAX HTML controls and web controls. The functionality of ASP.NET AJAX controls is similar but not identical to that of ASP.NET server controls. They provide a consistent, browser-independent model that enables JavaScript code to access and change client control properties. This would require considerable knowledge of JavaScript if attempted using controls outside theASP.NET AJAX framework. It would also take quite a knack for scripting workarounds to account for browser inconsistencies.

Table 14-1 lists controls available in the Futures release. The table lists the HTML elements with which the ASP.NET AJAX control works, along with the equivalent JavaScript DOM object or method you would otherwise use.

Table 14-1. ASP.NET AJAX controls

ASP.NET AJAX control	Description	HTML element	JavaScript equivalent
Sys.Preview.UI.Window	Implements JavaScript pop-up windows	N/A	window.alert(), window.confirm(), window.prompt()
Sys.Preview.UI.Label	Implements a span or label element	`<span>`, `<label>`	Label
Sys.Preview.UI.Image	Implements an image	`<img>`	Image
Sys.Preview.UI.HyperLink	Implements a link	`<a href="...">`	Link
Sys.Preview.UI.Button	Implements a button	`<input type="button">`, `<input type="submit">`, `<input type="reset">`, `<button>`	button
Sys.Preview.UI.CheckBox	Implements a checkbox	`<input type="checkbox">`	Checkbox
Sys.Preview.UI.Selector	Implements a list box or drop-down list	`<select>`	Select
Sys.Preview.UI.TextBox	Implements a text field	`<input type="text">`, `<input type="password">`, `<textarea>`	text, password, textarea

Using ASP.NET AJAX Controls

The ASP.NET AJAX framework uses two approaches with respect to the controls in Sys.Preview.UI. In one approach, some controls provide abstractions that make it easier to use JavaScript for various tasks. These are not controls in the ordinary sense of displaying a UI on the page. In the second approach, controls provide JavaScript access to HTML elements on the current page. Both ways are demonstrated in this section.

Accessing JavaScript Methods

One example of a control that abstracts JavaScript functionality is the client-side implementation of a message box using Sys.Preview.UI.Window. The JavaScript language supports three types of modal message boxes:

window.alert()
    Message box with an OK button

window.confirm()
    Message box with OK/Cancel or Yes/No buttons

window.prompt()
    Message box with an input field and an OK button

Inside the ASP.NET AJAX Sys.Preview.UI.Window class, the functionality for calling window.alert( ) or window.confirm( ) is encapsulated in the messageBox( ) method. The default behavior is to present a window.alert( ) box. This corresponds to the message box style Sys.Preview.UI.MessageBoxStyle.OK. The alternative is to use the Sys.Preview.UI.MessageBoxStyle.OKCancel style, which uses window.confirm( ) under the covers.

But what about the window.prompt( ) window? To be consistent with Visual Basic, this is implemented via the inputBox( ) method instead of the messageBox( ) method.

The following example implements all three variants of client modal window. Three client-side buttons are used to call the ASP.NET AJAX functionality:

```
<input type="button" value="MessageBoxOK" onclick="MessageBoxOKClick( );" />
<input type="button" value="MessageBoxOKCancel" onclick="MessageBoxOKCancelClick( );"
/>
<input type="button" value="InputBox" onclick="InputBoxClick( );" />
```

Each of the three functions—click1( ), click2( ), and click3( )—call a method of the ASP.NET AJAX Sys.Preview.UI.window object, as shown in the following code:

```
<script language="JavaScript" type="text/javascript">
function MessageBoxOKClick( ) {
  Sys.Preview.UI.Window.messageBox("Using Sys.Preview.UI.Window");
}
function MessageBoxOKCancelClick( ) {
  Sys.Preview.UI.Window.messageBox("Using Sys.Preview.UI.Window",
Sys.Preview.UI.MessageBoxStyle.OKCancel);
}

function InputBoxClick( ) {
  Sys.UI.Window.inputBox("Using Sys.Preview.UI.Window", "<enter text here>");
}
</script>
```

To use ASP.NET AJAX functionality in a page, you must include the ASP.NET AJAX library. The ASP.NET AJAX ScriptManager element takes care of that:

```
<asp:ScriptManager runat="server">
```

This loads the core ASP.NET AJAX library. However, in order to use functionality from Sys.Preview.UI, the Futures library must also be loaded. Unlike the core library, this is done manually, using this syntax:

```
<Scripts>
  <asp:ScriptReference Assembly="Microsoft.Web.Preview" Name="PreviewScript.js" />
</Scripts>
</asp:ScriptManager>
```

Example 14-1 shows the code you need for the first ASP.NET AJAX example in this chapter. Remember, to run any functionality involving the Futures release and the Sys.Preview.UI assembly, you must create a web site that is configured to include Futures functionality. For a refresher on how to do this, see Chapter 1.

Example 14-1. Modal JavaScript windows with ASP.NET AJAX

ControlMessageBox.aspx

```
<%@ Page Language="C#" %>

<!DOCTYPE html PUBLIC "-//W3C//DTD XHTML 1.0 Transitional//EN"
"http://www.w3.org/TR/xhtml1/DTD/xhtml1-transitional.dtd">
<html xmlns="http://www.w3.org/1999/xhtml">
<head runat="server">
  <title>ASP.NET AJAX</title>

  <script language="JavaScript" type="text/javascript">
  function MessageBoxOKClick( ) {
    Sys.Preview.UI.Window.messageBox("Using Sys.Preview.UI.Window");
  }

  function MessageBoxOKCancelClick( ) {
    Sys.Preview.UI.Window.messageBox("Using Sys.Preview.UI.Window",
Sys.Preview.UI.MessageBoxStyle.OKCancel);
  }

  function InputBoxClick( ) {
    Sys.Preview.UI.Window.inputBox("Using Sys.Preview.UI.Window", "<enter text here>");
  }
  </script>

</head>
<body>
  <form id="form1" runat="server">
    <asp:ScriptManager runat="server">
      <Scripts>
        <asp:ScriptReference Assembly="Microsoft.Web.Preview" Name="PreviewScript.js" />
      </Scripts>
    </asp:ScriptManager>
    <div>
      <input type="button" value="MessageBoxOK" onclick="MessageBoxOKClick( );" />
      <input type="button" value="MessageBoxOKCancel"
onclick="MessageBoxOKCancelClick( );" />
      <input type="button" value="InputBox" onclick="InputBoxClick( );" />
    </div>
  </form>
</body>
</html>
```

Figure 14-1 shows the result when you click the InputBox button.

This is nice functionality, but not of any particular value, as only very basic Java-Script functionality is encapsulated by the ASP.NET AJAX controls in use. However, other controls exist that provide more application functionality.

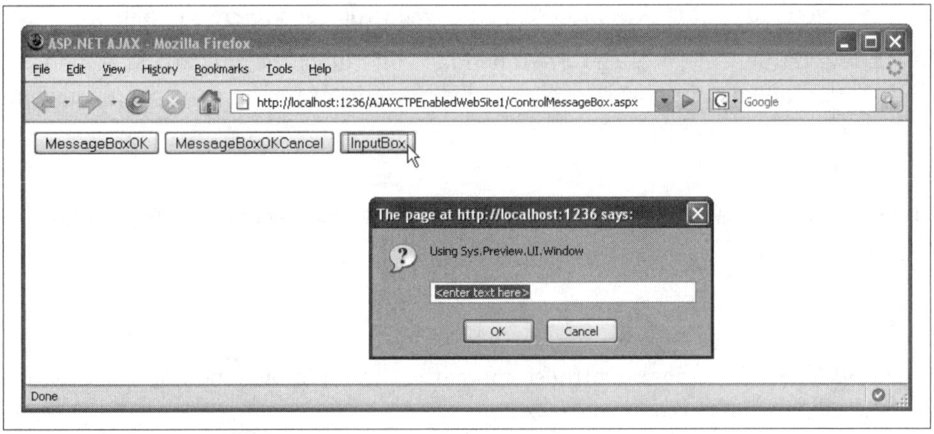

Figure 14-1. Clicking a button opens a JavaScript window

Accessing HTML Elements

ASP.NET AJAX controls also enable you to put HTML elements in the page and access them using an object-oriented, client-side approach. This means that even though you are using HTML elements, you can use a client-side abstraction layer to access their contents.

Initially, the syntax for using ASP.NET AJAX to access HTML elements can seem a bit strange. Let's consider a page that contains a <span> element such as the following:

```
<span id="Label1">This is a label</span>
```

Using JavaScript, you could access this element with the following code:

```
var label = document.getElementById("Label1")
```

But ASP.NET AJAX provides a nice shortcut to the method, $get( ):

```
var label = $get("Label1")
```

Properties for this element, including style information, could then be set. With JavaScript, you would need to write different code for different browsers. As stated earlier, this requires a fairly substantial knowledge of JavaScript and the DOM, beyond merely mastering the syntax.

The ASP.NET AJAX way is different. You *do* need to know the appropriate ASP.NET AJAX control class for the client-side element, but not too much more than that (refer back to Table 14-1). In this case, for the <span> element, you use Sys.Preview. UI.Label. The code must instantiate the class and provide the ID of the HTML element. However, the ID will be specified in a unique fashion—the aforementioned $get( ) method, with the actual ID in parentheses:

```
var label = new Sys.Preview.UI.Label($get("Label1"));
```

In effect, you are casting the object to a type when you get a reference to it.

Next, register the delegates and event handlers by calling the `initialize()` method. This step, though not mandatory for this specific example, is generally recommended for most other scenarios.

```
label.initialize();
```

If you do not use event handling (as in the next few examples), you can skip the call to `initialize()`.

Labels

The ASP.NET AJAX `Label` control supports the two additional methods that follow. Both are illustrated in Example 14-2.

`get_text()`
: Retrieves the current text of the element

`set_text()`
: Sets (changes) the text in the element

 JavaScript and the browser DOM don't offer an equivalent to ASP.NET's InnerText property. The property that both `get_text()` and `set_text()` access is innerHTML, so you always need to keep an eye open for special characters and escape them when necessary to avoid side effects.

Example 14-2 shows you how to manipulate a `label` control. The example demonstrates three actions:

1. It creates the client-side `Sys.Preview.UI.Label` object.

2. It reads the old text using the `get_text()` property method.

3. It writes new text using the `set_text()` property method.

Example 14-2. Using an ASP.NET AJAX Label control

```
ControlLabel.aspx

<%@ Page Language="C#" %>

<!DOCTYPE html PUBLIC "-//W3C//DTD XHTML 1.0 Transitional//EN"
"http://www.w3.org/TR/xhtml1/DTD/xhtml1-transitional.dtd">
<html xmlns="http://www.w3.org/1999/xhtml">
<head runat="server">
  <title>ASP.NET AJAX</title>

  <script language="JavaScript" type="text/javascript">
  function pageLoad() {
    var label = new Sys.Preview.UI.Label($get("Label1"));
    var d = new Date();
```

Example 14-2. Using an ASP.NET AJAX Label control (continued)

```
    var time = d.getHours() + ":" + d.getMinutes() + ":" + d.getSeconds();
    label.set_text(label.get_text() + time);
  }
  </script>

</head>
<body>
  <form id="form1" runat="server">
    <asp:ScriptManager runat="server">
      <Scripts>
        <asp:ScriptReference Assembly="Microsoft.Web.Preview" Name="PreviewScript.js" />
      </Scripts>
    </asp:ScriptManager>
    <div>
      <span id="Label1">time goes here: </span>
    </div>
  </form>
</body>
</html>
```

After the page loads, the current time is determined and then placed in the `<span>` element. Figure 14-2 displays the result. To see a new result, refresh the browser.

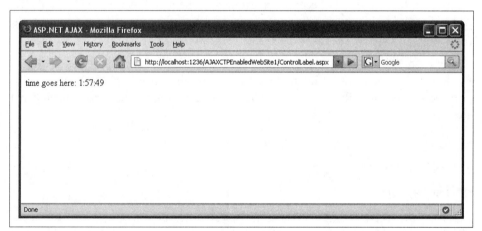

Figure 14-2. The current time appears in the label

Images

The HTML `<img>` element represents an image on the page. The Sys.Preview.UI. Image class implements an ASP.NET AJAX version of a client-side image (represented in the DOM with the Image object). In addition to the common methods listed earlier in this chapter, the ASP.NET AJAX Image class supports the following property methods:

get_alternateText( )
> Retrieves the value of the alt attribute

set_alternateText( )
> Changes the value of the alt attribute

get_height( )
> Gets the height of the image

set_height( )
> Sets the height of the image

get_width( )
> Gets the width of the image

set_width( )
> Sets the width of the image

get_imageURL( )
> Retrieves the relative or absolute URL of the image (src attribute)

set_imageURL( )
> Changes the relative or absolute URL of the image (src attribute)

Once again, standard DOM properties are encapsulated in a class. You don't need to learn much JavaScript, just become accustomed to the methods exposed by ASP.NET AJAX. Example 14-3 shows you how to manipulate the empty <img> element on the page. Initially it appears like this:

```
<img id="Image1" />
```

By default, the XHTML validation in Visual Studio will complain about missing attributes, but you will be using JavaScript code to set the required src and alt attributes.

Example 14-3. Using an ASP.NET AJAX Image control

ControlImage.aspx

```
<%@ Page Language="C#" %>

<!DOCTYPE html PUBLIC "-//W3C//DTD XHTML 1.0 Transitional//EN"
"http://www.w3.org/TR/xhtml1/DTD/xhtml1-transitional.dtd">
<html xmlns="http://www.w3.org/1999/xhtml">
<head runat="server">
  <title>ASP.NET AJAX</title>

  <script language="JavaScript" type="text/javascript">
  function pageLoad( ) {
    var image = new Sys.Preview.UI.Image($get("Image1"));
    image.set_imageURL("ajaxlogo.png");
    image.set_alternateText("ASP.NET AJAX logo");
  }
  </script>
```

Example 14-3. Using an ASP.NET AJAX Image control (continued)

```
</head>
<body>
  <form id="form1" runat="server">
    <asp:ScriptManager runat="server">
      <Scripts>
        <asp:ScriptReference Assembly="Microsoft.Web.Preview" Name="PreviewScript.js" />
      </Scripts>
    </asp:ScriptManager>
    <div>
      <img id="Image1" />
    </div>
  </form>
</body>
</html>
```

Figure 14-3 shows the result. For this example, you need the file *ajaxlogo.png* (taken from *http://ajax.asp.net/images/ajax-poster-photo-logo.png*) to reside in the root directory of the web site. You can find the file in the code downloads for this book (*http://www.oreilly.com/catalog/9780596514242*).

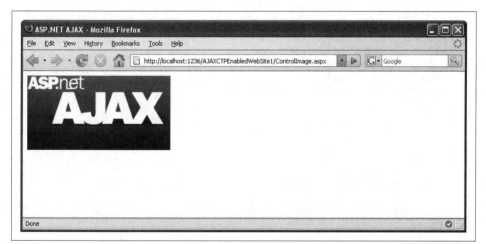

Figure 14-3. The Image control; the Properties window shows the alternate text

Hyperlinks

In HTML, the <a> element is used to link to other pages and to documents, and it is also used for bookmarks. In ASP.NET AJAX, hyperlinks are represented with the Sys.Preview.UI.HyperLink class. This class implements the get_navigateURL( ) and set_navigateURL( ) property methods to set the link target (only the target URL, not the target frame or window). It also provides a click event to which you can respond. (Event handling is covered later in this chapter in the section "Handling Control Events.")

In Example 14-4, an empty link (<a></a>) is created, with the link target added dynamically. In the example, the link is the same ASP.NET AJAX logo image used in the preceding example.

It is not possible to set the text of the link directly via the Link control. A link might not necessarily be a text link, but may also contain an image or another element. Therefore, the text of the link can be thought of as another object. If you want to set the link text, you need to place another element (with ID) inside the link.

Example 14-4. Using an ASP.NET AJAX Link control

ControlHyperLink.aspx

```
<%@ Page Language="C#" %>

<!DOCTYPE html PUBLIC "-//W3C//DTD XHTML 1.0 Transitional//EN"
"http://www.w3.org/TR/xhtml1/DTD/xhtml1-transitional.dtd">
<html xmlns="http://www.w3.org/1999/xhtml">
<head runat="server">
  <title>ASP.NET AJAX</title>

  <script language="JavaScript" type="text/javascript">
  function pageLoad( ) {
    var link = new Sys.Preview.UI.HyperLink($get("Link1"));
    link.set_navigateURL("http://ajax.asp.net/");
    var image = new Sys.Preview.UI.Image($get("Image1"));
    image.set_imageURL("ajaxlogo.png");
    image.set_alternateText("ASP.NET AJAX logo");
  }
  </script>

</head>
<body>
  <form id="form1" runat="server">
    <asp:ScriptManager runat="server">
      <Scripts>
        <asp:ScriptReference Assembly="Microsoft.Web.Preview" Name="PreviewScript.js" />
      </Scripts>
    </asp:ScriptManager>
    <div>
      <a id="Link1"><img id="Image1" /></a>
    </div>
  </form>
</body>
</html>
```

Figure 14-4 shows the result.

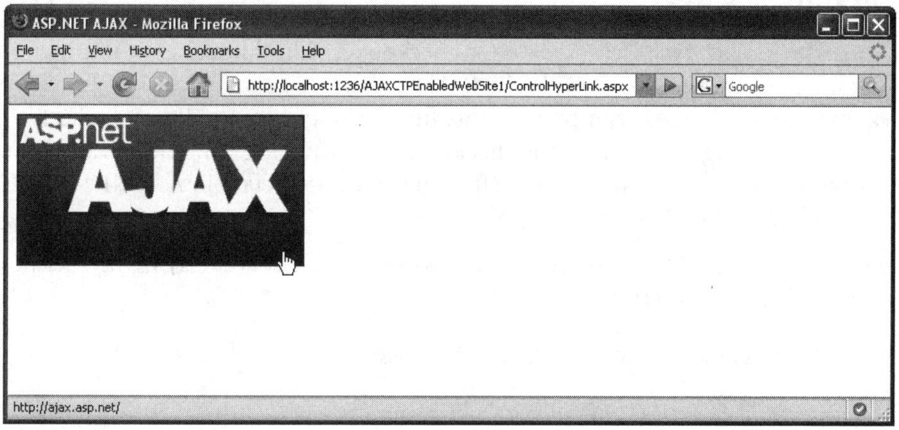

Figure 14-4. An Image control is now a hyperlink

Buttons

HTML supports various kinds of buttons. Some examples are `<input type="submit">` to submit a form; `<input type="reset">` to clear a form (reset it to its original state); and finally, `<input type="button">` and `<button>` to declare buttons with no predefined behavior that you can enrich with JavaScript. ASP.NET AJAX implements buttons with `Sys.Preview.UI.Button`. The following methods are supported:

`get_argument( )`
  Retrieves any argument that is sent along with the command when the button is clicked

`set_argument( )`
  Sets the argument of the button

`get_command( )`
  Retrieves the command that is sent when the button is clicked

`set_command( )`
  Sets the command of the button

Whenever you set the `argument` or `command` properties, the built-in event-handling mechanism (described later in this chapter) is activated. A different approach for binding functionality to buttons can be found in Chapter 16.

Checkboxes

HTML uses <input type="checkbox"> for checkboxes. Checkboxes exist in either one of two states: checked or not checked. These states can be set using JavaScript, meaning ASP.NET AJAX can provide this functionality as well. The set_checked( ) method can change the state of a checkbox (by providing a Boolean value), and get_checked( ) retrieves the current state. The associated class in ASP.NET AJAX is Sys.Preview.UI.CheckBox.

Example 14-5 uses HTML to create a checkbox, and ASP.NET AJAX/JavaScript to set its checked state to true.

Example 14-5. Using an ASP.NET AJAX CheckBox control

ControlCheckBox.aspx

```
<%@ Page Language="C#" %>

<!DOCTYPE html PUBLIC "-//W3C//DTD XHTML 1.0 Transitional//EN"
"http://www.w3.org/TR/xhtml1/DTD/xhtml1-transitional.dtd">
<html xmlns="http://www.w3.org/1999/xhtml">
<head runat="server">
  <title>ASP.NET AJAX</title>

  <script language="JavaScript" type="text/javascript">
  function pageLoad( ) {
    var checkbox = new Sys.Preview.UI.CheckBox($get("CheckBox1"));
    checkbox.set_checked(true);
  }
  </script>

</head>
<body>
  <form id="form1" runat="server">
    <asp:ScriptManager runat="server">
      <Scripts>
        <asp:ScriptReference Assembly="Microsoft.Web.Preview" Name="PreviewScript.js" />
      </Scripts>
    </asp:ScriptManager>
    <div>
      <input type="checkbox" id="CheckBox1" />
      <label for="CheckBox1">click me!</label>
    </div>
  </form>
</body>
</html>
```

Figure 14-5 shows the result displayed.

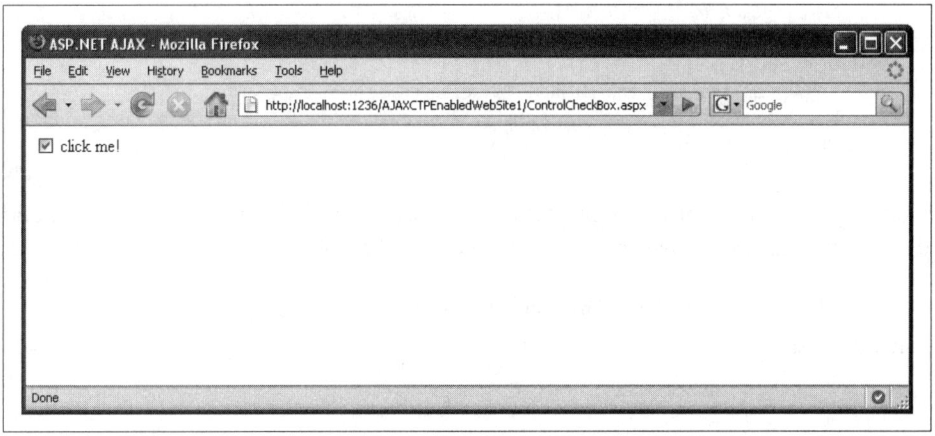

![ASP.NET AJAX - Mozilla Firefox browser window showing http://localhost:1236/AJAXCTPEnabledWebSite1/ControlCheckBox.aspx with a checked "click me!" checkbox]

Figure 14-5. ASP.NET AJAX has checked the checkbox

Selection Lists

HTML selection lists (`<select>...</select>`) come in two forms: a drop-down list that requires the user action to display all list elements, or a selection list in which some of the elements are already visible. Both types of lists are covered by ASP.NET AJAX with the `Sys.Preview.UI.Selector` class. Unlike JavaScript's treatment of a `<select>` element, ASP.NET AJAX classes *do not* provide the ability to set the individual values of the list's elements.

If the data for the list exists in the form of a .NET `DataTable` object, data binding is a possibility (otherwise, you would have to provide the list entries via markup). Chapter 17 explains this approach.

For now, however, we can demonstrate the `get_selectedValue()` method, which determines the value attribute of the currently selected item in the list.

When a form is sent to the server via HTTP GET or POST, it is not essential to set the value attribute, because the post process passes the caption of the element (the text between `<option>` and `</option>`) for value. However, JavaScript views a list item with no value property as empty. Therefore, you should *always* set the value property for all list elements.

Since event handling isn't covered until later in this chapter, the change event of the list in Example 14-6 is not captured. Instead, the state of the list is analyzed every second. This is done using the JavaScript function, `setInterval()`. This polling technique is used only for the sake of this example. Chapter 16 will detail a much better way to keep two elements in sync, namely through the use of data binding.

```
    function pageLoad( ) {
      window.setInterval(
        function( ) {
          //Access the list and output its selected value
        },
        1000);
    }
```

Example 14-6 shows how to use ASP.NET AJAX to check for a current selection and display its value in a <span> element (Sys.Preview.UI.Label).

Example 14-6. Using an ASP.NET AJAX Select control

ControlSelector.aspx

```
<%@ Page Language="C#" %>

<!DOCTYPE html PUBLIC "-//W3C//DTD XHTML 1.0 Transitional//EN"
"http://www.w3.org/TR/xhtml1/DTD/xhtml1-transitional.dtd">
<html xmlns="http://www.w3.org/1999/xhtml">
<head runat="server">
  <title>ASP.NET AJAX</title>

  <script language="JavaScript" type="text/javascript">
  var label;
  var select;

  function pageLoad( ) {
    label = new Sys.Preview.UI.Label($get("Label1"));
    select = new Sys.Preview.UI.Selector($get("Select1"));

    // Poll every second to determine whether a value has been selected.
    window.setInterval(
      function( ) {
        label.set_text(select.get_selectedValue( ));
      },
      1000);
  }
  </script>

</head>
<body>
  <form id="form1" runat="server">
    <asp:ScriptManager runat="server">
      <Scripts>
        <asp:ScriptReference Assembly="Microsoft.Web.Preview" Name="PreviewScript.js" />
      </Scripts>
    </asp:ScriptManager>
    <div>
      <select id="Select1" size="3">
        <option value="1">one</option>
        <option value="2">two</option>
        <option value="3">three</option>
      </select><br />
```

Example 14-6. Using an ASP.NET AJAX Select control (continued)

```
    Selected value: <label id="Label1"></label>
  </div>
 </form>
</body>
</html>
```

Figure 14-6 shows the result.

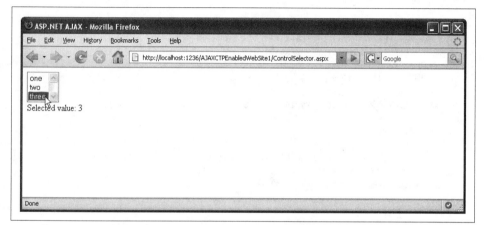

Figure 14-6. The selected value is written to the Label control

 Using get_selectedValue( ) may be convenient, but only for single-selection lists. If the list is set for multiple selections (<select multiple="multiple">), you the value of the first selected list element is returned, not all selected elements. To check all selected elements, you would need to use JavaScript code to loop through all the items individually, as shown in the following snippet:

```
var op = document.forms[0].elements["Select1"].options;
for (var i=0; i < op.length; i++) {
  if (op[i].selected) {
    //element is selected
  } else {
    //element is not selected
  }
}
```

Text Fields

A single-line text box is represented in HTML using <input type="text">. This element can be managed using the ASP.NET AJAX class Sys.Preview.UI.TextBox. The functionality provided by ASP.NET AJAX covers keyboard event handling and, of course, both read and write access for the text of the element itself. The methods for the latter are get_text( ) and set_text( ).

Example 14-7 displays the data entered into the text field using the same polling approach as in the preceding example (setInterval( )) to periodically copy the contents of the text box to an ASP.NET AJAX Label control.

Example 14-7. Using an ASP.NET AJAX TextBox control

ControlTextBox.aspx

```
<%@ Page Language="C#" %>

<!DOCTYPE html PUBLIC "-//W3C//DTD XHTML 1.0 Transitional//EN"
"http://www.w3.org/TR/xhtml1/DTD/xhtml1-transitional.dtd">
<html xmlns="http://www.w3.org/1999/xhtml">
<head runat="server">
  <title>ASP.NET AJAX</title>

  <script language="JavaScript" type="text/javascript">
  function pageLoad( ) {
    window.setInterval(
      function( ) {
        var label = new Sys.Preview.UI.Label($get("Label1"));
        var textbox = new Sys.Preview.UI.TextBox($get("TextBox1"));
        label.set_text(textbox.get_text( ));
      },
      1000);
  }
  </script>

</head>
<body>
  <form id="form1" runat="server">
    <asp:ScriptManager runat="server">
      <Scripts>
        <asp:ScriptReference Assembly="Microsoft.Web.Preview" Name="PreviewScript.js" />
      </Scripts>
    </asp:ScriptManager>
    <div>
      <input type="text" id="TextBox1" /><br />
      Entered value: <label id="Label1"></label>
    </div>
  </form>
</body>
</html>
```

Figure 14-7 shows the result.

 Single-line text fields (<input type="text">), multiline text fields (<textarea>), and password fields (<input type="password">) have one thing in common: from a JavaScript point of view, they are controlled in the same way. The value property provides read and write access to the contents of the field. So, you can use Sys.Preview.UI.TextBox for all three kinds of form fields.

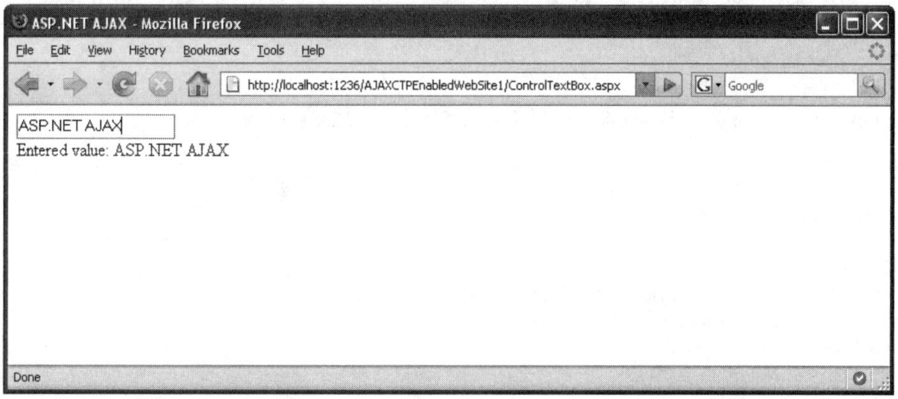

Figure 14-7. The text in the text box appears in the label

Base Methods

As discussed earlier in "Introducing ASP.NET AJAX Client Controls," ASP.NET AJAX supports common methods for each control within Sys.Preview.UI. Most of these set a property that JavaScript exposes for all controls. Two examples of this are the get_accessKey( ) and set_accessKey( ) methods that control the DOM accesskey property.

Methods with somewhat more visible results are those for controlling the CSS class of an element. This makes changing the layout of elements on the fly very easy. Here are the supported methods:

addCssClass( )
> Adds a CSS class to an element

removeCssClass( )
> Removes one CSS class from an element

toggleCssClass( )
> Adds the class to an element if it is not already there; otherwise, removes the class

Example 14-8 demonstrates the toggleCssClass( ) method. It also determines the current CSS class. To do so, the get_element( ) method of the label object returns the actual DOM element. The className property of the DOM element contains the list of CSS classes currently used.

In the page, the following three CSS classes are defined and can complement each other (i.e., every class covers another style):

```
<style type="text/css">
.style1 { font-family: Monospace; }
.style2 { border-style: solid; }
.style3 { color: #00f; }
</style>
```

The JavaScript code in the example selects one of these classes at random and then calls `toggleCssClass()`. A `Label` control periodically displays the current class or classes being used.

Example 14-8. Using the base CSS methods for ASP.NET AJAX controls

ControlCSS.aspx

```
<%@ Page Language="C#" %>

<!DOCTYPE html PUBLIC "-//W3C//DTD XHTML 1.0 Transitional//EN"
"http://www.w3.org/TR/xhtml1/DTD/xhtml1-transitional.dtd">
<html xmlns="http://www.w3.org/1999/xhtml">
<head runat="server">
  <title>ASP.NET AJAX</title>
  <style type="text/css">
  .style1 { font-family: Monospace; }
  .style2 { border-style: solid; }
  .style3 { color: #00f; }
  </style>

  <script language="JavaScript" type="text/javascript">
  function pageLoad( ) {
    window.setInterval(
      function( ) {
        var label = new Sys.Preview.UI.Label($get("Label1"));
        var rnd = Math.ceil(3 * Math.random( ));
        label.toggleCssClass("style" + rnd);
        label.set_text(label.get_element( ).className);
      },
      1000);
  }
  </script>

</head>
<body>
  <form id="form1" runat="server">
    <asp:ScriptManager runat="server">
      <Scripts>
        <asp:ScriptReference Assembly="Microsoft.Web.Preview" Name="PreviewScript.js" />
      </Scripts>
    </asp:ScriptManager>
    <div>
      CSS class(es):
      <label id="Label1">
      </label>
    </div>
  </form>
</body>
</html>
```

Figure 14-8 shows the result.

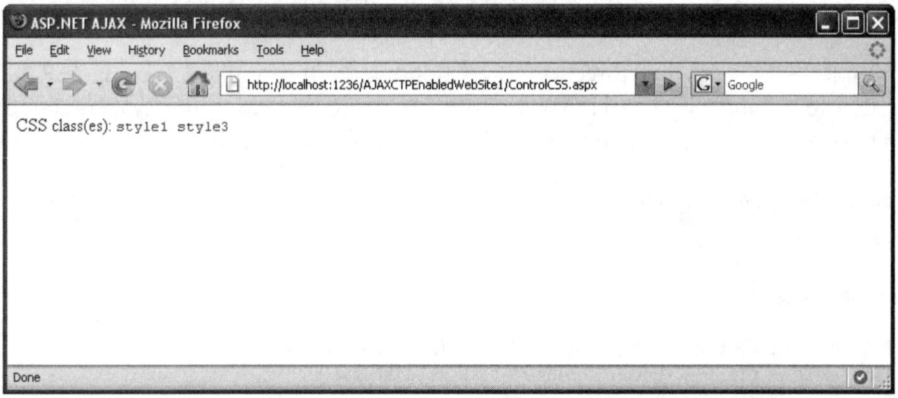

Figure 14-8. Two styles were applied at random

Handling Control Events

ASP.NET AJAX provides its client controls with an event handling mechanism. The mechanism works a bit differently than you might expect, but it's still intuitive.

The first and most important step is to call the `initialize( )` method of the element whose events you want to handle. This enables all the mechanisms that are internally used to capture events. Setting up events becomes a two-step process:

1. Write an event handling function that is called when the event occurs. As with the .NET Framework, the event handling function takes two arguments: one containing the object that raised the event, the other an event-specific object that, depending on the event, might contain additional information about the event.

2. Link the event handling function to the element using `<element>.add_<event name>(<method name>)`. The syntax is roughly reminiscent of the .NET Framework implementation of delegates.

Events for Buttons

Remember the example with the three modal pop-up windows from the beginning of this chapter? There, the JavaScript code that displayed the windows was added declaratively in the HTML button. This can also be done using the ASP.NET AJAX library, but in that case, you would not have gained much from using ASP.NET AJAX when compared to the "pure" JavaScript approach, except for the certainty that the ASP.NET AJAX library is fully loaded before attaching any JavaScript code to an element. However, the whole idea of the ASP.NET AJAX framework is to bring server-side and client-side development closer to each other and to bring new OOP capabilities and browser independence to the client. Therefore, using ASP.NET AJAX for tasks that you can do as easily in JavaScript still has benefits.

Example 14-9 revisits the "three windows" example from Example 4-1, using ASP.NET AJAX event handling. The HTML buttons are referenced using the Sys.Preview.UI. Button class, and the associated event is (somewhat obviously) click.

Example 14-9. Using ASP.NET AJAX Button control events

ControlEventButton.aspx

```
<%@ Page Language="C#" %>

<!DOCTYPE html PUBLIC "-//W3C//DTD XHTML 1.0 Transitional//EN"
"http://www.w3.org/TR/xhtml1/DTD/xhtml1-transitional.dtd">
<html xmlns="http://www.w3.org/1999/xhtml">
<head runat="server">
  <title>ASP.NET AJAX</title>

  <script language="JavaScript" type="text/javascript">
  function pageLoad( ) {
    var button1 = new Sys.Preview.UI.Button($get("MessageBoxOK"));
    var button2 = new Sys.Preview.UI.Button($get("MessageBoxOKCancel"));
    var button3 = new Sys.Preview.UI.Button($get("InputBox"));

    button1.initialize( );
    button2.initialize( );
    button3.initialize( );

    button1.add_click(MessageBoxOKClick);
    button2.add_click(MessageBoxOKCancelClick);
    button3.add_click(InputBoxClick);
  }

  function MessageBoxOKClick( ) {
    Sys.Preview.UI.Window.messageBox("Using Sys.Preview.UI.Window");
  }
  function MessageBoxOKCancelClick( ) {
    Sys.Preview.UI.Window.messageBox("Using Sys.Preview.UI.Window",
Sys.Preview.UI.MessageBoxStyle.OKCancel);
  }
  function InputBoxClick( ) {
    Sys.Preview.UI.Window.inputBox("Using Sys.Preview.UI.Window", "<enter text here>");
  }
  </script>

</head>
<body>
  <form id="form1" runat="server">
    <asp:ScriptManager runat="server">
      <Scripts>
        <asp:ScriptReference Assembly="Microsoft.Web.Preview" Name="PreviewScript.js" />
      </Scripts>
```

Example 14-9. Using ASP.NET AJAX Button control events (continued)

```
    </asp:ScriptManager>
    <div>
      <input type="button" value="MessageBoxOK" id="MessageBoxOK" />
      <input type="button" value="MessageBoxOKCancel" id="MessageBoxOKCancel" />
      <input type="button" value="InputBox" id="InputBox" />
    </div>
  </form>
</body>
</html>
```

There are two alternatives for adding an event handler to an element. First, you can call the $addHandler() function to assign a handler:

```
$addHandler(button1.get_element(), 'click', MessageBoxOK);
```

You've actually seen that addHandler function in action in previous chapters of this book, and we discussed it briefly in Chapter 4.

If you have more than one handler for an element, the $addHandlers() function comes in handy:

```
$addHandlers(
  <current element>.get_element(),
  {
    <event>: <handler function>,
    <another event>: <another handler function>
  }
);
```

Events for Lists

An event that is implemented for many ASP.NET AJAX client controls, and one that does not exist in this form in JavaScript, is propertyChanged. It is used generically for all controls to indicate that something has changed: a key was pressed, a list item was selected, and so on. In that case, the event passes you the name of the property that has changed.

It is also possible to work with individual change events for each form element so that you know exactly what values have changed. For example, when the selected element in a selection list changes, it raises the selectionChanged event (in JavaScript, the event is called change). Illustrating this event is again an opportunity to rewrite one of the previous examples (see Example 14-7). This time, we do not have to periodically check the selection list for changes; instead, we capture the associated event. Remember to call initialize(), otherwise, the event cannot be captured. Example 14-10 shows code that handles a Selector control's selectionChanged event.

Example 14-10. Using ASP.NET AJAX selection list events

ControlEventSelector.aspx

```
<%@ Page Language="C#" %>
```

Example 14-10. Using ASP.NET AJAX selection list events (continued)

```
<!DOCTYPE html PUBLIC "-//W3C//DTD XHTML 1.0 Transitional//EN"
"http://www.w3.org/TR/xhtml1/DTD/xhtml1-transitional.dtd">
<html xmlns="http://www.w3.org/1999/xhtml">
<head runat="server">
  <title>ASP.NET AJAX</title>

  <script language="JavaScript" type="text/javascript">
  var select;
  var label;

  function pageLoad( ) {
    select = new Sys.Preview.UI.Selector($get("Select1"));
    label = new Sys.Preview.UI.Label($get("Label1"));

    select.initialize( );
    select.add_selectionChanged (listHasChanged);
  }
  function listHasChanged(sender, args) {
    label.set_text(select.get_selectedValue( ));
  }
  </script>

</head>
<body>
  <form id="form1" runat="server">
    <asp:ScriptManager runat="server">
      <Scripts>
        <asp:ScriptReference Assembly="Microsoft.Web.Preview" Name="PreviewScript.js" />
      </Scripts>
    </asp:ScriptManager>
    <div>
      <select id="Select1" size="3">
        <option value="1">one</option>
        <option value="2">two</option>
        <option value="3">three</option>
      </select><br />
      Selected value: <label id="Label1"></label>
    </div>
  </form>
</body>
</html>
```

The performance of this code is much better than in the previous version of this
example, as the application reacts immediately when the selection in the list is
changed, not just at the end of each 1,000-millisecond interval. See Figure 14-9 for a
browser screenshot.

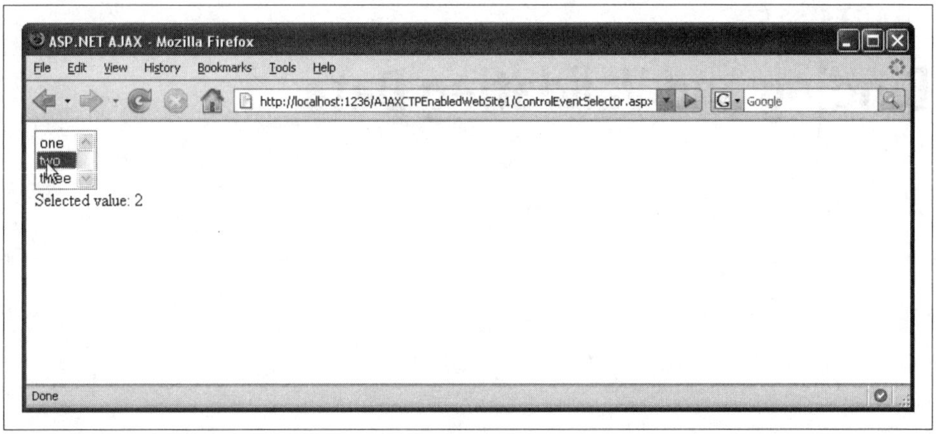

Figure 14-9. Clicking on the list immediately displays the selected item

Summary

This chapter showed you what ASP.NET AJAX offers in the client-side `Sys.Preview.UI` namespace—in particular, ways to write ASP.NET AJAX-specific JavaScript to work with HTML elements. It also covered event handling in ASP.NET AJAX. The next chapter will show you how to bind data to client-side elements so that you do not have to set the values manually. Data binding also enables you to sync elements— that is, to link them together so that a change in one element is reflected in the other, and vice versa.

For Further Reading

http://quickstarts.asp.net/Futures/ajax/doc/intro.aspx
    Pre-release Microsoft documentation on ASP.NET AJAX Futures Controls

CHAPTER 15

Binding and Validating Data

Data binding is the means by which a control (i.e., an HTML page element) is bound to data. Typically this is done so that it can be displayed to the user. For example, with data binding, you can tie the contents of a text box to a label element, or transform the data a user enters into something else (for instance, HTML) and process it further. Very often, data binding draws information from a database. This chapter covers the basics of ASP.NET AJAX data binding; Chapter 17 explains how to use ASP.NET AJAX to access data on the server.

The examples in Chapter 14 did not use declarative code to assign values to controls on the page, although the declarative coding model is one of the advantages of a framework like ASP.NET AJAX. Also, we found it necessary to use one or two hacks (or, put in more diplomatic terms, "less elegant" methods), such as using setInterval( ) to keep two HTML elements in sync. In this chapter, you'll learn xml-script, a declarative markup that ships with the Futures release of ASP.NET AJAX.

Data Binding

Data binding links data with an HTML element which maintains it for visual representation. In ASP.NET, data binding is used with controls such as the GridView, FormView, and DetailsView. Though of course, it's also possible to tie data to other objects, such as a bulleted list.

ASP.NET AJAX offers two approaches to data binding. One is programmatic, the other uses a unique kind of XML markup that ASP.NET AJAX interprets on the fly.

Using Code for Data Bindings

Programmatic data binding sounds more complicated than it actually is. Basically, you need to instantiate a class, then set some properties. The client-side class that is used for all ASP.NET AJAX bindings is Sys.Preview.Binding.

After you have created the binding by instantiating the class, you provide the following information:

A data context
> The name of the element that contains the data to bind to

A data path
> The name of the property to use as binding source

A property
> The name of the property to use as the binding target

A transformer
> Optional code that converts the source data in some fashion before writing it to the target

A binding direction
> A value specifying that the data is incoming, outgoing, or both

Some of this terminology will be new to ASP.NET users, such as the distinction between a data path and a property. It was selected to be compatible with the vocabulary that will be used for Windows Presentation Foundation (WPF) in Windows Vista. But the approach is quite straightforward: a binding object to which you can add the target element (this is why you need both the source element and its data path, but only the target property).

The data can be changed optionally during the binding process using a transformer. You can choose from the built-in transformers offered by ASP.NET AJAX, or you can define your own custom transformers as well. The transformers that ship with the Futures release include:

`Sys.Preview.BindingBase.Transformers.Invert`
> Converts `true` to `false` and `false` to `true`

`Sys.Preview.BindingBase.Transformers.ToString`
> Converts the value to a string, just as `String.Format()` would do; this permits the use of placeholders

`Sys.Preview.BindingBase.Transformers.Adds`
> Adds a value to the source value

`Sys.Preview.BindingBase.Transformers.Multiply`
> Multiplies the source value by another value

`Sys.Preview.BindingBase.Transformers.Compare`
> Compares the source value with a value and returns `true` if equal or `false` if not

`Sys.Preview.BindingBase.Transformers.CompareInverted`
> Compares the source value with a value and returns `false` if equal or `true` if not

Some of these transformers take an argument that can be set with the `set_transformerArgument()` method (for instance, the format for the `ToString` transformer).

Programmatic data binding using a built-in transformer

Let's return to actual code. Once again, in the interest of saving time and energy, we will recycle an existing example, this one from Chapter 14. Recall in Example 14-8, we created a text box and label. Changes in the text box also changed the text of the Label control. Now, we would like to connect these two controls using bindings. First, we need two elements in the HTML markup, such as the snippet below:

```
<input type="text" id="TextBox1" /><br />
<label id="Label1"></label>
```

Next, we need code to instantiate them in JavaScript:

```
function pageLoad( ) {
    var textbox = new Sys.Preview.UI.TextBox($get("TextBox1"));
    var label = new Sys.Preview.UI.Label($get("Label1"));
```

Now we're ready for binding. We first instantiate the Sys.Binding class:

```
var binding = new Sys.Preview.Binding( );
```

Then we must attach the binding's data source (data context). In this example, we are referencing the TextBox control:

```
binding.set_dataContext(textbox);
```

As the goal is to place text within the text box, the correct data path (property name) is text:

```
binding.set_dataPath("text");
```

The data will be written into the Label control's text property:

```
binding.set_property("text");
```

Now let's move on to a transformation. For this example we will use, ToString:

```
binding.add_transform(Sys.Preview.BindingBase.Transformers.ToString);
```

By default, the input data is used as the transformation argument. You can provide additional text to the argument as well, such as labels, sentence prefixes and suffixes, or even formatting information:

```
binding.set_transformerArgument("Text entered: {0}");
```

The binding is nearly complete. Next, you need to provide the target element, using the set_target( ) method:

```
binding.set_target(label);
```

Now to the tricky (and final) stage. Both controls and the binding must be initialized:

```
    textbox.initialize( );
    label.initialize( );
    binding.initialize( )
}
```

Why is this tricky? It's all in the timing. initialize( )needs to be called at the very end of the code, *after* you have created and attached the binding. If you call initialize( ) at an earlier stage, the binding will not be covered by the initialization and nothing will happen. In the previous chapter, intialize( ) was used for event handling, where no such constraints exist. A method can be called at any point. Here, however, it is important that the initialize( ) call is placed last. The order in which the other binding methods are called is inconsequential. In previous versions of ASP.NET AJAX/Atlas, it was not necessary to initialize the binding, so be aware of this when upgrading legacy code.

Finally, do not forget to load the *PreviewScript.js* file where all those bindings are implemented:

```
<asp:ScriptManager runat="server">
  <Scripts>
    <asp:ScriptReference Name="PreviewScript.js"
Assembly="Microsoft.Web.Preview" />
  </Scripts>
</asp:ScriptManager>
```

The complete code is shown in Example 15-1. When you enter some text in the text field, nothing happens at first. When you leave the text field, either by using the Tab key or by clicking outside the field, the propertyChanged event is triggered, the binding is executed, and your input appears in the label, as shown in Figure 15-1.

Example 15-1. Using ASP.NET AJAX data binding with a transformer

```
ControlBindingTextBox.aspx

<%@ Page Language="C#" %>

<!DOCTYPE html PUBLIC "-//W3C//DTD XHTML 1.0 Transitional//EN"
"http://www.w3.org/TR/xhtml1/DTD/xhtml1-transitional.dtd">
<html xmlns="http://www.w3.org/1999/xhtml">
<head id="Head1" runat="server">
  <title>ASP.NET AJAX</title>

  <script language="JavaScript" type="text/javascript">
  function pageLoad( ) {
    var textbox = new Sys.Preview.UI.TextBox($get("TextBox1"));
    var label = new Sys.Preview.UI.Label($get("Label1"));

    var binding = new Sys.Preview.Binding( );
    binding.set_dataContext(textbox);
    binding.set_dataPath("text");
    binding.set_property("text");
    binding.add_transform(Sys.Preview.BindingBase.Transformers.ToString);
    binding.set_transformerArgument("Text entered: {0}");
    binding.set_target(label);
```

```
      textbox.initialize( );
      label.initialize( );
      binding.initialize( );
    }
  </script>

</head>
<body>
  <form id="form1" runat="server">
    <asp:ScriptManager ID="ScriptManager1" runat="server">
      <Scripts>
        <asp:ScriptReference Name="PreviewScript.js" Assembly="Microsoft.Web.Preview" />
      </Scripts>
    </asp:ScriptManager>
    <div>
      <input type="text" id="TextBox1" /><br />
      <label id="Label1"></label>
    </div>
  </form>
</body>
</html>
```

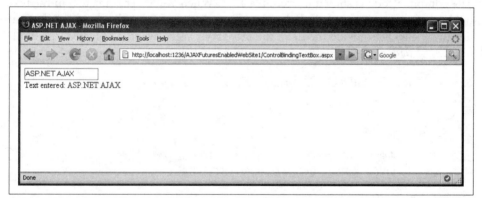

Figure 15-1. The Label control's text is bound to the TextBox control's text property

Binding direction

By default, a binding is "incoming," meaning that the data is copied from the source to the target. Imagine that you replace the Label control with a second text box and implement the binding as before. Then changes in the first text box are copied into the second one, but not vice versa. This behavior can be changed, however, by calling the Binding object's set_direction( ) method. The following values are possible:

Sys.Preview.BindingDirection.In
> The data is copied from the source to the target (default).

Sys.Preview.BindingDirection.Out
> The data is copied from the target to the source. This is particularly useful to reverse the effect of certain transformers.

```
Sys.Preview.BindingDirection.InOut
```
Changes to the data-bound properties in either target or source are copied to the other control.

The following command would make the binding bidirectional:

```
binding.set_direction(Sys.Preview.BindingDirection.InOut);
```

The binding direction is also important when using the Add or Multiply transformers. If you are using Sys.Preview.BindingDirection.InOut, ASP.NET AJAX processes the transformers backward, interpreting an Add transformer as subtract, and a Multiply transformer as divide.

Creating a custom transformer

If the built-in ASP.NET AJAX transformers are insufficient for your needs, it is easy to create a custom one. For example, the HTML markup in the text box of Example 15-1 is not escaped when the text is set in the Label control. If a user enters HTML in the text box, the markup (for instance, Text) is applied as HTML in the Label control instead of being displayed (in the example, this would make the text appear in boldface). If the text contains JavaScript, the code will be executed instead of displayed.

To avoid this behavior, you must write a custom transformer that converts HTML control characters, such as angle brackets and quotation marks—into their corresponding HTML entities.

Looking at the ASP.NET AJAX JavaScript source code (*Atlas.js*, to be exact), you can find out how such a transformer is implemented. The function signature for a transformation expects two parameters. The first, a sender and an event, is usually not used. The second parameter contains the data to be transformed:

```
function myTransformer(sender, args) {
   var value = args.get_value();
   ...
```

After the transformation, the value must be written back to the event argument using its set_value( ) method:

```
   ...
   args.set_value(value);
}
```

Here is a possible implementation of a transformer that escapes HTML markup using JavaScript regular expressions. The g modifier at the end of the expression ensures that all occurrences of ampersands, angle brackets, or quotes are replaced.

```
function customHtmlEncode(sender, args) {
   var value = args.get_value();
   var newValue = value.replace(/&/g, "&amp;")
                       .replace(/</g, "&lt;")
                       .replace(/>/g, "&gt;")
```

```
                        .replace(/"/g, "&quot;")
                        .replace(/'/g, "&apos;");
       args.set_value(newValue);
    }
```

The last step is to add this function as the transformer for the data binding, just as you would do with a built-in transformer. Example 15-2 shows the complete code for a page that uses a custom transformer. Figure 15-2 displays the results.

Example 15-2. Using a custom transformer

ControlBindingCustom.aspx

```
<%@ Page Language="C#" %>

<!DOCTYPE html PUBLIC "-//W3C//DTD XHTML 1.0 Transitional//EN"
"http://www.w3.org/TR/xhtml1/DTD/xhtml1-transitional.dtd">
<html xmlns="http://www.w3.org/1999/xhtml">
<head id="Head1" runat="server">
  <title>ASP.NET AJAX</title>

  <script language="JavaScript" type="text/javascript">
  function pageLoad( ) {
    var textbox = new Sys.Preview.UI.TextBox($get("TextBox1"));
    var label = new Sys.Preview.UI.Label($get("Label1"));

    var binding = new Sys.Preview.Binding( );
    binding.set_dataContext(textbox);
    binding.set_dataPath("text");
    binding.set_property("text");
    binding.add_transform(customHtmlEncode);
    binding.set_target(label);

    textbox.initialize( );
    label.initialize( );
    binding.initialize( );
  }

  function customHtmlEncode(sender, args) {
    var value = args.get_value( );
    var newValue = value.replace(/&/g, "&amp;")
                        .replace(/</g, "&lt;")
                        .replace(/>/g, "&gt;")
                        .replace(/"/g, "&quot;")
                        .replace(/'/g, "&apos;");
    args.set_value(newValue);
  }
  </script>

</head>
<body>
  <form id="form1" runat="server">
    <asp:ScriptManager ID="ScriptManager1" runat="server">
```

Example 15-2. Using a custom transformer (continued)

```
    <Scripts>
      <asp:ScriptReference Name="PreviewScript.js" Assembly="Microsoft.Web.Preview" />
    </Scripts>
  </asp:ScriptManager>
  <div>
    <input type="text" id="TextBox1" /><br />
    <label id="Label1"></label>
  </div>
  </form>
</body>
</html>
```

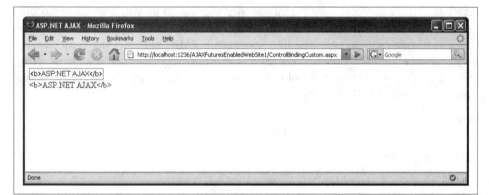

Figure 15-2. The HTML markup is escaped in the label

Using Markup for Data Binding: xml-script

The programmatic approach to data binding works beautifully, but a declarative approach has advantages as well. For example, with a declarative approach the issues that arise with use of the initialize( ) method (explained in the previous section) simply do not exist.

With its preview releases of ASP.NET AJAX, Microsoft introduced *xml-script*, a special markup format for adding functionality to ASP.NET AJAX pages. The ASP.NET AJAX team believed that using inline XML was a good way to provide needed information that the client's JavaScript interpreter can evaluate at runtime. It also offers developers a standards-compatible markup that is easy to read and might at one point even enjoy tool support. On the downside, there is no IntelliSense support for xml-script in Visual Studio. (For more details on this decision, read the blog entry at *http://www.nikhilk.net/AtlasXMLScript.aspx*). Somewhere along the line though, Microsoft decided to not pursue xml-script further. It is still available in the Futures release (and will therefore be used in this section), but chances that it will be promoted to the core ASP.NET AJAX Extensions are minimal.

The basic layout of xml-script is similar to the following:

```
<script type="text/xml-script">
  <page xmlns:script="http://schemas.microsoft.com/xml-script/2005">
    <components />
  </page>
</script>
```

ASP.NET AJAX relies on a markup element, <script>, but introduces the special type text/xml-script. This element is used to define ASP.NET AJAX functionality declaratively, data binding being a case in point. Within the <script> element, the <page> element is used to provide information about ensuing elements on the page and their bindings. The <components> section enables you to declaratively instantiate ASP.NET AJAX controls for elements on the page, such as you learned to do programmatically. The names of the tags for the supported HTML tags are very similar to the class names in Sys.Preview.UI, except the HTML tag names use camel casing, in which the initial word is lowercase and subsequent words uppercase (e.g., checkBox). The following is a list of the elements you can use in the <components> section to reference HTML elements:

<control>
> Generic element for any control

<label> *or* <span>
> A text label

> An image

<hyperLink>
> A link

<button>
> A button

<checkBox>
> A checkbox

<selector>
> A selection list

<textBox>
> A text field

To identify which of these tags represents which element on the page, you set the id property to the ID of the corresponding element:

```
<label id="Label1" />
```

Data bindings

A data binding is represented by the <binding> element, This element is declared as a child of the data binding control. Within the <binding> element, you can set the

---

properties listed in Table 15-1. These will be familiar to you from the examples earlier in this chapter.

Table 15-1. Properties for the <binding> element

Property	Description
dataContext	Element with the data to bind
dataPath	Property to be used as the binding source
property	Property to be used as the binding target
transformerArgument	Argument for the transformer
transform	Transformer to be used
direction	Direction in which to bind

It is probably obvious what the function of each of these properties is. One convenience you will appreciate is you do not need to provide the full namespace for transformers and directions. Instead, you can abbreviate using, for example, ToString in place of Sys.Preview.Binding.Transformers.ToString, or InOut rather than Sys.Preview.BindingDirection.InOut.

Using this xml-script markup, it is possible to bind data without writing code. One important fact though: referencing an HTML element in xml-script is equivalent to calling initialize( ) on it. Put another way, for any control that you must initialize, you must reference it in xml-script. Therefore, you also have to reference the text box in the xml-script markup, even though the binding is attached to the <label> element. Example 15-3 shows how this is done.

Example 15-3. Using ASP.NET AJAX bindings via xml-script markup

```
ControlBindingDeclarative.aspx

<%@ Page Language="C#" %>

<!DOCTYPE html PUBLIC "-//W3C//DTD XHTML 1.0 Transitional//EN"
"http://www.w3.org/TR/xhtml1/DTD/xhtml1-transitional.dtd">
<html xmlns="http://www.w3.org/1999/xhtml">
<head id="Head1" runat="server">
  <title>ASP.NET AJAX</title>
</head>
<body>
  <form id="form1" runat="server">
    <asp:ScriptManager runat="server">
      <Scripts>
        <asp:ScriptReference Name="PreviewScript.js" Assembly="Microsoft.Web.Preview" />
      </Scripts>
    </asp:ScriptManager>
    <div>
      <input type="text" id="TextBox1" /><br />
      <label id="Label1"></label>
    </div>
  </form>
```

Example 15-3. Using ASP.NET AJAX bindings via xml-script markup (continued)

```
      </form>
      <script type="text/xml-script">
        <page xmlns:script="http://schemas.microsoft.com/xml-script/2005">
          <components>
            <textBox id="TextBox1" />
            <label id="Label1">
              <bindings>
                <binding dataContext="TextBox1"
                         dataPath="text"
                         property="text"
                         transform="ToString"
                         transformerArgument="Text entered: {0}" />
              </bindings>
            </label>
          </components>
        </page>
      </script>
    </body>
    </html>
```

> If you are using a custom transformer, you do need code, but only for the transformer itself. You provide the transform function's name in the `transform` attribute, and the custom transformer is called when the binding occurs.

Event handling

Chapter 15 detailed client control event handling for ASP.NET AJAX. With xml-script, you can configure event handling in a fully declarative way.

As with data binding, everything takes place in the `<components>` section of the xml-script block. For each event (for example, `click`), there is an associated XML tag (`<click>`). Each event element supports the following three child elements:

`<setPropertyAction>` element
    Sets properties of an element

`<invokeMethodAction>` element
    Calls a method

`<button click="someFunction">`
    Declaratively adds an event handler

Let's begin with `<setPropertyAction>`. We will use a slightly modified version of Example 14-9, which changes CSS classes dynamically. This time, the CSS class is changed by setting the `class` property of the associated element.

The `<setPropertyAction>` tag supports the following attributes:

target

The element to access

property

The property to set

propertyKey

This property supports "dot" syntax (.) when using subproperties, such as style.borderStyle property must then be set to "element".

value

The new value

As an example, we want an action to be triggered when the user clicks a button. The \<click\> event is what you need to capture. The following code snippet changes the border style of a label when Button1 is pressed.

```
<label id="Label1" />
<button id="Button1">
  <click>
  <setProperty target="Label1"
              property="element"
              propertyKey="style.borderStyle"
              value="dotted" />
  </click>
</button>
```

This leads to the markup shown in Example 15-4, in which two buttons are defined, each with a different setPropertyAction definition. Figure 15-3 displays the result.

Example 15-4. Setting properties via xml-script

ControlDeclarativeProperty.aspx

```
<%@ Page Language="C#" %>

<!DOCTYPE html PUBLIC "-//W3C//DTD XHTML 1.0 Transitional//EN"
"http://www.w3.org/TR/xhtml1/DTD/xhtml1-transitional.dtd">
<html xmlns="http://www.w3.org/1999/xhtml">
<head id="Head1" runat="server">
  <title>ASP.NET AJAX</title>
</head>
<body>
  <form id="form1" runat="server">
    <asp:ScriptManager ID="ScriptManager1" runat="server">
      <Scripts>
        <asp:ScriptReference Name="PreviewScript.js" Assembly="Microsoft.Web.Preview" />
      </Scripts>
    </asp:ScriptManager>
    <div>
      <label id="Label1">This text will be reformatted</label>
    </div>
```

Example 15-4. Setting properties via xml-script (continued)

```
    <input type="button" id="Button1" value="Solid" />
    <input type="button" id="Button2" value="Dotted" />
  </form>
  <script type="text/xml-script">
    <page xmlns:script="http://schemas.microsoft.com/xml-script/2005">
      <components>
        <label id="Label1" />
        <button id="Button1">
          <click>
            <setPropertyAction target="Label1"
                               property="element"
                               propertyKey="style.borderStyle"
                               value="solid" />
          </click>
        </button>
        <button id="Button2">
          <click>
            <setPropertyAction target="Label1"
                               property="element"
                               propertyKey="style.borderStyle"
                               value="dotted" />
          </click>
        </button>
      </components>
    </page>
  </script>
</body>
</html>
```

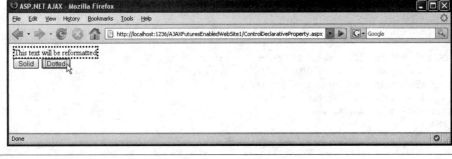

Figure 15-3. When you click a button, the CSS class of the text changes

Method invocation

Setting a property is convenient, but the ability to invoke a method when an event occurs is a must-have feature. As you might expect, this is also possible in xml-script. It requires two elements:

- The <invokeMethodAction> element
- The <parameters> element

`<invokeMethodAction>` supports the following attributes:

method

> Specifies which method to call

target

> Specifies the object whose method you are calling

You are not restricted merely to built-in functionality. For example, you can use the invokeMethodAction definition to call a web service method. Let's create a simple web service that returns one of two values: style1 or style2. Example 15-5 illustrates the code.

Example 15-5. The random CSS class web service

RandomCssClass.asmx

```
<%@ WebService Language="C#" Class="RandomCssClass" %>

using System;
using System.Web;
using System.Web.Services;
using System.Web.Services.Protocols;

[WebService(Namespace = "http://tempuri.org/")]
[WebServiceBinding(ConformsTo = WsiProfiles.BasicProfile1_1)]
[System.Web.Script.Services.ScriptService]
public class RandomCssClass  : System.Web.Services.WebService {

    [WebMethod]
    public string getRandomCssClass() {
      Random r = new Random();
      return "style" + r.Next(1, 3);
    }

}
```

Next, we want to use this web service to format an element according to the CSS class determined on the server. Here are the two CSS classes:

```
<style type="text/css">
  .style1 { font-family: Monospace; border-style: dotted; color: #0f0; }
  .style2 { font-family: Sans-Serif; border-style: solid; color: #0ff; }
</style>
```

The first step in xml-script is to define the web service so ASP.NET AJAX initializes it. To do this, we'll use the `<serviceMethodRequest>` element, which takes the following attributes:

id

> An identification that is used to refer to this web service method from other places in xml-script.

url

> The URL of the web service.

`methodName`

> The name of the web service method.

`useGet`

> Whether to use HTTP GET to call the web service. Set this to `false`, since HTTP GET is disabled by default.

```
<serviceMethodRequest id="randomCssMethod"
                      url="RandomCssClass.asmx"
                      methodName="getRandomCssClass"
                      useGet="false">
```

Whereas buttons can raise an event, such as `click`, a web service method request can handle the `<complete>` event, which is triggered once the web service returns data. When handling this event, we want to set the CSS class of a label appropriately. This is a case for `<setPropertyAction>`:

```
<completed>
  <setPropertyAction target="Label1"
                     property="element"
                     propertyKey="className">
```

The last step is crucial. We once again use ASP.NET AJAX data binding to bind the result of the web service call to the `className` property of the label. In the previous example, we set the property value of labels to hardcoded values. However, in the next example, we're setting a property to a dynamic value, which in this case is the result of the method call. For that, we need data binding.

Determining the values for `dataContext` ("randomCssMethod", the ID of the `<serviceMethodRequest>` element) and property ("value") is quite easy, but the `dataPath` value of `result` is something you need to look up (this is a reserved term). This leads to the following markup:

```
        <bindings>
          <binding dataContext="randomCssMethod"
                   dataPath="result"
                   property="value" />
        </bindings>
      </setPropertyAction>
    </completed>
  </serviceMethodRequest>
```

Finally, the method must be invoked when the button is clicked. By default, web service calls support the `userContext` property (see Chapter 5) to provide additional data to the call. The `<parameters>` element contains all parameters, in the form of attributes, so submitting one or more parameters to such a function is easy. These attributes have the format `parametername=parametervalue`, and as a result, subelements are not required.

The markup shown in the following snippet calls the web service method and provides an empty user context (which is the default, so you could actually omit `userContext` altogether).

```
<button id="Button1">
  <click>
    <invokeMethodAction target="randomCssMethod" method="invoke">
      <parameters userContext="" />
    </invokeMethodAction>
  </click>
</button>
```

That was a lot of effort, and scripting such as this is quite error-prone. For example, syntax errors in xml-script will surely catch your attention because the script does not work, but beyond that you do not get any additional clues. So, you might consider using an XML validator to check the xml-script. Example 15-6 contains the complete code, and Figure 15-4 shows the result in the browser.

Example 15-6. Invoking methods, web services, and data binding via xml-script

ControlDeclarativeMethod.aspx

```
<%@ Page Language="C#" %>

<!DOCTYPE html PUBLIC "-//W3C//DTD XHTML 1.0 Transitional//EN"
"http://www.w3.org/TR/xhtml1/DTD/xhtml1-transitional.dtd">
<html xmlns="http://www.w3.org/1999/xhtml">
<head id="Head1" runat="server">
  <title>ASP.NET AJAX</title>
  <style type="text/css">
  .style1 { font-family: Monospace; border-style: dotted; color: #0f0; }
  .style2 { font-family: Sans-Serif; border-style: solid; color: #0ff; }
  </style>
</head>
<body>
  <form id="form1" runat="server">
    <asp:ScriptManager ID="ScriptManager1" runat="server">
      <Services>
        <asp:ServiceReference Path="RandomCssClass.asmx" />
      </Services>
      <Scripts>
        <asp:ScriptReference Name="PreviewScript.js" Assembly="Microsoft.Web.Preview" />
      </Scripts>
    </asp:ScriptManager>
    <div>
      <label id="Label1">This text will be reformatted</label>
    </div>
    <input type="button" id="Button1" value="Random style" />
  </form>
    <script type="text/xml-script">
    <page xmlns:script="http://schemas.microsoft.com/xml-script/2005">
      <components>
        <label id="Label1" />
        <button id="Button1">
          <click>
            <invokeMethodAction target="randomCssMethod" method="invoke">
              <parameters userContext="" />
            </invokeMethodAction>
```

```
        </click>
      </button>
      <serviceMethodRequest id="randomCssMethod"
                            url="RandomCssClass.asmx"
                            methodName="getRandomCssClass"
                            useGet="false">
        <completed>
          <setPropertyAction target="Label1"
                             property="element"
                             propertyKey="className">
            <bindings>
              <binding dataContext="randomCssMethod"
                       dataPath="result"
                       property="value" />
            </bindings>
          </setPropertyAction>
        </completed>
      </serviceMethodRequest>
    </components>
  </page>
</script>
</body>
</html>
```

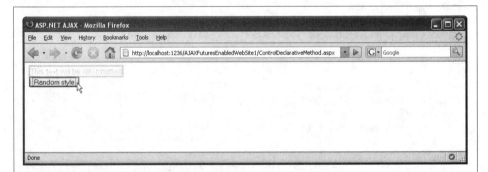

Figure 15-4. Clicking the button assigns a random CSS class to the label

 Although the web service is already referenced in xml-script, you still have to create the JavaScript proxy via the `ScriptManager` control, using the `<Services>` and `<asp:ServiceReference>` elements.

Data Validation

In addition to providing controls for data binding, the ASP.NET AJAX Futures release ships with its own client controls for validating user-entered data, a feature that many ASP.NET developers find useful. ASP.NET AJAX supports the following validators:

`requiredFieldValidator`

Checks whether the user has entered a value into a control

`regexValidator`

Checks the data in a control against a regular expression to match a pattern

`typeValidator`

Checks the data in a control against a data type

`rangeValidator`

Checks the data in a control against a value range

`customValidator`

Checks the data in a control using a custom validation function

> If you are working with an `UpdatePanel` control, you can use server-based ASP.NET validators to check input in any server controls within the panel. However, you need an updated version of these controls that is compatible with ASP.NET AJAX. For details, see the following blog entry by Matt Gibbs: *http://blogs.msdn.com/mattgi/archive/2007/05/12/validators-update-available.aspx*.

To implement data validation, you need:

- A control to validate
- A way to display an error message if the validation fails
- Code or markup to do the validation

In the following sections you'll see how to put each of the ASP.NET AJAX validators to work, including how to generate your own custom validation.

Checking a Required Field

The commonly used `requiredFieldValidator` class checks whether a control contains data. The following markup generates both an input field and a span in which to display any validator-generated:

```
<input type="text" id="TextBox1" />
<span id="Error1" style="color: red;">*</span>
```

As you can see, the label for the error message is not hidden by default. ASP.NET AJAX takes care of hiding it automatically.

In the xml-script for the page, add markup for the controls taking part in the validation—only the user-input elements, though, not any controls for displaying errors. In the `<validators>` subelement of an input control, specify the validator to use. The `errorMessage` property contains the text to display if validation fails. However, the ASP.NET AJAX validator is different than its ASP.NET counterpart.

In ASP.NET AJAX, the value of the errorMessage property is used as a tool tip that appears when you hold the mouse pointer over the error text (that is, over the ASP.NET AJAX validator control).

While we're on the subject of error text, there is no equivalent for the Text property of ASP.NET validation controls. The error text that appears in the label is the text that is already there. The following example shows the xml-script for defining a required field validator associated with a TextBox control:

```
<textBox id="TextBox1">
  <validators>
    <requiredFieldValidator errorMessage-"** TextBox1 value missing" />
  </validators>
</textBox>
```

The second step is to use the <validationErrorLabel> element. This element takes the following attributes:

id
> The ID of the control to display errors

associatedControl
> The ID of the element to validate

A complete page with validation is shown in Example 15-7.

Example 15-7. Using a validator for required fields

ControlValidationRequiredField.aspx

```
<%@ Page Language="C#" %>

<!DOCTYPE html PUBLIC "-//W3C//DTD XHTML 1.0 Transitional//EN"
"http://www.w3.org/TR/xhtml1/DTD/xhtml1-transitional.dtd">
<html xmlns="http://www.w3.org/1999/xhtml">
<head id="Head1" runat="server">
  <title>ASP.NET AJAX</title>
</head>
<body>
  <form id="form1" runat="server">
    <asp:ScriptManager ID="ScriptManager1" runat="server">
      <Scripts>
        <asp:ScriptReference Name="PreviewScript.js" Assembly="Microsoft.Web.Preview" />
      </Scripts>
    </asp:ScriptManager>
    <div>
      <input type="text" id="TextBox1" />
      <span id="Error1" style="color: red;">*</span>
      <br />
      <input type="submit" />
    </div>
  </form>
  <script type="text/xml-script">
    <page xmlns:script="http://schemas.microsoft.com/xml-script/2005">
      <components>
```

Example 15-7. Using a validator for required fields (continued)

```
        <textBox id="TextBox1">
          <validators>
            <requiredFieldValidator errorMessage="** TextBox1 value missing" />
          </validators>
        </textBox>
        <validationErrorLabel id="Error1" associatedControl="TextBox1" />
      </components>
    </page>
  </script>
</body>
</html>
```

Load the page, enter some data in the text field, and then leave the field (which raises the change event—don't click the button to submit the page). Now, enter the field again, delete its contents and exit the field. The change event is raised once more, this time triggering the validation control. As shown in Figure 15-5, error displays appear as a tool tip and as a (longer) text message in a display label.

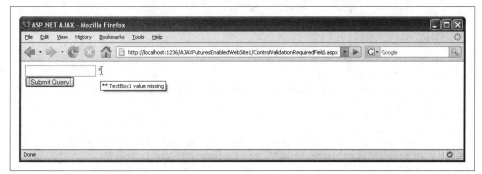

Figure 15-5. The error text, including more information in the tool tip

In this case, the validator displays an error if the user doesn't enter data, but the user can still submit the page. The validator is informational only. Later in the chapter we'll see how to prevent a page from being submitted if validation doesn't pass.

Checking Against a Regular Expression

Using a regular expression to check data validity functions just like the ASP.NET RegularExpressionValidation control, but the name of the XML element and its attributes are different. The regex property (or attribute, depending on whether you are using code or markup) provides the regular expression against which the validator checks the data:

```
        <regexValidator regex="/\d*/" errorMessage="** digits only" />
```

The code shown in Example 15-8 contains two validators: one checks whether there is *anything* in the text field, the other allows only digits. You could also achieve this using a data type check, but I want to demonstrate the regexValidator control here.

Example 15-8. Using an ASP.NET AJAX validator with a regular expression

ControlValidationRegex.aspx

```
<%@ Page Language="C#" %>

<!DOCTYPE html PUBLIC "-//W3C//DTD XHTML 1.0 Transitional//EN"
"http://www.w3.org/TR/xhtml1/DTD/xhtml1-transitional.dtd">
<html xmlns="http://www.w3.org/1999/xhtml">
<head id="Head1" runat="server">
  <title>ASP.NET AJAX</title>
</head>
<body>
  <form id="form1" runat="server">
    <asp:ScriptManager ID="ScriptManager1" runat="server">
      <Scripts>
        <asp:ScriptReference Name="PreviewScript.js" Assembly="Microsoft.Web.Preview" />
      </Scripts>
    </asp:ScriptManager>
    <div>
      <input type="text" id="TextBox1" />
      <span id="Error1" style="color: red;">*</span>
      <br />
      <input type="submit" />
    </div>
  </form>
  <script type="text/xml-script">
    <page xmlns:script="http://schemas.microsoft.com/xml-script/2005">
      <components>
        <textBox id="TextBox1">
          <validators>
            <requiredFieldValidator errorMessage="** TextBox1 value missing" />
            <regexValidator regex="/\d*/" errorMessage="** digits only" />
          </validators>
        </textBox>
        <validationErrorLabel id="Error1" associatedControl="TextBox1" />
      </components>
    </page>
  </script>
</body>
</html>
```

Checking the Data Type

The <typeValidator> element checks the data type of a value. The only data type currently supported is Number, but other types might be added in future releases. The type property of the <typeValidator> element contains the data type:

```
<typeValidator type="Number" errorMessage="** numbers only" />
```

The code shown in Example 15-9 uses both a requiredFieldValidator and typeValidator to check for numeric values only.

Example 15-9. Using avalidator for a data type check

ControlValidationType.aspx

```
<%@ Page Language="C#" %>

<!DOCTYPE html PUBLIC "-//W3C//DTD XHTML 1.0 Transitional//EN"
"http://www.w3.org/TR/xhtml1/DTD/xhtml1-transitional.dtd">
<html xmlns="http://www.w3.org/1999/xhtml">
<head runat="server">
  <title>ASP.NET AJAX</title>
</head>
<body>
  <form id="form1" runat="server">
    <asp:ScriptManager ID="ScriptManager1" runat="server">
      <Scripts>
        <asp:ScriptReference Name="PreviewScript.js"
          Assembly="Microsoft.Web.Preview" />
      </Scripts>
    </asp:ScriptManager>
    <div>
      <input type="text" id="TextBox1" />
      <span id="Error1" style="color: red;">*</span>
      <br />
      <input type="submit" />
    </div>
  </form>
  <script type="text/xml-script">
    <page xmlns:script="http://schemas.microsoft.com/xml-script/2005">
      <components>
        <textBox id="TextBox1">
          <validators>
            <requiredFieldValidator errorMessage="** TextBox1 value missing" />
            <typeValidator type="Number" errorMessage="** numbers only" />
          </validators>
        </textBox>
        <validationErrorLabel id="Error1"
                              associatedControl="TextBox1" />
      </components>
    </page>
  </script>
</body>
</html>
```

Checking a Range

Sometimes a value must not only be numeric, but must also have a value that falls within a certain range (for instance, this is often true for time intervals or dates). For these tasks, you can use the `<rangeValidator>` element. The lower and upper limits are set in the `lowerBound` and `upperBound` properties. The following markup shows how to check for a value between 1 and 6:

```
<rangeValidator lowerBound="1" upperBound="6" errorMessage="** 1 to 6 only" />
```

Example 15-10 builds on the preceding example. The data is checked not only with a requiredFieldValidator and a typeValidator, but now with a rangeValidator as well.

Example 15-10. Using a validator to verify a valid range

ControlValidationRange.aspx

```
<%@ Page Language="C#" %>

<!DOCTYPE html PUBLIC "-//W3C//DTD XHTML 1.0 Transitional//EN"
"http://www.w3.org/TR/xhtml1/DTD/xhtml1-transitional.dtd">
<html xmlns="http://www.w3.org/1999/xhtml">
<head runat="server">
  <title>ASP.NET AJAX</title>
</head>
<body>
  <form id="form1" runat="server">
    <asp:ScriptManager ID="ScriptManager1" runat="server">
      <Scripts>
        <asp:ScriptReference Name="PreviewScript.js"
          Assembly="Microsoft.Web.Preview" />
      </Scripts>
    </asp:ScriptManager>
    <div>
      <input type="text" id="TextBox1" />
      <span id="Error1" style="color: red;">*</span>
      <br />
      <input type="submit" />
    </div>
  </form>
  <script type="text/xml-script">
    <page xmlns:script="http://schemas.microsoft.com/xml-script/2005">
      <components>
        <textBox id="TextBox1">
          <validators>
            <requiredFieldValidator errorMessage="** TextBox1 value missing" />
            <typeValidator type="Number" errorMessage="** numbers only" />
            <rangeValidator lowerBound="1" upperBound="6" errorMessage="** 1 to 6 only" />
          </validators>
        </textBox>
        <validationErrorLabel id="Error1"
                              associatedControl="TextBox1" />
      </components>
    </page>
  </script>
</body>
</html>
```

Custom Validation

To achieve the greatest flexibility, you can write a custom function to validate user data. The signature for your validation function is as follows:

```
function <name>(sender, args) { }
```

The first parameter contains the element which caused the validation, but more important is the second parameter that provides the validation value, which can be retrieved using get_value( ). After validation, call the set_isValid( ) method. If validation succeeds, pass true as a parameter. If it fails, pass false.

Just for purposes of illustration, let's consider that for some inexplicable reason only square numbers may now be entered into the text field. The following function performs the validation:

```
function validateSquare(sender, args) {
  var value = args.get_value( );
  args.set_isValid(Math.sqrt(value) == Math.floor(Math.sqrt(value)));
}
```

In the xml-script, the <customValidator> element must include a validateValue attribute that references your new custom validation function:

```
<customValidator validateValue="validateSquare" errormessage="** square numbers
only" />
```

The Visibility Mode of a Validation Control

We have yet to cover a particular property of validation controls, visibilityMode. To be more accurate, it is a property of the <validationErrorLabel> element and takes one of two possible values (via the Sys.UI.VisibilityMode enumeration):

- Collapse
- Hide

The display style (or in JavaScript: *element*.style.display) is set to this mode. If no visibility mode is provided, "none" is used (which makes the error message invisible and also makes the area it consumed on the page available to other elements). This controls how the validation error Label control is hidden when the page has been loaded.

Example 15-11 shows the complete code for this custom validator.

Example 15-11. Using a custom validator

ControlValidationCustom.aspx

```
<%@ Page Language="C#" %>

<!DOCTYPE html PUBLIC "-//W3C//DTD XHTML 1.0 Transitional//EN"
"http://www.w3.org/TR/xhtml1/DTD/xhtml1-transitional.dtd">
<html xmlns="http://www.w3.org/1999/xhtml">
<head id="Head1" runat="server">
  <title>ASP.NET AJAX</title>
```

Example 15-11. Using a custom validator (continued)

```
<script type="text/javascript">
function validateSquare(sender, args) {
  var value = args.get_value();
  args.set_isValid(Math.sqrt(value) == Math.floor(Math.sqrt(value)));
}
</script>
</head>
<body>
  <form id="form1" runat="server">
    <asp:ScriptManager ID="ScriptManager1" runat="server">
      <Scripts>
        <asp:ScriptReference Name="PreviewScript.js" Assembly="Microsoft.Web.Preview" />
      </Scripts>
    </asp:ScriptManager>
    <div>
      <input type="text" id="TextBox1" />
      <span id="Error1" style="color: red;">*</span>
      <br />
      <input type="submit" />
    </div>
  </form>
  <script type="text/xml-script">
    <page xmlns:script="http://schemas.microsoft.com/xml-script/2005">
      <components>
        <textBox id="TextBox1">
          <validators>
            <requiredFieldValidator errorMessage="** TextBox1 value missing" />
            <typeValidator type="Number" errorMessage="** numbers only" />
            <customValidator validateValue="validateSquare" errorMessage="** square
numbers only" />
          </validators>
        </textBox>
        <validationErrorLabel id="Error1" associatedControl="TextBox1" />
      </components>
    </page>
  </script>
</body>
</html>
```

Programmatic Validation

The declarative approach fares well in practice, but there is a programmatic approach to validation as well (which basically adds the validation at runtime).

It still requires some declarations though, such as we can see in the following snippet:

```
<textBox id="TextBox1">
</textBox>
<validationErrorLabel id="Error1"
                      associatedControl="TextBox1" />
```

You can then create the validator using JavaScript code. Two steps are required:

1. Add the validator: *element*.get_validators( ).add(*validator*).

2. If you want to use a callback function (a function to be called when the validation has occurred), use *element*.add_validated(*function*).

You cannot make the element available for validation with the usual new Sys. Preview.UI.*XXX* approach. Instead, you must use the peculiar-looking syntax that was presented during the discussion on preventing form submissions:

```
var textbox = $get("TextBox1").control;
```

The client-side element is accessed using the dollar sign, then you may access its control property. Example 15-12 shows a complete page utilizing a programmatic approach to validation. This example performs the same required-field validation highlighted in Example 15-7, but it adds the validator to the text box using Java-Script code.

Example 15-12. Using a custom validator programmatically

ControlValidationCustomProgrammatic.aspx

```
<%@ Page Language="C#" %>

<!DOCTYPE html PUBLIC "-//W3C//DTD XHTML 1.0 Transitional//EN"
"http://www.w3.org/TR/xhtml1/DTD/xhtml1-transitional.dtd">
<html xmlns="http://www.w3.org/1999/xhtml">
<head id="Head1" runat="server">
  <title>ASP.NET AJAX</title>
  <script type="text/javascript">
  function pageLoad( ) {
    var textbox = $get("TextBox1").control;
    validator = new Sys.Preview.UI.RequiredFieldValidator( );
    validator.set_errorMessage("** enter some data");
    textbox.get_validators( ).add(validator);
    textbox.add_validated(validationComplete);
  }

  function validationComplete(sender, args) {
  }
  </script>
</head>
<body>
  <form id="form1" runat="server">
    <asp:ScriptManager ID="ScriptManager1" runat="server">
      <Scripts>
        <asp:ScriptReference Name="PreviewScript.js" Assembly="Microsoft.Web.Preview" />
      </Scripts>
    </asp:ScriptManager>
    <div>
      <input type="text" id="TextBox1" />
      <span id="Error1" style="color: red;">*</span>
      <br />
```

Example 15-12. Using a custom validator programmatically (continued)

```
      <input type="submit" />
    </div>
  </form>
  <script type="text/xml-script">
    <page xmlns:script="http://schemas.microsoft.com/xml-script/2005">
      <components>
        <textBox id="TextBox1">
        </textBox>
        <validationErrorLabel id="Error1"
                              associatedControl="TextBox1" />
      </components>
    </page>
  </script>
</body>
</html>
```

This also works for more complex validators, including the custom validator. The syntax for declaring a custom validation function is the following:

validator.add_validateValue(*validation function*);

Example 15-13 demonstrates how to add validators to input controls both declaratively and programmatically. The required field and type validators are added declaratively; the custom validator is added programmatically. The result is the same as has been demonstrated in earlier examples.

Example 15-13. Adding validation declaratively and programmatically

ControlValidationRequiredFieldProgrammatic.aspx

```
<%@ Page Language="C#" %>

<!DOCTYPE html PUBLIC "-//W3C//DTD XHTML 1.0 Transitional//EN"
"http://www.w3.org/TR/xhtml1/DTD/xhtml1-transitional.dtd">
<html xmlns="http://www.w3.org/1999/xhtml">
<head id="Head1" runat="server">
  <title>ASP.NET AJAX</title>
  <script language="JavaScript" type="text/javascript">
  function validateSquare(sender, args) {
    var value = args.get_value();
    args.set_isValid(Math.sqrt(value) == Math.floor(Math.sqrt(value)));
  }
  function pageLoad() {
    var textbox = $get("TextBox1").control;
    validator = new Sys.Preview.UI.CustomValidator();
    validator.set_errorMessage("Square numbers only");
    validator.add_validateValue(validateSquare);
    textbox.get_validators().add(validator);
    textbox.add_validated(validationComplete);
  }
  function validationComplete(sender, args) {
```

Example 15-13. Adding validation declaratively and programmatically (continued)

```
    }
    </script>
</head>
<body>
    <form id="form1" runat="server">
        <asp:ScriptManager ID="ScriptManager1" runat="server">
            <Scripts>
                <asp:ScriptReference Name="PreviewScript.js" Assembly="Microsoft.Web.Preview" />
            </Scripts>
        </asp:ScriptManager>
        <div>
            <input type="text" id="TextBox1" />
            <span id="Error1" style="color: red;">*</span>
            <br />
            <input type="submit" />
        </div>
    </form>
    <script type="text/xml-script">
        <page xmlns:script="http://schemas.microsoft.com/xml-script/2005">
            <components>
                <textBox id="TextBox1">
                    <validators>
                        <requiredFieldValidator errorMessage="** TextBox1 value missing" />
                        <typeValidator type="Number" errorMessage="** numbers only" />
                    </validators>
                </textBox>
                <validationErrorLabel id="Error1"
                                      associatedControl="TextBox1" />
            </components>
        </page>
    </script>
</body>
</html>
```

Validation Groups

Validation controls can be grouped together allowing multiple controls to be validated as a single unit. Validation groups are created using the <validationGroup> element. All the validators in a group perform their test individually, but the group can be tested as a whole. If any individual validation check fails, the entire group fails. Not surprisingly, on the other hand, if all the controls validate, then the group passes. Grouping is particularly useful for being able to enable and disable sets of validators conditionally. In the following example you will see how to make an element visible only if all validator conditions are met.

The validation group exposes a method, isValid( ) to determine whether the validation failed or not. This can be used in conjunction with data binding to display a message depending on whether the validation succeeds or fails.

First, you must provide an element to display the message:

```
<div id="Errors">-no errors-</div>
```

Next, bind this element's visible property to the validation group's isValid()
method. If all the validators in the group have passed, the <div> element will be
visible.

```
<label id="Errors">
  <bindings>
    <binding dataContext="group" dataPath="isValid" property="visible" />
  </bindings>
</label>
```

To make the <div> element visible if the validation *fails*, use the Invert transformer:

```
<binding dataContext="group" dataPath="isValid" property="visible"
transform="Invert" />
```

At this point, apart from the actual validators, only one thing is missing: the validation group itself. The group is represented by the <validationGroup> element. It
needs an ID (the preceding markup for data binding is using "group" as the target
ID), and within the group element, all form elements that take part in the validation
are referenced, as shown here:

```
<validationGroup id="group" >
  <associatedControls>
    <reference component="TextBox1" />
    <reference component="TextBox2" />
  </associatedControls>
</validationGroup>
```

Example 15-14 shows a page with a validation group. In the page, the <div> element
displays -no errors- when all the text boxes have passed validation. The first text
box has a required field validator, meaning the <div> element is displayed only when
that text box has received some input. The second text box requires a numeric value
that's a square number. Figure 15-6 displays the result.

Example 15-14. Using a validation group bound to a label

CustomValidationGroup.aspx

```
<%@ Page Language="C#" %>

<!DOCTYPE html PUBLIC "-//W3C//DTD XHTML 1.0 Transitional//EN"
"http://www.w3.org/TR/xhtml1/DTD/xhtml1-transitional.dtd">
<html xmlns="http://www.w3.org/1999/xhtml">
<head id="Head1" runat="server">
  <title>ASP.NET AJAX</title>
  <script language="JavaScript" type="text/javascript">
  function validateSquare(sender, args) {
    var value = args.get_value();
    args.set_isValid(Math.sqrt(value) == Math.floor(Math.sqrt(value)));
  }
```

Example 15-14. Using a validation group bound to a label (continued)

```
    </script>
</head>
<body>
  <form id="form1" runat="server">
    <asp:ScriptManager ID="ScriptManager1" runat="server">
      <Scripts>
        <asp:ScriptReference Name="PreviewScript.js" Assembly="Microsoft.Web.Preview" />
      </Scripts>
    </asp:ScriptManager>
    <div>
      Anything: <input type="text" id="TextBox1" />
      <span id="Error1" style="color: red;">*</span>
      <br />
      A square: <input type="text" id="TextBox2" />
      <span id="Error2" style="color: red;">*</span>
      <br />
      <input type="submit" />
    </div>
    <div id="Errors">-no errors-</div>
  </form>
  <script type="text/xml-script">
    <page xmlns:script="http://schemas.microsoft.com/xml-script/2005">
      <components>
        <textBox id="TextBox1">
          <validators>
            <requiredFieldValidator errorMessage="** TextBox1 value missing" />
          </validators>
        </textBox>
        <validationErrorLabel id="Error1"
                              associatedControl="TextBox1" />
        <textBox id="TextBox2">
          <validators>
            <requiredFieldValidator errorMessage="** TextBox2 value missing" />
            <typeValidator type="Number" errorMessage="** numbers only" />
            <customValidator validateValue="validateSquare" errorMessage="** square
numbers only" />
          </validators>
        </textBox>
        <validationErrorLabel id="Error2"
                              associatedControl="TextBox2" />
        <validationGroup id="group">
          <associatedControls>
            <reference component="TextBox1" />
            <reference component="TextBox2" />
          </associatedControls>
        </validationGroup>
        <label id="Errors">
          <bindings>
            <binding dataContext="group" dataPath="isValid" property="visible" />
          </bindings>
        </label>
      </components>
```

Example 15-14. Using a validation group bound to a label (continued)

```
        </page>
      </script>
  </body>
</html>
```

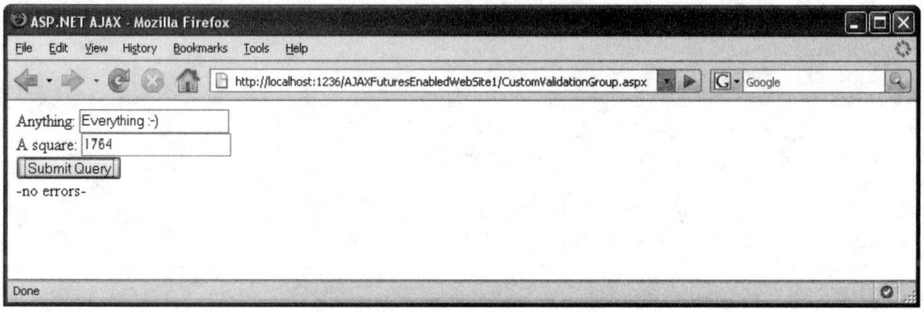

Figure 15-6. The label appears only when all text boxes are filled correctly

Preventing Form Submission

The validation controls that come with the ASP.NET AJAX Futures release are quite useful, but they do not include a form submission mechanism. So, even if a validation fails, a form can be submitted. Usually this is no great concern, as all form data must be revalidated on the server anyway (JavaScript could be deactivated, so you can never truly rely on client-side validation). However, the usability of the form may be better if it can only be submitted when all values are correct.

Adding this functionality requires a bit of custom code, but it's not difficult. We will start with Example 15-7 (the validator for required fields) and add the feature to prevent form submission. The trick is to hook an event that is raised by the <form> tag. Thanks to the event handler system, we can execute JavaScript code when the form is being submitted (the event submit is triggered). If this code is return false, the form submission is cancelled. This is how the <form> tag is modified:

```
<form id="form1" runat="server" onsubmit="return validateForm( );">
```

The validateForm( ) method returns false if the form is incomplete, otherwise, it returns true. This can be easily achieved by using the get_isInvalid( ) helper method, which is defined as a method of the text box control (use the control property of the associated HTML element):

```
function validateForm( ) {
  var textbox = $get("TextBox1").control;
  return !(textbox.get_isInvalid( ));
}
```

The complete code is displayed in Example 15-15.

Example 15-15. Using a validation group bound to a label

CustomValidationGroup.aspx

```
<%@ Page Language="C#" %>

<!DOCTYPE html PUBLIC "-//W3C//DTD XHTML 1.0 Transitional//EN"
"http://www.w3.org/TR/xhtml1/DTD/xhtml1-transitional.dtd">
<html xmlns="http://www.w3.org/1999/xhtml">
<head id="Head1" runat="server">
  <title>ASP.NET AJAX</title>
  <script type="text/javascript">
  function validateForm( ) {
    var textbox = $get("TextBox1").control;
    return !(textbox.get_isInvalid( ));
  }
  </script>
</head>
<body>
  <form id="form1" runat="server" onsubmit="return validateForm( );">
    <asp:ScriptManager ID="ScriptManager1" runat="server">
      <Scripts>
        <asp:ScriptReference Name="PreviewScript.js" Assembly="Microsoft.Web.Preview" />
      </Scripts>
    </asp:ScriptManager>
    <div>
      <input type="text" id="TextBox1" />
      <span id="Error1" style="color: red;">*</span>
      <br />
      <input type="submit" />
    </div>
  </form>
  <script type="text/xml-script">
    <page xmlns:script="http://schemas.microsoft.com/xml-script/2005">
      <components>
        <textBox id="TextBox1">
          <validators>
            <requiredFieldValidator errorMessage="** TextBox1 value missing" />
          </validators>
        </textBox>
        <validationErrorLabel id="Error1" associatedControl="TextBox1" />
      </components>
    </page>
  </script>
</body>
</html>
```

Expanding this code for more form elements is straightforward; the validateForm( )
function then simply returns something like this:

```
!(formelement1.get_isInvalid( ) || formelement2.get_isInvalid( ) || ...)
```

Summary

In this chapter, you were introduced to data binding and the client-side validation controls that are a part of ASP.NET AJAX Futures release. When compared to ASP.NET validation controls, they lack some features. Using the ASP.NET AJAX controls is also a bit unusual when compared with their server equivalents. They do not integrate in the form submission mechanism of the browser, which means that the form can be submitted even if errors exist. Finally, and most important, validation works only on the client side and only with JavaScript. ASP.NET validation controls work on both the server-side and the client-side and therefore cannot be circumvented by merely disabling JavaScript. This makes them the preferable choice if the option is available. However, if the web site uses ASP.NET AJAX for all client-side effects, the ASP.NET AJAX validators integrate well with other ASP.NET AJAX features.

For Further Reading

http://blogs.msdn.com/mattgi/archive/2007/05/12/validators-update-available.aspx
> Blog entry by Matt Gibbs regarding an updated version of the validators that also work within UpdatePanel controls

http://quickstarts.asp.net/Futures/ajax/doc/bindings.aspx
> Pre-release Microsoft documentation on data bindings

http://quickstarts.asp.net/Futures/ajax/doc/validation.aspx
> Pre-release Microsoft documentation on validators

CHAPTER 16

Using Behaviors and Components

Handling events with script code or xml-script can be a practical way to create user experiences that are more interactive, but sometimes this approach just requires too much code. This is especially true when you wish to tie a specific action to a particular control, such as one that is a reaction to a user clicking or hovering over it. Fortunately, ASP.NET AJAX offers viable alternatives that will be introduced and discussed in this chapter: ASP.NET AJAX *behaviors* and *components*.

Whereas ASP.NET AJAX behaviors contain JavaScript functionality and are always tied to visible HTML page elements, ASP.NET AJAX components, which consist of JavaScript, might or might not have a graphical representation. One example of this, the `Timer` control was discussed in Chapter 6, which demonstrated an instance of a component that is not represented graphically on the page.

In this chapter, we will explore the behaviors and components that ship with the ASP.NET AJAX Futures release and demonstrate how to use them.

Using Behaviors

ASP.NET AJAX behaviors are similar to those introduced by Microsoft for Internet Explorer in that you can attach a predefined ASP.NET AJAX behavior to an HTML element just as you can attach an Internet Explorer behavior. For instance, one behavior that ships with Internet Explorer allows you to do something when the mouse pointer hovers over an element, such as a button, perhaps altering its color or font.

The ASP.NET AJAX Futures release actually ships with only one behavior—`Sys.Preview.UI.ClickBehavior`. Other behaviors are defined in additional ASP.NET AJAX Futures libraries that can be reference in your application. These include:

- `Sys.Preview.UI.FloatingBehavior` (defined in *PreviewDragDrop.js*, discussed later in this chapter)
- `Sys.Preview.UI.OpacityBehavior` (defined in *PreviewGlitz.js* in Chapter 19)
- `Sys.Preview.UI.LayoutBehavior` (also defined in *PreviewGlitz.js*)

Using the Click Behavior

`Sys.Preview.UI.ClickBehavior` ties a click on an element to an executable action (the name kind of says it all).

The example shown in this section demonstrates this in more detail. This example simulates tabbed browsing, a popular feature of browsers such as Firefox, Opera, and Internet Explorer 7.

 This example creates tabs for the purposes of demonstrating a simple way to work with behaviors. If you want to include tabs in your application, use the Tabs control from the Control Toolkit. Refer to Chapter 12 for a detailed discussion.

Two `<div>` elements represent the two tabs; the user can toggle between them using two `<span>` elements:

```
<div>
  <span id="Show1" style="background-color: Fuchsia;">Tab 1</span>
  <span id="Show2" style="background-color: Fuchsia;">Tab 2</span>
</div>
<div id="Panel1" style="visibility: visible; position: absolute; top: 35px; left:
10px">
  This is the first tab.<br />
  It is full of ASP.NET AJAX information.<br />
  Although it seems to be full of dummy text.
</div>
<div id="Panel2" style="visibility: hidden; position: absolute; top: 35px; left:
10px">
  This is the second tab.<br />
  It is full of ASP.NET AJAX information as well.<br />
  Although it seems to be full of dummy text, too.
</div>
```

The rest of the page will consist of declarative elements only, so no code is required. Once again, xml-script will come in handy. First, the two `<div>` elements must be registered to make them accessible later to behaviors. Recall there is no client-side web control in `Sys.Preview.UI` that represents a `<div>` panel, but a generic `<control>` element can be used, as shown in the following snippet:

```
<control id="Panel1" />
<control id="Panel2" />
```

The behaviors must be attached to the individual `<span>` elements that constitute the actual tabs. First, the elements must be registered:

```
<label id="Show1">
...
</label>
```

Then, a set of subelements comes into play:

- A <behaviors> element, which will contain all behaviors to be attached to the element.

- An element for each behavior to implement. For this example, a <clickBehavior> element must be used.

- Within this element, a <click> subelement must be defined, which identifies the event associated with this behavior. (It is possible for some behaviors to monitor more than one event.) Here's the markup for one <span> element, or, one tab:

```
<label id="Show1">
  <behaviors>
    <clickBehavior>
      <click>
      ...
      </click>
    </clickBehavior>
  </behaviors>
</label>
```

At this point, the <setPropertyAction> or <invokeMethodAction> elements introduced in Chapter 15 enter the stage. When a user clicks the first <span> element, the first panel is made visible, and the second invisible. Here's the markup to accomplish this:

```
<label id="Show1">
  <behaviors>
    <clickBehavior>
      <click>
        <setPropertyAction target="Panel1" property="visible" value="true" />
        <setPropertyAction target="Panel2" property="visible" value="false" />
      </click>
    </clickBehavior>
  </behaviors>
</label>
```

When the second <span> element is clicked, the first panel becomes invisible and the second, visible. Example 16-1 shows the complete markup required to implement a tabbed page.

Example 16-1. Using the click behavior

```
BehaviorClick.aspx

<%@ Page Language="C#" %>

<!DOCTYPE html PUBLIC "-//W3C//DTD XHTML 1.0 Transitional//EN"
"http://www.w3.org/TR/xhtml1/DTD/xhtml1-transitional.dtd">
<html xmlns="http://www.w3.org/1999/xhtml">
<head id="Head1" runat="server">
```

Example 16-1. Using the click behavior (continued)

```
  <title>ASP.NET AJAX</title>
</head>
<body>
  <form id="form1" runat="server">
    <asp:ScriptManager runat="server" ID="ScriptManager1">
      <Scripts>
        <asp:ScriptReference name="PreviewScript.js"
assembly="Microsoft.Web.Preview" />
      </Scripts>
    </asp:ScriptManager>
    <div>
      <span id="Show1" style="background-color: Fuchsia;">Tab 1</span>
      <span id="Show2" style="background-color: Fuchsia;">Tab 2</span>
    </div>
    <div id="Panel1" style="visibility: visible; position: absolute; top: 35px;
left: 10px">
      This is the first tab.<br />
      It is full of ASP.NET AJAX information.<br />
      Although it seems to be full of dummy text.
    </div>
    <div id="Panel2" style="visibility: hidden; position: absolute; top: 35px; left:
10px">
      This is the second tab.<br />
      It is full of ASP.NET AJAX information, as well.<br />
      Although it seems to be full of dummy text, too.
    </div>
  </form>

  <script type="text/xml-script">
    <page xmlns:script="http://schemas.microsoft.com/xml-script/2005">
      <components>
        <control id="Panel1" />
        <control id="Panel2" />
        <label id="Show1">
          <behaviors>
            <clickBehavior>
              <click>
                <setPropertyAction target="Panel1"
property="visible" value="true" />
                <setPropertyAction target="Panel2"
property="visible" value="false" />
              </click>
            </clickBehavior>
          </behaviors>
        </label>
        <label id="Show2">
          <behaviors>
            <clickBehavior>
              <click>
                <setPropertyAction target="Panel1"
property="visible" value="false" />
                <setPropertyAction target="Panel2"
```

Example 16-1. Using the click behavior (continued)

```
property="visible" value="true" />
            </click>
          </clickBehavior>
        </behaviors>
      </label>
    </components>
  </page>
</script>
</body>
</html>
```

Figure 16-1 shows the page displayed by the markup in Example 16-1.

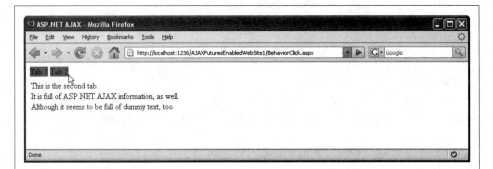

Figure 16-1. Clicking on the labels loads the associated tab

 Unlike when hovering over a hyperlink, the mouse cursor does not change when hovering over the click area. If you would like this effect on your page, it can be implemented using the CSS style cursor: hand:

```
<span id="Show1" style="background-color: Fuchsia;
cursor: hand">Tab 1</span>

<span id="Show2" style="background-color: Fuchsia;
cursor: hand">Tab 2</span>
```

Using the Drag-and-Drop Behavior

Unlike the click behavior described earlier, the drag-and-drop behavior of the Futures release does not have a self-descriptive name, such as DragDropBehavior, or something similar. Rather, it labors under the ambiguous name FloatingBehavior. Drag-and-drop is a feature that is widely used by web portals nowadays, but is not part of the *PreviewScript.js* JavaScript library that ships with the ASP.NET AJAX Futures CTP. Instead, the functionality resides in the extra file *PreviewDragDrop.js* (there is the term "DragDrop").

Implementing drag-and-drop using ASP.NET AJAX is simple. First, you need an ASP.NET Panel control to drag. An HTML <div> would work as well, but using the Panel makes it easy to put a random value within, as you will see in a moment.

In this example, we use the panel to create a small status bar to simulate a display that shows the number of messages in a user's inbox:

```
<asp:Panel CssClass="mailbox" ID="DragPanel" runat="server">
  <p>
    You currently have <asp:Label id="inbox" runat="server"></asp:Label>
    e-mail messages in your <a href="http://www.hotmail.com/">inbox</a>.
  </p>
</asp:Panel>
```

In this case, the "inbox" will contain a random number of new email messages (as appears to be the number of messages showing on the Windows XP login screen). The code to create our random number of messages is as follows:

```
<script runat="server">

  protected void Page_Load(object sender, EventArgs e)
  {
    inbox.Text = new Random().Next(0, 100).ToString();
  }
</script>
```

The CSS-style class `mailbox`, referenced by the `Panel` control, does not contain anything extraordinary, but it should include a border and a width setting:

```
<style type="text/css">
.mailbox { border: solid 2px black; width: 150px; }
</style>
```

Now all that's left is to add a `<floatingBehavior>` element into xml-script and associate it with the panel. Set the handle property to the ID of the element that serves as the drag handle. In our case, the whole mail status panel is the drag handle, so you can reuse the ID.

```
<script type="text/xml-script">
  <page xmlns:script="http://schemas.microsoft.com/xml-script/2005">
    <components>
      <control id="DragPanel">
        <behaviors>
          <floatingBehavior handle="DragPanel" />
        </behaviors>
      </control>
    </components>
  </page>
</script>
```

Example 16-2 presents the complete code.

Example 16-2. Adding drag-and-drop behavior to a panel

DragDrop.aspx

```
<%@ Page Language="C#" %>

<!DOCTYPE html PUBLIC "-//W3C//DTD XHTML 1.0 Transitional//EN"
```

Example 16-2. Adding drag-and-drop behavior to a panel (continued)

```
"http://www.w3.org/TR/xhtml1/DTD/xhtml1-transitional.dtd">

<script runat="server">
  protected void Page_Load(object sender, EventArgs e)
  {
    inbox.Text = new Random().Next(0, 100).ToString( );
  }
</script>

<html xmlns="http://www.w3.org/1999/xhtml">
<head id="Head1" runat="server">
  <title>ASP.NET AJAX</title>
  <style type="text/css">
  .box { border: solid 2px black; }
  .mailbox { border: solid 2px black; width: 150px; }
  </style>
</head>
<body>
  <form id="form1" runat="server">
    <asp:ScriptManager ID="ScriptManager1" runat="server">
      <Scripts>
        <asp:ScriptReference name="PreviewScript.js"
assembly="Microsoft.Web.Preview" />
        <asp:ScriptReference name="PreviewDragDrop.js"
assembly="Microsoft.Web.Preview" />
      </Scripts>
    </asp:ScriptManager>
    <asp:Panel ID="ContentPanel" CssClass="box" runat="server">
      <h1>My Portal</h1>
      <p>
        Welcome to your personal portal, powered by Microsoft ASP.NET AJAX.
        The mail status window is freely draggable. Welcome to your personal portal,
powered by ASP.NET AJAX.
        The mail status window is freely draggable. Welcome to your personal portal,
powered by ASP.NET AJAX.
        The mail status window is freely draggable.
      </p>
      [...]
    </asp:Panel>
    <asp:Panel CssClass="mailbox" ID="DragPanel" runat="server">
      <p>
        You currently have <asp:Label id="inbox" runat="server"></asp:Label>
        mails in your <a href="http://www.hotmail.com/">inbox</a>.
      </p>
    </asp:Panel>

  </form>
<script type="text/xml-script">
  <page xmlns:script="http://schemas.microsoft.com/xml-script/2005">
    <components>
      <control id="DragPanel">
        <behaviors>
          <floatingBehavior handle="DragPanel" />
```

Example 16-2. Adding drag-and-drop behavior to a panel (continued)

```
        </behaviors>
      </control>
    </components>
  </page>
</script>
</body>
</html>
```

Run the example and view it in the browser. You can drag and drop the inbox wherever you like within the confines of the defined page (for example, you can't drag the panel to the bottom of the screen, because that would place it outside the HTML-defined page). As you can see in Figure 16-2, the underlying panel and text is visible through the panel as it is dragged about the page. Note that the panel will return to its original position when you refresh the page. Later in this chapter you will learn how to maintain its position between browser sessions.

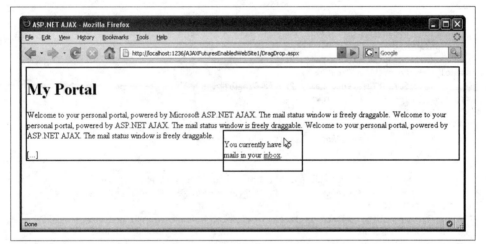

Figure 16-2. You can drag the inbox around

Using the Drag-and-Drop Extender

Some behaviors are also available as web controls. FloatingBehavior has a web control counterpart, DragOverlayExtender. This is a nonvisual control that you can put on a page to enrich ("extend") a control with drag-and-drop capabilities. You do not need xml-script and can use server-code to access the extender's properties.

Inside the extender, you will need the following properties:

Enabled
    Activates the effect

TargetControlID
    References the panel you want to define as draggable

In case you are wondering why this component contains an Enabled property, this gives you the ability to switch the effect on and off programmatically in script code.

This control allows the inbox panel to be dragged throughout the page (within the limits described following Example 16-2):

```
<asp:DragOverlayExtender ID="DragOverlayExtender1" runat="server"
   TargetControlID="DragPanel" Enabled="true" />
```

Example 16-3 shows the complete example, including another panel with dummy text to give us a place to drag the inbox.

Example 16-3. Adding drag-and-drop behavior to a panel using an extender

DragDropExtender.aspx

```
<%@ Page Language="C#" %>

<!DOCTYPE html PUBLIC "-//W3C//DTD XHTML 1.0 Transitional//EN"
"http://www.w3.org/TR/xhtml1/DTD/xhtml1-transitional.dtd">

<script runat="server">
  protected void Page_Load(object sender, EventArgs e)
  {
    inbox.Text = new Random().Next(0, 100).ToString();
  }
</script>

<html xmlns="http://www.w3.org/1999/xhtml">
<head id="Head1" runat="server">
  <title>ASP.NET AJAX</title>
  <style type="text/css">
  .box { border: solid 2px black; }
  .mailbox { border: solid 2px black; width: 150px; }
  </style>
</head>
<body>
  <form id="form1" runat="server">
    <asp:ScriptManager ID="ScriptManager1" runat="server">
      <Scripts>
        <asp:ScriptReference name="PreviewScript.js"
assembly="Microsoft.Web.Preview" />
        <asp:ScriptReference name="PreviewDragDrop.js"
assembly="Microsoft.Web.Preview" />
      </Scripts>
    </asp:ScriptManager>
    <asp:Panel ID="ContentPanel" CssClass="box" runat="server">
      <h1>My Portal</h1>
      <p>
        Welcome to your personal portal, powered by Microsoft ASP.NET AJAX.
        The mail status window is freely draggable. Welcome to your personal portal,
powered by ASP.NET AJAX.
```

Example 16-3. Adding drag-and-drop behavior to a panel using an extender (continued)

```
        The mail status window is freely draggable. Welcome to your personal portal,
powered by ASP.NET AJAX.
        The mail status window is freely draggable.
      </p>
      [...]
    </asp:Panel>
    <asp:Panel CssClass="mailbox" ID="DragPanel" runat="server">
      <p>
        You currently have <asp:Label id="inbox" runat="server"></asp:Label>
        mails in your <a href="http://www.hotmail.com/">inbox</a>.
      </p>
    </asp:Panel>
    <asp:DragOverlayExtender ID="DragOverlayExtender1" runat="server"
      TargetControlID="DragPanel" Enabled="true" />
  </form>
</body>
</html>
```

Personalized Drag-and-Drop

There is a limitation to the previous examples. As has been demonstrated, our simulated inbox panel can move freely about the page. However, if you leave the page and return to it later, the most recent position of the inbox is not maintained. This limitation can be overcome.

Once again, code reuse is the key. ASP.NET 2.0 already comes with a means for personalization in the form of profile properties (see "For Further Reading," at the end of this chapter, for information regarding ASP.NET 2.0 profiles, and refer to Chapter 7 to review these capabilities). ASP.NET AJAX supports profile properties in some of its controls, including DragDropExtender. The DragOverlayExtender component property, ProfileProperty, can be set to preserve dragged panel's location.

To store the position data, create a profile property in the *Web.config* file with the following markup:

```
<configuration xmlns="http://schemas.microsoft.com/.NetConfiguration/v2.0">
  <system.web>
    <anonymousIdentification enabled="true" />
    <profile>
      <properties>
        <add name="DragPanelPosition" allowAnonymous="true" />
      </properties>
    </profile>
    [...]
  </system.web>

  <system.web.extensions>
    <scripting>
      <webServices>
        <profileService enabled="true"
          writeAccessProperties="DragPanelPosition"
```

```
            readAccessProperties="DragPanelPosition" />
          [...]
        </webServices>
      </scripting>
    </system.web.extensions>

  </configuration>
```

 If you do not include the element `<anonymousIdentification
enabled="true" />`, only authenticated users (users who are logged in
or otherwise authenticated) receive a profile and can have their panel
position saved.

Apply these changes to the existing *Web.config* in your application. Then you need to
enable the profile script service on your page by adding the `<asp:ProfileService>`
element. Be sure to set `AutoSave` to `"true"` so the updated panel position is saved
upon every drag-and-drop operation.

```
    <asp:ProfileService ID="ProfileService1" runat="server" AutoSave="true" />
```

Finally, the `DragDropExtender` declaration, updated with a reference to the profile
property that will be used to store the location of the box. The `ProfileServiceID`
property of the `DragDropExtender` needs to match the ID of the `ProfileService` control we have just added to the page.

```
    <asp:DragOverlayExtender ID="DragOverlayExtender1" runat="server"
      TargetControlID="DragPanel" Enabled="true"
      ProfileProperty="DragPanelPosition" ProfileServiceID="ProfileService1" />
```

When you reload the page, the element is returned to its saved position. If you look
closely, you will see that the page is rendered first with the panel in its default position, then it moves to its previously saved position. Example 16-4 illustrates the complete code.

Example 16-4. Adding drag-and-drop behavior to a panel and remembering its position

```
DragDropExtenderProfile.aspx

<%@ Page Language="C#" %>

<!DOCTYPE html PUBLIC "-//W3C//DTD XHTML 1.0 Transitional//EN"
"http://www.w3.org/TR/xhtml1/DTD/xhtml1-transitional.dtd">

<script runat="server">
  protected void Page_Load(object sender, EventArgs e)
  {
    inbox.Text = new Random().Next(0, 100).ToString();
  }
</script>

<html xmlns="http://www.w3.org/1999/xhtml">
<head id="Head1" runat="server">
```

```
<title>ASP.NET AJAX</title>
<style type="text/css">
.box { border: solid 2px black; }
.mailbox { border: solid 2px black; width: 150px; }
</style>
</head>
<body>
  <form id="form1" runat="server">
    <asp:ScriptManager ID="ScriptManager1" runat="server">
      <Scripts>
        <asp:ScriptReference name="PreviewScript.js"
assembly="Microsoft.Web.Preview" />
        <asp:ScriptReference name="PreviewDragDrop.js"
assembly="Microsoft.Web.Preview" />
      </Scripts>
    </asp:ScriptManager>
    <asp:Panel ID="ContentPanel" CssClass="box" runat="server">
      <h1>My Portal</h1>
      <p>
        Welcome to your personal portal, powered by Microsoft ASP.NET AJAX.
        The mail status window is freely draggable. Welcome to your personal portal,
powered by ASP.NET AJAX.
        The mail status window is freely draggable. Welcome to your personal portal,
powered by ASP.NET AJAX.
        The mail status window is freely draggable.
      </p>
      [...]
    </asp:Panel>
    <asp:Panel CssClass="mailbox" ID="DragPanel" runat="server">
      <p>
        You currently have <asp:Label id="inbox" runat="server"></asp:Label>
        mails in your <a href="http://www.hotmail.com/">inbox</a>.
      </p>
    </asp:Panel>
    <asp:DragOverlayExtender ID="DragOverlayExtender1" runat="server"
      TargetControlID="DragPanel" Enabled="true"
      ProfileProperty="DragPanelPosition" ProfileServiceID="ProfileService1" />
    <asp:ProfileService ID="ProfileService1" runat="server" AutoSave="true" />
  </form>
</body>
</html>
```

The first time this example is run, it will take a noticeable amount of time before
anything is displayed in the browser. This is as a result of ASP.NET creating the
database in which it will store profile information. The profile database is created in
the App_Data directory of your web site. It is available in via the *ASPNETDB.MDF*
file. If you open it, you will notice there is an entry for the panel position in the
aspnet_Profile database (see Figure 16-3). Every time you change the position of the
panel, ASP.NET AJAX will send out an HTTP request to update the profile data (see
Figure 16-4).

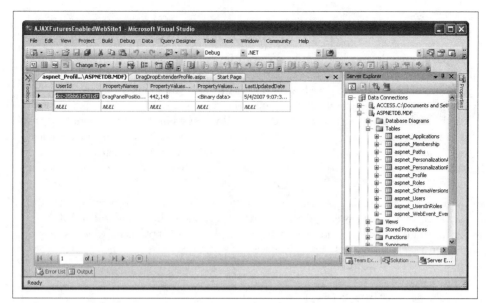

Figure 16-3. The position of the panel is saved in a profile property

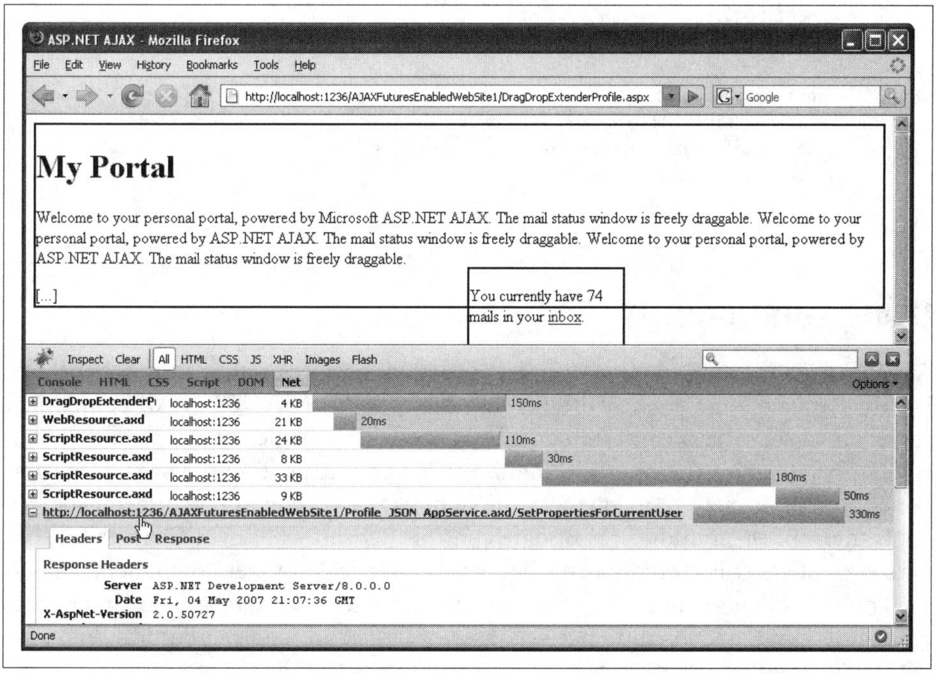

Figure 16-4. ASP.NET AJAX sends an HTTP request in the background to update the profile

Drag-and-Drop Best Practices

Implementing drag-and-drop behavior with JavaScript is difficult, particularly if the code needs to run on all browsers. The ASP.NET AJAX Futures CTP works surprisingly well, however there are a few things you of which you should be aware. First, the drop point for any element must be within the content area of the current page. This is one of the reasons why so much dummy text was used in the inbox example: there needs to be some place to which to drag the inbox. Without it, you might experience the "Snap Back" effect, where you drop a an item outside the content area of the page, and the item snaps back to its original position. This effect is particularly pronounced in older versions of the ASP.NET AJAX Futures CTP.

When scrolling and window resizing come into play, the situation becomes worse as the scroll position is not always correctly taken into account by the extender. The ASP.NET AJAX Control Toolkit contains a small JavaScript fix for this problem, which is shown here in a slightly modified form. Whenever the window is resized, the height of the content area is reset accordingly:

```
<script type="text/javascript">
  function fixBodyHeight( ) {
     document.body.style.height =
Math.max(document.documentElement.scrollHeight,
document.body.scrollHeight) + "px";
  }

  function pageLoad( ) {
    fixBodyHeight( );
    $addHandler(window, "resize", fixBodyHeight);
  }
</script>
```

Using Components

An ASP.NET AJAX component is encapsulated JavaScript that is not bound to HTML elements on a page, rather, it stands alone. An ASP.NET AJAX component aggregates a set of JavaScript functionality to provide a single interface to be used in code. A behavior must always be bound to a specific element on the page, so a component can offer more functionality. The Futures release comes with several components, most of them in the area of data controls (as you will see in Chapter 17), but here we will cover one component that is very practical: a timer component. This is the xml-script equivalent to the Timer server control demonstrated in Chapter 6, providing the same functionality, but—in case of xml-script and the Futures release—without official support from Microsoft.

Using the Timer Component

Apart from using the `<asp:Timer>` web control (see Chapter 6), there are two alternative ways to use a timer with the ASP.NET AJAX Futures CTP. You can either use xml-script, or you can use code.

Let's start with xml-script. The element used for a timer is called `<timer>`, which takes the following properties:

`enabled`
> Set to true to activate the timer

`interval`
> The number of milliseconds after which the timer's `tick` event is triggered

> The timing units in milliseconds suggest the ASP.NET AJAX Futures CTP timer is internally using the JavaScript `window.setInterval()` method. And indeed, that's how it's done.

The remaining script is straightforward. The `tick` event needs to be handled using `<invokeMethodAction>` or `<setPropertyAction>`:

```
<timer id="Timer1" interval="5000" enabled="true">
  <tick>
    <invokeMethodAction ... />
    <setPropertyAction ... />
  </tick>
</timer>
```

An alternative, programmatic approach is to use JavaScript to create a timer object:

```
var timer = new Sys.Preview.Timer();
```

Now, you can use setter (and getter) methods to configure the timer:

```
timer.set_enabled(true);
timer.set_interval(5000);
```

Do not forget to add a tick event handler:

```
timer.add_tick(function() {
  // ...
});
```

Finally, initialize the timer, otherwise it won't work:

```
timer.initialize();
```

Let's use this control with the tabbed-panels sample (from Example 16-1). Example 16-5 employs both ways of adding a timer to a page. The first timer uses xml-script and displays the second tab every five seconds. The second timer is created with JavaScript code. It displays the first tab, also every five seconds. However, the code uses `window.setTimeout()` to delay 2.5 seconds before creating the second timer.

Therefore, each timer is on a 5-second interval, but they are offset by 2.5 seconds, so that the visible panel changes every 2.5 seconds.

Example 16-5. Two different timers at once

Timer.aspx

```
<%@ Page Language="C#" %>

<!DOCTYPE html PUBLIC "-//W3C//DTD XHTML 1.0 Transitional//EN"
"http://www.w3.org/TR/xhtml1/DTD/xhtml1-transitional.dtd">
<html xmlns="http://www.w3.org/1999/xhtml">
<head id="Head1" runat="server">
  <title>ASP.NET AJAX</title>
  <script type="text/javascript">
  function pageLoad() {
    setTimeout("setupTimer();", 2500);
  }

  function swapPanels() {
    $get("Panel1").style.visibility = "hidden";
    $get("Panel2").style.visibility = "visible";
  }

  function setupTimer() {
    swapPanels();
    var timer = new Sys.Preview.Timer();
    timer.set_enabled(true);
    timer.set_interval(5000);
    timer.add_tick(swapPanels);
    timer.initialize();
  }
  </script>
</head>
<body>
  <form id="form1" runat="server">
    <asp:ScriptManager runat="server" ID="ScriptManager1">
      <Scripts>
        <asp:ScriptReference name="PreviewScript.js"
assembly="Microsoft.Web.Preview" />
      </Scripts>
    </asp:ScriptManager>
    <div id="Panel1" style="visibility: visible; position: absolute; top: 35px;
left: 10px">
      This is the first tab.<br />
      It is full of ASP.NET AJAX information.<br />
      Although it seems to be full of dummy text.
    </div>
    <div id="Panel2" style="visibility: hidden; position: absolute; top: 35px; left:
10px">
      This is the second tab.<br />
      It is full of ASP.NET AJAX information, as well.<br />
      Although it seems to be full of dummy text, too.
```

Example 16-5. Two different timers at once (continued)

```
    </div>
  </form>

  <script type="text/xml-script">
    <page xmlns:script="http://schemas.microsoft.com/xml-script/2005">
      <components>
        <control id="Panel1" />
        <control id="Panel2" />
        <timer id="Timer1" interval="5000" enabled="true">
          <tick>
            <setPropertyAction target="Panel1" property="visible" value="true" />
            <setPropertyAction target="Panel2" property="visible" value="false" />
          </tick>
        </timer>
      </components>
    </page>
  </script>
</body>
</html>
```

Summary

This chapter covered ASP.NET AJAX behaviors, such as click and drag-and-drop. It also went into ASP.NET AJAX components, which, as was demonstrated, can be referenced using xml-script. Although controls are implemented internally in Java-Script, xml-script provides a declarative method to add functionality to your controls and web site.

For Further Reading

http://quickstarts.asp.net/Futures/ajax/doc/behaviors.aspx
   Pre-release Microsoft documentation on ASP.NET AJAX Futures behaviors

CHAPTER 17

Using Server Data

The ASP.NET AJAX features introduced thus far all contribute to a considerable savings in development time and effort. Yet, there are more, very powerful features and functionality yet to come.

In this chapter, you'll learn how to use ASP.NET AJAX to connect to databases and bind data from these sources to page elements. This functionality isn't limited to simple, static controls like text fields, but lets you bind complex data as well. With ASP.NET AJAX, you can use tables and HTML lists to display data and, as with so many other features we've explored, you can create your own custom data source.

In Chapter 16, you were introduced to client control data binding. However, servers were not a part of this discussion. This chapter will expand upon what you learned about data binding, dealing with data from a server. You will write a web service that retrieves data from the data source and return it. You will then use the client ASP.NET AJAX controls and xml-script markup to display that data in HTML.

Using a ListView Control

The best way to display data in ASP.NET AJAX is using the ListView control (in xml-script, the <listView> element). This control can iterate through a *list* so that the user can *view* the result—hence, the name of the control.

Within a <listView> xml-script element, you can define two display templates:

<layoutTemplate>
    To specify the layout and appearance of the data

<itemTemplate>
    To specify the layout for each individual element (item) of the data

In addition, you set a number of attributes (which will be detailed in the following section) and can bind the data to the elements. You can choose any suitable HTML element as a target element. Static lists (numbered or bulleted), selection lists

(`<select>` element), and tables are the elements most commonly used as they exist precisely to display lists of data.

Binding a ListView Control to Data

An obvious vehicle for displaying data from a server data source is an unordered list. The following example will query data from a server database and display it as an HTML bulleted list.

Before we dig deep into xml-script, let's add the HTML markup used to display the data from the data source. First, you'll need a container, typically a `<div>` element, to hold the data-display list. Here's the markup:

```
<div id="output">
  vendor list goes here</div>
```

Next, you need to put the templates (layout and item) in a different container, the layout container. The style of this container will be set to invisible (`display:none`). The layout container does not directly display data, it just serves as a container for HTML elements that are used to lay the data out and style it. The data will actually appear in the container that was just illustrated, which initially functions only as a placeholder.

In the layout container, we need a number of elements (and associated IDs):

- An outer container that represents the `<layoutTemplate>` element, typically a `<div>` element.
- An inner container that reflects the `<itemTemplate>` element.
- Individual elements that act as placeholders for data items (such as `<span>` elements) from the data source.

If you are familiar with the ASP.NET `Repeater` control, this arrangement is similar (for example, the layout container is the `Repeater` control itself). The difference is that the output container (the original `<div>` element illustrated above) is a container for the `Repeater` control itself.

The following snippet presents an example that can be used for an unordered list (a `<ul>` element). As an outer container, a `<div>` element is used. The individual data item is displayed using a `<li>` element (its parent element being the `<ul>` element). This leads to the following markup serving as the placeholder:

```
<div style="display:none;"> <!-- hide the placeholders -->
  <div id="vendorsLayout"> <!-- layout template container -->
    <ul id="vendorsItemParent"> <!-- item template container -->
      <li id="vendorsItem"><span id="vendorsName">vendor name goes here
        </span> </li>
    </ul>
  </div>
</div>
```

You can't eliminate an element by merging the outer, invisible <div> and the layout template element (vendorsLayout, in the example). If you do, the output will be invisible, too, even after being inserted into the output element. You need the additional <div> element (reflecting <itemTemplate>), which itself isn't hidden via CSS (only the outer <div> is).

Before we continue creating a page to display the data, we need to create the data with which we will work. We will do this by creating a web service. You need something that exposes the data you want as properties of the object returned by the web service. The ASP.NET AJAX data binding mechanism for the listView element does not accept ADO.NET datasets directly. The two most used options are:

- A DataTable object, or specifically, a DataRowCollection inside a DataTable
- A custom class in which all data is put in class members

The custom class gives you more flexibility, but usually also means more code. Using a DataRowCollection object, on the other hand, is rather easy. A DataSet object is created, then its Table[0].Rows property is accessed to return the desired collection of rows with all data in it. As has been the case since Chapter 1, we will use the *AdventureWorks* database for sample data. In this example, the fields AccountNumber and Name from the Vendor table are queried. The code shown in Example 17-1 highlights the web service that returns the *AdventureWorks* data as a DataRowCollection object. Do not forget to use the [ScriptService] attribute for all web services that will be consumed by ASP.NET AJAX, and the [WebMethod] attribute for individual methods that will be exposed in the web service.

 If you test this web service directly in the browser, you will likely see the error message, "System.Data.DataRow cannot be serialized because it does not have a parameterless constructor." This message can be ignored. It does not affect the functionality of the web service when you call it from client script.

Example 17-1. A web service that returns a DataRowCollection object

ListViewVendors.asmx

```
<%@ WebService Language="C#" Class="Vendors" %>

using System;
using System.Web;
using System.Web.Services;
using System.Web.Services.Protocols;
using System.Data;
using System.Data.SqlClient;

[WebService(Namespace = "http://hauser-wenz.de/")]
[WebServiceBinding(ConformsTo = WsiProfiles.BasicProfile1_1)]
[System.Web.Script.Services.ScriptService]
public class Vendors : System.Web.Services.WebService
```

Example 17-1. A web service that returns a DataRowCollection object (continued)

```
{
    [WebMethod]public DataRowCollection GetVendors( )
    {
        SqlConnection conn = new SqlConnection(
            "server=(local)\\SQLEXPRESS; Integrated Security=true; Initial
Catalog=AdventureWorks");
        conn.Open( );
        SqlCommand comm = new SqlCommand(
            "SELECT TOP 10 AccountNumber, Name FROM Purchasing.Vendor",
            conn);
        SqlDataAdapter adap = new SqlDataAdapter(comm);
        DataSet ds = new DataSet( );
        adap.Fill(ds);
        return ds.Tables[0].Rows;
    }
}
```

 Pre-release versions of ASP.NET AJAX (Atlas) worked with DataTable objects directly. ASP.NET AJAX, however, requires that the web service return a DataRowCollection object. Otherwise, the server also sends general information about all columns to the client, which will cause confusion with the ASP.NET AJAX component responsible for displaying that data.

When using DataRowCollection, you should be aware that ASP.NET AJAX introduced one issue. When you try to consume the web service from JavaScript, you receive an error message indicating a circular reference that could not be resolved. This is caused by the inability of ASP.NET to serialize DataTable objects and DataRowCollection objects without some assistance. This "assistance" is provided by a couple of converters that need to be put into *Web.config*. Look for the <webServices> section (if it does not exist there, create one within the <scripting> sub node of the <system.web.extensions> node). This is of particular interest when migrating Atlas code to ASP.NET AJAX, but is always required.

Now, add the following markup:

```
<jsonSerialization maxJsonLength="500000000">
  <converters>
    <add name="DataSetConverter"
type="Microsoft.Web.Preview.Script.Serialization.Converters.DataSetConverter,
Microsoft.Web.Preview"/>
    <add name="DataRowConverter"
type="Microsoft.Web.Preview.Script.Serialization.Converters.DataRowConverter,
Microsoft.Web.Preview"/>
    <add name="DataTableConverter"
type="Microsoft.Web.Preview.Script.Serialization.Converters.DataTableConverter,
Microsoft.Web.Preview"/>
  </converters>
</jsonSerialization>
```

This first sets the maximum length of any JSON string during serialization. You can use a large or small value here, depending on your specific scenario. Then, three converters are added, for `DataSet`, `DataRow`, and `DataTable` objects. These take care of the data objects we are about to use.

Alternatively, the web service can be written to return a custom array based on the data, instead of returning a `DataRowCollection` object directly. As the example web service you are building is written to use the `AccountNumber` and `Name` fields from *AdventureWorks*, if you create a custom type, that type must return two string properties with the names `AccountNumber` and `Name`. The following code snippet shows how you might implement the custom type:

```
public class Vendor
{
  string _AccountNumber;
  string _Name;

  public string AccountNumber
  {
    get
    {
      return _AccountNumber;
    }
    set
    {
      _AccountNumber = value;
    }
  }

  public string Name
  {
    get
    {
      return _Name;
    }
    set
    {
      _Name = value;
    }
  }

  public Vendor(string AccountNumber, string Name)
  {
    this._AccountNumber = AccountNumber;
    this._Name = Name;
  }

  public Vendor()
  {
  }
}
```

The empty constructor public Vendor( ) { } is required so the class can be serialized. If you omit this class constructor and use this class in a Web service, you get an error when calling the *.asmx* file directly in your browser. However, the web service still works and can be called from script. This additional constructor makes testing a web service in the browser easier, but does not add any functionality to the script that is required.

A rewritten web service that uses the custom type queries the Purchasing.Vendors table in *AdventureWorks* and selects items (in our example, the first 10 entries), as the previous example did:

```
[WebMethod]
public Vendor[] GetVendors( )
{
  SqlConnection conn = new SqlConnection(
    "server=(local)\\SQLEXPRESS; Integrated Security=true; Initial
Catalog=AdventureWorks");
  conn.Open( );
  SqlCommand comm = new SqlCommand(
    "SELECT TOP 10 AccountNumber, Name FROM Purchasing.Vendor",
    conn);
  SqlDataReader dr = comm.ExecuteReader( );
```

Rather than returning a DataRowCollection, the code iterates through the list and creates a Vendor element for each entry in the data table. This list is then converted into an array and returned from the service:

```
List<Vendor> v = new List<Vendor>( );

while (dr.Read( ))
{
  v.Add(new Vendor(
    dr["AccountNumber"].ToString( ),
    dr["Name"].ToString( )));
}
return v.ToArray( );
}
```

This example uses a construct that's new in the .NET Framework version 2.0: generics. To use generics, you need to import the associated namespaces (System. Collections for List support, and System.Collections.Generic). Example 17-2 presents the completed code for a version of the web service that works with the custom Vendor type.

Example 17-2. This web service returns a custom type

ListViewVendorsCustom.asmx

```
<%@ WebService Language="C#" Class="Vendors" %>
```

Example 17-2. This web service returns a custom type (continued)

```
using System;
using System.Web;
using System.Web.Services;
using System.Web.Services.Protocols;
using System.Data;
using System.Data.SqlClient;
using System.Collections;
using System.Collections.Generic;

public class Vendor
{
  string _AccountNumber;
  string _Name;

  public string AccountNumber
  {
    get
    {
      return _AccountNumber;
    }
    set
    {
      _AccountNumber = value;
    }
  }

  public string Name
  {
    get
    {
      return _Name;
    }
    set
    {
      _Name = value;
    }
  }

  public Vendor(string AccountNumber, string Name)
  {
    this._AccountNumber = AccountNumber;
    this._Name = Name;
  }
  public Vendor()
  {
  }
}

[WebService(Namespace = "http://hauser-wenz.de/")]
[WebServiceBinding(ConformsTo = WsiProfiles.BasicProfile1_1)]
[System.Web.Script.Services.ScriptService]
public class Vendors : System.Web.Services.WebService
```

Example 17-2. This web service returns a custom type (continued)

```
{
  [WebMethod]
  public Vendor[] GetVendors( )
  {
    SqlConnection conn = new SqlConnection(
      "server=(local)\\SQLEXPRESS; Integrated Security=true;
Initial Catalog=AdventureWorks");
    conn.Open( );
    SqlCommand comm = new SqlCommand(
      "SELECT TOP 10 AccountNumber, Name FROM Purchasing.Vendor",
      conn);
    SqlDataReader dr = comm.ExecuteReader( );
    List<Vendor> v = new List<Vendor>( );

    while (dr.Read( ))
    {
      v.Add(new Vendor(
        dr["AccountNumber"].ToString( ),
        dr["Name"].ToString( )));
    }
    return v.ToArray( );
  }
}
```

 In the source code downloads for this book, both variants of the web service—one using a DataRowCollection and one using a custom type—are included under *ListViewVendors.asmx* and *ListViewVendorsCustom.asmx*. You can use both of them for the following examples; they are interchangeable.

Now back to the ASP.NET page, where the web service is called. Web services have already been covered in greater detail in Chapter 5, so here is just a refresher of what must be done to use them. First, the *.asmx* file must be referenced in the xml-script. Then, a client-side proxy is generated—a local object that exposes the behavior of the remote web service. That means that the local object has the same methods the remote service has; calling the local methods in turn calls the remote methods. This call is done asynchronously (just as XMLHttpRequest calls were done in Chapter 3). A callback function is used to process the results of the call after the web service returns data.

When including the ASP.NET AJAX ScriptManager, control, be sure to first reference the web service's *.asmx* file. Here's the markup you need:

```
<asp:ScriptManager runat="server">
  <Services>
    <asp:ServiceReference Path="ListViewVendors.asmx" />
  </Services>
</asp:ScriptManager>
```

When the page has been loaded, you need to call the web service. However, the term "when the page has been loaded" is a bit misleading. The following code, for instance, would not work:

```
<script type="text/javascript">
  window.onload = function() {
    Vendors.GetVendors(callComplete);
  }
</script>
```

The load event of an HTML page occurs when the HTML of the page has been fully loaded. However at this point, it is possible that the ASP.NET AJAX library and the web service proxy have not yet been fully loaded themselves. Therefore, this code could fail with JavaScript displaying an error message such as "Vendors is not defined." Therefore, it is better to add a delay. You could use JavaScript's window.setTimeout() method, or you wait and have the user click a button to get the data, using syntax such as the following (the function loadVendors() will be implemented in the next step):

```
<input type="button" value="Load Vendors" onclick="loadVendors();" />
```

The best way is to use the special pageLoad() method that ASP.NET AJAX provides:

```
<script type="text/javascript">
  function pageLoad() {
    Vendors.GetVendors(callComplete);
  }
</script>
```

Then, you can call the web service:

```
<script type="text/javascript">
  function loadVendors() {
    Vendors.GetVendors(callComplete, callError);
  }
```

You will receive the results in the first callback function (or an error in the second one). In the callback function, you need to do the following:

1. Get a reference to the element to which you want to display the data (in the example, that's <div id="output" />).

2. Access its control property and call its set_data() method, submitting the result of the web service call.

This leads to the following code:

```
function callComplete(result) {
  $get("output").control.set_data(result);
}
</script>
```

There is only one task remaining: create the xml-script markup. This is a little tricky to do, although starting off is relatively easy. Begin by creating a `<script>` element, then nest a `<page>` element, finally, nest a `<components>` element:

```
<script type="text/xml-script">
  <page xmlns="http://schemas.microsoft.com/xml-script/2005">
    <components>
    ...
    </components>
  </page>
</script>
```

Now within `<components>`, you can place the `<listView>` element. This tag requires several attributes:

`itemTemplateParentElementId`

> The ID of the element that is the parent of the individual item elements. It sounds confusing, but basically it references the `<ul>` element in the example.

`id`

> The ID of the element where the result will be placed.

The following markup is the result for the unordered list example:

```
<listView itemTemplateParentElementId="vendorsItemParent" id="output">
...
</listView>
```

Within `<listView>`, the layout template and the item template must be defined. The former is easy—you simply need to reference the outer `<div>`:

```
<listView itemTemplateParentElementId="vendorsItemParent" id="output">
  <layoutTemplate>
    <template layoutElement="vendorsLayout" />
  </layoutTemplate>
  ...
</listView>
```

The `<itemTemplate>` is a bit trickier. This time, you need to reference the individual item. In the example, that item is the `<li>` element.

```
<listView itemTemplateParentElementId="vendorsItemParent" id="output">
  <layoutTemplate>
    <template layoutElement="vendorsLayout" />
  </layoutTemplate>
  <itemTemplate>
    <template layoutElement="vendorsItem">
    ...
    </template>
  </itemTemplate>
</listView>
```

Within the <template> element, you have to define the bindings for each item. Since you want to output text, you can use the <label> element, which provides a representation of the ASP.NET AJAX Label web control. In the markup code, the following two properties are required:

dataPath
    The name of the class property you want to bind

property
    The property of the Label control to which you want to bind

This leads to the following markup:

```
<listView itemTemplateParentElementId="vendorsItemParent" id="output">
  <layoutTemplate>
    <template layoutElement="vendorsLayout" />
  </layoutTemplate>
  <itemTemplate>
    <template layoutElement="vendorsItem">
      <label id="vendorsName">
        <bindings>
          <binding dataPath="Name" property="text" />
        </bindings>
      </label>
    </template>
  </itemTemplate>
</listView>
```

This is a lot of work, and all without the support of IntelliSense. But the result is rewarding. The final step is to load the *PreviewScript.js* JavaScript library from the Futures release that contains the actual client functionality:

```
<asp:ScriptManager runat="server">
  <Services>
    <asp:ServiceReference Path="ListViewVendors.asmx" />
  </Services>
  <Scripts>
    <asp:ScriptReference Name="PreviewScript.js"
Assembly="Microsoft.Web.Preview" />
  </Scripts>
</asp:ScriptManager>
```

Example 17-3 shows the complete markup and script for the page.

Example 17-3. Binding data to an HTML list

ListViewUnorderedList.aspx

```
<%@ Page Language="C#" %>

<!DOCTYPE html PUBLIC "-//W3C//DTD XHTML 1.0 Transitional//EN"
"http://www.w3.org/TR/xhtml1/DTD/xhtml1-transitional.dtd">
<html xmlns="http://www.w3.org/1999/xhtml">
<head id="Head1" runat="server">
```

Example 17-3. Binding data to an HTML list (continued)

```
  <title>ASP.NET AJAX</title>

  <script type="text/javascript">
    function loadVendors() {
      Vendors.GetVendors(callComplete, callError);
    }

    function callComplete(result) {
      $get("output").control.set_data(result);
    }
    function callError(result) {
      $get("output").innerHTML = "Error: " + result.get_message();
    }
  </script>

</head>
<body>
  <form id="form1" runat="server">
    <asp:ScriptManager runat="server">
      <Services>
        <asp:ServiceReference Path="ListViewVendors.asmx" />
      </Services>
      <Scripts>
          <asp:ScriptReference Name="PreviewScript.js"
Assembly="Microsoft.Web.Preview" />
      </Scripts>
    </asp:ScriptManager>
    <input type="button" value="Load Vendors" onclick="loadVendors();" />
    <div id="output">
      vendor list goes here</div>
    <div style="display:none;">
      <div id="vendorsLayout">
        <ul id="vendorsItemParent">
          <li id="vendorsItem"><span id="vendorsName">
vendor name goes here</span></li>
        </ul>
      </div>
    </div>
  </form>

<script type="text/xml-script">
  <page xmlns="http://schemas.microsoft.com/xml-script/2005">
    <components>
      <listView itemTemplateParentElementId="vendorsItemParent" id="output">
        <layoutTemplate>
          <template layoutElement="vendorsLayout" />
        </layoutTemplate>
        <itemTemplate>
          <template layoutElement="vendorsItem">
            <label id="vendorsName">
              <bindings>
                <binding dataPath="Name" property="text" />
```

Example 17-3. Binding data to an HTML list (continued)

```
            </bindings>
          </label>
        </template>
      </itemTemplate>
    </listView>
  </components>
</page>
</script>

</body>
</html>
```

Figure 17-1 displays the results of loading the page and clicking on the Load Vendors button.

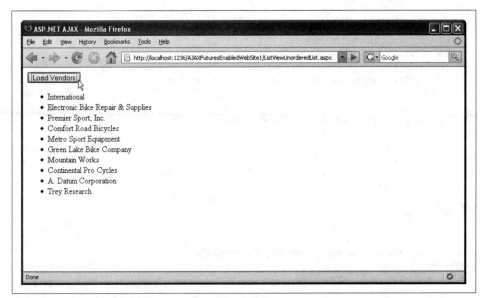

Figure 17-1. Upon clicking the button, the list is populated

The following is a synopsis of what actually happens:

1. When you click the button, the web service is called.

2. Once the web service returns data, the callback function is executed.

3. The JavaScript code iterates through the result set from the web service.

4. According to the data in the xml-script, the placeholders are filled with data and the list is created in the invisible `<div>` element.

5. The list is copied (using DOM functions) to the final destination, the output `<div>` element.

Binding Data to an HTML Table

Instead of an unordered list, you can use an HTML table to display data—an ASP.NET AJAX version of an ASP.NET `GridView` data control, so to speak. To do so, you need to change the HTML markup a bit. Instead of the `<ul>` and `<li>` elements, you will use `<table>` and `<tr>` elements. Also, since a table can show multiple columns, all the data from the web service can be used, including both the `Name` *and* `AccountNumber` fields.

For every data item, you create a table row (`<tr>`). Within this row, create two cells (`<td>`), one for each database column returned from the web service.

Using an HTML Selection List

Unfortunately, the approach from Example 17-3 does not work with HTML `<select>` list elements. Take a look at how a `<select>` element normally appears:

```
<select>
  <option value="1">one</option>
  <option value="2">two</option>
  <option value="3">three</option>
</select>
```

Within an `<option>` element, no other HTML is allowed. So, you might want to try something like this:

```
<select>
  <option value="1"><span id="text1">one</span></option>
  <option value="2">two</option>
  <option value="3">three</option>
</select>
```

However, this will not work. Therefore, you cannot use the approach from Example 17-3 to fill a selection list with data from a data source. You can, however, use one of the other ASP.NET AJAX techniques covered in this book to fill the list dynamically: the Future release `Select` client-side control also supports data binding!

Here is the (hidden) placeholder containing a `<table>` element to which ASP.NET AJAX binds server-side data:

```
<div style="display: none;">
  <div id="vendorsLayout">
    <table id="vendorsItemParent">
      <tr><th>Account Number</th><th>Name</th></tr>
      <tr id="vendorsItem">
        <td><span id="vendorsAccountNumber">vendor account number goes
here</span></td>
        <td><span id="vendorsName">vendor name goes here</span></td>
      </tr>
    </table>
  </div>
</div>
```

However, there is a problem. Mozilla browsers display the table, but in Internet Explorer, the browser remains blank. Internet Explorer is very particular about the structure of the dynamically generated HTML table. This is an interesting result in light of the fact that Internet Explorer has a history of being very tolerant of incorrect HTML markup.

So, to make the data-bound HTML table work, you have to create the table with a <thead> and a <tbody> section. The <tbody> section is the parent element of each data item, as rendered using a <tr> element.

You could also add an optional <tfoot> element, but this must occur before the <tbody> element. This example does not need <tfoot>.

```
<table>
  <thead>
    <tr><th>Account Number</th><th>Name</th></tr>
  </thead>
  <tbody id="vendorsItemParent">
    <tr id="vendorsItem">
      <td id="vendorsAccountNumber">vendor account number goes here</td>
      <td id="vendorsName">vendor name goes here</td>
    </tr>
  </tbody>
</table>
```

In xml-script, you have to add the additional binding for the new placeholder element. Then, the example works as before: when you click the HTML button, the web service is called, its result is parsed into the vendorsLayout element, and the result is copied into the ouput element. Example 17-4 shows the complete code, with changes highlighted in bold.

Example 17-4. Binding data to an HTML table

ListViewTable.aspx

```
<%@ Page Language="C#" %>

<!DOCTYPE html PUBLIC "-//W3C//DTD XHTML 1.0 Transitional//EN"
"http://www.w3.org/TR/xhtml1/DTD/xhtml1-transitional.dtd">
<html xmlns="http://www.w3.org/1999/xhtml">
<head id="Head1" runat="server">
  <title>ASP.NET AJAX</title>

  <script language="JavaScript" type="text/javascript">
    function loadVendors() {
      Vendors.GetVendors(callComplete, callError);
    }

    function callComplete(result) {
      $get("output").control.set_data(result);
    }
    function callError(result) {
```

Example 17-4. Binding data to an HTML table (continued)

```
      $get("output").innerHTML = "Error: " + result.get_message( );
    }
  </script>

</head>
<body>
  <form id="form1" runat="server">
    <asp:ScriptManager runat="server">
      <Services>
        <asp:ServiceReference Path="ListViewVendors.asmx" />
      </Services>
      <Scripts>
        <asp:ScriptReference Name="PreviewScript.js"
Assembly="Microsoft.Web.Preview" />
      </Scripts>
    </asp:ScriptManager>
    <input type="button" value="Load Vendors" onclick="loadVendors( );" />
    <div id="output">
      vendor list goes here</div>
    <div style="display: none;">
      <div id="vendorsLayout">
        <table>
          <thead>
            <tr><th>Account Number</th><th>Name</th></tr>
          </thead>
          <tbody id="vendorsItemParent">
            <tr id="vendorsItem">
              <td id="vendorsAccountNumber">vendor account number goes here</td>
              <td id="vendorsName">vendor name goes here</td>
            </tr>
          </tbody>
        </table>
      </div>
    </div>
  </form>

  <script type="text/xml-script">
    <page xmlns="http://schemas.microsoft.com/xml-script/2005">
      <components>
        <listView itemTemplateParentElementId="vendorsItemParent" id="output">
          <layoutTemplate>
            <template layoutElement="vendorsLayout" />
          </layoutTemplate>
          <itemTemplate>
            <template layoutElement="vendorsItem">
              <label id="vendorsAccountNumber">
                <bindings>
                  <binding dataPath="AccountNumber" property="text" />
                </bindings>
              </label>
              <label id="vendorsName">
```

Example 17-4. Binding data to an HTML table (continued)

```
                    <bindings>
                      <binding dataPath="Name" property="text" />
                    </bindings>
                  </label>
              </template>
          </itemTemplate>
      </listView>
    </components>
  </page>
</script>


</body>
</html>
```

Figure 17-2 shows the results of displaying the page.

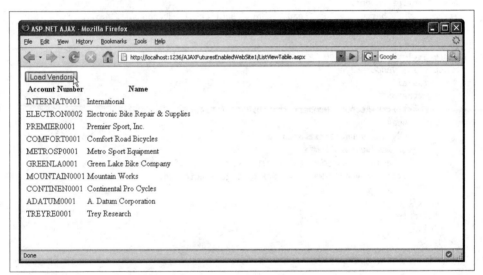

Figure 17-2. Clicking the button generates and fills the table

Creating a Custom Data Source

If you want more flexibility for the data access and do not want to stick to the structure provided by the data source, you can implement a data source yourself, as a server-side ASP.NET class. Since ASP.NET AJAX relies heavily on web services, you need to implement a DataService class. The associated class is implemented in the Microsoft.Web.Preview.Services namespace defined in the Futures release. Within the DataService class, you need to implement the default methods for a data object. These methods are listed in the System.ComponentModel.DataObjectMethodType enumeration and include the following:

- Delete
- Insert
- Select
- Update

Displaying Data from a Custom Data Source

For demonstration purposes, we will first implement a web service SELECT method, which again retrieves data from the Purchasing.Vendors table in the *AdventureWorks* database.

As in previous examples, you can implement a method that returns the desired data. By using the [DataObjectMethod(DataObjectMethodType.Select)] attribute, you declare the specific method as the "select" method. The actual naming is arbitrary. As the data type of the method's return value, you can again use a custom type, as shown in Example 17-5.

Example 17-5. Returning a custom type

ListViewVendorsDataServiceCustomType.asmx, excerpt

```
[DataObjectMethod(DataObjectMethodType.Select)]
public Vendor[] GetVendors( )
{
  SqlConnection conn = new SqlConnection(
    "server=(local)\\SQLEXPRESS; Integrated Security=true; Initial
Catalog=AdventureWorks");
  conn.Open( );
  SqlCommand comm = new SqlCommand(
    "SELECT TOP 10 AccountNumber, Name FROM Purchasing.Vendor",
    conn);
  SqlDataReader dr = comm.ExecuteReader( );
  List<Vendor> v = new List<Vendor>( );

  while (dr.Read( ))
  {
    v.Add(new Vendor(
      dr["AccountNumber"].ToString( ),
      dr["Name"].ToString( )));
  }
  return v.ToArray( );
}
```

As an alternative, you can also return a DataTable, which requires less code, as shown in Example 17-6. Choosing this return type does require a DataTable, not a DataRowCollection!

Example 17-6. Returning a DataTable

ListViewVendorsDataService.asmx

```
<%@ WebService Language="C#" Class="VendorsDataService" %>
using System;
using System.Web;
using System.Web.Services;
using System.Web.Services.Protocols;
using System.Data;
using System.Data.SqlClient;
using Microsoft.Web.Preview.Services;using System.ComponentModel;

[WebService(Namespace = "http://hauser-wenz.de/")]
[WebServiceBinding(ConformsTo = WsiProfiles.BasicProfile1_1)]
[System.Web.Script.Services.ScriptService]
public class VendorsDataService : DataService
{[DataObjectMethod(DataObjectMethodType.Select)]
  public DataTable GetVendors()
  {
    SqlConnection conn = new SqlConnection(
      "server=(local)\\SQLEXPRESS; Integrated Security=true;
InitialCatalog=AdventureWorks");
    conn.Open();
    SqlCommand comm = new SqlCommand(
      "SELECT TOP 10 AccountNumber, Name FROM Purchasing.Vendor",
      conn);
    SqlDataAdapter adap = new SqlDataAdapter(comm);
    DataSet ds = new DataSet();
    adap.Fill(ds);
    return ds.Tables[0];
  }
}
```

These *.asmx* files do not contain something explicitly labeled with [WebMethod].
However, when you call one of these web services in the browser directly, you see
that they have two web methods: GetData() and SaveData() (see Figure 17-3). Both
expect a parameters array with additional information. ASP.NET AJAX automatically generates the required parameters, so you just call the methods under the fixed
DataObjectMethodType names; Delete, Insert, Select, and Update.

> Example 17-6 comes in two flavors: DataTable and custom type.
> You can find in the code downloads for this book under the filenames
> *ListViewVendorsDataService.asmx* and *ListViewVendorsDataService-
> Custom.asmx*. The custom type has *.txt* appended to its filename to
> avoid data type conflicts with *ListViewVendorsCustom.asmx*.

Over on the ASP.NET side, two items are required: HTML markup to define the output template and xml-script markup to do the data binding. The former is, as before,
an HTML table. Remember to use <thead> and <tbody> to satisfy Internet Explorer.

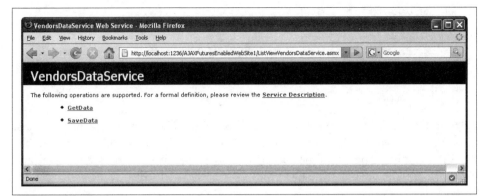

Figure 17-3. The methods provided by the base class

The following HTML markup serves as the placeholder to which ASP.NET AJAX binds the data from the custom data source:

```
<div id="output">
  vendor list goes here</div>
<div style="display: none;">
  <div id="vendorsLayout">
    <table>
    <thead>
        <tr><th>Account Number</th><th>Name</th></tr>
    </thead>
      <tbody id="vendorsItemParent">
        <tr id="vendorsItem">
          <td id="vendorsAccountNumber">vendor account number goes here</td>
          <td id="vendorsName">vendor name goes here</td>
        </tr>
    </tbody>
    </table>
  </div>
</div>
```

However, the xml-script part requires some changes from the preceding example. It starts off as usual:

```
<script type="text/xml-script">
  <page xmlns="http://schemas.microsoft.com/xml-script/2005">
    <components>
    ...
    </components>
  </page>
</script>
```

Then, the data source needs to be referenced. Since this is no ordinary web service, the ScriptManager object will not work to reference the web service. Instead, the <dataSource> xml-script element is used. Provide the URL and an ID—you will need the latter later on!

```
<script type="text/xml-script">
  <page xmlns="http://schemas.microsoft.com/xml-script/2005">
    <components>
      <dataSource id="vendorSource" serviceURL="ListViewVendorsDataService.asmx" />
      ...
    </components>
  </page>
</script>
```

Next up is the ListView control, and by extension, the <listView> element. The most important step is to bind the data source from the preceding code snippet to the ListView control. The properties dataPath and property must be set to data, and dataContext must reference the ID of the <dataSource> element:

```
<listView id="vendorsList" itemTemplateParentElementId="vendorsItemParent"
targetElement="output">
  <bindings>
    <binding dataContext="vendorSource" dataPath="data" property="data" />
  </bindings>
  ...
</listView>
```

The <layoutTemplate> and <itemTemplate> elements are the same as before, binding the data to the <table> element and its subelements.

One thing is missing, however. The data is bound, but has not yet been loaded. The data source supports the property autoLoad. If set to "true", this automatically calls the Select method of the data source.

See Example 17-7 for the complete code for this task.

Example 17-7. Displaying data from a custom data source

ListViewDataService.aspx

```
<%@ Page Language="C#" %>

<!DOCTYPE html PUBLIC "-//W3C//DTD XHTML 1.0 Transitional//EN"
"http://www.w3.org/TR/xhtml1/DTD/xhtml1-transitional.dtd">
<html xmlns="http://www.w3.org/1999/xhtml">
<head id="Head1" runat="server">
  <title>ASP.NET AJAX</title>
</head>
<body>
  <form id="form1" runat="server">
    <asp:ScriptManager runat="server">
      <Scripts>
        <asp:ScriptReference Name="PreviewScript.js"
Assembly="Microsoft.Web.Preview" />
      </Scripts>
    </asp:ScriptManager>
```

Example 17-7. Displaying data from a custom data source (continued)

```html
  <div id="vendorsList">
    vendor list goes here</div>
  <div style="display: none;">
    <div id="vendorsLayout">
      <table>
        <thead>
          <tr><th>Account Number</th><th>Name</th></tr>
        </thead>
        <tbody id="vendorsItemParent">
          <tr id="vendorsItem">
            <td id="vendorsAccountNumber">vendor account number goes here</td>
            <td id="vendorsName">vendor name goes here</td>
          </tr>
        </tbody>
      </table>
    </div>
  </div>
</form>

<script type="text/xml-script">
  <page xmlns="http://schemas.microsoft.com/xml-script/2005">
    <components>
      <dataSource id="vendorSource" serviceURL="ListViewVendorsDataService.asmx"
        autoLoad="true" />
      <listView id="vendorsList" itemTemplateParentElementId="vendorsItemParent">
        <bindings>
          <binding dataContext="vendorSource" dataPath="data" property="data" />
        </bindings>
        <layoutTemplate>
          <template layoutElement="vendorsLayout" />
        </layoutTemplate>
        <itemTemplate>
          <template layoutElement="vendorsItem">
            <label id="vendorsAccountNumber">
              <bindings>
                <binding dataPath="AccountNumber" property="text" />
              </bindings>
            </label>
            <label id="vendorsName">
              <bindings>
                <binding dataPath="Name" property="text" />
              </bindings>
            </label>
          </template>
        </itemTemplate>
      </listView>
    </components>
  </page>
</script>

</body>
</html>
```

There is no actual coding involved (except of the `DataService` web service), just declarations. The output shows the first 10 elements in the `Purchasing.Vendors` table, formatted in an HTML `<table>` element. Therefore, the output of this script is identical to the one in Figure 17-2.

Managing Data

Displaying data is just the first step. The logical consequence would be to implement the other methods defined in `System.ComponentModel.DataObjectMethodType`. Then you can page through the data, update it, and more. This creates a whole new set of possibilities. However you would achieve better performance and realize more efficiencies in development by using the ASP.NET `GridView` control (or any other suitable data control). If you are concerned about the postbacks and page refreshes that are fundamental to the `GridView` control, have a look at Chapter 6 where a method was presented that overcomes this limitation—with the use of ASP.NET AJAX, of course.

Summary

This chapter demonstrated how to access server-side data from the client. We implemented a web service, then used ASP.NET AJAX's data binding and special client controls such as `ListView` to display the server information.

For Further Reading

http://quickstarts.asp.net/Futures/ajax/doc/data.aspx
> Pre-release Microsoft documentation on using data services from ASP.NET AJAX

http://astoria.mslivelabs.com/
> A Microsoft project codenamed "Astoria" that attempts to enable applications to expose data as data services

http://download.microsoft.com/download/5/9/c/59cd0dc5-4691-4c3e-840c-66d865f27692/listview.xps
> Specification of a new (server) web control in .NET Framework 3.5, also called ListView

Using Remote Web Services

Chapters 5 and 17 discussed consuming ASP.NET web services with ASP.NET AJAX. The XMLHttpRequest object that fuels all Ajax applications runs in a restricted environment and is forbidden access to anything outside the current domain. If you need data from a remote web service (one that is on a different server), there is only one solution: create a proxy on your server and then call this proxy from your JavaScript code. This in turn allows creating *mashups*. Mashups are web applications that use data from different sources to "mix 'n mash" them into something new. This chapter shows you how to make remote web services data accessible to JavaScript. From there you can use JavaScript to combine various external sources into something new.

The ASP.NET AJAX Futures release supports proxy implementation for such web services calls through a technology referred to as a web service bridge. In the following sections, we will create pages that receive data from two of the most popular commercial web services, the Google search web service and the Amazon e-commerce web service. The techniques shown here can easily be adapted to any other SOAP web service.

The secret behind this rests in a new file extension that the ASP.NET AJAX Futures release web site template registers in *Web.config*: *.asbx*. Files with this extension can contain XML markup that provides information about a local (server-based) proxy class for a web service. The web page's JavaScript code simply connects with the *.asbx* file, which then takes care of communication with the remote service. Figure 18-1 shows this mechanism.

If you are using the ASP.NET AJAX Futures CTP web site template, the *Web.config* file is already prepared. Before moving on, be aware that the January 2007, May 2007, and July 2007 releases of ASP.NET AJAX Futures contain a bug, which can be found in the following line:

```
<add extension="*.asbx" type="Microsoft.Web.Preview.Services.BridgeBuildProvider"/>
```

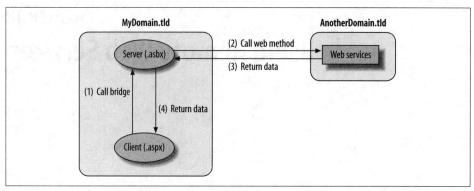

Figure 18-1. *The client page calls the server bridge, which then calls the remote web service*

The * character is wrong here. This is not an error you would have noticed immediately, but only later when some scripts inform you that "There is no build provider registered for the extension '.asbx'." The following fix will solve the problem:

```
<add extension=".asbx" type="Microsoft.Web.Preview.Services.BridgeBuildProvider"/>
```

Make this change in any web sites you have that rely on features of the ASP.NET Futures. You will also need to fix any new Futures-enabled web sites you create. (Alternatively, you can change the *Web.config* file template so that new sites have the correction already. The templates for *Web.config* files are in the ASP.NET Futures installation location, which by default is *%programdir%\Microsoft ASP.NET\ASP.NET Futures July 2007\v1.2.61025\web_config*.)

Using the Google Web Service

The Google web service provides convenient programmatic access to the search engine, using both a SOAP and a REST interface. For our example, we will use the SOAP interface for the ASP.NET AJAX web service bridge.

Using the Google web service requires you to register with Google. To make the request, go to *http://www.google.com/apis/soapsearch*. Google will send you a 32-byte license key, which you will need to send with every search request to the service.

> As of this writing, Google has at least temporarily discontinued issuing new license keys. If you already have a key, you can continue to work with the web service. If you do not have a license key available, don't worry; the section "Using the Amazon Web Service," later in this chapter, develops two sample applications for which new license keys are still happily issued.

Of course, it would be a terrible idea to store this (secret!) license key in JavaScript code in the page. Putting the key in the ASP.NET server code is also not recommended.

Manual .asbx Registration

If you cannot run the *.msi* ASP.NET AJAX installer, the *.asbx* extension will not be mapped with your IIS web server. In that case, run the IIS management console and map the *.asbx* file extension to the *aspnet_isapi.dll* file, which allows the HTTP verbs GET, POST, and HEAD. Also, add the following markup to the *Web.config* file of any web site that uses a web service bridge so that the bridge files are recognized:

```
<compilation>
  <buildProviders>
  ...
    <add extension=".asbx" type="Microsoft.Web.Preview.Services.
BridgeBuildProvider"/>
  </buildProviders>
</compilation>
...
<httpHandlers>
  ...
  <add verb="GET,HEAD,POST" path="*.asbx" type="System.Web.Script.Services.
ScriptHandlerFactory, System.Web.Extensions, Version=1.2.61025.0,
Culture=neutral, PublicKeyToken=31bf3856ad364e35" validate="false"/>
```

If you are using IIS 7, add the following element in the <handlers> subnode of the <system.webServer> node in *Web.config*:

```
<add name="ASBXHandler" verb="GET,HEAD,POST" path="*.asbx"
preCondition="integratedMode"
  type="System.Web.Script.Services.ScriptHandlerFactory, System.Web.Extensions,
Version=1.2.61025.0, Culture=neutral, PublicKeyToken=31bf3856ad364e35"/>
```

However, you can put the license key in the <appSettings> section of the *Web.config* file, as demonstrated in this snippet:

```
<appSettings>
  <add key="GoogleLicenseKey" value="***" />
</appSettings>
```

Obviously, the *Web.config* file available as part of the source code downloads for this chapter does *not* contain this license key yet. you will need to obtain and fill in your own key. You should also use the encryption feature of *Web.config* entries to encrypt your secret API key. This feature is outside the scope of our discussion, so we will not be including it in the examples that follow in this chapter.

The Google Web API Developer's Kit is available for download on the Google API web site. It also contains a WSDL description file named *GoogleSearch.wsdl* that describes the web service interface. The tool *wsdl.exe* (part of the .NET Framework SDK) can use this WSDL information to generate a proxy class.

Download the *GoogleSearch.wsdl* file or extract it as part of the Google API SDK. You can also view the *.wsdl* file in the browser at *http://api.google.com/GoogleSearch.wsdl*, then copy and paste it into a local file. Open a Windows Command window and run the following command (be sure to use an uppercase "GOOGLE," as this will be a case-sensitive namespace when you work with it later):

```
wsdl.exe /namespace:Google GoogleSearch.wsdl
```

 To run the `wsdl.exe` command at the command line, you might need to set a PATH variable to the folder containing the .NET SDK utilities. By default, the utilities are in the folder *%windir%\Program Files\ Microsoft Visual Studio 8\SDK\v2.0\Bin.*

This generates a named *GoogleSearch.cs* file that contains a class and methods for calling the Google search API. As Figure 18-2 shows, you will receive some warnings, but you can safely ignore them for this web service. Also, notice that we provide a namespace for the class to prevent a potential name conflict with other classes in our web application.

```
Visual Studio 2005 Command Prompt                                        _ □ x
C:\Documents and Settings\Christian\My Documents>wsdl.exe /namespace:Google
GoogleSearch.wsdl
Microsoft (R) Web Services Description Language Utility
[Microsoft (R) .NET Framework, Version 2.0.50727.42]
Copyright (C) Microsoft Corporation. All rights reserved.
Warning: This web reference does not conform to WS-I Basic Profile v1.1.
R2706: A wsdl:binding in a DESCRIPTION MUST use the value of "literal" for the u
se attribute in all soapbind:body, soapbind:fault, soapbind:header and soapbind:
headerfault elements.
    - Input element soapbind:body of operation 'doGetCachedPage' on portType 'Goo
gleSearchBinding' from namespace 'urn:GoogleSearch'.
    - Output element soapbind:body of operation 'doGetCachedPage' on portType 'Go
ogleSearchBinding' from namespace 'urn:GoogleSearch'.
    - Input element soapbind:body of operation 'doSpellingSuggestion' on portType
 'GoogleSearchBinding' from namespace 'urn:GoogleSearch'.
    - Output element soapbind:body of operation 'doSpellingSuggestion' on portTyp
e 'GoogleSearchBinding' from namespace 'urn:GoogleSearch'.
    - Input element soapbind:body of operation 'doGoogleSearch' on portType 'Goog
leSearchBinding' from namespace 'urn:GoogleSearch'.
    - Output element soapbind:body of operation 'doGoogleSearch' on portType 'Goo
gleSearchBinding' from namespace 'urn:GoogleSearch'.

For more details on the WS-I Basic Profile v1.1, see the specification
at http://www.ws-i.org/Profiles/BasicProfile-1.1.html.

Writing file 'C:\Documents and Settings\Christian\My Documents\GoogleSearchServi
ce.cs'.

C:\Documents and Settings\Christian\My Documents>_
```

Figure 18-2. Creating the web service proxy for the Google web service

Put the generated class file, *GoogleSearchService.cs*, in the *App_Code* folder of an ASP.NET Futures-enabled web application. (If the web site doesn't already have an *App_Code* folder, create one.) This enables you to use the class without manual compilation.

In the next step, you have to create a wrapper in server code for the web service proxy, one that calls the search method. Going into great detail about the Google web service API is beyond the scope of this book. But the most important information is that the web service exposes a doGoogleSearch( ) method, which accepts two parameters: the Google license key and the search string. The wrapper just calls this method and returns the results, as shown in Example 18-1. Create a class file named *GoogleSearch-ServiceWrapper.cs* in the *App_Code* folder, delete any code already in the file, and then copy the code from Example 18-1 into it.

Example 18-1. A Google web service wrapper class

```
GoogleSearchServiceWrapper.cs

using Google;

public class GoogleSearchServiceWrapper
{
  public GoogleSearchResult Search(string licenseKey, string query)
  {
    GoogleSearchService gss = new GoogleSearchService( );
    return gss.doGoogleSearch(
      licenseKey,
      query,
      0, // offset of the first result
      10, // maximum number of results
      false, // whether to filter similar results
      "", // subset of Google to restrict search to
      false, // whether to filter adult content
      "", // language to restrict search to
      "", // ignored, as is the next parameter
      "");
  }
}
```

Now we can use the ASP.NET AJAX web service bridge. To activate the web service bridge, you need to provide all relevant web service information in an *.asbx* file. Create an XML file named *Google.asbx* in the root of your web site.

In the *.asbx* file, provide the name of your (custom) namespace where the bridge will reside (namespace attribute) and the name of the class you want to implement with the bridge (className attribute).

```
<bridge namespace="OReilly.AspNetAJAX" className="Google" >
```

The <proxy> element holds the name of the wrapper class and where to find it:

```
<proxy type="GoogleSearchServiceWrapper, App_Code" />
```

Next, all methods in the web service are listed, including the names of the parameters. All the parameters specified here can be used in JavaScript calls later. However, don't forget that the required license key is stored in the *Web.config* file. The parameter for the Google license key therefore cannot be set using JavaScript. Instead, you can use the following syntax to load the key at runtime from the <appSettings> section:

```
<parameter name="licenseKey" value="% appsettings : GoogleLicenseKey %"
serverOnly="true" />
```

The serverOnly="true" syntax makes the licenseKey parameter unavailable for the JavaScript code, so the value for it is always taken from *Web.config*.

That wraps it up. Example 18-2 contains the complete code for the bridge file.

Example 18-2. The web service bridge for the Google web service

Google.asbx

```xml
<?xml version="1.0" encoding="utf-8" ?>
<bridge namespace="OReilly.AspNetAJAX" className="Google" >
  <proxy type="GoogleSearchServiceWrapper, App_Code" />
  <method name="Search">
    <input>
      <parameter name="licenseKey"
                 value="% appsettings : GoogleLicenseKey %"
                 serverOnly="true" />
      <parameter name="query" />
    </input>
  </method>
</bridge>
```

Now all that is left to do is to write the ASP.NET AJAX-powered *.aspx* page. Our page needs a text box for the search query, a button to run the query, and some placeholders to display the results.

The markup might look like the following:

```html
<div>
  <input type="text" id="Query" />
  <input type="button" value="Search" onclick="Search();" />
</div>
<div>
  <p>Approx. <span id="Count">0</span> results.</p>
  <ul id="Results">
  </ul>
</div>
```

Of course, the page must contain a ScriptManager control. In its <Services> sub-element, the web service is referenced—naturally, as an *.asbx* file. Also, the *PreviewScript.js* script library (see Chapter 15) is loaded since it will be used in the JavaScript code.

```
<asp:ScriptManager ID="ScriptManager1" runat="server">
  <Services>
    <asp:ServiceReference Path="~/Google.asbx" />
  </Services>
  <Scripts>
    <asp:ScriptReference Assembly="Microsoft.Web.Preview" Name="PreviewScript.js" />
  </Scripts>
</asp:ScriptManager>
```

This loads the bridge and exposes our `OReilly.AspNetAJAX` namespace to JavaScript. You can then call the `Search()` method from the web service wrapper as you would call any local web service. Notice how you provide the parameters—you use an array with the parameter names as the indexes:

```
OReilly.AspNetAJAX.Google.Search(
  { "query": query },
  callComplete, callError
);
```

The return data from the web service is a JavaScript representation of the SOAP objects returned by the server. For a Google search, the return data has a property (or subelement) named `resultElements`, which contains an array of all individual URLs found by this search. Each of these URLs has, among other things, `title` and `URL` properties that we will display in the page.

The complete code in Example 18-3 contains some other nifty JavaScript effects. For example, when the results from the web service arrive, they are dynamically added to the selection list (a `<ul>` HTML element). The `clearList()` helper function clears that list when a new search is executed. The search results from Google are visible on the local page (Figure 18-3), thanks to the ASP.NET AJAX web service bridge (see Figure 18-1 earlier in this chapter).

Example 18-3. Calling the Google web service

Google.aspx

```
<%@ Page Language="C#" %>

<!DOCTYPE html PUBLIC "-//W3C//DTD XHTML 1.0 Transitional//EN"
"http://www.w3.org/TR/xhtml1/DTD/xhtml1-transitional.dtd">
<html xmlns="http://www.w3.org/1999/xhtml">
<head runat="server">
  <title>ASP.NET AJAX</title>

  <script language="JavaScript" type="text/javascript">
  function clearList() {
    var list = $get("Results");
    while (list.firstChild != null) {
      list.removeChild(list.firstChild);
    }
  }

  function Search() {
    var query = new Sys.Preview.UI.TextBox($get('Query'))
    $get("Button").disabled = true;
    clearList();
    OReilly.AspNetAJAX.Google.Search(
      { "query": query.get_text() },
      callComplete, callError
```

Example 18-3. Calling the Google web service (continued)

```
    );
    new Sys.Preview.UI.Label($get('Count')).set_text("...");
  }

  function callComplete(result)  {
    new
Sys.Preview.UI.Label($get('Count')).set_text(result.estimatedTotalResultsCount);
    if (result.resultElements != null) {
      for (var i = 0; i < result.resultElements.length; i++) {
        var page = result.resultElements[i];
        var li = document.createElement("li");
        var a = document.createElement("a");
        a.setAttribute("href", page.URL);
        a.innerHTML = page.title;
        li.appendChild(a);
        $get("Results").appendChild(li);
      }
    }
    $get("Button").disabled = false;
  }
  function callError(result) {
    window.alert("Error! " + result.get_message());
    new Sys.Preview.UI.Label($get('Count')).set_text("0");
    $get("Button").disabled = false;
  }
  </script>

</head>
<body>
  <form id="form1" runat="server">
    <asp:ScriptManager ID="ScriptManager1" runat="server">
      <Services>
        <asp:ServiceReference Path="~/Google.asbx" />
      </Services>
      <Scripts>
        <asp:ScriptReference Assembly="Microsoft.Web.Preview"
Name="PreviewScript.js" />
      </Scripts>
    </asp:ScriptManager>
    <div>
      <input type="text" id="Query" />
      <input type="button" id="Button" value="Search" onclick="Search();" />
    </div>
    <div>
      <p>Approx. <span id="Count">0</span> results.</p>
      <ul id="Results">
      </ul>
    </div>
  </form>
</body>
</html>
```

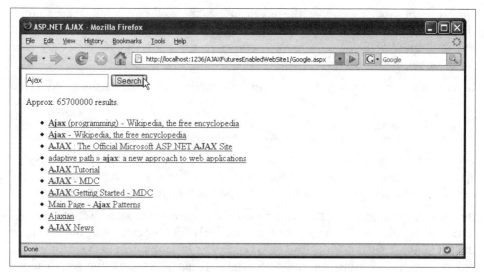

Figure 18-3. Searching with the Google API and an ASP.NET AJAX web services bridge

 While working on this book, the Google web services server had some outages from time to time, so don't immediately assume there is a problem with your code if you don't see results right away. It could be the remote server that causes issues. Refer to Appendix A for information on debugging Ajax applications and how to have a look at the HTTP traffic.

Using the Amazon Web Service

The preceding section showed you how to use the Google web service, a relatively unsophisticated service with no custom types as parameters and a simple method that handles everything. In this section, we will cover the more complex Amazon web service. It supports several types that together make up a search request. Again, the implementation details of the Amazon web service are of no particular interest, but the way ASP.NET AJAX can use this data is.

Once again you will need a license key (Amazon calls it an *access key*). As with the Google web service, this requires registration; the URL of the Amazon web service documentation site is *http://www.amazon.com/gp/aws/landing.html*. As with the Google key, you must put the access key in the <appSettings> section of the *Web.config* file (Amazon's key is 20 bytes long).

The sample file you can download for this book does not contain this key, so you need to put yours in:

```
<appSettings>
  <add key="AmazonAccessKey" value="***" />
</appSettings>
```

Similar to the Google example, the next step uses the *wsdl.exe* tool to create a proxy class from the WSDL description of the Amazon web service. You can download the Amazon WSDL file at *http://webservices.amazon.com/AWSECommerceService/AWSECommerceService.wsdl*.

Use the following command in a Command window to generate the proxy class, *AWSECommerceService.cs*:

```
wsdl.exe /namespace:Amazon
http://webservices.amazon.com/AWSECommerceService/AWSECommerceService.wsdl
```

Copy the resulting *.cs* file to your application's *App_Code* folder. If an error message appears, it may be caused by the usual list of server hiccups; just use the *AWSECommerceService.cs* class provided as part of the this book's downloads.

Implementing the wrapper class is a bit more difficult this time, as the web service uses some custom objects. Create a class file named *AWSECommerceServiceWrapper.cs* in the site's *App_Code* folder. In the class, you must instantiate an ItemSearchRequest object to which you provide the search term (what to search), the search index (where to search for it), and the response group (how much data to return):

```
public Amazon.Items Search(string accessKey, string query)
{
   ItemSearchRequest searchRequest = new ItemSearchRequest();
   searchRequest.Keywords = query;
   searchRequest.ResponseGroup = new string[] { "Small" };
   searchRequest.SearchIndex = "Books";
```

The next step is to instantiate an ItemSearch object, which provides the Amazon access key and the newly created ItemSearchRequest object:

```
   ItemSearch search = new ItemSearch();
   search.AWSAccessKeyId = accessKey;
   search.Request = new ItemSearchRequest[1] { searchRequest };
```

Finally, you instantiate the main class, AWSECommerceService, and call the ItemSearch() method, providing the ItemSearch object as a parameter. The return data is an array of the responses of all search queries sent (it is possible to send multiple queries in one call).

Since we were sending only one query, we expect only one result:

```
   AWSECommerceService awse = new AWSECommerceService();
   ItemSearchResponse searchResponse = awse.ItemSearch(search);
   return searchResponse.Items[0];
}
```

Example 10-8 has the complete code for *AWSECommerceServiceWrapper.cs* wrapper class.

Example 18-4. The Amazon web service wrapper class

AWSECommerceServiceWrapper.cs

```csharp
using Amazon;

public class AWSECommerceServiceWrapper
{
  public Amazon.Items Search(string accessKey, string query)
  {
    ItemSearchRequest searchRequest = new ItemSearchRequest();
    searchRequest.Keywords = query;
    searchRequest.ResponseGroup = new string[] { "Small" };
    searchRequest.SearchIndex = "Books";

    ItemSearch search = new ItemSearch();
    search.AWSAccessKeyId = accessKey;
    search.Request = new ItemSearchRequest[1] { searchRequest };

    AWSECommerceService awse = new AWSECommerceService();
    ItemSearchResponse searchResponse = awse.ItemSearch(search);
    return searchResponse.Items[0];
  }
}
```

The rest of this Amazon demo application is more or less the same as the Google example. An *Amazon.asbx* file serves as the bridge to the external web service. The accessKey data is read from *Web.config*, and the query parameter will come from the client application. Example 18-5 shows you the XML for the *Amazon.asbx* file.

Example 18-5. The web service bridge for the Amazon web service

Amazon.asbx

```xml
<?xml version="1.0" encoding="utf-8" ?>
<bridge namespace="OReilly.AspNetAJAX " className="Amazon" >
  <proxy type="AWSECommerceServiceWrapper, App_Code"  />
  <method name="Search">
    <input>
      <parameter name="accessKey"
                 value="% appsettings : AmazonAccessKey %"
                 serverOnly="true" />
      <parameter name="query" />
    </input>
  </method>
</bridge>
```

Not only is sending data to the Amazon web service complicated, getting the data out of it is also complex. The wrapper's return data (which is an array of type Amazon.Item) contains a list of books. Most of the interesting data in this array is put in the ItemAttributes property, another custom object.

Example 18-6 shows an ASP.NET page that contains code to extract the author(s) of all books that satisfied the search parameters along with the book title, then put the results in a <ul> element. Figure 18-4 shows the result.

Example 18-6. Calling the Amazon web service

```
Amazon.aspx

<%@ Page Language="C#" %>

<!DOCTYPE html PUBLIC "-//W3C//DTD XHTML 1.0 Transitional//EN"
"http://www.w3.org/TR/xhtml1/DTD/xhtml1-transitional.dtd">
<html xmlns="http://www.w3.org/1999/xhtml">
<head runat="server">
  <title>ASP.NET AJAX</title>

  <script type="text/javascript">
  function clearList( ) {
    var list = $get("Results");
    while (list.firstChild != null) {
      list.removeChild(list.firstChild);
    }
  }

  function Search( ) {
    var query = new Sys.Preview.UI.TextBox($get('Query'))
    $get("Button").disabled = true;
    clearList( );
    OReilly.AspNetAJAX.Amazon.Search(
      { "query": query.get_text( ) },
      callComplete, callError
    );
    new Sys.Preview.UI.Label($get('Count')).set_text("...");
  }

  function callComplete(result)  {
    new Sys.Preview.UI.Label($get('Count')).set_text(result.TotalResults);
    if (result.Item != null) {
      for (var i = 0; i < result.Item.length; i++) {
        var article = result.Item[i];
        var author = (article.ItemAttributes.Author != null ?
          join(article.ItemAttributes.Author) + ": " : "");
        var title = article.ItemAttributes.Title;
        var li = document.createElement("li");
        var liText = document.createTextNode(author + title);
        li.appendChild(liText);
        $get("Results").appendChild(li);
      }
    }
    $get("Button").disabled = false;
  }
```

Example 18-6. Calling the Amazon web service (continued)

```
  function callError(result) {
    window.alert("Error! " + result.get_message());
    new Sys.Preview.UI.Label($get('Count')).set_text("0");
    $get("Button").disabled = false;
  }

  function join(a) {
    var s = "";
    for (var i=0; i < a.length - 1; i++) {
      s += a[i] + "/";
    }
    s += a[a.length - 1];
    return s;
  }
  </script>

</head>
<body>
  <form id="form1" runat="server">
    <asp:ScriptManager ID="ScriptManager1" runat="server">
      <Services>
        <asp:ServiceReference Path="~/Amazon.asbx" />
      </Services>
      <Scripts>
        <asp:ScriptReference Assembly="Microsoft.Web.Preview"
Name="PreviewScript.js" />
      </Scripts>
    </asp:ScriptManager>
    <div>
      <input type="text" id="Query" />
      <input type="button" id="Button" value="Search" onclick="Search();" />
    </div>
    <div>
      <p>
        <span id="Count">0</span> results.</p>
      <ul id="Results">
      </ul>
    </div>
  </form>
</body>
</html>
```

 Interestingly, both Google and Amazon offer a SOAP and a REST interface to their services. Both interfaces provide the same functionality. The REST usage numbers are much higher in both cases than the SOAP numbers. One reason is certainly the increased complexity of using SOAP. However, with the ASP.NET AJAX web service bridge, most of that complexity is taken care of for you.

Figure 18-4. Searching the Amazon catalog using an ASP.NET AJAX bridge

Transforming a Web Service Result with XSLT

The data returned from a web service is generally XML (at least if SOAP or REST is used). This XML is represented in your ASP.NET AJAX page as a JavaScript object, from which you can extract what you need, then display using HTML elements.

Another way to convert the web service data from XML to HTML output, though, is to use an XSL transformation (XSLT). Explaining the use of XSLT is beyond the scope of this book, but I have cited some excellent sources of information in the "For Further Reading" section at the end of this chapter. Modern web browsers (Mozilla, Internet Explorer, Opera 9+) support XSLT via JavaScript, but very inconsistently. Therefore, a better approach is to perform the transformation in server code. This is possible using custom .NET code, or by letting ASP.NET AJAX components do all the work. In this section, we'll transform the return data from the Google search service into an HTML fragment, which will then be displayed on the web page.

The ASP.NET AJAX web service bridge supports two built-in transformers that can convert objects into another format. The `Microsoft.Web.Preview.Services.XmlBridgeTransformer` class converts an object into XML, and the `Microsoft.Web.Preview.Services.XsltBridgeTransformer` class performs an XSL conversion of XML data into any output format (usually, HTML).

As before, we will prepare a bridge, a wrapper class, and JavaScript code in the page that sets the search in motion. The JavaScript code will send the search request from the page to the bridge, which will call the wrapper, which performs the search. The results come back to the wrapper as an object (as we saw earlier, we can work with the object as an array). The wrapper sends this to the bridge. However, this time, the bridge does not send the results back down to the page as is.

Unlike examples earlier in the chapter, the bridge this time performs a pair of transforms on the results. The first transform converts the result object into XML. The second applies an XSLT transformation to the converted XML to produce HTML. Indeed, it produces the actual HTML that we want to use to display the result list. The bridge sends this HTML to the page, where a single line of JavaScript can simply insert the finished HTML into a waiting container.

We will use variations on the three files that we created for the earlier Google search example. However, we need one additional item: XSLT created as an *.xsl* file. This is the transformation that will be called by the bridge to convert the XML to HTML.

In the root folder of your web application, add a new XSLT file named *Google.xsl*. This file will hold the XSLT instructions for transforming Google search results into HTML.

As in the previous Google example, we want to display the search results as an HTML <ul> list. Therefore, the XSLT must iterate over all the matches returned by the search as XML, which we can do with an XSL for each loop. There is one small hurdle though. Every search result resides in a <resultElement> element, the ASP.NET AJAX XML transformer converts this into <ResultElement>. XSL is lowercase, therefore accessing resultElement will not work, we need to use ResultElement instead:

```
<xsl:for-each select="//resultElements/ResultElement">
...
</xsl:for-each>
```

For each search result item, an <li> element is created. The text of the <li> element is a link (an <a> element) that points to the web page for that particular result. XSLT processors escape HTML entities, but the Google web service returns the page's title as HTML (since the search terms are highlighted in bold). Therefore, we will need to use the disable-output-encoding attribute for the title.

One other point: since we want to create an HTML fragment, in the XSLT's <xsl:output> element we need to include the omit-xml-declaration attribute to prevent the transformation from creating a result that starts with <?xml ?>. Example 18-7 shows the complete XSLT file.

Example 18-7. The XSLT file for the Google web service

Google.xsl

```
<?xml version="1.0" encoding="utf-8"?>

<xsl:stylesheet version="1.0"
    xmlns:xsl="http://www.w3.org/1999/XSL/Transform">

  <xsl:output method="html" encoding="utf-8" omit-xml-declaration="yes" />

  <xsl:template match="/">
```

Example 18-7. The XSLT file for the Google web service (continued)

```
   <p>
     Approx. <xsl:value-of select="//estimatedTotalResultsCount" /> matches!
     <ul>
        <xsl:for-each select="//resultElements/ResultElement">
   <li>
   <a>
   <xsl:attribute name="href">
   <xsl:value-of select="URL" />
   </xsl:attribute>
   <xsl:value-of select="title" disable-output-escaping="yes" />
   </a>
   </li>
        </xsl:for-each>
     </ul>
   </p>
 </xsl:template>

</xsl:stylesheet>
```

For the next step, we need a new entry for the XSL transformation. This will set up the object transformation to XML (via `XmlBridgeTransformer`) and the XML transformation into HTML (via `XsltBridgeTransformer`). Usually, you would create a new method in the web service wrapper for the search that generates the results for the object transformation, but for this example, there is no new business logic to implement.

 You could also use a new bridge file, but then you would have to use a different class name than earlier, otherwise Visual Studio would complain during compilation (you could still run the page, though).

In prerelease versions of ASP.NET AJAX, within the bridge, the `serverName` attribute of the `<method>` element could be used to redirect requests to the wrapper method:

```
   <method name="SearchXslt" serverName="Search">
   ...
   </method>
```

This exposes a method called `SearchXslt( )` that is accessible in JavaScript, but it just executes the existing `Search( )` method in the wrapper.

Recent ASP.NET AJAX versions no longer support that hook. Therefore, you need to do a server-side redirection by patching the *GoogleSearchServiceWrapper.cs* file as shown in Example 18-8.

Example 18-8. The updated Google search service wrapper

```
GoogleSearchServiceWrapper.cs

using Google;
```

Example 18-8. The updated Google search service wrapper (continued)

```
public class GoogleSearchServiceWrapper
{
  public GoogleSearchResult Search(string licenseKey, string query)
  {
    GoogleSearchService gss = new GoogleSearchService( );
    return gss.doGoogleSearch(
      licenseKey,
      query,
      0,
      10,
      false,
      "",
      false,
      "",
      "",
      "");
  }

  public GoogleSearchResult SearchXslt(string licenseKey, string query)
  {
    return Search(licenseKey, query);
  }
}
```

But back to the bridge file. In the <method> element, the <input> element remains the same, as the parameters do not change. However, a new <transforms> element is introduced, which specifies the two transformers. For the XSLT transformer, you must, of course, provide the XSL file to use. Example 18-9 shows the XML markup for the updated bridge file.

Example 18-9. The updated XSLT web service bridge for the Google web service

Google.asbx

```
<?xml version="1.0" encoding="utf-8" ?>
<bridge namespace="OReilly.AspNetAJAX" className="Google" >
  <proxy type="GoogleSearchServiceWrapper, App_Code" />
  <method name="Search">
    <input>
      <parameter name="licenseKey"
                 value="% appsettings : GoogleLicenseKey %"
                 serverOnly="true" />
      <parameter name="query" />
    </input>
  </method>
  <method name="SearchXslt" serverName="Search">
    <input>
      <parameter name="licenseKey"
                 value="% appsettings : GoogleLicenseKey %"
                 serverOnly="true" />
      <parameter name="query" />
    </input>
```

```
    <transforms>
      <transform type="Microsoft.Web.Preview.Services.XmlBridgeTransformer" />
      <transform type="Microsoft.Web.Preview.Services.XsltBridgeTransformer">
        <data>
          <attribute name="stylesheetFile" value="~/Google.xsl" />
        </data>
      </transform>
    </transforms>
  </method>
</bridge>
```

All that remains to be done is to call this bridge. As the bridge returns an HTML fragment, the result from the web service call can simply be assigned to the innerHTML property of a <div> container. This significantly simplifies the JavaScript code.

Example 18-10 shows a complete ASP.NET page with markup and JavaScript code. The output of this page is identical to that of Example 18-3, which was displayed in Figure 18-3.

Example 18-10. Calling the Google web service with XSLT

GoogleXslt.aspx

```
<%@ Page Language="C#" %>

<!DOCTYPE html PUBLIC "-//W3C//DTD XHTML 1.0 Transitional//EN"
"http://www.w3.org/TR/xhtml1/DTD/xhtml1-transitional.dtd">
<html xmlns="http://www.w3.org/1999/xhtml">
<head runat="server">
  <title>ASP.NET AJAX</title>

  <script language="JavaScript" type="text/javascript">
  function clearList() {
    $get("Results").innerHTML = "";
  }

  function Search() {
    var query = new Sys.Preview.UI.TextBox($get('Query'))
    $get("Button").disabled = true;
    clearList();
    OReilly.AspNetAJAX.Google.SearchXslt(
      { "query": query.get_text() },
      callComplete, callError
    );
  }

  function callComplete(result) {
    $get("Results").innerHTML = result;
    $get("Button").disabled = false;
  }
  function callError(result) {
    window.alert("Error! " + result.get_message());
```

Example 18-10. Calling the Google web service with XSLT (continued)

```
      $get("Button").disabled = false;
    }
  </script>

</head>
<body>
  <form id="form1" runat="server">
    <asp:ScriptManager ID="ScriptManager1" runat="server">
      <Services>
        <asp:ServiceReference Path="~/Google.asbx" />
      </Services>
      <Scripts>
        <asp:ScriptReference Assembly="Microsoft.Web.Preview"
Name="PreviewScript.js" />
      </Scripts>
    </asp:ScriptManager>
    <div>
      <input type="text" id="Query" />
      <input type="button" id="Button" value="Search" onclick="Search();" />
    </div>
    <div id="Results">
    </div>
  </form>
</body>
</html>
```

Of course, this approach also works with the Amazon web service. First, we need to update the web services bridge file. Example 18-11 shows the new code.

Example 18-11. The updated Amazon web services bridge

Amazon.asbx

```
<?xml version="1.0" encoding="utf-8" ?>
<bridge namespace="OReilly.AspNetAJAX" className="Amazon" >
  <proxy type="AWSECommerceServiceWrapper, App_Code"  />
  <method name="Search">
    <input>
      <parameter name="accessKey"
                 value="% appsettings : AmazonAccessKey %"
                 serverOnly="true" />
      <parameter name="query" />
    </input>
  </method>
  <method name="SearchXslt" serverName="Search">
    <input>
      <parameter name="accessKey"
                 value="% appsettings : AmazonAccessKey %"
                 serverOnly="true" />
      <parameter name="query" />
    </input>
    <transforms>
```

Example 18-11. The updated Amazon web services bridge (continued)

```
      <transform type="Microsoft.Web.Preview.Services.XmlBridgeTransformer" />
      <transform type="Microsoft.Web.Preview.Services.XsltBridgeTransformer">
        <data>
          <attribute name="stylesheetFile" value="~/Amazon.xsl" />
        </data>
      </transform>
    </transforms>
  </method>
</bridge>
```

We must also provide a dummy function in the web service wrapper to redirect calls of SearchXslt( ) to Search( ), as shown in Example 18-12.

Example 18-12. The updated Amazon web services wrapper

```
AWSECommerceServiceWrapper.cs

using Amazon;

public class AWSECommerceServiceWrapper
{
  public Amazon.Items Search(string accessKey, string query)
  {
    ItemSearchRequest searchRequest = new ItemSearchRequest( );
    searchRequest.Keywords = query;
    searchRequest.ResponseGroup = new string[] { "Small" };
    searchRequest.SearchIndex = "Books";

    ItemSearch search = new ItemSearch( );
    search.AWSAccessKeyId = accessKey;
    search.Request = new ItemSearchRequest[1] { searchRequest };

    AWSECommerceService awse = new AWSECommerceService( );
    ItemSearchResponse searchResponse = awse.ItemSearch(search);
    return searchResponse.Items[0];
  }

  public Amazon.Items SearchXslt(string accessKey, string query)
  {
    return Search(accessKey, query);
  }
}
```

Next, we need an XSL transformation that converts the XML returned from the Amazon SOAP service into HTML. Example 18-13 presents one possible approach.

Example 18-13. The stylesheet to transform Amazon web services results into HTML

```
Amazon.xsl

<?xml version="1.0" encoding="utf-8"?>
```

Example 18-13. The stylesheet to transform Amazon web services results into HTML (continued)

```
<xsl:stylesheet version="1.0"
    xmlns:xsl="http://www.w3.org/1999/XSL/Transform">

  <xsl:output method="html" encoding="utf-8" omit-xml-declaration="yes" />

  <xsl:template match="/">
    <p>
      <xsl:value-of select="//TotalResults" /> matches found!
      <ul>
        <xsl:for-each select="//Items/Item/ItemAttributes">
          <li>
            <xsl:value-of select="Author" />:
            <xsl:value-of select="Title" />
          </li>
        </xsl:for-each>
      </ul>
    </p>
  </xsl:template>

</xsl:stylesheet>
```

Finally, we use code very similar to Example 18-10 to run the transformation. Example 18-14 contains the complete listing.

Example 18-14. Calling the Amazon web service with XSLT

AmazonXslt.aspx

```
<%@ Page Language="C#" %>

<!DOCTYPE html PUBLIC "-//W3C//DTD XHTML 1.0 Transitional//EN"
"http://www.w3.org/TR/xhtml1/DTD/xhtml1-transitional.dtd">
<html xmlns="http://www.w3.org/1999/xhtml">
<head id="Head1" runat="server">
  <title>ASP.NET AJAX</title>

  <script language="JavaScript" type="text/javascript">
  function clearList( ) {
    $get("Results").innerHTML = "";
  }

  function Search( ) {
    var query = new Sys.Preview.UI.TextBox($get('Query'))
    $get("Button").disabled = true;
    clearList( );
    OReilly.AspNetAJAX.Amazon.SearchXslt(
      { "query": query.get_text() },
      callComplete, callError
    );
  }

  function callComplete(result)  {
```

Example 18-14. Calling the Amazon web service with XSLT (continued)

```
    $get("Results").innerHTML = result;
    $get("Button").disabled = false;
  }
  function callError(result) {
    window.alert("Error! " + result.get_message());
    $get("Button").disabled = false;
  }
  </script>

</head>
<body>
  <form id="form1" runat="server">
    <asp:ScriptManager ID="ScriptManager1" runat="server">
      <Services>
        <asp:ServiceReference Path="~/Amazon.asbx" />
      </Services>
      <Scripts>
        <asp:ScriptReference Assembly="Microsoft.Web.Preview"
Name="PreviewScript.js" />
      </Scripts>
    </asp:ScriptManager>
    <div>
      <input type="text" id="Query" />
      <input type="button" id="Button" value="Search" onclick="Search();" />
    </div>
    <div id="Results">
    </div>
  </form>
</body>
</html>
```

Figure 18-5 displays the output. You will note some visual flaws. For example, books for which no author is listed, such as encyclopedias and other reference works, look a little disjointed with the colon at the beginning of the entry. This is something that is easier to compensate with code than with XSL. But there are workarounds for this, as well.

Using the Yahoo! Web Service (and REST and XPath)

In the final example of this chapter, we will use yet another web service, this time the Yahoo! web service. This service does not currently provide a SOAP interface, but uses REST exclusively.

Therefore, on the server, we need to send a GET request instead of a POST SOAP request. The ASP.NET AJAX Futures release comes with support for this, but first you need to register with Yahoo! in order to be able to use the service.

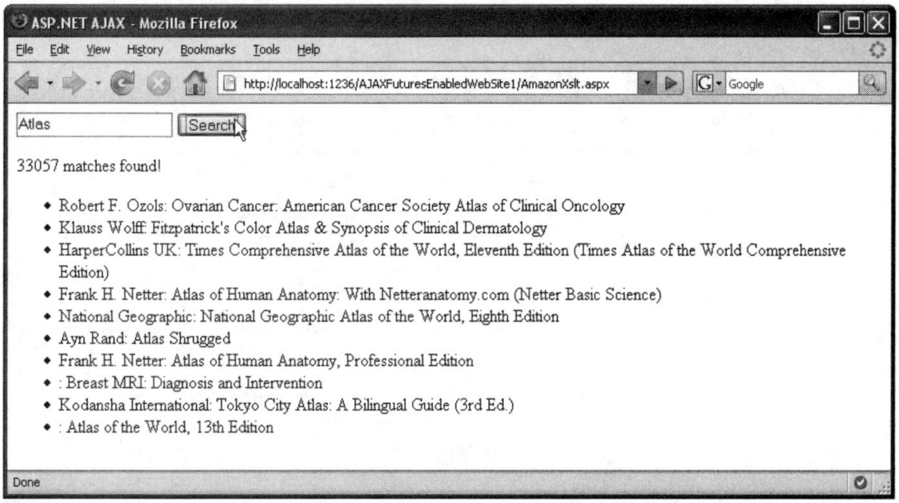

Figure 18-5. Searching the Amazon catalog using an ASP.NET AJAX bridge and an XSL transformation

A Moment for REST

REST stands for "REpresential State Transfer," a concept taken from Roy Fielding's University of California PhD dissertation, "Architectural Styles and the Design of Network-based Software Architectures." (Fielding is one of the authors of the HTTP specification.) The theory behind REST is not pertinent for our example and we won't go into any further detail here. What we do need to know is that REST web service calls usually work in the following fashion: a GET (!) request is sent to the server, all request data (which method to call, which arguments to pass) being parts of the URL. The return data from this GET call is usually XML, but it can also come in different formats—for instance, plain text, CSV, or JSON.

Yahoo! expects you to register each application, and as a result provides you with several keys in case you need to use more than one. To apply for such an application ID, go to *http://search.yahooapis.com/webservices/register_application*. You need to sign in to Yahoo! in order to access this page. If you do not currently have a Yahoo! account, you can set one up at no cost. Then, you will get to the questionnaire shown in Figure 18-6, where you need to provide background information about the application. The web page, including the application key, is displayed in Figure 18-7 (which for publishing purposes has been redacted, for understandable reasons).

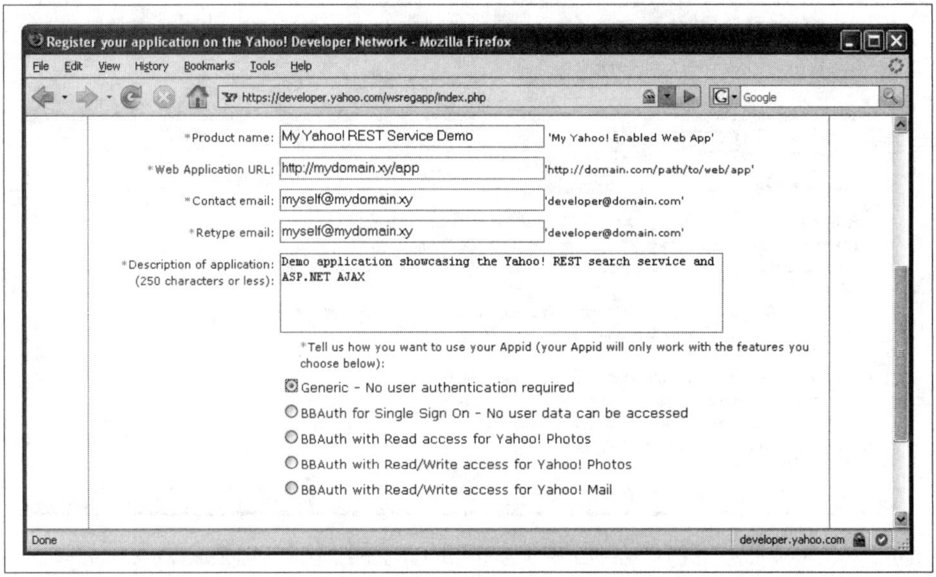

Figure 18-6. Providing information regarding your application

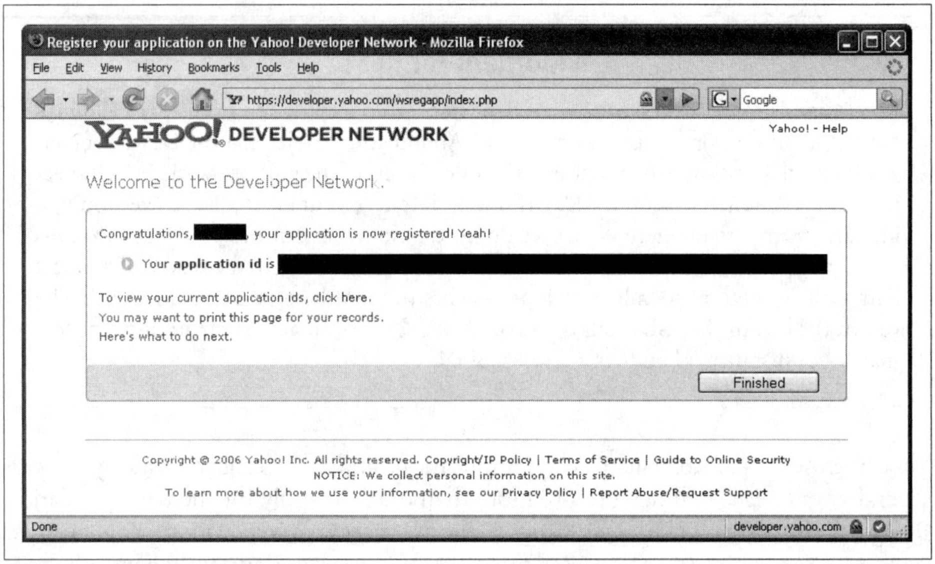

Figure 18-7. The newly generated application key (for obvious reasons the key itself is not shown here)

Store the new application key in your site's *Web.config*, under the name YahooApplicationID. Including the previous examples, *Web.config* now should contain a section that appears as follows:

```
<appSettings>
  <add key="AmazonAccessKey" value="***" />
  <add key="GoogleLicenseKey" value="***" />
  <add key="YahooAppID" value="***" />
</appSettings>
```

A REST call to the Yahoo! search service is scripted as follows (see Figure 18-8 for what this XML can look like):

```
http://api.search.yahoo.com/WebSearchService/V1/webSearch?
appid=***&output=xml&query=***
```

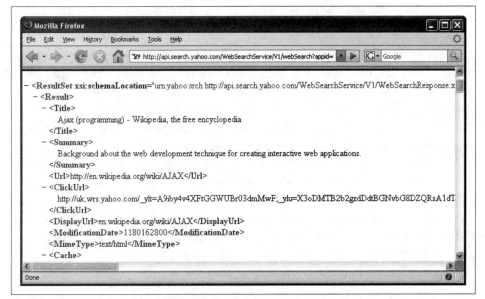

Figure 18-8. The XML output of the Yahoo! search service REST call

This URL consists of a base path (*http://api.search.yahoo.com/WebSearchService/V1/ webSearch*) and several arguments as part of the query string. The *.asbx* bridge file we create for this example will configure the application to send a request to such a URL.

First, the correct proxy type must be used. This time we do not have a SOAP wrapper based on a WSDL service description, but can use a provider that ships with the ASP.NET AJAX Futures release: `Microsoft.Web.Preview.Services.BridgeRestProxy`. The `serviceURL` property of the `<proxy>` element points to the base path of the Yahoo! search service:

```
<?xml version="1.0" encoding="utf-8" ?>
<bridge namespace="OReilly.AspNetAJAX" className="Yahoo">
  <proxy type="Microsoft.Web.Preview.Services.BridgeRestProxy"
          serviceUrl="http://api.search.yahoo.com/WebSearchService/V1/webSearch" />
```

As in the previous examples, a method is defined with the `<method>` element. The two arguments `appid` and `output` come from the server, but the query argument (the actual search term) will be provided by the JavaScript code:

```
<method name="Search">
  <input>
    <parameter name="appid"
               value="% appsettings : YahooAppID %"
               serverOnly="true" />
    <parameter name="output"
               value="xml"
               serverOnly="true" />
    <parameter name="query" />
  </input>
```

This would actually already work. If you called the `OReilly.AspNetAJAX.Yahoo.Search()` method, you would get XML quite similar to the one from Figure 18-8 in return. This XML could then be parsed with JavaScript code, and the data from it displayed on the web page.

However, parsing XML with JavaScript can be a tedious task, that does not work equally well on all browsers, and is simply unnecessary here. Another helpful feature of ASP.NET AJAX Futures is the `XPathBridgeTransformer`. The approach is similar to that of of the `XsltBridgeTransformer`, but this time ASP.NET AJAX does not transform the XML into HTML, but XML into a JavaScript object.

This is the idea: you can use `XPath` queries to access specific nodes in the resulting XML. The results of the `XPath` queries are converted into JavaScript objects and are then readily available to client script.

Usually, you need the following steps:

1. Use `<attribute name="selector" value="`*XPath expression*`" />` to query one or more nodes in the XML.

2. Optional: if you need to use a namespace, use a `<dictionary>` item to define this namespace (the following example will demonstrate how this is done).

3. Use a `<dictionary>` element to select nodes from the XPath result and convert them into JavaScript object properties.

The XML returned from the Yahoo! search service appears as follows (shortened version):

```
<ResultSet xsi:schemaLocation="urn:yahoo:srch
http://api.search.yahoo.com/WebSearchService/V1/WebSearchResponse.xsd">
  <Result>
    <Title>Ajax (programming) - Wikipedia, the free encyclopedia</Title>
    <Url>http://en.wikipedia.org/wiki/AJAX</Url>
  </Result>
  <Result>
    ...
  </Result>
</ResultSet>
```

In order to select all individual results, the XPath query `ResultSet/Result` or just `Result` can be used. However, there is one issue: the XML uses a namespace for the schema information: `urn:yahoo:srch`. This namespace has to be defined in the bridge, as well. This is how you can do it:

```
<transforms>
  <transform type="Microsoft.Web.Preview.Services.XPathBridgeTransformer">
    <data>
      <attribute name="selector" value="y:Result" />
      <dictionary name="namespaceMapping">
        <item name="y" value="urn:yahoo:srch" />
      </dictionary>
```

The `y` prefix now denotes the `urn:yahoo:srch` namespace. The previous markup selects all `Result` nodes. With a `<dictionary>` element, you can now access specific result nodes and properties. In this example, we are interested in the search result's title and url, which are denoted by `<Title>` and `<Url>` elements. The following markup selects these elements, and also provides JavaScript property names for them (`resultTitle` and `resultUrl`):

```
      <dictionary name="selectedNodes">
        <item name="resultTitle" value="y:Title" />
        <item name="resultUrl" value="y:Url" />
      </dictionary>
    </data>
  </transform>
</transforms>
    </method>
  </bridge>
```

Example 18-15 shows the complete markup for the bridge.

Example 18-15. The web service bridge for the Yahoo! REST web service

Yahoo.asbx

```
<?xml version="1.0" encoding="utf-8" ?>
<bridge namespace="OReilly.AspNetAJAX" className="Yahoo">
  <proxy type="Microsoft.Web.Preview.Services.BridgeRestProxy"
         serviceUrl="http://api.search.yahoo.com/WebSearchService/V1/webSearch" />
  <method name="Search">
    <input>
      <parameter name="appid"
                 value="% appsettings : YahooAppID %"
                 serverOnly="true" />
      <parameter name="output"
                 value="xml"
                 serverOnly="true" />
      <parameter name="query" />
    </input>
    <transforms>
      <transform type="Microsoft.Web.Preview.Services.XPathBridgeTransformer">
        <data>
```

```
        <attribute name="selector" value="y:Result" />
        <dictionary name="namespaceMapping">
          <item name="y" value="urn:yahoo:srch" />
        </dictionary>
        <dictionary name="selectedNodes">
          <item name="resultTitle" value="y:Title" />
          <item name="resultUrl" value="y:Url" />
        </dictionary>
      </data>
    </transform>
  </transforms>
  </method>
</bridge>
```

Once the bridge is in place, the rest of the application is "business as usual" and quite similar to the previous examples. Create a new ASP.NET file, and reference the *.asbx* file and the Futures release in the ScriptManager control:

```
<asp:ScriptManager ID="ScriptManager1" runat="server">
  <Services>
    <asp:ServiceReference Path="~/Yahoo.asbx" />
  </Services>
  <Scripts>
    <asp:ScriptReference Assembly="Microsoft.Web.Preview" Name="PreviewScript.js" />
  </Scripts>
</asp:ScriptManager>
```

Then, add some UI to let users enter a search term. Once the Submit button is clicked, this code needs to be executed:

```
function Search() {
  var query = new Sys.Preview.UI.TextBox($get('Query'))
  $get("Button").disabled = true;
  clearList();
  OReilly.AspNetAJAX.Yahoo.Search(
    { "query": query.get_text() },
    callComplete, callError
  );
}
```

In the callComplete() function, the result from the web service call is automatically provided as the first argument. This argument is a JavaScript array of all search results (the Yahoo! web service by default returns ten results, unless less matches were found). Each of these array elements is an object with the properties resultTitle and resultUrl, as specified in the bridge file. It is then quite easy to use this data and apply it to the page:

```
function callComplete(result) {
  for (var i = 0; i < result.length; i++) {
    var li = document.createElement("li");
    var a = document.createElement("a");
    a.setAttribute("href", result[i].resultUrl);
```

```
      a.innerHTML = result[i].resultTitle;
      li.appendChild(a);
      $get("Results").appendChild(li);
    }
    $get("Button").disabled = false;
  }
```

Example 18-16 shows the complete code for this example, and Figure 18-9 shows the results (note the good ranking of the ASP.NET AJAX home page when searching for "Ajax" ;-)).

Example 18-16. Calling the Google REST web service

Yahoo.aspx

```
<%@ Page Language="C#" %>

<!DOCTYPE html PUBLIC "-//W3C//DTD XHTML 1.0 Transitional//EN"
"http://www.w3.org/TR/xhtml1/DTD/xhtml1-transitional.dtd">
<html xmlns="http://www.w3.org/1999/xhtml">
<head id="Head1" runat="server">
  <title>ASP.NET AJAX</title>

  <script language="JavaScript" type="text/javascript">
  function clearList( ) {
    $get("Results").innerHTML = "";
  }

  function Search( ) {
    var query = new Sys.Preview.UI.TextBox($get('Query'))
    $get("Button").disabled = true;
    clearList( );
    OReilly.AspNetAJAX.Yahoo.Search(
      { "query": query.get_text( ) },
      callComplete, callError
    );
  }

  function callComplete(result)  {
    for (var i = 0; i < result.length; i++) {
      var li = document.createElement("li");
      var a = document.createElement("a");
      a.setAttribute("href", result[i].resultUrl);
      a.innerHTML = result[i].resultTitle;
      li.appendChild(a);
      $get("Results").appendChild(li);
    }
    $get("Button").disabled = false;
  }
  function callError(result) {
    window.alert("Error! " + result.get_message( ));
    $get("Button").disabled = false;
  }
  </script>
```

Example 18-16. Calling the Google REST web service (continued)

```
</head>
<body>
  <form id="form1" runat="server">
    <asp:ScriptManager ID="ScriptManager1" runat="server">
      <Services>
        <asp:ServiceReference Path="~/Yahoo.asbx" />
      </Services>
      <Scripts>
        <asp:ScriptReference Assembly="Microsoft.Web.Preview"
Name="PreviewScript.js" />
      </Scripts>
    </asp:ScriptManager>
    <div>
      <input type="text" id="Query" />
      <input type="button" id="Button" value="Search" onclick="Search();" />
    </div>
    <div id="Results">
    </div>
  </form>
</body>
</html>
```

Figure 18-9. The result of the Yahoo! search service

 One kind of web service that is quite often used for mashups is maps. There are many companies offering a map API, including Google, Yahoo!, and Microsoft. When they have a SOAP or REST interface, you can use the techniques presented in this chapter to include the mapping functionality in your web application. Even better, many of those services have special Ajax interfaces: you only need to use some JavaScript code and HTML markup and the map is included on your page, with no server code to be written on your part.

Caching Bridge Requests

You might want to consider caching requests using the web service bridge. To do that, add the following XML element in your .asbx bridge file (anywhere under the `<bridge>` node):

```
<caching >
  <cache type="Microsoft.Web.Preview.Services.BridgeCache" />
</caching>
```

This might improve the performance of your web service calls, but can be a real obstacle during development and testing, so you should turn it off until the code works as planned.

Summary

This chapter featured an exciting feature of the ASP.NET AJAX Futures release: the ability to call external web services, overcoming the security restrictions of the `XMLHttpRequest` object via a server bridge.

For Further Reading

http://www.amazon.com/gp/aws/landing.html
> Registration for, and documentation of, the Amazon e-commerce web service

http://www.google.com/apis
> Registration for, and documentation of, the Google search web service

http://developer.yahoo.com
> Yahoo! API developer site

http://www.w3schools.com/xsl/
> An XSLT tutorial including an XSL reference

Fitzgerald, Michael. Learning XSLT (O'Reilly)
> A great introduction to the technology

http://www.ics.uci.edu/~fielding/pubs/dissertation/rest_arch_style.htm
> Roy Fielding's University of California PhD dissertation, "Architectural Styles and the Design of Network-Based Software Architectures," which introduced the REST principle

Using Animations

Slick transitions between pages or elements make for nice eye candy, but they can be tricky to implement and can sometimes only be achieved using a variety of transformations. For example, visual changes in an element's opacity or position can be accomplished by gradual shifts in the number value of the element, thus creating the illusion of animation. A number going from 0 to 100 can be used as the opacity value of an element to animate a change in appearance from transparent to opaque.

Luckily, the ASP.NET AJAX Futures release comes with several built-in animations. They are all defined in a library called *PreviewGlitz.js* (which is embedded in the Futures assembly).

In this chapter, you'll learn how to use ASP.NET AJAX animations to change an element's position and opacity. You will also learn the range of animations and how to work with them.

Using Animations

Since the animations reside in an external library, the *PreviewGlitz.js* file must be included manually in any page that uses them. The file also depends on the *PreviewScript.js* file, the "core" JavaScript library for the Futures release. There are several possibilities for including this file. The best way is to add an ASP.NET AJAX ScriptReference element, as shown in the following snippet:

```
<asp:ScriptManager runat="server" ID="ScriptManager1">
  <Scripts>
    <asp:ScriptReference Name="PreviewGlitz.js" Assembly="Microsoft.Web.Preview" />
  </Scripts>
</asp:ScriptManager>
```

Table 19-1 lists the animations offered in the *PreviewGlitz.js* file.

Table 19-1. Animations included in the PreviewGlitz.js library

Animation	Description
Sys.Preview.UI.Effects.PropertyAnimation	Animates a property (e.g., the left or top position) of an element
Sys.Preview.UI.Effects.InterpolatedAnimation	Animates a property value and interpolates (calculates) the intermediate animation steps
Sys.Preview.UI.Effects.DiscreteAnimation	Animates a value over a specified list of values
Sys.Preview.UI.Effects.NumberAnimation	Animates a number value
Sys.Preview.UI.Effects.ColorAnimation	Animates the color of an element
Sys.Preview.UI.Effects.LengthAnimation	Animates a number and rounds every intermediate step to a whole number
Sys.Preview.UI.Effects.CompositeAnimation	Aggregates several animations in one
Sys.Preview.UI.Effects.FadeAnimation	Animates the opacity of an element

All of these animations can be used declaratively in xml-script, and most of them can also be accessed programmatically. You'll learn to use both techniques in the following examples.

Every animation has a play( ) method that starts the animation. Internally, the method uses a few of properties defined in the class. The following three properties are the most useful ones:

_duration
    How long the animation will run (in seconds)

_fps
    The number of animation steps (frames) per second

_target
    The target element of the animation

Whenever a step of the animation is executed, the setValue( ) method is called. How it operates is up to its implementation. This method can be implemented by each animation, or the setValue( ) method of the base animation class in Sys.Preview.UI. Effects.Animation is used. Depending on the animation, the method's implementation involves quite sophisticated calculations or just jumps to the next element in an array.

For alpha transparency (a graphical concept defining degrees of transparency, which enables effects like semitransparency), Internet Explorer uses the DXImageTransform.Microsoft.Alpha DirectX filter, whereas other browsers, such as Mozilla, Firefox, etc., have built-in support for opacity.

Using an Animation to Create a Fade Effect

You can create an impressive fade effect by changing the opacity of an element. Let's start with the programmatic approach. In the pageLoad( ) function, we create a new Sys.Preview.UI.Effects.FadeAnimation object:

```
var ani = new Sys.Preview.UI.Effects.FadeAnimation( );
```

Then we set the target element, a label element, <span> we create on the page:

```
ani.set_target($get("Label1").control);
```

The default behavior for the fading animation is that the element fades in. However, the Sys.Preview.UI.Effects.FadeEffect enumeration defines two options, FadeIn and FadeOut, which you can change by calling the set_effect( ) property method:

```
ani.set_effect(Sys.Preview.UI.Effects.FadeEffect.FadeOut);
```

Next, define the length of time the animation should run. The default value is one second; the following code triples that:

```
ani.set_duration(3);
```

Finally, we run the animation:

```
ani.play( );
```

The complete code is illustrated in Example 19-1.

Example 19-1. Using a fading animation

FadeAnimation.aspx

```
<%@ Page Language="C#" %>

<!DOCTYPE html PUBLIC "-//W3C//DTD XHTML 1.0 Transitional//EN"
"http://www.w3.org/TR/xhtml1/DTD/xhtml1-transitional.dtd">
<html xmlns="http://www.w3.org/1999/xhtml">
<head id="Head1" runat="server">
  <title>ASP.NET AJAX</title>

  <script language="JavaScript" type="text/javascript">
  function pageLoad( ) {
    var ani = new Sys.Preview.UI.Effects.FadeAnimation( );
    ani.set_target($get("Label1").control);
    ani.set_effect(Sys.Preview.UI.Effects.FadeEffect.FadeOut);
    ani.set_duration(3);
    ani.play( );
  }
  </script>

</head>
<body>
  <form id="form1" runat="server">
    <asp:ScriptManager runat="server" ID="ScriptManager1">
```

Example 19-1. Using a fading animation (continued)

```
    <Scripts>
        <asp:ScriptReference name="PreviewScript.js"
assembly="Microsoft.Web.Preview" />
        <asp:ScriptReference name="PreviewGlitz.js"
assembly="Microsoft.Web.Preview" />
    </Scripts>
  </asp:ScriptManager>
  <div>
    <label id="Label1" style="display: inline-block; background-color: Red;">
    See me fading ...</label>
  </div>
</form>

<script type="text/xml-script">
  <page xmlns:script="http://schemas.microsoft.com/xml-script/2005">
    <components>
        <label id="Label1" />
    </components>
  </page>
</script>

</body>
</html>
```

Note that the `display: inline-block` CSS command is used, Otherwise, Internet Explorer will not show the animation (for reasons I have been unable to determine). When the page is loaded, the element fades over the course of three seconds. Figure 19-1 shows how the page appears as the `Label` control is fading.

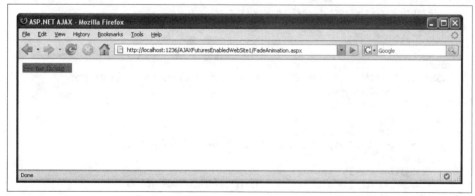

Figure 19-1. The Label is fading into the background

Naturally, this effect can also be implemented in a declarative way. As always, you create an xml-script element whose name is a camel-case version of the class, so FadeAnimation becomes a `<fadeAnimation>` element. It is important to provide an ID for the animation, because you need to be able to refer to it to start it.

You can start it not only with code, but also by using xml-script, as follows:

```
<application>
  <load>
    <invokeMethodAction target="ani" method="play" />
  </load>
</application>
```

This approach is explained in greater detail in Chapter 17.

Figure 19-2 shows the complete code, with important page elements in bold. In this case, we're not setting an explicit duration, so the animation lasts for the default value of one second.

Example 19-2. Implementing a fading animation with xml-script

FadeAnimationDeclarative.aspx

```
<%@ Page Language="C#" %>

<!DOCTYPE html PUBLIC "-//W3C//DTD XHTML 1.0 Transitional//EN"
"http://www.w3.org/TR/xhtml1/DTD/xhtml1-transitional.dtd">
<html xmlns="http://www.w3.org/1999/xhtml">
<head id="Head1" runat="server">
  <title>ASP.NET AJAX</title>
</head>
<body>
  <form id="form1" runat="server">
    <asp:ScriptManager runat="server" ID="ScriptManager1">
      <Scripts>
        <asp:ScriptReference name="PreviewScript.js"
assembly="Microsoft.Web.Preview" />
        <asp:ScriptReference name="PreviewGlitz.js"
assembly="Microsoft.Web.Preview" />
      </Scripts>
    </asp:ScriptManager>
    <div>
    <label id="Label1" style="display: inline-block; background-color: Red;">
    See me fading ...</label>
    </div>
  </form>
  <script type="text/xml-script">
    <page xmlns:script="http://schemas.microsoft.com/xml-script/2005">
      <components>
        <label id="Label1" />
        <fadeAnimation id="ani" target="Label1" effect="FadeOut" />
        <application>
          <load>
            <invokeMethodAction target="ani" method="play" />
          </load>
        </application>
      </components>
    </page>
  </script>
</body>
</html>
```

Using an Animation to Move an Element

Changing an element's opacity is an animation that is tied to a specific task. A different (and more general) kind of animation provided by ASP.NET AJAX is one that simply increments the value of a number at set intervals. You can then use the changing number value in some useful way, typically to set an element property. One example that immediately comes to mind is animating an element by continually changing left and top properties.

The ASP.NET AJAX Sys.Preview.UI.Effects.NumberAnimation class animates numbers from a start value to an end value. By setting the animation's duration and frames-per-second values, you control the number of intermediate steps and how long the whole animation takes.

We will again use a Label control as an example. The code instantiates the Sys.Preview.UI.Effects.NumberAnimation class and sets the required properties, except for the frames per second, where the default value of 25 is used:

```
var ani = new Sys.Preview.UI.Effects.NumberAnimation( );
ani.set_target($get("Label1").control);
ani.set_startValue(0);
ani.set_endValue(300);
ani.set_duration(3);
ani.set_integralValues(true);
```

 In this case, the animation takes three seconds and there are 25 frames per second, so for each step the value increases by 4. (Three seconds with 25 frames each makes 75 animation steps; since the number is animated from 0 to 300, this leads to a step size of 4.) Therefore, all values are whole numbers—that is, integral. However, there are cases in which the relationship of duration and intervals does not result in integral values. Since we want to position the label only at integral positions, the resulting values must be rounded. The NumberAnimation class has a built-in support for that in the form of the integralValues property.

Because the NumberAnimation class is generic—there are no assumptions about how you will use the changing numeric values—it does not implement a method that you can call directly to translate the numeric values into an element property. Instead, you set the NumberAnimation class's setValue property to a function that performs the work you want to do. This has the advantage that you can manipulate the numeric values as needed. For example, some browsers (like the Mozilla-based ones) only accept values for positioning that include a unit, such as "20px" instead of just "20", so your setMethod( ) function can add a unit to the number.

One challenge is referencing the element to be animated without making the code too specific (for instance, with document.getElementById( ) or $get( ), and a fixed ID). The animation class enables you to get a reference to the target object using the get_target( ) property method, and the result's element property grants access to the associated DOM element (using the get_element( ) method). You can combine this reference with your implementation of setValue( ) and then start the animation. Your code might look like the following:

```
ani.setValue = function(value) {
  this.get_target().get_element().style.left = value + "px";
  this.get_target().get_element().style.top = value + "px";
}
ani.play();
```

Instead of manually setting the position of the label, you can also use the Sys.UI. DomElement.setLocation( ) method that ASP.NET AJAX provides, which also takes care of providing the correct units:

```
ani.setValue = function(value) {
  Sys.UI.DomElement.setLocation(
    this.get_target().get_element(),
    value,
    value);
}
ani.play();
```

Example 19-3 shows a complete listing for a page that animates a Label control, moving it around on the page.

Example 19-3. Moving an element with an animation

NumberAnimation.aspx

```
<%@ Page Language="C#" %>

<!DOCTYPE html PUBLIC "-//W3C//DTD XHTML 1.0 Transitional//EN"
"http://www.w3.org/TR/xhtml1/DTD/xhtml1-transitional.dtd">
<html xmlns="http://www.w3.org/1999/xhtml">
<head id="Head1" runat="server">
  <title>ASP.NET AJAX</title>
  <script type="text/javascript">
  function pageLoad( ) {
    var ani = new Sys.Preview.UI.Effects.NumberAnimation( );
    ani.set_target($get("Label1").control);
    ani.set_startValue(0);
    ani.set_endValue(300);
    ani.set_duration(3);
    ani.set_integralValues(true);
    ani.setValue = function(value) {
      Sys.UI.DomElement.setLocation(
        this.get_target().get_element(),
        value,
        value);
    }
    ani.play( );
  }
  </script>
</head>
<body>
```

Example 19-3. Moving an element with an animation (continued)

```
<form id="form1" runat="server">
  <asp:ScriptManager runat="server" ID="ScriptManager1">
    <Scripts>
      <asp:ScriptReference name="PreviewScript.js"
assembly="Microsoft.Web.Preview" />
      <asp:ScriptReference name="PreviewGlitz.js"
assembly="Microsoft.Web.Preview" />
    </Scripts>
  </asp:ScriptManager>
  <div>
    <label id="Label1" style="background-color: Red; position: relative;">
    See me moving ...</label>
  </div>
</form>
<script type="text/xml-script">
  <page xmlns:script="http://schemas.microsoft.com/xml-script/2005">
    <components>
      <label id="Label1" />
    </components>
  </page>
</script>
</body>
</html>
```

Once the page has been loaded, the `label` element moves across the page at a 45-degree angle. Notice how the `position: relative` CSS property is used to make this possible—you do need to set the position. Figure 19-2 is a snapshot of the result.

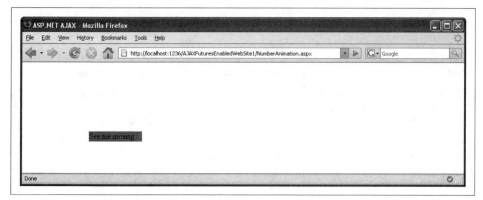

Figure 19-2. The element moves across the screen

Using a Length Animation to Move an Element

The preceding code can also be written declaratively. As noted earlier, to be sure an animation can work with all browsers, the `top` and `left` properties of an element must not be set to a number but must contain a unit. The `NumberAnimation` class can provide the unit only when you create a custom `setValue( )` method.

However, ASP.NET AJAX also provides a class called LengthAnimation that is capable of performing the task more directly.

It works like NumberAnimation, but with two differences:

- The values for each animation step are always rounded.
- The value of the unit property (the default is "px") is appended to the numeric value.

So, the LengthAnimation class looks like a "better" way to move an element than the NumberAnimation class from the previous example. Both work though, and that's why both are shown here.

Still, using the LengthAnimation class to animate a Label control is a bit tricky. The left and top properties are part of the element's style, which is not directly accessible as a property. However, a behavior called <layoutBehavior> provides access to style this information, and therefore, to the positioning values.

 Another useful behavior is <opacityBehavior>, which can be used to control the opacity of an element if you want to manually create a fade animation or other animation that involves changing the visibility of an element.

To move a Label control around the page, add the <layoutBehavior> behavior to the label in xml-script and assign it an ID:

```
<label id="Label1">
  <behaviors>
    <layoutBehavior id="Label1Style" />
  </behaviors>
</label>
```

Then create an animation—or two, since we are modifying two style values:

```
<lengthAnimation id="ani1" target="Label1Style" duration="3" property="left"
  startValue="0" endValue="300" />
<lengthAnimation id="ani2" target="Label1Style" duration="3" property="top"
  startValue="0" endValue="300" />
```

In the <application><load> section, you must, of course, start both animations. Example 19-4 shows the resulting code.

Example 19-4. Moving an element with xml-script

LengthAnimation.aspx

```
<%@ Page Language="C#" %>

<!DOCTYPE html PUBLIC "-//W3C//DTD XHTML 1.0 Transitional//EN"
"http://www.w3.org/TR/xhtml1/DTD/xhtml1-transitional.dtd">
<html xmlns="http://www.w3.org/1999/xhtml">
```

Example 19-4. Moving an element with xml-script (continued)

```
<head id="Head1" runat="server">
  <title>ASP.NET AJAX</title>
</head>
<body>
  <form id="form1" runat="server">
    <asp:ScriptManager runat="server" ID="ScriptManager1">
      <Scripts>
        <asp:ScriptReference name="PreviewScript.js"
assembly="Microsoft.Web.Preview" />
        <asp:ScriptReference name="PreviewGlitz.js"
assembly="Microsoft.Web.Preview" />
      </Scripts>
    </asp:ScriptManager>
    <div>
      <label id="Label1" style="background-color: Red; position: relative;">
        See me moving ...</label>
    </div>
  </form>
  <script type="text/xml-script">
    <page xmlns:script="http://schemas.microsoft.com/xml-script/2005">
      <components>
        <label id="Label1">
          <behaviors>
            <layoutBehavior id="Label1Style" />
          </behaviors>
        </label>
        <lengthAnimation id="ani1" target="Label1Style" duration="3"
          property="left" startValue="0" endValue="300" />
        <lengthAnimation id="ani2" target="Label1Style" duration="3"
          property="top" startValue="0" endValue="300" />
        <application>
          <load>
            <invokeMethodAction target="ani1" method="play" />
            <invokeMethodAction target="ani2" method="play" />
          </load>
        </application>
      </components>
    </page>
  </script>
</body>
</html>
```

Compositing (Grouping) Animations

When the effect you're looking for involves more than one animation, the markup
can get ugly: you get several animations that start in sequence (but hopefully are executed in parallel). The preceding example (Example 19-4) contained two separate
animations, one for the horizontal value and one for the vertical value, each of which
you had to define separately, including their duration.

You can simplify things by grouping animations using the Sys.Preview.UI.Effects. CompositeAnimation class. Grouping animations helps make sure that animations execute in parallel.

You can do this using the xml-script <compositeAnimation> element. Within the element, the <animation> element contains the xml-script definitions for all animations that should be executed together. You can then specify an id attribute and a duration attribute for the <compositeAnimation> element that then apply to the group as a whole:

```
<compositeAnimation id="ani" duration="3">
  <animations>
    <lengthAnimation target="Label1Style" property="left"
                     startValue="0" endValue="300" />
    <lengthAnimation target="Label1Style" property="top"
                     startValue="0" endValue="300" />
    <fadeAnimation target="Label1" effect="FadeOut" />
  </animations>
</compositeAnimation>
```

You can start the composited animation using <invokeMethod>:

```
<application>
  <load>
    <invokeMethodAction target="ani" method="play" />
  </load>
</application>
```

Example 19-5 shows the complete code for a page that contains a set of grouped animations.

Example 19-5. Grouping animations on a page

CompositeAnimation.aspx

```
<%@ Page Language="C#" %>

<!DOCTYPE html PUBLIC "-//W3C//DTD XHTML 1.0 Transitional//EN"
"http://www.w3.org/TR/xhtml1/DTD/xhtml1-transitional.dtd">
<html xmlns="http://www.w3.org/1999/xhtml">
<head id="Head1" runat="server">
  <title>ASP.NET AJAX</title>
</head>
<body>
  <form id="form1" runat="server">
    <asp:ScriptManager runat="server" ID="ScriptManager1">
      <Scripts>
        <asp:ScriptReference name="PreviewScript.js"
assembly="Microsoft.Web.Preview" />
        <asp:ScriptReference name="PreviewGlitz.js"
assembly="Microsoft.Web.Preview" />
```

Example 19-5. Grouping animations on a page (continued)

```
          </Scripts>
      </asp:ScriptManager>
      <div>
          <label id="Label1" style="display: inline-block; background-color: Red;
position: relative;">
              See me fading and moving ...</label>
      </div>
  </form>
  <script type="text/xml-script">
      <page xmlns:script="http://schemas.microsoft.com/xml-script/2005">
          <components>
              <label id="Label1">
                  <behaviors>
                      <layoutBehavior id="Label1Style" />
                  </behaviors>
              </label>
              <compositeAnimation id="ani" duration="3">
                  <animations>
                      <lengthAnimation target="Label1Style" property="left"
                                      startValue="0" endValue="300" />
                      <lengthAnimation target="Label1Style" property="top"
                                      startValue="0" endValue="300" />
                      <fadeAnimation target="Label1" effect="FadeOut" />
                  </animations>
              </compositeAnimation>
              <application>
                  <load>
                      <invokeMethodAction target="ani" method="play" />
                  </load>
              </application>
          </components>
      </page>
  </script>
</body>
</html>
```

This group is composed of three separate animations that each finish at the same time (see Figure 19-3):

- The element fades out
- The element is moved right
- The element is moved down

Even though the real-world use of animations is a bit limited, ASP.NET AJAX makes it very convenient to add some entertaining visual effects to a web application. Since these features all reside in an external JavaScript file, the *PreviewScript.js* library itself is not bloated by including this functionality by default.

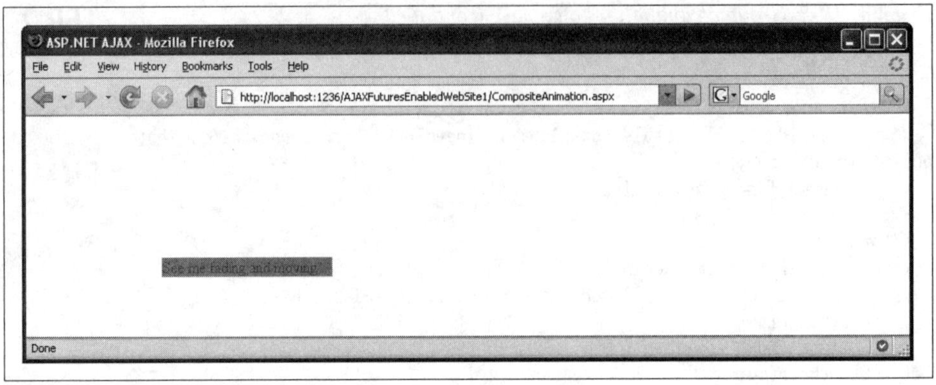

Figure 19-3. The label moves and fades at the same time

Summary

The ASP.NET AJAX Futures release offers several animations that can be used to animate or modify elements. These animations can be applied both programmatically and declaratively for maximum flexibility during development.

For Further Reading

http://blogs.msdn.com/phaniraj/archive/2007/03/15/howto-sys-preview-ui-effects-fadeanimation.aspx

Blog entry on FadeAnimation

Fixing Bookmarks and Back/Forward Buttons

Ajax applications have a number of distinct advantages over "classic" web applications, but the disadvantages inherent in the concept should not be ignored. One of the more glaring shortcomings is that it won't work without JavaScript and a fairly modern browser. Right out of the gate, this excludes between 5 and 10 percent of users (this number can be significantly different depending on your specific target audience). One of the more annoying shortcomings is its lack of support for browser bookmarks ("favorites" in Internet Explorer) and the forward and back buttons—two fundamentals of the browser interface.

Breaking with such traditions is not only considered rude, but usually comes at a price. In 2006, Live.com was launched. Its search engine module made use of a lot of Ajax effects. So much so, in fact, that it actually knocked the back button out of commission. A public outcry ensued, and back button support was added within a few days. This required a considerable amount of JavaScript sleight-of-hand and ended up causing some clicking sounds in Internet Explorer (due to information in a hidden frame being reloaded in some scenarios). More public outcry followed, and a third version finally stripped the offending functionality. Live.com now works as expected, with both bookmarking support and forward and back buttons enabled.

The reason for the missing bookmark functionality lies in the fact that Ajax applications try their best to avoid a complete page refresh. The state of one page may change, but the URL does not. Therefore, it is usually not feasible to bookmark an Ajax-enabled page, since the state of that page is not part of the URL. As a result, the back and forward buttons in the web browser also do not work. You can only navigate between URLs. No new URL is equivalent to no new entry in the history of the browser (Firefox: chronic), rendering navigation impossible.

As these two problems are related to one another, so too are their solutions. The main objective is to change the URL whenever the state of a page changes. Changing the URL in most cases results in reloading the page. This is an effect we wanted to avoid in the first place. The only exception is changing the hash (the part of the URL starting at the # sign) of a URL. When the page currently loaded is *Page.aspx* and

JavaScript code converts that to *Page.aspx#anyData*, no reload happens (some browsers scroll back to the top of the page, an effect that is very hard to avoid).

Fixing with Code

The source of the problem—not changing—leads to a simple solution for the bookmark problem: whenever the state of the current page changes, this state information is put in the hash of the current page. Whenever a page is loaded, any data from the hash of the URL is applied to the page, recreating the state when the page was bookmarked. Two pieces of JavaScript code are required. The first, shown below, places information about any changes on a page in the hash:

```
function somethingChanged() {
  location.hash = "#" + getCurrentPageState();
}
```

The second piece of code is run when the page is initially loaded. If there is state information in the hash, it must be applied to the current page:

```
function pageLoad() {
  if (location.hash.length > 0) {
    applyPageState(location.hash);
  }
}
```

You need to implement the getCurrentPageState() and applyPageState() functions, which can be quite an obstacle. The main challenge often is how to serialize the current page state and put it in the URL, then how to deserialize it back to the page. No universal solution exists, but the approach in solving the problem remains the same.

Fixing the back and forward buttons is a bit trickier. Here, browsers behave quite differently. Mozilla browsers automatically create a history entry when the URL hash has changed.

For example, an Ajax application loads three URLs, *Page.aspx#1*, *Page.aspx#2*, and *Page.aspx#3*. When the current page, *Page.aspx#3* is loaded and the user clicks on the back button, the browser loads *Page.aspx#2*. Actually, only the URL changes, but the page is not reloaded, so the pageLoad() function is not executed. All that remains to do is to periodically check the URL to check if any new information has been added. If so, the new information must be reapplied to the page.

For Internet Explorer, some extra steps are required. The Microsoft browser only creates a history entry when an HTTP request has been created. Changing the URL hash does not result in such a request that we of course want to avoid, as it conflicts with one of the basic goals of this book, avoiding page reloads.

A page state serialization approach I often find in security audits is to use JSON. Some web pages that do support bookmarking serialize the page state by writing page elements and their values or contents into a JSON string such as the following:

```
{"TextBox1": "My Data", "Label1": "Some other data", "DropDownList1": "2"}
```

This data is then URL-encoded (using JavaScript's escape( ) function) and appended to the URL. To this point, there is no problem with this approach. However, the difficulties start when the data from the URL is reintegrated in the page. The easiest way to convert the JSON string back into a JavaScript object is to use JavaScript's eval( ) function as demonstrated below:

```
var o = eval("(" + location.hash.substring(1) + ")");
```

Let's consider this code for a minute. Data from the URL is evaluated as JavaScript code. This is a classic example of Cross-Site Scripting (XSS) and represents a significant danger. A malicious attacker could craft some dangerous JavaScript code, append it to the URL of the page, and then send this URL to victims. If the URL is accessed, it would execute the JavaScript code in the browser.

Always consider that the URL information could be tainted. Do not use it to place sensitive information, and be particularly careful when reapplying this information to the page.

As is so often the case, there is a workaround. If a page contains an internal frame (also called iframe, which is derived from the HTML element, <iframe>, that we are about to use), and this internal frame creates an HTTP request, this HTTP request is written in the global browser history of the outer page.

This leads directly to a possible solution for the back/forward buttons dilemma. If the JavaScript code detects Internet Explorer, an <iframe> HTML element is dynamically created and appended to the page. The iframe is made invisible using CSS, as we do not want any extraneous or unintended visual effects.

Whenever the state of the page changes, a new page is loaded in the iframe, creating a new browser history entry. Now, when the user then clicks the browser's back or forward buttons, the iframe loads the previous or next page. JavaScript code detects that a new page has been loaded and applies the appropriate page state.

The JavaScript code required for this workaround is not trivial. Moreover, most Internet Explorer versions generate a clicking sound when loading a new page, which might be irritating to some users. However, with most Ajax applications, this extra work is really worth the effort.

Fixing Bookmarks and Back/Forward Buttons with Controls Using UpdateHistory

ASP.NET AJAX is all about exciting JavaScript effects without the tedium and rigor of too much coding. So, you might have already anticipated that fixes for the bookmarks and back/forward buttons will not need to be coded in JavaScript, but instead use an external module.

Microsoft's own Nikhil Kothari (architect on the ASP.NET AJAX team, father of Script#, known for his very informative weblog *http://nikhilk.net/*) wrote a control that comes in very handy here. The UpdateHistory control does not do everything for you automatically, but it does take care of the most cumbersome aspects, including all JavaScript code. There is also a component in the Futures Release which will be covered in the section "Fixing Bookmarks and Back/Forward Buttons with Controls Using the ASP.NET AJAX Futures," later in this chapter.

At this writing, version 1.1 of Kothari's UpdateHistory control is the most current. You can find the blog entry for this version at *http://www.nikhilk.net/UpdateControls11.aspx*. When a new version comes out, the blog entry will point you to the new module.

When you download Kothari's code, look for the *nStuff.UpdateControls.dll* file in the site's *bin* directory. Copy it to your ASP.NET AJAX' *bin* directory. Alternatively, you can copy it to the Global Assembly Cache (GAC), as the control is even signed.

Next, create a new *.aspx* file. The following directive loads the assembly and also defines a tag prefix:

```
<%@ Register Assembly="nStuff.UpdateControls" TagPrefix="nk"
Namespace="nStuff.UpdateControls" %>
```

Among other things, this assembly defines the UpdateHistory control. This is a nonvisual control that can handle history entries and provides hooks when a page is loaded, either by initially loading it (typing in the URL, clicking on a link) or by using the back/forward buttons. The following markup includes the control and also prepares the event handling mechanism for page loading:

```
<nk:UpdateHistory ID="UpdateHistory1" runat="server" OnNavigate="historyNavigate" />
```

The UpdateHistory control is limited to server-side hooks only. To call server code without reloading the whole page, an UpdatePanel control should be used.

As a sample scenario, the ASP.NET 2.0 Wizard control will be used. When it is put in an UpdatePanel, the back and forward buttons do not work, so navigating back to a previous step cannot be done using the browser toolbar.

```
<asp:UpdatePanel ID="UpdatePanel1" runat="server" UpdateMode="Conditional">
  <ContentTemplate>
    <asp:Wizard ID="Wizard1" runat="server" OnActiveStepChanged="stepChanged">
      <WizardSteps>
        <asp:WizardStep runat="server" Title="Step 1">
```

```
        <h1>Ready ...</h1>
      </asp:WizardStep>
      <asp:WizardStep runat="server" Title="Step 2">
        <h1>Set ...</h1>
      </asp:WizardStep>
      <asp:WizardStep runat="server" Title="Step 3">
        <h1>Go!</h1>
      </asp:WizardStep>
    </WizardSteps>
  </asp:Wizard>
 </ContentTemplate>
</asp:UpdatePanel>
```

There are two items in the preceding markup that should be noted. First, the UpdateMode of the UpdatePanel control is set to "Conditional"; we later want to use server-side code to update the panel's contents when we detect that the back or forward button of the browser has been pressed. Second, whenever the user navigates to another step of the Wizard (OnActiveStepChanged property), a method called stepChanged( ) is executed. In this method, the current step number is written in the UpdateHistory control.

For this, the AddEntry( ) method can be called. It expects a string parameter; other data types have to be previously converted. Here is the code:

```
protected void stepChanged(object sender, EventArgs e)
{
  UpdateHistory1.AddEntry(((Wizard)sender).ActiveStepIndex.ToString( ));
}
```

The historyNavigate( ) method is called when the page or content on it is loaded. The UpdateHistory control automatically provides the associated history entry. All that remains to do is read out this entry and convert it into the appropriate wizard step. Remember to validate the information to stop attackers when they try to append invalid data to the URL:

```
protected void historyNavigate(object sender, HistoryEventArgs e)
{
  int step = 0;
  if (e.EntryName != null)
  {
    int.TryParse(e.EntryName.ToString( ), out step);
  }
  if (step >= 0 && step < Wizard1.WizardSteps.Count)
  {
    Wizard1.ActiveStepIndex = step;
  }
  UpdatePanel1.Update( );
}
```

Example 20-1 contains the complete code for this example. In the example, the UpdateControls assembly is loaded, an UpdateHistory control is added, and the required code is provided to enable bookmarks and back/forward buttons.

Example 20-1. Fixing bookmarks and back/forward buttons

Bookmarks.aspx

```
<%@ Page Language="C#" %>

<%@ Register Assembly="nStuff.UpdateControls" TagPrefix="nk"
Namespace="nStuff.UpdateControls" %>

<!DOCTYPE html PUBLIC "-//W3C//DTD XHTML 1.0 Transitional//EN"
"http://www.w3.org/TR/xhtml1/DTD/xhtml1-transitional.dtd">

<script runat="server">

  protected void stepChanged(object sender, EventArgs e)
  {
    UpdateHistory1.AddEntry(((Wizard)sender).ActiveStepIndex.ToString());
  }

  protected void historyNavigate(object sender, HistoryEventArgs e)
  {
    int step = 0;
    if (e.EntryName != null)
    {
      int.TryParse(e.EntryName.ToString(), out step);
    }
    if (step >= 0 && step < Wizard1.WizardSteps.Count)
    {
      Wizard1.ActiveStepIndex = step;
    }
    UpdatePanel1.Update();
  }


</script>

<html xmlns="http://www.w3.org/1999/xhtml">
<head runat="server">
  <title>ASP.NET AJAX</title>
</head>
<body>
  <form id="form1" runat="server">
    <asp:ScriptManager ID="ScriptManager1" runat="server" />
    <nk:UpdateHistory ID="UpdateHistory1" runat="server"
OnNavigate="historyNavigate" />
    <asp:UpdatePanel ID="UpdatePanel1" runat="server" UpdateMode="Conditional">
      <ContentTemplate>
        <asp:Wizard ID="Wizard1" runat="server" OnActiveStepChanged="stepChanged">
          <WizardSteps>
            <asp:WizardStep runat="server" Title="Step 1">
              <h1>Ready ...</h1>
            </asp:WizardStep>
            <asp:WizardStep runat="server" Title="Step 2">
              <h1>Set ...</h1>
```

Example 20-1. Fixing bookmarks and back/forward buttons (continued)

```
            </asp:WizardStep>
            <asp:WizardStep runat="server" Title="Step 3">
              <h1>Go!</h1>
            </asp:WizardStep>
          </WizardSteps>
        </asp:Wizard>
      </ContentTemplate>
    </asp:UpdatePanel>
  </form>
</body>
</html>
```

Figure 20-1 shows how the page looks when it is initially loaded. Note how the URL changes after the second wizard step is activated (see Figure 20-2). A click on the browser's back button would go back to wizard step 1. If you copy the URL from Figure 20-2 into another browser, this browser would also show wizard step 2 (see Figure 20-3), so bookmark support is available once again.

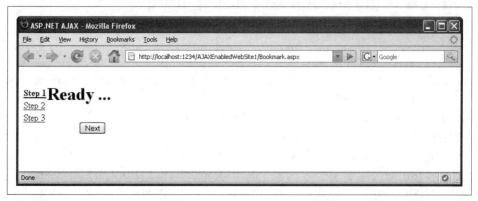

Figure 20-1. The initial state of the page

Figure 20-2. The second wizard step has been activated

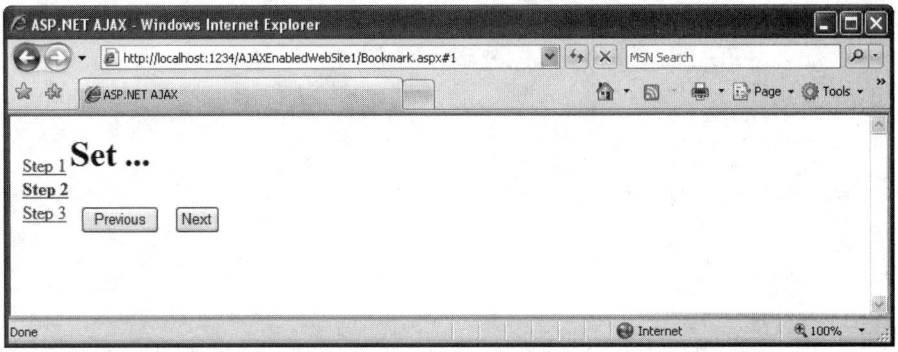

Figure 20-3. The second wizard step in Internet Explorer

Fixing Bookmarks and Back/Forward Buttons with Controls Using the ASP.NET AJAX Futures

Beginning with the May (2007) CTP of the Futures release, ASP.NET AJAX also comes with a control to fix the bookmarks and the back/forward buttons issue. This control is very similar to those previously used in this chapter, however the API changes a little bit. Since all contents of the Futures are subject to change, this chapter covers both controls.

There are several differences between the `UpdateHistory` control and the corresponding control in the Futures release:

- The name of the control changed to `History`.
- You can write the current state information into the History object using the `AddHistoryPoint()` method. This expects both a key and a value, as every history entry is a `Dictionary` object.
- You can access the current state information using the `State` property of the `HistoryEventArgs` object. As just mentioned, this is a dictionary.

Example 20-2 shows the updated code, which now uses the Futures control, not Kothari's control. Note that we're using `"myHistory"` as the key for the state information. This value can be chosen arbitrarily; you simply need to use the same value for reading and writing data. Figure 20-4 shows the new example in the browser; the URL now contains more information, since a dictionary is used instead of a static string.

Example 20-2. Fixing bookmarks and back/forward buttons with the Futures release

`BookmarksUpdatePanel.aspx`

```
<%@ Page Language="C#" %>

<!DOCTYPE html PUBLIC "-//W3C//DTD XHTML 1.0 Transitional//EN"
"http://www.w3.org/TR/xhtml1/DTD/xhtml1-transitional.dtd">
```

Example 20-2. Fixing bookmarks and back/forward buttons with the Futures release (continued)

```
<script runat="server">

  protected void stepChanged(object sender, EventArgs e)
  {
    History1.AddHistoryPoint("myHistory",
((Wizard)sender).ActiveStepIndex.ToString( ));
  }

  protected void historyNavigate(object sender, HistoryEventArgs e)
  {
    int step = 0;
    if (e.State.ContainsKey("myHistory"))
    {
      int.TryParse(e.State["myHistory"].ToString( ), out step);
    }
    if (step >= 0 && step < Wizard1.WizardSteps.Count)
    {
      Wizard1.ActiveStepIndex = step;
    }
    UpdatePanel1.Update( );
  }


</script>

<html xmlns="http://www.w3.org/1999/xhtml">
<head runat="server">
  <title>ASP.NET AJAX</title>
</head>
<body>
  <form id="form1" runat="server">
    <asp:ScriptManager ID="ScriptManager1" runat="server" />
    <asp:History ID="History1" runat="server" OnNavigate="historyNavigate" />
    <asp:UpdatePanel ID="UpdatePanel1" runat="server" UpdateMode="Conditional">
      <ContentTemplate>
        <asp:Wizard ID="Wizard1" runat="server" OnActiveStepChanged="stepChanged">
          <WizardSteps>
            <asp:WizardStep runat="server" Title="Step 1">
              <h1>Ready ...</h1>
            </asp:WizardStep>
            <asp:WizardStep runat="server" Title="Step 2">
              <h1>Set ...</h1>
            </asp:WizardStep>
            <asp:WizardStep runat="server" Title="Step 3">
              <h1>Go!</h1>
            </asp:WizardStep>
          </WizardSteps>
        </asp:Wizard>
      </ContentTemplate>
    </asp:UpdatePanel>
  </form>
</body>
</html>
```

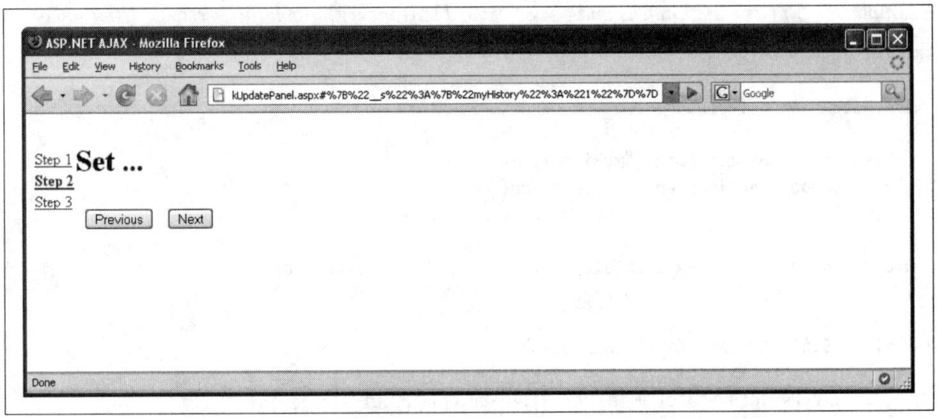

Figure 20-4. The Wizard with Back/Forward button support—note the longer URL

One advantage of the Futures control is that it also exposes a JavaScript API. So, you do not even need an UpdatePanel control. If you are using JavaScript to maintain state information, you can use the History control's JavaScript API to write state information (which in turn appends data to the URL hash). Also, the control automatically executes the pageNavigate() JavaScript function. This is the place where you can then recreate the page's state using the data from the History control.

For this example, we try to recreate a client-side version of the ASP.NET 2.0 Wizard control, albeit a limited one. The three wizard steps are modeled in three HTML table rows, which are all initially invisible:

```
<table cellspacing="0" cellpadding="0" border="0" style="height: 100%; width: 100%;
  border-collapse: collapse;">
  <tr id="Wizard1_Step1" style="height: 100%; display: none;">
    <td>
      <h1>
        Ready ...</h1>
    </td>
  </tr>
  <tr id="Wizard1_Step2" style="height: 100%; display: none;">
    <td>
      <h1>
        Set ...</h1>
    </td>
  </tr>
  <tr id="Wizard1_Step3" style="height: 100%; display: none;">
    <td>
      <h1>
        Go!</h1>
    </td>
  </tr>
</table>
```

For navigation between the wizard steps, the three links in the left sidebar are used, this time using a custom JavaScript implementation:

```
<table id="Wizard1_SideBarContainer_SideBarList" cellspacing="0"
border="0" style="border-collapse: collapse;">
  <tr>
    <td id="Wizard1_SideBar1">
      <a id="Wizard1_SideBarContainer_SideBarList_ctl00_SideBarButton"
href="javascript:gotoStepClick(1)">
        Step 1</a></td>
  </tr>
  <tr>
    <td id="Wizard1_SideBar2">
      <a id="Wizard1_SideBarContainer_SideBarList_ctl01_SideBarButton"
href="javascript:gotoStepClick(2)">
        Step 2</a></td>
  </tr>
  <tr>
    <td id="Wizard1_SideBar3">
      <a id="Wizard1_SideBarContainer_SideBarList_ctl02_SideBarButton"
href="javascript:gotoStepClick(3)">
        Step 3</a></td>
  </tr>
</table>
```

The gotoStepClick( ) function first adds a new history point. The corresponding JavaScript method for the server-side addHistoryPoint( ) method of the History control looks like this:

```
function gotoStepClick(nr) {
  Sys.Application.get_history( ).addHistoryPoint({myHistory: nr});
```

Then the gotoStepClick( ) function calls another helper function, gotoStep( ):

```
  gotoStep(nr);
}
```

The gotoStep( ) function takes care of displaying the correct wizard step (and hiding the other one). Also, the link for the current step is made bold:

```
function gotoStep(nr) {
  if (nr >= 1 && nr <= 3) {
    $get("Wizard1_Step1").style.display = "none";
    $get("Wizard1_Step2").style.display = "none";
    $get("Wizard1_Step3").style.display = "none";
    $get("Wizard1_SideBar1").style.fontWeight = "normal";
    $get("Wizard1_SideBar2").style.fontWeight = "normal";
    $get("Wizard1_SideBar3").style.fontWeight = "normal";
    $get("Wizard1_Step" + nr).style.display = "";
    $get("Wizard1_SideBar" + nr).style.fontWeight = "bold";
  }
}
```

The final piece of this sample is the code that recovers the page state when the user clicks on the forward or back button in the browser. As mentioned earlier, this can be handled in the pageNavigate( ) JavaScript function. The second argument that is passed automatically to this function contains all state variables. The get_state( ) methods return them. Because we were using `myHistory` when adding the history point, you can use `get_state( ).myHistory` to retrieve the specific state we set previously.

```
function pageNavigate(sender, e) {
  var step = 1;
  if (e.get_state( ).myHistory != null) {
    step = e.get_state( ).myHistory;
  }
  gotoStep(step);
}
```

And that's it! Example 20-3 contains the complete code for the example, and Figure 20-5 shows the custom wizard in the browser.

Example 20-3. Fixing bookmarks and back/forward buttons with JavaScript code

BookmarksJavaScript.aspx

```
<%@ Page Language="C#" %>

<!DOCTYPE html PUBLIC "-//W3C//DTD XHTML 1.0 Transitional//EN"
"http://www.w3.org/TR/xhtml1/DTD/xhtml1-transitional.dtd">

<html xmlns="http://www.w3.org/1999/xhtml">
<head id="Head1" runat="server">
  <title>ASP.NET AJAX</title>
  <script type="text/javascript">
  function pageLoad( ) {
    gotoStep(1);
  }

  function gotoStepClick(nr) {
    Sys.Application.get_history( ).addHistoryPoint({myHistory: nr});
    gotoStep(nr);
  }

  function gotoStep(nr) {
    if (nr >= 1 && nr <= 3) {
      $get("Wizard1_Step1").style.display = "none";
      $get("Wizard1_Step2").style.display = "none";
      $get("Wizard1_Step3").style.display = "none";
      $get("Wizard1_SideBar1").style.fontWeight = "normal";
      $get("Wizard1_SideBar2").style.fontWeight = "normal";
      $get("Wizard1_SideBar3").style.fontWeight = "normal";
      $get("Wizard1_Step" + nr).style.display = "";
      $get("Wizard1_SideBar" + nr).style.fontWeight = "bold";
    }
  }

  function pageNavigate(sender, e) {
    var step = 1;
    if (e.get_state( ).myHistory != null) {
      step = e.get_state( ).myHistory;
```

Example 20-3. Fixing bookmarks and back/forward buttons with JavaScript code (continued)

```
    }
    gotoStep(step);
  }
  </script>
</head>
<body>
  <form id="form1" runat="server">
    <asp:ScriptManager ID="ScriptManager1" runat="server" />
    <asp:History ID="History1" runat="server" />
    <table cellspacing="0" cellpadding="0" border="0" id="Wizard1" style="border-
collapse:collapse;">
        <tr>
            <td style="height:100%;"><table
id="Wizard1_SideBarContainer_SideBarList" cellspacing="0" border="0" style="border-
collapse:collapse;">
                <tr>
                    <td id="Wizard1_SideBar1"><a
id="Wizard1_SideBarContainer_SideBarList_ctl00_SideBarButton"
href="javascript:gotoStepClick(1)">Step 1</a></td>

                </tr><tr>
                    <td id="Wizard1_SideBar2"><a
id="Wizard1_SideBarContainer_SideBarList_ctl01_SideBarButton"
href="javascript:gotoStepClick(2)">Step 2</a></td>
                </tr><tr>
                    <td id="Wizard1_SideBar3"><a
id="Wizard1_SideBarContainer_SideBarList_ctl02_SideBarButton"
href="javascript:gotoStepClick(3)">Step 3</a></td>
                </tr>
            </table></td><td style="height:100%;"><table cellspacing="0"
cellpadding="0" border="0" style="height:100%;width:100%;border-
collapse:collapse;">
                <tr id="Wizard1_Step1" style="height:100%;display:none;">
                    <td>

            <h1>Ready ...</h1>
        </td>
                </tr>
                <tr id="Wizard1_Step2" style="height:100%;display:none;">
                    <td>

            <h1>Set ...</h1>
        </td>
                </tr>
                <tr id="Wizard1_Step3" style="height:100%;display:none;">
                    <td>

            <h1>Go!</h1>
        </td>
                </tr>
            </table></td>
```

Example 20-3. Fixing bookmarks and back/forward buttons with JavaScript code (continued)

```
                </tr>
            </table>
        </form>
    </body>
</html>
```

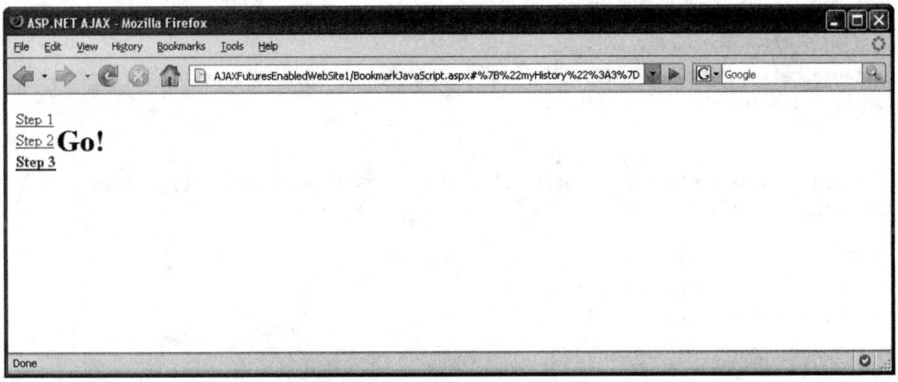

Figure 20-5. The simulated Wizard control

Creating Permalinks

A *permalink* describes a permanent link for a web page, including its state. You have probably noticed that the URLs of the sample applications in this chapter change whenever the state changes (and we have included code to handle that). So, whenever you bookmark the current page, the URL contains all the information to reproduce the page state.

The History control also offers a helper method to retrieve the bookmark URL information. You could, of course, read out the location.href JavaSscript property. You can also resort to the following methods:

getStateString( )
    Server method to retrieve the bookmark URL

Sys.Application.get_history().get_stateString( )
    Client method to retrieve the bookmark URL

Some web pages include a permalink hyperlink. Whenever the page state changes, the URL of this hyperlink is updated appropriately.

Summary

This chapter introduced two well-known problems of many Ajax applications: lack of bookmark support, and nonfunctional back/forward browser buttons. However, this chapter also provided solutions for these problems. These may require some extra effort, but can make the usability of an Ajax-powered page so much better.

For Further Reading

http://quickstarts.asp.net/futures/ajax/doc/history.html
    Documentation for the History control

Wenz, Christian. Ajax, Software & Support (Entwickler Press)
    Introduces code solutions to solve the bookmark and back/forward button problems

CHAPTER 21

Web Parts

Using Ajax can help you make web applications behave more like desktop applications. And the more web applications become like desktop applications, the more developers tend to design and reuse components to deliver greater functionality to their pages.

ASP.NET AJAX offers several ways to reuse components toward adding functionality to browser-based clients. The control extenders in the ASP.NET AJAX Control Toolkit are a prime example. This chapter covers another one, Web Parts, an ASP.NET feature (introduced in ASP.NET 2.0), that benefits from an extra boost thanks to the ASP.NET AJAX Futures release.

Using ASP.NET AJAX with ASP.NET Web Parts

This section will show how you can use ASP.NET AJAX with ASP.NET Web Parts to give users more control over the layout and content of an ASP.NET AJAX page. ASP.NET Web Parts are a set of controls enabling users to add, remove, and change elements on a page at runtime. Web Parts offer the ability to create pages such as the Google personalized home page (*http://www.google.com/ig*) in ASP.NET.

Web Parts are enabled using client script to support drag-and-drop, expand and collapse, and other similar features. However, a limitation of Web Parts as shipped with ASP.NET 2.0 is that most of their functionality is available only in Internet Explorer. Therefore, ASP.NET Web Parts are mostly used in intranet environments that can rely on working with Internet Explorer.

Of course, Internet Explorer is not the only browser available and many web users have Firefox or other browsers. So, although Web Parts are a nice feature, they are not necessarily suitable for broadly-accessed public web sites.

ASP.NET AJAX compensates for this limitation. With the ASP.NET AJAX Futures release, it is now possible to use Web Parts that are equally functional in Internet

Explorer and Firefox. If you are developing a public web site and need cross-browser support, ASP.NET AJAX Web Parts are a very appealing option.

In this section, you'll learn how to implement Web Parts using ASP.NET AJAX. I won't provide background information on Web Parts (which is a rather large subject), so if you want more information about the basics of Web Parts, you might try the documentation. A good place to start might be the ASP.NET Web Parts pages (*http://msdn2.microsoft.com/en-US/library/e0s9t4ck.aspx*).

In the example that that will follow, we'll use ASP.NET AJAX Web Parts to package a calendar control and a wizard control, then we'll enable drag-and-drop functionality for both so the user can arrange them to personal preference in a browser. These changes are persisted (maintained), so if cookies are activated and the page is visited again, the two controls will be at the same position as the previous visit.

There are two ways to work with ASP.NET AJAX-specific Web Parts. One is to remap the existing ASP.NET Web Parts tags to equivalent ASP.NET AJAX tags—in which case, `<asp:WebPartZone>` uses the ASP.NET AJAX version of Web Parts. You might do this if you have existing pages that use Web Parts and you want to extend the controls to use ASP.NET AJAX but do not want to build the site from scratch again.

To remap the tags, you can use a `<tagMapping>` element in the site's *Web.config* file. This element redirects all tag references of a certain type to one of another type.

The following snippet from a *Web.config* file shows how to remap two ASP.NET Web Parts tags (defined in the `System.Web.UI.WebControls.WebParts.WebPartManager` namespace), to the equivalent ASP.NET AJAX Web Parts (defined in the `Microsoft.Web.Preview.UI.Controls.WebParts.WebPartManager` namespace).

```
<pages>
<!-- Other page settings -->
  <tagMapping>
    <add tagType="System.Web.UI.WebControls.WebParts.WebPartManager"
      mappedTagType="Microsoft.Web.Preview.UI.Controls.WebParts.WebPartManager"/>
    <add tagType="System.Web.UI.WebControls.WebParts.WebPartZone"
      mappedTagType="Microsoft.Web.Preview.UI.Controls.WebParts.WebPartZone"/>
  </tagMapping>
</pages>
```

This markup remaps the default ASP.NET `WebPartManager` and `WebPartZone` types to their ASP.NET AJAX counterparts. (Generally, the type provided in the `tagType` attribute gets mapped to the type provided in the `mappedTagType` attribute.) This strategy maps *all* Web Part tags for the application.

The second way to work with ASP.NET AJAX-specific Web Parts is to simply use the Web Parts control directly. This enables you to use Web Parts on individual pages without affecting the application as a whole.

To do this, you need to register the `Microsoft.Web.Preview.UI.Controls.WebParts` namespace. Enter the following markup in the `<system.web>` element in the *Web.config* file:

```
<pages>
  <!-- Other page settings -->
  <controls>
    <!-- Other control namespaces -->
    <add
      namespace="Microsoft.Web.Preview.UI.Controls.WebParts"
      assembly="Microsoft.Web.Preview"
      tagPrefix="ajax" />
  </controls>
</pages>
```

Now you can access the ASP.NET AJAX Web Part elements using the `ajax` prefix, for instance `<ajax:WebPartManager>`.

In this chapter we will use the former approach (tag mapping), so we do not need to introduce an additional tag prefix. Be sure you add the `<tagMapping>` element to the *Web.config* file before you run the example in this chapter. Also keep in mind this will remap *all* the Web Parts controls in the web site.

Now you can create an ASP.NET page with ASP.NET AJAX Web Parts. As always, a `ScriptManager` control is required. You must also add a `WebPartManager` control to enable Web Parts support:

```
<asp:WebPartManager ID="WebPartManager1" runat="server" />
```

Web Part zones are areas on the page where Web Parts can appear—in effect, containers for Web Parts. You can drag Web Parts between zones, and you can hide or show zones to hide or show the Web Parts inside them. You create a zone with the `WebPartZone` control whose child element, `<ZoneTemplate>`, contains the contents of that Web Part. Here are two Web Part zones, each containing an ASP.NET `Calendar` and `Wizard` control:

```
<asp:WebPartZone ID="WebPartZone1" HeaderText="Zone 1" runat="server">
  <ZoneTemplate>
    <asp:Calendar ID="Calendar1" runat="server"></asp:Calendar>
  </ZoneTemplate>
</asp:WebPartZone>
<asp:WebPartZone ID="WebPartZone2" HeaderText="Zone 2" runat="server">
  <ZoneTemplate>
    <asp:Wizard ID="Wizard1" runat="server">
      <WizardSteps>
        <asp:WizardStep ID="Step1" runat="server" Title="Step 1" />
        <asp:WizardStep ID="Step2" runat="server" Title="Step 2" />
      </WizardSteps>
    </asp:Wizard>
  </ZoneTemplate>
</asp:WebPartZone>
```

To give your Web Part drag-and-drop functionality, you need to set the `DisplayMode` property of the `WebPartManager` control to `DesignDisplayMode`. The display mode cannot be set declaratively, but the following server-side C# code comes to the rescue:

```
void Page_Init ()
{
  WebPartManager1.DisplayMode =
Microsoft.Web.Preview.UI.Controls.WebParts.WebPartManager
.DesignDisplayMode;
}
```

 Because you now have two `WebParts` namespaces (one for ASP.NET 2.0 and one for ASP.NET AJAX), references to `WebPartManager.DesignDisplayMode` are ambiguous. Therefore, you must fully qualify any reference to the display mode.

Example 21-1 contains the complete code for this example. In Figure 21-1, you can see the result as displayed in Firefox—dragging and dropping a Web Part is now supported. The first time you run the example, there will be a delay as ASP.NET configures the database in which the Web Parts information is stored. When you drag a Web Part or close a zone, information about the state of the Web Parts is persisted between browser sessions.

 Remember you need to configure the tag mapping in the *Web.config* file.

Example 21-1. Web Parts with ASP.NET AJAX

WebParts.aspx

```
<%@ Page Language="C#" %>

<!DOCTYPE html PUBLIC "-//W3C//DTD XHTML 1.0 Transitional//EN"
"http://www.w3.org/TR/xhtml1/DTD/xhtml1-transitional.dtd">

<script runat="server">
  void Page_Init( )
  {
    WebPartManager1.DisplayMode =
Microsoft.Web.Preview.UI.Controls.WebParts.WebPartManager.DesignDisplayMode;
  }
</script>

<html xmlns="http://www.w3.org/1999/xhtml">
<head id="Head1" runat="server">
  <title>ASP.NET AJAX</title>
</head>
<body>
```

Example 21-1. Web Parts with ASP.NET AJAX (continued)

```
<form id="form1" runat="server">
  <asp:ScriptManager ID="ScriptManager1" runat="server" />
  <div>
    <asp:WebPartManager ID="WebPartManager1" runat="server" />
    <table>
      <tr>
        <td>
          <asp:WebPartZone ID="WebPartZone1" HeaderText="Zone 1" runat="server">
            <ZoneTemplate>
              <asp:Calendar ID="Calendar1" runat="server"></asp:Calendar>
            </ZoneTemplate>
          </asp:WebPartZone>
        </td>
        <td>
        <asp:WebPartZone ID="WebPartZone2" HeaderText="Zone 2" runat="server">
          <ZoneTemplate>
            <asp:Wizard ID="Wizard1" runat="server">
              <WizardSteps>
                <asp:WizardStep ID="Step1" runat="server" Title="Step 1" />
                <asp:WizardStep ID="Step2" runat="server" Title="Step 2" />
              </WizardSteps>
            </asp:Wizard>
          </ZoneTemplate>
        </asp:WebPartZone>
        </td></tr>
    </table>
  </div>
  </form>
</body>
</html>
```

Moving elements between Web Parts always causes a postback, which leads to a browser refresh. If you put an ASP.NET AJAX UpdatePanel control on the page and include the WebPartManager and the two WebPartZone controls in it, moving the Web Parts controls no longer requires a full postback. However, you currently can only drag and drop elements once, then the feature stops working. (If you refresh the browser, you can move the elements again—one time per browser refresh.) It is expected that future versions of the ASP.NET AJAX Futures release will provide a fix that enables you to put an UpdatePanel control in each WebPartZone.

Mike Harder's blog (see "For Further Reading," at the end of this chapter) describes three scenarios that either work or don't work with ASP.NET AJAX web parts:

- Cross-browser web parts work
- Web parts within an UpdatePanel control currently do not work, but may work with the next version of Visual Studio (Visual Studio 2008)
- UpdatePanel controls within web parts work

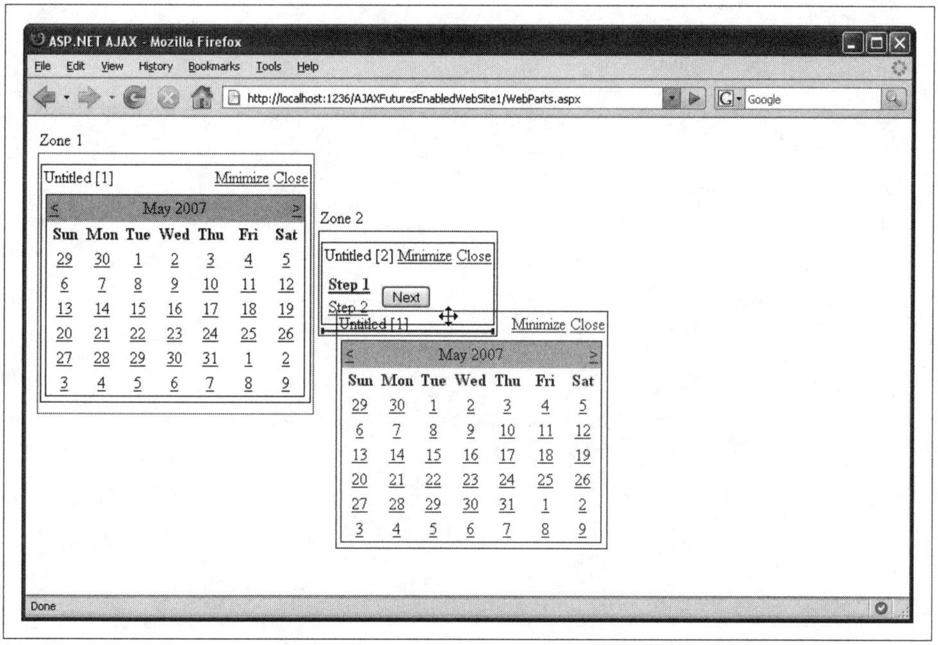

Figure 21-1. ASP.NET AJAX Futures CTP Web Parts support for drag-and-drop in Mozilla browsers

Summary

This chapter explored one very unique approach to using (and reusing) ASP.NET AJAX components. Web parts are rarely used at present, but are gaining momentum. Unlike their ASP.NET 2.0 counterparts, the ASP.NET AJAX Futures CTP, web parts work in a browser-agnostic fashion.

For Further Reading

http://msdn2.microsoft.com/en-US/library/e0s9t4ck.aspx
   MSDN library section for ASP.NET 2.0 Web Parts

http://blogs.msdn.com/mharder/archive/2007/01/23/webparts-and-asp-net-ajax-1-0.aspx
   Blog entry by Mike Harder regarding ASP.NET AJAX and web parts

Microsoft AJAX Library

CHAPTER 22

Using ASP.NET AJAX with Other Server Technologies

As discussed at the outset of this book in Chapter 1, ASP.NET AJAX includes both client-side and server-side components. The ASP.NET AJAX server components rely heavily on ASP.NET 2.0 controls, but the client components are delivered as JavaScript libraries. Even though the client libraries are embedded into pages by the `<script>` tag that references *WebResource.axd*, the libraries are actually standalone *.js* files that come in the form of embedded resources in the ASP.NET AJAX Library.

The Microsoft AJAX Library was also first mentioned in Chapter 1. It is a JavaScript-only subset of the ASP.NET AJAX Library. But as it has no dependency on ASP.NET, this library can also be used with any other server-side scripting language.

By using this library, you can take advantage of some ASP.NET AJAX features while using other (non-ASP.NET) server technologies. You are not limited to just the client scripting features of ASP.NET AJAX, but you can also use its more advanced server features. However, to implement ASP.NET AJAX functionality on platforms other than ASP.NET 2.0 and IIS, some of the ASP.NET AJAX functionality and certain server controls (i.e., `ScriptManager`), need to be emulated with non-ASP.NET technology.

This chapter demonstrates how to use the ASP.NET AJAX web services support with PHP. The code for it has come a long way. Initially, Shanku Niyogi wrote a demonstration version and published it in his blog (see the "For Further Reading" section at the end of this chapter). We exchanged a few emails and he posted an updated version some time later. In early 2007, Steve Marx (Microsoft's "Developer Evangelist" for ASP.NET AJAX) set up a project on Codeplex to illustrate using PHP to plug into the Microsoft AJAX Library. The code of this CodePlex project is essentially an updated version of Niyogi's code.

The following sections demonstrate what is possible with the library and give you an idea of what's required for using the library with PHP. We will also have a brief look at the code. What you will see here is how to build a server-based PHP module that emulates a web service. You will invoke this pseudo-web service from an ordinary HTML page (not an *.aspx* page). We will use JavaScript code to invoke the service using ASP.NET AJAX functionality to call the PHP module.

Using ASP.NET AJAX with PHP

To use ASP.NET AJAX with PHP, you will create an HTML web page. This demonstration page contains an HTML text box and sends the text in this box to a web service. To add the ASP.NET AJAX functionality we need to make the web-service call, the ASP.NET AJAX client libraries must be loaded into the HTML page.

Prepare the ASP.NET AJAX library by creating a new folder in your web site named *AjaxLibrary*. (For example, if your web site is at *C:\Document and Settings\JaneDoe\AJAXEnabledWebSite1*, you would create a folder named *C:\Document and Settings\JaneDoe\AJAXEnabledWebSite1\AjaxLibrary*.) Download the Microsoft AJAX Library from *http://ajax.asp.net/downloads/default.aspx?tabid=47* and copy the *System.Web.Extensions* folder into the new *AjaxLibrary* folder.

Next, download the Microsoft AJAX Library for PHP from *http://codeplex.com/phpmsajax* (as with ASP.NET AJAX; the "NoSource" package suffices). Unzip the library and copy the two PHP files *MSAjaxService.php* and *MSAjaxProxyGenerator.php* into the web site's root directory.

> This chapter assumes that you have PHP working on your computer. You can download the PHP libraries from *http://www.php.net/downloads.php*. You need at least PHP version 5.2.0; earlier versions do not support some features (such as JSON serialization) that are required for the web service code. Follow the installation instructions carefully!
>
> To run a PHP file under IIS, you must use IIS (the ASP.NET Development Server will not run *.php* files). The PHP installation instructions include information on performing PHP installation on IIS as well as on other web servers, such as Apache. Do not install PHP files into a folder that contains spaces in the name—*C:\Program Files*, for example. A space in the ISAPI mapping can render IIS unable to find the appropriate *.dll* files.
>
> If you use the PHP *.msi* installer, the installer configures IIS so that it dispatches requests for *.php* files to the PHP ISAPI handler. Otherwise, you'll need to map the *.php* extension manually.

For the PHP part of the example, you need to create a PHP web service that can be called from ASP.NET AJAX. Actually, the code we are about to develop is not a "real" SOAP-based web service using WSDL; instead, it is code that is compatible with the way ASP.NET AJAX communicates with web services.

Create a text file in the root of your web site and name it *PHPHelloWorldService.php*. In the PHP file, first load the part of the PHP for Microsoft AJAX library that handles creating a "compatible" web service.

```php
<?php
    require_once 'MSAjaxService.php';
```

The code in *MSAjaxService.php* creates an extendable class suited for creating services that can be called from ASP.NET AJAX. Now, we create a simple PHP class with a really simple "Hello World" method, quite similar to the one used in Chapter 1:

```php
class PHPHelloWorldService extends MSAjaxService {
  function sayHello($name) {
    return "Hello $name, says the server!";
  }
}
```

Finally, the PHP script must initiate the new `PHPHelloWorldService` class and call its `ProcessRequest()` method so that PHP handles incoming requests from ASP.NET AJAX:

```php
$ps = new PHPHelloWorldService();
$ps->ProcessRequest();
?>
```

Example 22-1 contains the complete code for our PHP web service

Example 22-1. The PHP ASP.NET AJAX compatible pseudo-web service

PHPHelloWorldService.php

```php
<?php
  require_once 'MSAjaxService.php';

  class PHPHelloWorldService extends MSAjaxService {
    function sayHello($name) {
      return "Hello $name, says the server!";
    }
  }

  $ps = new PHPHelloWorldService();
  $ps->ProcessRequest();
?>
```

The main effect of the PHP code is that once again a JavaScript proxy is created. Figure 22-1 shows the JavaScript code that is generated when you call the URL *PHPHelloWorldService.php/js*.

Now you need to write JavaScript code to call this service. Using client script, we need to load the Microsoft Ajax library you unzipped into the *AjaxLibrary* subfolder. We are using a relative path here—check whether this path also exists in your web site, and change the path if necessary:

```html
<script type="text/javascript"
  src="AjaxLibrary/System.Web.Extensions/1.0.61025.0/MicrosoftAjax.js"></script>
```

You also need to load the web service JavaScript proxy. Remember, simply append */js* to the URL of the web service file:

```html
<script type="text/javascript" src="PHPHelloWorldService.php/js"></script>
```

Figure 22-1. The new service generates a JavaScript proxy

The latter `<script>` element generates JavaScript code that lets you execute a web method using the format *<classname>.<methodname>*, thus in this case PHPHelloWorldService.sayHello( ). Example 22-2 contains the complete code for the HTML page that calls the PHP service using the Microsoft Ajax Library. Figure 22-2 shows the result in the browser.

Example 22-2. Calling the PHP ASP.NET AJAX compatible pseudo-web service

PHPHelloWorldService.html

```
<!DOCTYPE html PUBLIC "-//W3C//DTD XHTML 1.1//EN"
"http://www.w3.org/TR/xhtml11/DTD/xhtml11.dtd">
<html xmlns="http://www.w3.org/1999/xhtml">
<head>
  <title>ASP.NET AJAX</title>

  <script type="text/javascript"
    src="AjaxLibrary/System.Web.Extensions/1.0.61025.0/MicrosoftAjax.js"></script>
  <script type="text/javascript" src="PHPHelloWorldService.php/js"></script>

  <script language="Javascript" type="text/javascript">
  function callService(f) {
    PHPHelloWorldService.sayHello(
      f.elements["name"].value,
      callComplete,
      callError);
  }

  function callComplete(result) {
```

Example 22-2. Calling the PHP ASP.NET AJAX compatible pseudo-web service (continued)

```
    window.alert(result);
  }
  function callError(result) {
    window.alert("Error! " + result);
  }
  </script>

</head>
<body>
  <form id="form1">
    <div>
      <input type="text" id="name" name="name" />
      <input type="button" value="Call Service" onclick="callService(this.form);" />
    </div>
  </form>

</body>
</html>
```

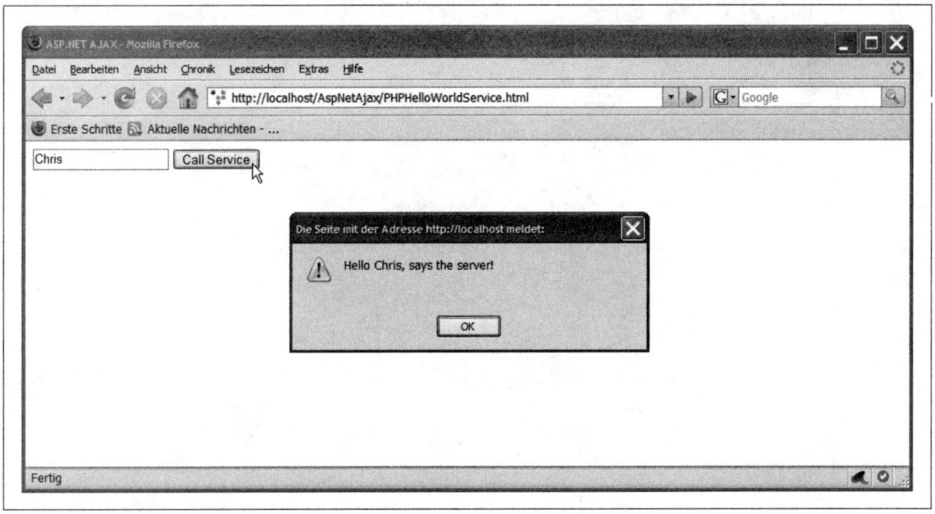

Figure 22-2. The window displays data from the PHP service

Summary

This chapter showed how to use ASP.NET AJAX from PHP, using the Microsoft AJAX framework from another server technology (and also from another operating system, if desired). The client-side components of ASP.NET AJAX can easily be used with other languages since it is all platform-agnostic JavaScript; the server-side components, on the other hand, need to be emulated. This emulation is of course language-agnostic, so the example in this book could have also been written in JSP, Perl, ColdFusion, or even in classic ASP.

The PHP for Microsoft AJAX project facilitates using ASP.NET AJAX from PHP, since a lot of the tricky code (e.g., generation of the JavaScript proxy) has already been implemented for you.

For Further Reading

http://www.shankun.com/AtlasPhp.aspx
   The original blog entry, demonstrating how to use Atlas with PHP

http://www.shankun.com/Atlas_Php_2.aspx
   A more recent version of Shanku Niyogi's code, with some bugs fixed

http://codeplex.com/phpmsajax
   PHP for Microsoft AJAX Library

Appendixes

Debugging ASP.NET AJAX Applications

In a perfect world, every line of code we write would be flawless. There may actually be some developers out there who never make mistakes—I am not one of them. Debugging ASP.NET AJAX applications, or JavaScript applications in general, is much more difficult than finding errors in "regular" programs. An Ajax application runs on both the client and the server. This leads to some obstacles for debugging: some server errors are not shown in the client. Also, very often an error is caused by the data sent between client and server, which you need to inspect as well.

This appendix presents some useful tools that will enable you to effectively debug ASP.NET AJAX applications running in the browser (and any JavaScript code). We will also have a look at debugging features provided by ASP.NET AJAX itself.

Debugging Tools

When asked what the best way is to test JavaScript during the development process, many developers answer, "Do not use Internet Explorer." Whereas the most recent versions of all the major browsers are really quite good, the quality of JavaScript error reporting differs greatly between them. The reporting for IE suffers the most. Take a look at the error message for identical JavaScript errors generated by different browsers. Figure A-1 shows the output in Firefox, which includes a line number, the name of the file, which caused the error, and also (when clicking on the filename) the erroneous code in question. Not great, but at least it is something with which you can work. Figure A-2, on the other hand, shows the output in Internet Explorer, with a not-so-descriptive error message, a different filename, and also a different line number.

Please don't misunderstand; I am sure there are good reasons why Internet Explorer displays limited and simplified error information. During development though, this can prove to be wholly inadequate and very frustrating. Therefore, additional tools are required. In fact, both Internet Explorer *and* Firefox can take advantage of add-on tools for debugging.

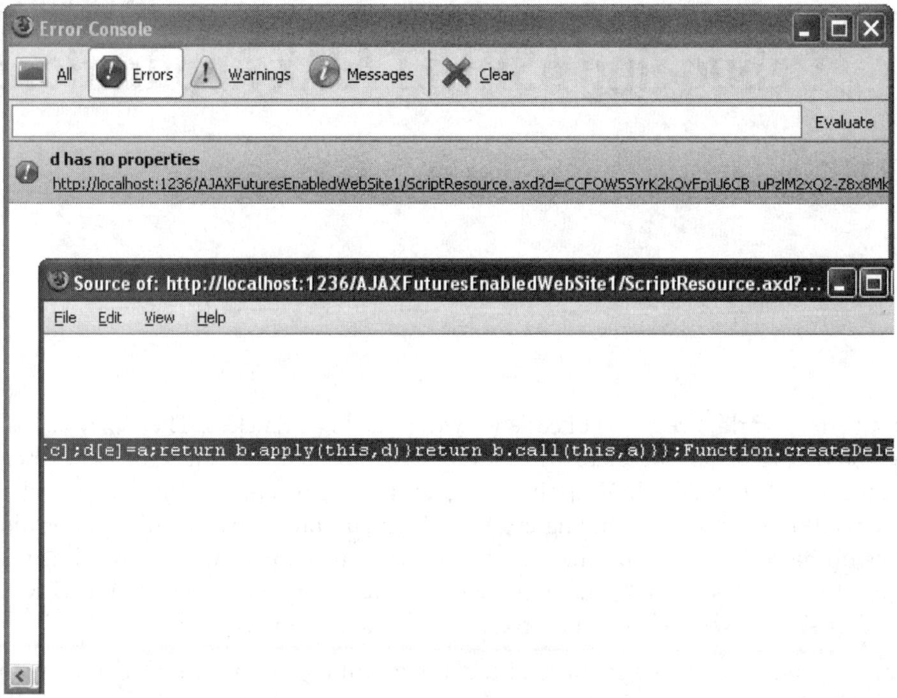

Figure A-1. A JavaScript error in Firefox

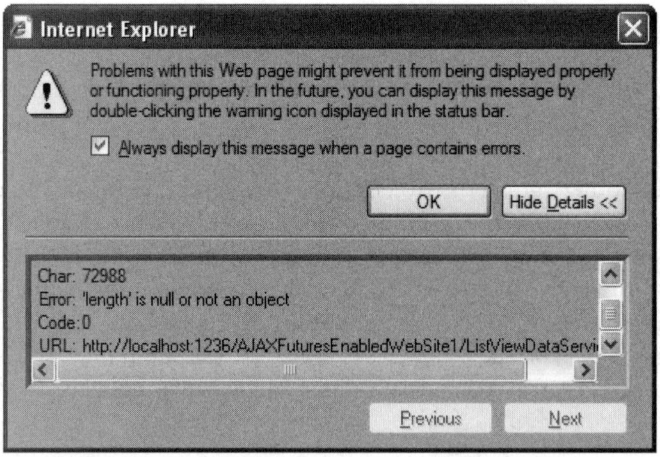

Figure A-2. A JavaScript error in Internet Explorer

This appendix focuses on the most popular browsers at the moment: Internet Explorer and Firefox. Other browsers like Opera and Safari do not as yet provide a large ecosystem for extensions, however, there are good solutions available for those programs as well.

Firebug for Firefox

One of the best web development extensions for Firefox browsers is Firebug. It features seamless integration into the browser and provides numerous debugging features for web sites. After installation is complete, press F12 in Firefox to launch Firebug. When it starts, Firebug gathers and displays all the relevant information for the current page. Beginning with the DOM (including write access!), it continues with detailed JavaScript error messages. Firebug even includes a feature that brings you directly to an offending line of code simply by clicking on an error message. It also offers a detailed list of all HTTP requests sent by the page (invaluable for debugging XMLHttpRequest calls).

To install Firebug, go to *http://www.getfirebug.com/* and click on the Download button. You may need to allow the *getfirebug.com* domain to install Firefox add-ons. Figure A-3 shows Firebug in action.

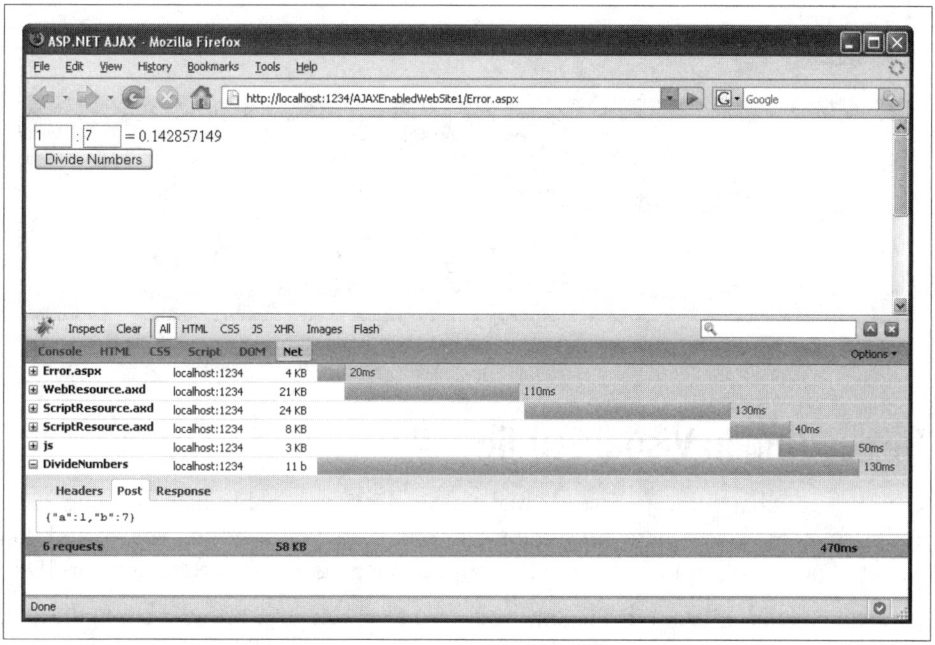

Figure A-3. The Firebug Firefox extension

Web Development Helper (for Internet Explorer)

For quite some time, debugging JavaScript applications and especially Ajax applications with Internet Explorer was quite hard. There were some plug-ins, but none of them offered all the features required for debugging modern web sites. Finally, Microsoft's own Nikhil Kothari (architect on the ASP.NET AJAX team and developer of the UpdateHistory control [presented in chapter 10], among other achievements) wrote his own tool, the Web Development Helper. You can download it at *http://www.nikhilk.net/projects/WebDevHelperDebuggingTools.aspx*. The add-in integrates into both Internet Explorer 6 and 7. To activate it, choose View → Explorer Bar → Web Development Helper. Internet Explorer displays the add-in on top of the page. The Web Development Helper not only provides access to page information, but also to special, ASP.NET-specific features like ViewState and tracing information (features Firebug currently lacks). You can also activate HTTP logging, access an interactive JavaScript console, and even capture a screenshot. Figure A-4 illustrates the Web Development Helper interface.

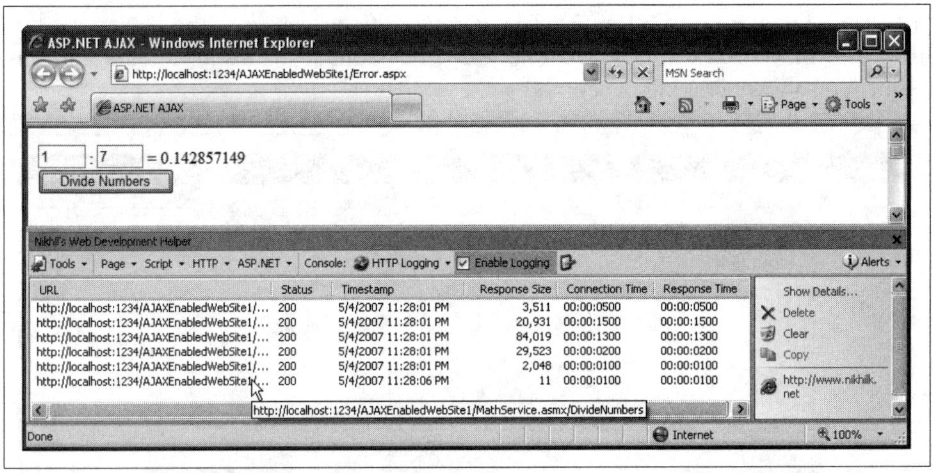

Figure A-4. The Web Development Helper Internet Explorer add-in

Debugging in Visual Studio

Contrary to what some believe, Visual Studio 2005 is capable of debugging JavaScript code. However there are some issues and traps you need to avoid—and you need to find a (well-hidden) feature for script debugging that is in the Microsoft IDE.

Before you actually begin debugging, you need to check your browser configuration. We are assuming that Internet Explorer is launched from Visual Studio; if you are using another browser by default, use the "Browser With" setting to use IE this time. Choose Tools → Internet Options and select the Advanced Tab. In Internet Explorer 6 and 7, you will find the following two options:

- Disable Script Debugging (Internet Explorer)
- Disable Script Debugging (Other)

Older Internet Explorer versions contain this option:

- Disable Script Debugging

Whether your browser displays one or two options, uncheck them all, otherwise, debugging from Visual Studio 2005 will not work. Figure A-5 shows the recommended settings.

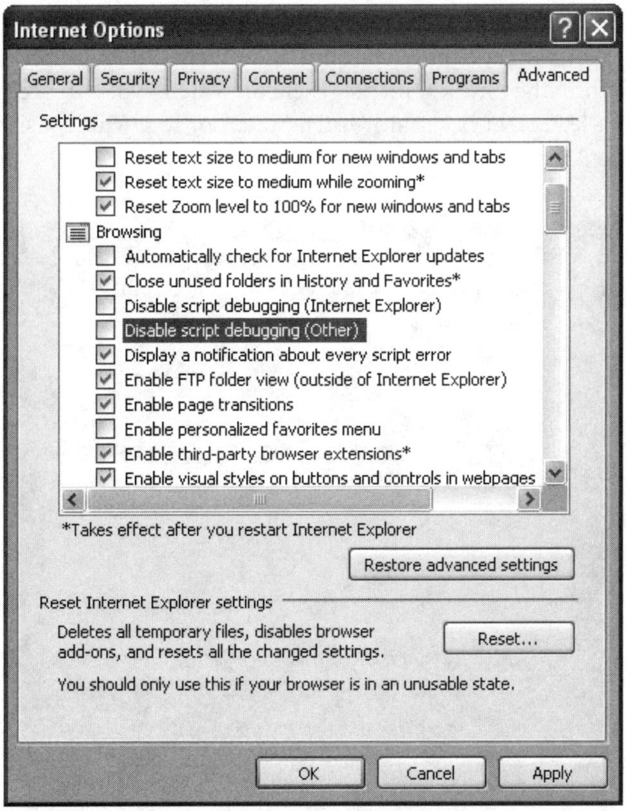

Figure A-5. Internet Explorer needs to be configured to allow script debugging

Now, load the *.aspx* file you want to debug into Visual Studio. There are three options to make Internet Explorer jump into the debugger while running the file:

- Add a breakpoint from the Debug menu or by pressing F9. However, this does not work for JavaScript code in a `<script>` block, only for external *.js* files. (There are also some known issues with hitting breakpoints in the debugger— see the discussion a little later in this section.)

- Add a line in the JavaScript code with the following content: `debugger;` (works for Firefox and Internet Explorer, does not work for Safari or Opera).

- Use the `Sys.Debug.fail()` or `Sys.Debug.assert()` methods provided by ASP. NET AJAX (see the section "Debugging Features in ASP.NET AJAX," later in this chapter).

After setting up the JavaScript code, run the ASP.NET page from Visual Studio in debug mode (press F5). If you have not run the debugger before in this Web site, you will be prompted to change the *Web.config* file to add a debug option—accept that option. Wait until the breakpoint is reached, which will—if everything goes as planned—either lead right back into Visual Studio or to a window similar to the one shown in Figure A-6.

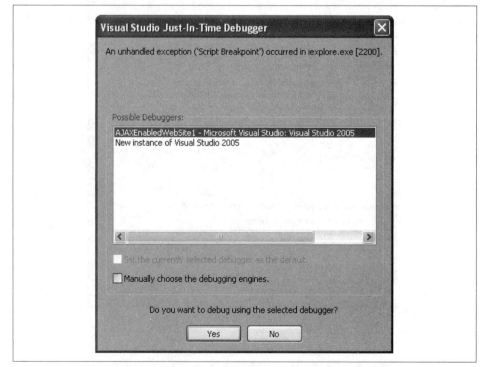

Figure A-6. Internet Explorer wants to break into a debugger and provides a list

Visual Studio is now active in debug mode. However, in many cases you will not see the current line of the script that caused the browser to exit to the debugger. Instead, you might see the message, "There is no source code available for the current location" (Figure A-7), or "No debug symbols have been loaded." This can have several causes, including the fact that an ASP.NET AJAX page dynamically loads various JavaScript libraries (i.e., the script files are dynamically appended to the current page's DOM and are not hard-linked to the page using `<script>` elements).

Figure A-7. Visual Studio does not find the source code—yet

If you encounter an issue as a result of a breakpoint, you can work around it with a little-known feature in Visual Studio 2005: the *Script Explorer*. This tool is only available in debug mode (which might be why few people know about it) and is accessible via Debug → Windows → Script Explorer. You can also customize the Visual Studio layout to display the Script Explorer window by default.

To begin, open Script Explorer. From there, you can open all JavaScript files loaded by the current page and perform the following:

- Step through the code
- Look at current variables
- Execute JavaScript commands on the fly, and much more.

Figure A-8 shows a debugging session using Script Explorer.

 The JavaScript handling features of Visual Studio will be improved with the next version (Visual Studio 2008). At the time of this writing, the second beta version of Visual Studio 2008 is already available, so you can have a preview of what the next version might bring.

Debugging Features in ASP.NET AJAX

ASP.NET AJAX comes with additional debugging features that work well with the techniques covered in this chapter thus far. However, to have access to these ASP.NET AJAX features, you must use the debug versions of any JavaScript code in your application.

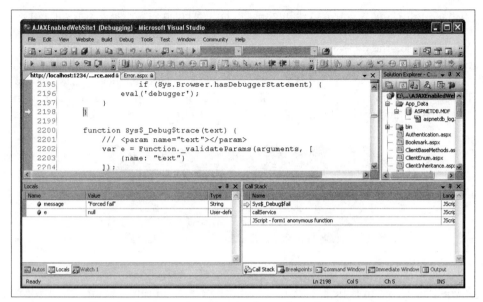

Figure A-8. Visual Studio's Script Explorer feature also works with JavaScript

Debugging with Firefox

When you install the Firebug browser extension, you have all you need for debugging, as Firebug also includes these tools. When a script launches a debugger—the Java-Script debugger statement, for example—Firebug leaps into action and displays the current executed line in the script, as shown in Figure A-9.

There is also a very competent JavaScript debugger for Firefox, called Venkman (download at *https://addons.mozilla.org/firefox/addon/216*). It provides everything you can ask of a debugger, except for the integrated IDE experience offered by Visual Studio. On the other hand, Venkman very handily integrates in the web browser. To launch the debugger, choose Tools → JavaScript Debugger.

Note that when using Venkman, some Firefox versions have a particularly annoying bug; you can only open the debugger once per browser session. If this is the case and you close the debugger window, you may need to restart the browser to be able to open the window again. It's much better to leave the debugger window open continuously while debugging an application. Figure A-10 shows how Venkman appears.

There are two ways to do so. First, set the web page to run in debug mode, either by adding the <compilation debug="true"> element to *Web.config* or by pressing F5 in Visual Studio. Alternatively, set the ScriptMode property of the ScriptManager control to "Debug". In both cases, this causes ASP.NET AJAX to automatically use the

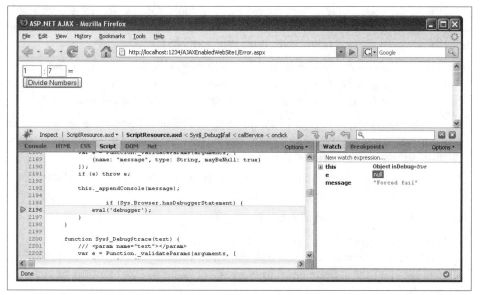

Figure A-9. Firefox also comes with a JavaScript debugger

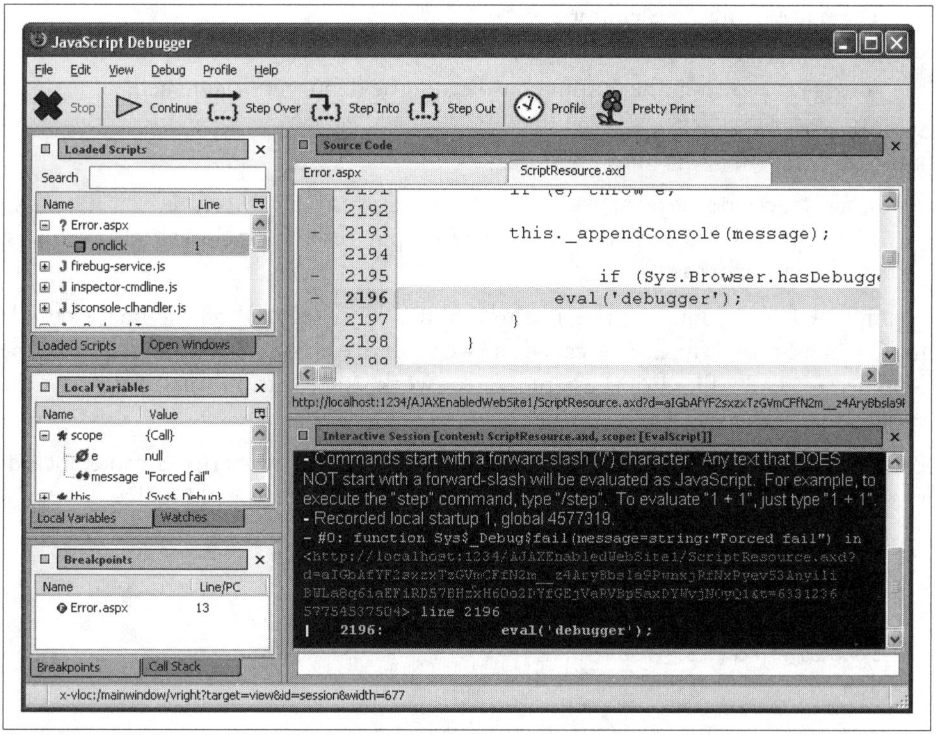

Figure A-10. Venkman, a JavaScript debugger for Firefox and other Mozilla browsers

versions of the code libraries that support debug tools. Of course this is only viable for development systems; on a production system, you should use the (smaller and therefore better performing) release versions of ASP.NET AJAX.

In the debug versions of the libraries, the Sys.Debug class provides five handy methods for debugging. Most of those methods interact with a JavaScript output console. There are two different ways ASP.NET AJAX interacts with that console:

- The debug messages appear in the JavaScript console of either the browser or of a special browser extension (like Firefox). This obviously depends on the browser used and on the availability of special browser extensions.

- The debug messages appear in an HTML <textarea> element whose ID is TraceConsole, if such an element exists.

These methods are provided in Sys.Debug:

Sys.Debug.assert(condition, message, displayCaller)
> If condition is not met, message is shown in the output console (including the name of the calling function, if displayCaller is set to true) and the debugger is launched.

Sys.Debug.clearTrace( )
> The output console is emptied.

Sys.Debug.fail(message)
> message is shown in the output console and the debugger is launched.

Sys.Debug.trace(text)
> text is shown in the output console.

Sys.Debug.traceDump(object, name)
> The content of object is shown in the output console (including all members, and an optional name!).

Example A-1 uses some of these methods and is loosely based on the final example in Chapter 5, in which we called a web service. This example requires the *MathService.asmx* file from Chapter 5 to work (the version that supports the ExtendedDivideNumbers( ) method).

Before the web service is called, information is sent to the JavaScript console, including information about the JavaScript web service proxy object, MathService:

```
Sys.Debug.trace("Calling MathService");
Sys.Debug.traceDump(MathService, "MathService: ");
```

Data received from the service is displayed in the console:

```
Sys.Debug.trace("Received result!");
Sys.Debug.traceDump(result, "result: ");
```

In case of an error, this error is displayed in the JavaScript console, as well (depending on the browser and its configuration). Additionally, the script exits to the JavaScript debugger (if available):

```
function callError(result) {
  Sys.Debug.fail(
    result.get_exceptionType() +
    ": " +
    result.get_message() +
    "\n" +
    result.get_stackTrace());
}
```

Refer to Example A-1 for the complete code, and to Figure A-11 to see how it might look in a browser. The beauty of the debugging support of ASP.NET AJAX is that this code only affects the page in debug mode. If you configure the application or the page to run in release mode, no data is sent to the JavaScript console. Therefore, you do not have to remove the debug code from your application, apart from the <textarea> output console, if applicable. (On the other hand, if you do remove all Sys.Debug.* calls, your script gets a bit smaller, which is also beneficial to the page's performance.)

Example A-1. Using ASP.NET AJAX debugger features

Debug.aspx

```
<%@ Page Language="C#" %>

<!DOCTYPE html PUBLIC "-//W3C//DTD XHTML 1.0 Transitional//EN"
"http://www.w3.org/TR/xhtml1/DTD/xhtml1-transitional.dtd">

<html xmlns="http://www.w3.org/1999/xhtml">
<head id="Head1" runat="server">
  <title>ASP.NET AJAX</title>

  <script language="Javascript" type="text/javascript">
  function callService(f) {
    document.getElementById("c").innerHTML = "";
    Sys.Debug.trace("Calling MathService");
    Sys.Debug.traceDump(MathService, "MathService: ");
    MathService.ExtendedDivideNumbers(
      parseInt(f.elements["a"].value),
      parseInt(f.elements["b"].value),
      callComplete,
      callError);
  }

  function callComplete(result) {
    Sys.Debug.trace("Received result!");
    Sys.Debug.traceDump(result, "result: ");
```

Example A-1. Using ASP.NET AJAX debugger features (continued)

```
   document.getElementById("c").innerHTML =
     result.result +
     " (calculated at " +
     result.calculationTime +
     ")";
}

function callError(result) {
  Sys.Debug.fail(
    result.get_exceptionType() +
    ": " +
    result.get_message() +
    "\n" +
    result.get_stackTrace());
}
</script>

</head>
<body>
  <form id="form1" runat="server">
    <asp:ScriptManager ID="ScriptManager1" runat="server"
      ScriptMode="Debug">
      <Services>
        <asp:ServiceReference Path="MathService.asmx" />
      </Services>
    </asp:ScriptManager>
    <div>
      <nobr>
        <input type="text" id="a" name="a" size="2" />
        :
        <input type="text" id="b" name="b" size="2" />
        =
        <span id="c" style="width: 50px;"></span>
      </nobr>
      <br />
      <input type="button" value="Divide Numbers"
onclick="callService(this.form);" />
      <br />
      <textarea id="TraceConsole" rows="10" cols="50">Debug information:
</textarea>
    </div>
  </form>
</body>
</html>
```

Summary

This appendix should have dispelled rumors that Ajax applications cannot be debugged. There are, in fact, several options and tools. And although debugging Windows applications is still much more convenient, JavaScript is bit by bit getting there (pardon the pun…).

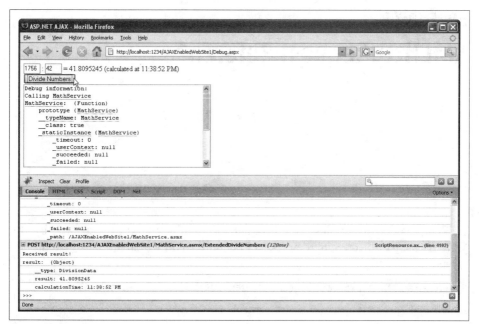

Figure A-11. The JavaScript console information appears both in the text field and in the Firebug add-on

For Further Reading

http://ajax.asp.net/docs/overview/ASPNETAJAXDebuggingAndTracingOverview.aspx
Microsoft documentation topic on debugging ASP.NET AJAX web applications. It includes information on known issues when debugging Internet Explorer.

http://chrispederick.com/work/webdeveloper/
Another useful Firefox browser add-in including JavaScript debugger.

XMLHttpRequest Reference

This Appendix assembles all the methods and properties exposed by the XMLHttpRequest object. Square brackets [] denote an array; parentheses () indicate a method.

To create an XMLHttpRequest object for Internet Explorer, you must use ActiveX:

```
XMLHTTP = new ActiveXObject("Microsoft.XMLHTTP");
```

With other browsers, the XMLHttpRequest object is a built-in type and can be instantiated directly, as in the following snippet:

```
XMLHTTP = new XMLHttpRequest();
```

Once the XMLHttpRequest object is instantiated, the following cross-browser methods and properties are supported.

Methods

Method	Description
abort()	Terminates the request and discards any response.
getAllResponseHeaders()	Returns all headers of the HTTP response.
getResponseHeader(header)	Returns the value of the given HTTP response header.
open(method, url, async, username, password)	Creates and sends an HTTP request with the given method (GET or POST) to the target URL. The other parameters are optional: whether or not to use an asynchronous call (default), and credentials for HTTP authentication. (Note that credentials are sent in clear text; if you are concerned about security, use HTTPS protocol for the page.)
send(content)	Sends the HTTP request; optionally providing data to send along with it (POST information).
setRequestHeader(name, value)	Adds a header with the given name and value to the HTTP request.

Properties

Property	Description
readyState	Status of HTTP request (0=uninitialized, 1=loading, 2=loaded, 3=waiting, 4=complete).
responseText	Data returned in the HTTP response as text.
responseXML	Data returned in the HTTP response as an XML DOM object.
status	HTTP status code of the HTTP response.
statusText	HTTP status message of the HTTP response.

DOM Reference

This Appendix assembles all DOM methods and properties exposed by JavaScript. The DOM used is the W3C DOM supported by recent versions of Internet Explorer, Mozilla, Safari/Konqueror, and Opera. Methods and properties that are not supported by either of the two "main" browsers—Internet Explorer and Mozilla brands—are not mentioned.

Square brackets [ ] denote an array; parentheses ( ) indicate a method.

Generic Methods and Properties

The methods and properties in this section exist for all DOM elements.

Methods

Method	Description
appendChild(node)	Appends a child node to the element
appendData(data)	Appends data (HTML or text) to a node; does not overwrite existing data
blur()	Removes the focus from the element
click()	Simulates a click on the element
cloneNode(deep)	Creates a copy of the node (if deep is true, all subnodes are copied as well)
deleteData(start, length)	Deletes a number of characters from the data in a node
focus()	Gives the focus to the element
getAttribute(attribute)	Returns the value of the given attribute
getAttributeNode(attribute)	Returns the node containing the given attribute
getElementsByTagName(name)	Returns an array of all elements with the given tag name
hasChildNodes()	Returns a value that indicates whether the element has subnodes
insertBefore(node)	Inserts a node before the element

Method	Description
insertData(position, data)	Inserts data (HTML or text) at a certain position
removeAttribute(attribute)	Removes the given attribute and its value from the element
removeChild(node)	Removes the given subnode from the element
replaceChild(newnode, oldnode)	Replaces the given old subnode with the given subnode
replaceData(start, length, newdata)	Replaces data (from a given position on, with a given length) with new data
setAttribute(name, value)	Sets the value of the specified attribute to the given value
setAttributeNode(node)	Adds a new attribute node, replacing any existing one

Properties

Property	Description
attributes[]	Gets or sets an array that contains the element's attributes and values
childNodes[]	Gets or sets a list of element's subnodes
className	Gets or sets the name of an element's CSS class
data	Gets or sets character data (in a text node)
dir	Gets or sets the reading direction of element
firstChild	Gets the element's first subnode
id	Gets or sets the ID of the element
innerHTML	Gets or sets the HTML content of an element (not W3C-compatible, but implemented in all relevant browsers)
lang	Gets or sets the language (lang attribute) of element
lastChild	Gets the element's last subnode
length	Gets or sets the length of the element
localName	Gets or sets the local element tag name (without namespace, if any)
namespaceURI	Gets or sets the URI of the element's namespace
nextSibling	Gets or sets the element after the current element in the DOM tree
nodeName	Gets or sets the tag name of the element node
nodeType	Gets or sets the node type of the element node
nodeValue	Gets or sets the value in the element node
ownerDocument	Gets the document that the element resides in
parentNode	Gets the element's parent node
prefix	Gets or sets the namespace prefix used in the node
previousSibling	Gets or sets the element before the current element in the DOM tree
style	Gets or sets the element's style information
tabIndex	Gets or sets the element's tab order index
tagName	Gets or sets the name of the element's tag
title	Gets or sets the title of the element

Document Methods and Properties

The methods and properties in this section are implemented for the document object. Methods and properties already covered in the previous section are not repeated.

Methods

Method	Description
clear( )	Empties the document
close( )	Ends the write access (started with open( )) to the document
createAttribute(attribute)	Creates an attribute with the given name
createDocumentFragment( )	Creates a document fragment
createElement(name)	Creates an element with the given tag name
createTextNode(text)	Creates a text node with the given text
getElementById(id)	Returns the element with the given ID
getElementsByTagName(name)	Returns an array with all elements with the given name
open(mime, replace)	Opens the document for write access, sets the MIME type, and if the optional replace parameter is true, replaces the old contents (otherwise, appends data)
write(text)	Writes data to the document
writeln(text)	Writes data and a linefeed (\r\n) to the document

Properties

Property	Description
alinkColor	Gets or sets the color for active links
anchors[]	Gets an array of all anchors in the document
applets[]	Gets an array of all Java applets in the document
bgColor	Gets or sets the background color of the document
body	Gets or sets the body portion of the document
compatMode	Gets or sets a value that indicates whether the rendering engine uses a compatibility mode for older content
cookie	Gets or sets the cookies that the document can access
documentElement	Gets or sets the DOM node for the document
domain	Gets the domain of the document
embeds[]	Gets or sets an array of all embedded objects
fgColor	Gets or sets the foreground (text) color of the document
forms[]	Gets or sets an array of all form elements in the document; in ASP.NET pages, there can be only one form element, which is always forms[0]
images[]	Gets an array of all images in the document
lastModified	Gets the date and time of the last modification of the document on the server

Property	Description
linkColor	Gets or sets the color for links
links[]	Gets an array of all links in the document
location	Gets URL information about the document
referrer	Gets the URL of the document that the user came from to the current document
styleSheets[]	Gets an array all CSS style sheets referenced in the document
URL	Gets the URL of the document
vlinkColor	Gets or sets the color for visited links

ASP.NET AJAX Reference

ASP.NET AJAX provides several JavaScript helper APIs and adds new functionality to existing JavaScript objects. This appendix shows a selective list of the most important functions and methods.

Helper Functions

ASP.NET AJAX comes with several useful helper functions. The most important ones have shortcut function names prefixed with a dollar sign ($).

Property	Description
$addHandler(element, eventName, handler);	Adds an event handler for an event to a DOM element
$addHandlers(element, events, handlerOwner)	Adds several event handlers to a DOM element
$clearHandlers(element)	Removes all event handlers attached to a DOM element
$create(type, properties, events, references, element)	Creates a component and initializes it
$find(id, parent)	Searches for a component by its ID
$get(id, element)	Searches for a DOM element by its ID
$removeHandler(element, eventName, handler)	Removes one specific event handler from a DOM element

Object Extensions

ASP.NET AJAX extends some standard JavaScript objects like strings and Booleans with additional methods. The extensions for the JavaScript Error object are mostly used internally, but the other object extensions are also suitable for custom code.

Array Extensions

All `Array` methods need to be called statically (e.g., `Array.add( )`).

Method	Description
`add(array, item)`	Adds an element to the array
`addRange(array, items)`	Adds elements to the array
`clear(array)`	Empties the array
`clone(array)`	Creates a copy of the array
`contains(array, item)`	Whether the array contains an item or not
`dequeue(array)`	Removes (and returns) the first element of an array
`enqueue(array, item)`	Adds an element to the array (should not be called directly, use `add( )` instead)
`forEach(array, method, contxt)`	Iterate over an array and call a method for each element
`indexOf(array, item, start)`	Returns the zero-based index of the element in the array, or −1 if not found
`insert(array, index, item)`	Adds an item at the given position to the array
`parse(value)`	Converts a JSON string into an array
`remove(array, item)`	Removes an item from the array
`removeAt(array, index)`	Removes the item at the given position from the array

Boolean Extensions

The one available `Boolean` method needs to be called statically (`Boolean.parse( )`).

Method	Description
`parse(value)`	Converts the value into a Boolean

Date Extensions

Unless otherwise noted, all `Date` methods need to be called on an object instance (e.g., `(new Date()).format( )`).

Method	Description
`format(format)`	Formats a date according to a format string
`localeFormat(format)`	Formats a date according to a format string and to the current culture; may also be called statically
`parseLocale(value, formats)`	Parses a string for a date, according to the current culture; may also be called statically
`parseInvariant(value, formats)`	Parses a string for a date, according to the invariant culture; may also be called statically

Number Extensions

Unless otherwise noted, all Number methods need to be called on an object instance.

Method	Description
format(format)	Formats a number according to the invariant culture
localeFormat(format)	Formats a number according to the current culture
parseInvariant(value)	Parses a string for a number, according to the invariant culture; may also be called statically
parseLocale(value)	Parses a string for a number, according to the current culture; may also be called statically

Object Extensions

All Object methods need to be called statically (e.g., Object.getType( )).

Method	Description
getType(instance)	Returns the type of the instance
getTypeName(instance)	Returns the type name of the instance

String Extensions

Unless otherwise noted, all String methods need to be called on an object instance.

Method	Description
endsWith(suffix)	Whether a string ends with the given suffix or not
format(format, args)	Replaces placeholders {0}, {1}, … in the string with values provided as additional parameters; needs to be called statically
localeFormat(format, args)	Replaces placeholders {0}, {1},… in the string with values provided as additional parameter, using the current culture for dates and numbers; needs to be called statically
startsWith(prefix)	Whether a string starts with the given prefix or not
trim( )	Removes whitespace at both ends of the string
trimLeft( )	Removes whitespace at the beginning of the string
trimRight( )	Removes whitespace at the end of the string

ScriptManager, UpdatePanel, UpdateProgress, and Timer Declarative Reference

In this Appendix, the properties of four of the most important ASP.NET AJAX server controls are covered: ScriptManager, UpdatePanel, UpdateProgress, and Timer. All available properties are described (when using the controls declaratively), with the exception of ID and runat="server". Also, properties inherited from Control are omitted from the list.

ScriptManager

The ScriptManager is the most important control on an ASP.NET AJAX-powered web site since it is responsible for loading the client libraries and can also generate web services proxies.

Properties

Property	Description
AllowCustomErrorsRedirect	Allows (*true*, default) or disallows (*false*) whether errors occurring during an asynchronous postback will lead to a custom redirect (if enabled in *Web.config*)
AsyncPostBackErrorMessage	Error message when an error occurs during an asynchronous postback
AsyncPostBackSourceElementID	ID of the element that triggered the asynchronous postback
AuthenticationService-Path	Path of the authentication service
EnablePageMethods	Enables (*true*) or disables (*false*, default) the use of static inline web methods (page methods)
EnablePartialRendering	Enables (*true*, default) or disables (*false*) the partial rendering implemented by UpdatePanel
EnableScriptGlobalization	Enables (*true*) or disables (*false*, default) the use of cultures from ASP.NET AJAX
EnableScriptLocalization	Enables (*true*) or disables (*false*, default) the use of localized content from ASP.NET AJAX

Property	Description
LoadScriptsBeforeUI	Loads the JavaScript libraries before (*true*, default) or after (*false*) the page's markup has been loaded
ProfileService-LoadProperties	Profile properties available to client script code
ProfileService-Path	Path of a profile web service
ScriptMode	Whether to use Debug or Release versions of the JavaScript libraries
ScriptPath	Root folder for ASP.NET AJAX and custom JavaScript libraries

AuthenticationService

The <Authentication> subelement of the ScriptManager control is used to enable authentication service support; the following property is supported.

Property	Description
Path	Path and filename of the (custom) authentication web service

ProfileService

The <ProfileService> subelement of the ScriptManager control is used to enable profile service support; the following properties are supported.

Property	Description
LoadProperties	List of profile properties to make available to client script code

Scripts

The <Scripts> subelement of the ScriptManager control contains all client-side scripts that will be loaded using the <asp:ScriptReference> control. This control supports the following properties.

Property	Description
Assembly	Assembly that contains the script
IgnoreScriptPath	Whether to ignore the ScriptManager ScriptPath property (*true*) or not (*false*, default)
Name	Name of the embedded script resource to use
NotifyScriptLoaded	Whether to automatically add code to the end of the script (*true*, default) or not (*false*) to notify the ScriptManager control that the script has been loaded.
Path	Path and filename of the script to load
ResourceUICultures	List of UI cultures to use
ScriptMode	Whether to use the Debug or Release version of the script
Path	Path and filename of the (custom) profile web service

UpdatePanel

With the `UpdatePanel` control, a section of an ASP.NET-AJAX-powered page can be updated independently from the rest of the page; the content resides in the `<ContentTemplate>` subelement of `<asp:UpdatePanel>`.

Properties

Property	Description
ChildrenAsTriggers	Whether postbacks in child elements trigger a refresh of the UpdatePanel control (*true*, default) or not (*false*)
RenderMode	How to render the contents of the UpdatePanel: in a `<div>` element (Block, default) or in a `<span>` element (Inline)
UpdateMode	When to refresh: Always (i.e., whenever a postback occurs) or Conditional (i.e., only when a trigger causes the refresh)

Triggers

The `<Triggers>` subelement of the `UpdatePanel` control contains triggers that can cause the refresh of the `UpdatePanel`'s contents. Two triggers are available with these properties, `<asp:AsyncPostBackTrigger>` and `<asp:PostBackTrigger>`.

Property	Description
ControlID	ID of the control that can pull the trigger
EventName	Event that causes the trigger to be pulled (`<asp:AsyncPostBackTrigger>` only)

UpdateProgress

The `UpdateProgress` control displays a waiting screen while an `UpdatePanel` control is updated. The actual content of the waiting screen resides in the `<ProgressTemplate>` subelement of `<asp:UpdateProgress>`.

Properties

Property	Description
AssociatedUpdatePanelID	The ID of the associated UpdatePanel control
DisplayAfter	Number of milliseconds after which the waiting screen is shown (defaults to 500).
DynamicLayout	Whether to reserve space on the page for the waiting screen (*false*) or to dynamically make space once the waiting screen needs to appear (*true*, default).

Timer

The Timer control triggers events and creates postbacks at timed intervals.

Properties

Property	Description
Enabled	Enables (*true*, default) or disables (*false*) the timer
Interval	Number of milliseconds between Timer actions (defaults to 60000).

Index

We'd like to hear your suggestions for improving our indexes. Send email to *index@oreilly.com*.

C

O

object-oriented programming (see OOP)
objects
    ASP.NET AJAX
        clients, 83–87
        extensions to existing, 70
        OOP features for JavaScript, 71–83
    built-in, JavaScript, 32–34
    creating, 61
    DataRowCollection, 316
    document, 38
    enumerations, 85
    extensions, 432, 434
    HistoryEventArgs, 388
    ItemSearchRequest, 346
    JSON, 61–64
        serialization/deserialization, 100–105
    Sys.Preview.UI.Effects.FadeAnimation,
        370
    XMLDocument, 55–60
    XMLHttpRequest, 45–55
        references, 426
OKControlID property, 212
onreadystatechange property, 49
OOP (object-oriented programming), 4
    features for JavaScript, 71–83
    JavaScript, 34–38
open( ) method, 49
opening windows, 245
operators
    Boolean, 28
    comparison, 28
    typeof, 47
Outlook Web Access (see OWA)
OWA (Outlook Web Access), 45

P

packages, ASP.NET AJAX, 6
page elements, accessing, 38–42
page methods, 93–95
Page_Load event handlers, 50
pageLoad( ) function, 69, 149
pageLoad( ) method, 322
PageMethods class, 93
pageNavigate( ) function, 391
PageRequestManager class, 128
PageRequestManager instance, 128
panels, drag-and-drop, 194
panes
    Accordian control, 197–199
    collapsing, 210

<Panes> element, 198
parameters
    base type, 72
    baseArguments, 78
    failedCallback, 135
    instance, 78
    interface type, 72
    loadCompletedCallback, 135
    methodName, 78
    name, 72
    propertyNames, 135
    UserContext, 135
passwords, profiles, 144
patch utility, 228
patches
    packaging, 234
    saving, 233
    uploading, 237
paths, data, 265
permalinks, creating, 394
personalized drag-and-drop, 306–310
PHP, applying with ASP.NET
        AJAX, 406–409
PHPHelloWorldService class, 407
PHPHelloWorldService.php file, 406
play( ) method, 369
plugins, Firebug, 140
PopupControlID property, 212
popups, generating, 211–214
positioning HTML elements, 199–201
POST command, 54
postbacks
    triggering, 121, 122
    UpdatePanel control, 116
        regions, 116–131
PostBackTrigger, 122
preventDefault( ) method, 224
preventing form submission, 294–296
PreviewDragDrop.js file, 301
PreviewGlitz.js file, 368
ProcessRequest( ) method, 407
profileError( ) function, 137, 142
profileLoadedError( ) function, 136
profiles
    accessing, 135–139, 139–144
    service support, 436
    web sites, preparing, 133–135
ProfileService class, 135
programmatic data binding, 266–268
programmatic validation, 288–291
programmatically updating
        sections, 123–126

uploading patches, 237
url attributes, 277
URLs (Uniform Resource Locators),
    JavaScript, 25
useGet attribute, 278
user names, profiles, 139
userContext parameter, 135
UserData property, 134

V

validation
    customization, 287–288
    data, 280–296
    groups, 291–294
    programmatic, 288–291
validators, 280
value attribute, 275
values, onreadystatechange property, 49
variables
    custom functions, writing, 33
    dateformat, 156
    daynames, 156
    JavaScript, 26
VerticalSide property, 200
viewing
    custom data sources, 334
    wait screens, 126–128
views, Design, 118
Virtual Earth, 3
visibilityMode, 287
Visual Studio 2005, 5
    debugging, 416–421
    installation, 7
Visual Studio Integration (VSI), 178
Visual Web Developer Express Edition
    installation, 7
VSI (Visual Studio Integration), 178

W

wait screens
    canceling, 130
    displaying, 126–128
WCF (Windows Communication
    Foundation), 88
Web Development Helper, 416
web pages
    Ajax architecture, 3
    animation
        drag-and-drop, 193–195
        framework, 185–190
        programming, 190–193

ASP.NET, 5
ASP.NET AJAX
    clients, 83–87
    extensions to existing objects, 70
    OOP features for JavaScript, 71–83
    shortcuts, 67–70
JavaScript
    arrays, 27
    built-in objects, 32–34
    control structures, 27–31
    DOM methods, 42–43
    methods, 25
    OOP, 34–38
    overview of, 24–25
    page element access, 38–42
    variables, 26
    life cycles of, 14
    popups, generating, 211–214
Web Parts (ASP.NET), 396–401
web services
    complex data, exchanging, 100–105
    error handling, 88–92
    Internet Explorer and, 106–108
    JavaScript, consuming with, 105–114
    ListView control, 321
    Mozilla and, 108–112
    page methods, 93–95
    PHP, 407
    remote, 337
        Amazon, 345–367
        Google, 338–344
        Yahoo!, 358–367
    results, transforming with
        XSLT, 350–358
    session state, maintaining, 95–101
Web Services Description Language
    (WSDL), 106
web sites
    Control Toolkit, 178
        applying, 181–184
    globalization, 169–172
    localization, 156
        satellite resources, 159–169
        scripts, 156–159
    profiles, preparing for, 133–135
Web.config file, 133
WebPartManager control, 398
while loops, 31
whitelist approach, 204
window.setInterval( ) method, 122
window.setTimeout( ) method, 122

About the Author

Christian Wenz is a trainer and consultant who has written more than 50 books. He works with both open source and closed source web technologies, has been awarded a Microsoft MVP for ASP/ASP.NET, and is listed in Zend's Who's Who of PHP. Christian is also listed in Mozilla's credits (about:credits) and is considered an expert in browser-agnostic JavaScript.

Colophon

The animal on the cover of *Programming ASP.NET AJAX* is a black murex snail (*hexaplex nigritus*). The black murex is found off the coast of California and Mexico. As it ages, its shell turns from white to predominately black. However, pure white or black shells are very rare. Mature black murexes are about 6 inches (15 centimeters) long.

Black murex snails are carnivorous gastropods. Their diet is composed of bivalve mollusks, including oysters, clams, and sea anemone. Gastropods kill their prey by various means, including smothering, tearing, or boring into the shell by using an acidic mucus to weaken the outside surface.

The murex snail played a crucial role in the culture and trade of the ancient Phoenicians. They crushed the murex in order to extract a purple-red secretion used to dye fabric. It is estimated that some 10,000 snails were needed to dye one toga. As a result, only royalty could afford the precious dye for clothing. When the dye was combined with silk imported from China, the purple garments were worth more than their weight in gold. Purple has since been equated with royalty, but the red of papal robes and the blue in the flag of Israel are also derivative of murex snail dye.

The cover image is from *Johnson's Natural History*. The cover font is Adobe ITC Garamond. The text font is Linotype Birka; the heading font is Adobe Myriad Condensed; and the code font is LucasFont's TheSans Mono Condensed.

Related Titles from O'Reilly

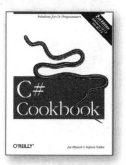

.NET

ADO.NET Cookbook

ASP.NET 2.0 Cookbook, *2nd Edition*

ASP.NET 2.0: A Developer's Notebook

C# Cookbook, *2nd Edition*

C# in a Nutshell, *2nd Edition*

C# Language Pocket Reference

Learning C# 2005, *2nd Edition*

Learning WCF

MCSE Core Elective Exams in a Nutshell

.NET and XML

.NET Gotchas

Programming .NET Components, *2nd Edition*

Programming .NET Security

Programming .NET Web Services

Programming ASP.NET, *3rd Edition*

Programming Atlas

Programming C#, *4th Edition*

Programming MapPoint in .NET

Programming Visual Basic 2005

Programming WCF Services

Programming Windows Presentation Foundation

Visual Basic 2005: A Developer's Notebook

Visual Basic 2005 Cookbook

Visual Basic 2005 in a Nutshell, *3rd Edition*

Visual Basic 2005 Jumpstart

Visual C# 2005: A Developer's Notebook

Visual Studio Hacks

Windows Developer Power Tools

XAML in a Nutshell